Yearbook of Corpus Linguistics and Pragmatics

2016

More information about this series at http://www.springer.com/series/11559

Jesús Romero-Trillo
Editor

Yearbook of Corpus Linguistics and Pragmatics 2016

Global Implications for Society and Education in the Networked Age

Springer

Editor
Jesús Romero-Trillo
Departamento de Filología Inglesa/
Facultad de Filosofía
Universidad Autónoma de Madrid
Madrid, Spain

ISSN 2213-6819 ISSN 2213-6827 (electronic)
Yearbook of Corpus Linguistics and Pragmatics
ISBN 978-3-319-41732-5 ISBN 978-3-319-41733-2 (eBook)
DOI 10.1007/978-3-319-41733-2

Library of Congress Control Number: 2015946312

Printed on acid-free paper

This Springer imprint is published by Springer Nature
The registered company is Springer International Publishing AG Switzerland

Contents

Contributors

Carolina P. Amador-Moreno Filología Inglesa/Facultad de Filosofía, Universidad de Extremadura, Cáceres, Spain

Nancy E. Avila-Ledesma Filología Inglesa/Facultad de Filosofía, Universidad Autónoma de Madrid, Madrid, Spain

Ramona Bongelli Department of Political Sciences, Communication and International Relations, University of Macerata, Macerata, Italy

Roberto Burro Department of Philosophy, Education, Psychology, University of Verona, Verona, Italy

Claire Childs School of English Literature, Language and Linguistics, Newcastle University, Newcastle Upon Tyne, UK

Edie Furniss Department of Hispanic Studies and Modern and Classical Languages, University of Houston, Houston, TX, Texas, USA

Karen Kinloch Linguistics and English Language Department, Lancaster University, Lancaster, UK

Fiona MacArthur Filología Inglesa/Facultad de Filosofía Y Letras, Universidad de Extremadura, Cáceres, Spain

Sofia Malamatidou Department of Modern Languages, University of Birmingham, Birmingham, UK

Eva M. Mestre-Mestre Lingüística Aplicada/Escola Politècnica Superior de Gandia, Universitat Politècnica de València, Camí Vera s/n, València, Spain

María Muelas Gil Universidad Autónoma de Madrid, Madrid, Spain

Departamento de Filología Moderna/Facultad de Educación, Universidad de Castilla-La Mancha, Cuenca, Spain

Ilaria Riccioni Department of Education, Cultural Heritage and Tourism, University of Macerata, Macerata, Italy

Jesús Romero-Trillo Departamento de Filología Inglesa/Facultad de Filosofía, Universidad Autónoma de Madrid, Madrid, Spain

Carmen Santamaría-García Filología Moderna/Facultad de Filosofía Y Letras, Universidad de Alcalá, Alcalá de Henares, Madrid, Spain

Andrea Scibetta Linguistica e Didattica Della Lingua Italiana a Stranieri, Università per Stranieri di Siena (University for Foreigners of Siena), Siena, Italy

Keiko Tsuchiya International Education Centre, Tokai University, Hiratsuka, Kanagawa, Japan

Massimiliano Valotto Department of Mathematics, Computer Science and Physics, University of Udine, Udine, Italy

Francisco Yus Departamento de Filología Inglesa, Universidad de Alicante, Alicante, Spain

Andrzej Zuczkowski Department of Education, Cultural Heritage and Tourism, University of Macerata, Macerata, Italy

Introduction: Global Implications for Society and Education in the Networked Age

Jesús Romero-Trillo

It cannot be denied that we live in the age of information access and that information processing defines the way we live and think and, also, the way we consume goods and services (Rifkin 2001). In this sense, the enormous surge in the amount of information that we receive every day has coincided with the financial crisis that has affected the so-called developed world since 2008, with its subsequent domino-effect on the political and economic situation in less developed countries (Caparrós 2015). The fact that social media is increasingly reliant on language has made politicians and journalists become aware of the role of language in the explanation of the dramatic changes that are shaping a new horizon in geopolitical and human relations. Some authors, like Bauman and Bordoni (2014), believe that globalisation has grown parallel to the emptying of the power of states and institutions, which cannot longer manage (and control) social and economic processes. The result is that citizens have begun to mistrust institutions and that social networks have become the new agora where individuals can vent their anger or express their hopes.

For this reason, the fourth volume of the series Yearbook of Corpus Linguistics and Pragmatics 2016 is published at an opportune moment as it offers an accurate and theory-principled view on reality based on the linguistic investigation of

J. Romero-Trillo (✉)
Departamento de Filología Inglesa/Facultad de Filosofía, Universidad Autónoma de Madrid, Madrid, Spain
e-mail: jesus.romero@uam.es

J. Romero-Trillo (ed.), *Yearbook of Corpus Linguistics and Pragmatics 2016*,
Yearbook of Corpus Linguistics and Pragmatics 4,
DOI 10.1007/978-3-319-41733-2_1

social and educational challenges in our networked times. Its contributors have strived to look at reality from a corpus pragmatic perspective and have evidenced the importance of digital access to society, information and language teaching methodology.

The volume is divided into three sections. The first section is called ‘Society, social networks and corpus pragmatics’, the second section is entitled ‘Linguistic and educational implications of corpus pragmatics’, and the third section contains relevant book reviews.

The first section, ‘Society, social networks and corpus pragmatics’, starts with a contribution entitled ‘Towards a cyberpragmatics of mobile instant messaging’, by Francisco Yus. The author, who previously explored cyberpragmatics from a contextual perspective (Yus 2011), approaches internet-mediated communication from a cognitive-relevance theoretical angle. The aim of the chapter is to investigate the inferential strategies to process information on the Net by “addressee users”. The author describes in detail the main research issues the study of mobile instant messaging applications. The ultimate aim of cyberpragmatics is to explain how users make sense of messages on the Net and, in the case of mobile phone-mediated interaction, the author’s suggestion is the need not only to include propositional but also non-propositional aspects of communication.

The next chapter, by Carmen Santamaría-García, has the title ‘Connected parents: combining online and off-line parenthood in blogs and vlogs’ and explores evaluative discourse in a corpus sample of parents’ vlogs (video blogs) and blogs. The parents discuss family tasks and responsibilities online about the issue of parenthood. Specifically, the author investigates the meanings of affect, judgment and appreciation, as well as positive politeness in the online and off-line construction of parenthood. The study shows two main patterns in parents’ practices: the quest for perfection through juggling and multi-tasking, and the resistance to social and familiar demands vis-a-vis their parental duties.

‘Healing and comfort on the net: Gender and emotions in violent domestic environments’, by Eva M. Mestre-Mestre, also deals with domestic realms. The article explores the online expression of emotions in distressing contexts through Computer Mediated Communication. Specifically, the author studies the language used in a corpus of cases of violence against women, and the expression of painful and supportive attitudes. The study opens new paths in the understanding of how women suffer and how they are consoled by other women on the net, which can surely be a useful tool for therapists and social workers to approach these painful situations anonymously.

The following chapter is entitled ‘“The more please [places] I see the more I think of home”: On gendered discourse of Irishness and migration experiences’ and is authored by Nancy E. Avila-Ledesma, & Carolina P. Amador-Moreno. The aim of the investigation is to analyse the challenges faced by Irish emigrants and their diasporic identities in new communities far from their homes. Specifically, the article explores gender and the conceptualization of Irishness in post-famine emigrants’ letters. Methodologically speaking, the paper takes an interdisciplinary approach combining sociolinguistics (Chamber 2009) and corpus pragmatics (Romero-Trillo 2008, 2013) to understand better the emotional load of the key terms that contribute to the gender differentiation in the negotiation of Irishness in emigrants.

The chapter 'A cross-linguistic study of conceptual metaphors in financial discourse' by María Muelas-Gil, analyses the explanatory strength of conceptual metaphors in economics and financial reporting. According to the author, one particular feature of this discourse is its heavy metaphorical nature due to its specific terminology. The article investigates the most salient metaphorical expressions in the field and shows their different cognitive conceptualisation by experts and non-experts, both in English and Spanish. The analysis of financial and economic metaphors in the article comprises three generic groups: the Great Chain of Being, the Image-Schema and the Events metaphor. The results indicate that cross-linguistic studies of metaphors can raise translators' and E.S.P. teachers' awareness of their relevance.

The second section of the volume, 'Linguistic and educational implications of corpus pragmatics', verses on the role of corpora and pragmatic awareness in language teaching. The first chapter of this section, by Edie Furniss, is entitled 'Teaching pragmatics with corpus data: The development of a corpus-referred website for the instruction of routine formulas in Russian', avers although recent studies in computer-assisted language learning (CALL) applications have incorporated pragmatics instruction, they have not fully implemented corpus data. The chapter shows the methodology used in the construction of a corpus-based online instructional website for the teaching of routine formulae in Russian. The author's intention is to promote the use of corpus methodologies in pragmatics instruction as well as to recommend specific strategies for other scholars interested in CALL.

Fiona MacArthur contributes to the volume with the chapter 'Beyond engaged listenership: Assessing Spanish undergraduates' active participation in academic mentoring sessions in English as academic lingua franca'. The study focuses on the language used in the academic mentoring of undergraduate students in their L2. The article examines a corpus of conversations recorded at several European universities in which Spanish Erasmus students sought advice from their lecturers about various aspects of their academic work. The particular topic under research is the student responses to the advice given by their mentors and how the students position themselves in the tutorial sessions. The final aim of the linguistic analysis is to find out ways to improve the secondary role of students so that they can find academic mentoring sessions more advantageous in their educational process.

The next chapter, 'Focusing on content or language?: comparing paired conversations in CLIL and EFL classrooms, using a corpus', by Keiko Tsuchiya, compares two dyad interactions of Japanese learners of English in a Content and Language Integrated Learning classroom (CLIL) and in a General English class (GE) at a Japanese university. The analysis showed differences between the two teaching styles in turns (regarding length and quantity), in the modes of endorsement to others' discourse, and in the types of repair. Apart from the clear linguistic implications of the two styles of classroom interaction, the author also points to the different consequences of these forms regarding the theory of communicative action.

The following chapter, 'Writers' uncertainty in a corpus of scientific biomedical articles with a diachronic perspective', is authored by Andrzej Zuczkowski, Ramona Bongelli, Ilaria Riccioni, Massimiliano Valetta and Roberto Burro and focuses on how science communicates uncertainty from a diachronic perspective based on a corpus of the British Medical Journal.

They base their analysis on the number of Uncertainty Markers (UMs) and their linguistic scope along 167 years, and they try to link this to the fact that the translation of scientific discoveries to practice may be related to how uncertainty is portrayed in the academic literature. Andrea Scibetta's contribution ends the second part of the volume. His chapter 'Chinese University Students' Development of Pragmatic Skills in L2 Italian: a Corpus-Based Study' focuses on the pragmatic development of Chinese University students' learning Italian. The paper follows an experimental approach in which students perform written and oral activities about specific pragmatic skills to deepen the knowledge about the difficulties as well as the specificities of Chinese students. Also, and based on the results, the paper suggests some effective teaching techniques to help the students develop their pragmatic competence faster.

The last section of the volume presents the reviews of three books of interest to pragmaticians and corpus linguists. The first, written by Claire Childs, is a review of the book edited by Bamford, Cavalieri and Diani (2013) entitled 'Variation and Change in Spoken and Written Discourse: Perspectives from Corpus Linguistics'. The second review is by Sofia Malamatidou on the volume by Kruger, Wallmach and Munday (2011) with the title 'Corpus-Based Translation Studies: Research and Applications'. The third review is on the volume by Hyland, Huat and Handford (2012) entitled 'Corpus Applications in Applied Linguistics', and is authored by Karen Donnelly.

References

Bauman, Z., & Bordoni, C. (2014). *State of crisis*. Cambridge: Polity Books Ltd.

Caparrós, M. (2015). *El Hambre*. Madrid: Anagrama.

Chamber, J. K. (2009). *Sociolinguistic theory* (Rev. ed.). Oxford: Wiley-Blackwell.

Rifkin, J. (2001). *The age of access: The new culture of Hypercapitalism*. New York: TarcherPerigee.

Romero-Trillo, J. (Ed.). (2008). *Pragmatics and corpus linguistics: A mutualistic Entente*. Berlin: Mouton de Gruyter.

Romero-Trillo, J. (Ed.). (2013). *The yearbook of corpus linguistics and pragmatics 2013: New domains and methodologies*. Dordrecht: Springer.

Yus, F. (2011). *Cyberpragmatics*. Amsterdam: John Benjamins.

Part I
Society, Social Networks and Corpus Pragmatics

Towards a Cyberpragmatics of Mobile Instant Messaging

Francisco Yus

Abstract Cyberpragmatics analyses Internet-mediated communication from a cognitive pragmatics, relevance-theoretic perspective. It focuses on the inferential strategies that "addressee users" engage in while processing information located on the Net or the one exchanged with other users through this virtual medium. In this sense, the theory underlines the role that the interfaces play in the eventual (ir)relevant outcome of the acts of communication that take place on the Net. In this chapter, I will sketch the main research issues that cyberpragmatics should address when studying mobile instant messaging applications (*WhatsApp*, *WeChat*, *Snapchat*...). As a theory grounded in cognitive pragmatics, cyberpragmatics aims at explaining how users make sense of messages when transmitted on the Net. However, in order to achieve that, an extension of analysis is proposed as necessary for this kind of mobile phone-mediated interaction, so as to cover not only propositional aspects of communication (i.e. the relevance of the information exchanged), but also non-propositional constraints and effects associated with this kind of communication and which play a major role in the eventual (dis)satisfaction. New terminology will be added to the general relevance-theoretic formula of positive cognitive effects vs. mental effort, opening up interesting paths for future research on why mobile-mediated interactions end up (ir)relevant to the users.

Keywords WhatsApp • Mobile instant messaging • Cyberpragmatics • Contextual constraints • Non-propositional effects

1 Cognitive Pragmatics and Cyberpragmatics

Relevance Theory (Sperber and Wilson 1995, henceforth RT) claims that all human cognition is relevance-oriented, to the extent that all the stimuli that humans pay attention to are selected due to their potential interest while many others are discarded due to their irrelevance. This general tendency to focus on potentially

F. Yus (✉)
Departamento de Filología Inglesa, Universidad de Alicante,
Apartado 99, E-03080 Alicante, Spain
e-mail: francisco.yus@ua.es

J. Romero-Trillo (ed.), *Yearbook of Corpus Linguistics and Pragmatics 2016*,
Yearbook of Corpus Linguistics and Pragmatics 4,
DOI 10.1007/978-3-319-41733-2_2

relevant inputs is covered by the *cognitive principle of relevance*: "Human beings are geared to the maximization of relevance". With this evolved cognitive ability, humans are really good at minimising mental effort by selecting from context only the quantity and quality of information that is bound to aid in deriving relevant conclusions from any input. An example is provided in Yus (2011a) concerning a doctorate student that comes across a yellow Mercedes while walking on campus:

(1) New information (visual input):
A yellow Mercedes is parked near our Department.
(2) Information already available (from encyclopaedic knowledge):
a. Professor Smith, who supervises my thesis, owns a yellow Mercedes.
b. Professor Smith usually takes the bus to the university.
c. Only when he intends to stay at university till late in the evening does he drive his car to university (since there are no late buses returning to where he lives).
(3) (Relevant) conclusion (inferred by combining (1) and (2)):
This evening I will be able to discuss with him at length how my thesis is progressing.

RT would claim that in a situation where (1) is processed, (3) would be relevant since it can only result from the combination of (1) and (2). A similar procedure also applies to linguistic communication (see below) and, as is claimed within cyberpragmatics, also to Internet-mediated communication. This cognitive principle is at work in the processing of any kind of stimulus, both verbal and visual (and also applies to one's own thoughts in a specific situation, some of which are more likely to be entertained than others).

However, RT is more interested in narrowing down this broad application of the cognitive principle to the specific analysis of verbal communication, as we can deduce from the main objective of RT: "to identify underlying mechanisms, rooted in human psychology, which explain how humans communicate with one another" (Sperber and Wilson 1995: 32). Again, and included in the aforementioned *cognitive principle*, there is another principle but communication-centred: the *communicative principle of relevance*: "Every act of ostensive communication conveys the presumption of its own optimal relevance". This presumption sets inferential strategies in motion in order to turn the schematic meaning of the words uttered by the speaker into a contextualised and meaningful proposition matching the intended interpretation. To accomplish this choice of interpretations, addressees invariably tend to choose the first interpretation that provides an optimal balance between the following two conditions (square brackets now added):

Condition a. An assumption [*information*, in plain words] is relevant to an individual to the extent that the positive cognitive effects [its *interest*, in plain words] achieved when it is optimally processed are large.

Condition b. An assumption is relevant to an individual to the extent that the [*mental*] effort required to achieve these positive cognitive effects is small.

Needless to say, to determine which is the first, most relevant interpretation depends enormously on context accessibility. According to the *underdeterminacy thesis*, all utterances communicate more information than the meaning that is literally coded, and the addressee has to use context to turn this schematic meaning into a fully contextualised and relevant interpretation. This applies to the explicit level of interpretation (*explicatures*), since addressees often have to engage in reference resolution (4a), disambiguation, resolution of the domain of quantifiers (4b), concept adjustment (4c), saturation of unarticulated constituents (4d), etc. And of course, the gap between what is coded and what is meant and interpreted is even higher in the case of implicit communication (*implicatures*), which are inferred beyond the propositional information of the utterance with the aid of contextual information. In this way, that same utterance may convey utterly different implicatures when contextual support varies. An example is provided in Mike's answer to John in (5). If John can access the intended contextual information (6a–c), he will derive the different implicatures (6a′–c′).

(4) a. I saw *her there* talking to *Peter*.
I saw [*whom?*] [*where?*] talking to [*whom?*].
b. I've got *nothing* to wear for the party.
I've got nothing [*elegant, classy*] to wear for the party.
c. John *drinks* too much.
John drinks [*alcohol*] too much.
d. She is a better candidate.
She is a better candidate [*than whom?*] [*for what?*].

(5) John: Now, tell me, how's your girlfriend?
Mike: She's no longer my girlfriend.

(6) a. [*Mike and his girlfriend have been preparing the wedding ceremony*].
a′ Implicature: Mike and his girlfriend are now married.
b. [*A woman normally stops being a girlfriend when she splits up with her boyfriend*].
b′ Implicature: Mike and his girlfriend have split up.
c. [*Mike's girlfriend was suffering from terminal cancer*].
c′ Implicature: Mike's girlfriend has passed away.

Cyberpragmatics (Yus 2001, 2010, 2011a, 2013) aims to apply these relevance-theoretic claims to the specific environment of Internet-mediated communication. One of the central aims is to determine why Internet users often resort to and find relevance in plain text-based communication even though several options with a higher level of contextualisation (video, sound) are also available in many interfaces used nowadays for Internet-mediated interactions. It also analyses how users fill the gap between what is coded and what is interpreted, and the role of technological aspects in the eventual assessment of relevance (cognitive effects vs. processing effort, as mentioned above). In this sense, it should be stressed that the inferential strategies used for interpreting discourses sent through the Net do not differ from the ones used in the interpretation of utterances in situations of physical co-presence. There is only one biologically rooted ability to obtain relevant interpretations, regardless of the type of utterance, the channel used, and the richness of contextual information.

Similarly, users expect their virtual interlocutors to retrieve from context some specific information that will enable them to reach the intended interpretation of their messages. However, the characteristics of the different applications for Internet communication (chatrooms, Messenger, e-mail, Web pages, etc.) affect the quality and quantity of contextual information accessed by users, the mental effort devoted to interpretation, and the choice of an interpretation. In short, cyberpragmatics analyses exchanges that take place in all forms of Internet-mediated communication, and what we can label the "material qualities" of the interfaces (basically their position on the verbal-visual and oral-written scales in terms of options for contextualisation) will have an impact on the balance of cognitive effects (i.e., interest) and mental effort obtained during the relevance-seeking interpretation of these utterances.

2 SMS, IM and MIM

Mobile phone applications such as *WhatsApp*, *Snapchat* or *WeChat*, among many others, are initially intended to provide users with the possibility to send typed messages to friends or contacts. As such, they look as if they are actually an evolution of SMS communication, but in reality typing words on the screen is the only similarity with SMS, since they are closer to the instant messaging programs (IM) that were so popular several years ago, among them the once ubiquitous *Messenger*, now extinct. This is why these applications are generically labelled *mobile instant messaging* (henceforth MIM) and their options for communication are also higher. Among the qualities that these applications exhibit, we should underline the fact that MIM apps offer users a whole range of types of discourse that may be communicated. Apart from typed texts, users may send photos, audio files, videos, links to websites, information on physical location, etc. Lately, they have also incorporated the possibility of making free phone calls directly from the application. In any case, MIM is felt as quasi-conversational, more fluid than SMS. In Church and de Oliveira (2013: 354), a user comments that "with *WhatsApp* maybe you type more, but the conversation is more fluid. You type a sentence and someone sends a sentence and then you type another one. I have the feeling that if it's *WhatsApp*, it's an open conversation. It is similar to if you were talking in person".

Besides, MIM is mainly meant to sustain communication with friends that the user knows already and with whom he/she already interacts in physical, face-to-face scenarios. Nevertheless, these applications have also proved essential to maintain contact with people who live far away, as in the case of students who interact with their parents when they are living abroad (Awan and Gauntlett 2013: 118). In general MIM is a clear example of the convergence (and clash) of increasingly *virtualised* physical settings for interactions and a growing *physicalisation* of virtual environments for interactions. Since communication has evolved towards a total hybridisation of physical-virtual scenarios in personal networks (Yus 2007), MIM allows for (mainly) synchronic text or audio file-based conversations that substitute physical interactions or complement them efficiently. As Ahad and Lim (2014: 190) summarise, MIM (specifically *WhatsApp*) allows for better accessibility and ease of communication offering real-time messaging, empowerment, sense of belongingness and sociability, enjoyment, quick information-sharing and cost benefits. It is commonly adopted for convenience in communication and because it saves money, and is also popular for entertainment purposes such as to share jokes or funny photos or audios. On the other hand, it is also used to 'dwell' with people in the virtual space, with effects such as a sense of group membership, as well as a secured and committed bond (see below).

In fact, this kind of mediated text- or file-based interaction has become the norm, being now preferred to traditional phone calls. Indeed, very often users prefer exchanging texts or recorded audio files that resemble a phone conversation rather than engaging in an actual phone call. A possible explanation lies in the synchronous-asynchronous interface. SMS is typically asynchronous, although it can reproduce a quasi-synchronous conversation if the system manages to send the messages fast. On the other hand, MIM is typically synchronous, with long exchanges of conversations taking place between users, but it also possesses an asynchronous potential. Park and Sundar (2015: 122) point in the same direction when they comment that IM-sustained interactions tend to exhibit the classic features of informal face-to-face communications, being diplomatic, brief, dyadic and full of context. "The relative synchronicity of IM allows participants to determine one's availability at very short notice and carry out communications with greater potential for immediacy behaviours that are known to engender a higher psychological sense of social presence".

Users may also prefer to send a typed message or an audio file, which provides the interlocutor with a certain freedom to reply any time they want, than an intrusive phone call that demands instant attention and participation by the interlocutor. Additionally, MIM may be more convenient than phone or face-to-face communication if the user has to coordinate actions with a number of people simultaneously. As Knop et al. (2016: 1078) correctly remark, as the number of interaction partners increases, it becomes more and more difficult to coordinate and communicate with each other in a face-to-face situation. Therefore, social groups might value the opportunity of communicating via MIM and receiving immediate feedback.

IM and MIM also share the capability for notifications regarding who has contacted the user though these programs or applications, which is a nice example of the duality of intentions suggested within RT: the *informative intention* (the intention to inform the interlocutor of something) and the *communicative intention* (the intention to alert the interlocutor to this informative intention). With the latter, the speaker can effectively draw the interlocutor's attention and direct it to his/her intentions. In this case, the stimulus acquires an ostensive quality. In this duality of intentions, linguistic communication is very useful because, whenever a person talks to us, we immediately identify at least his/her communicative intention. Similarly, IM generates pop-up windows on the taskbar that warn users of an in-coming message while, at the same time, a sound is heard; and MIM applications display a message on the mobile phone screen, alerting the user to an in-coming message. From a cyberpragmatic point of view, this "visual warning" is useful to stress the user's communicative intention underlying his/her informative intention. However, it may also produce disturbances in the user's task at hand, a negative non-intended non-propositional effect, as will be labelled below.

In both IM and MIM, we can also find default messages available on the user's profile, called *away messages* in IM and *status messages* in MIM. These are often personalised and are available even when the user is not logged onto the system. Specifically, away messages are a useful tool for the management of interactive availability in a type of interaction where, as Baym (2010: 43) explains, "everything from the onscreen activity with its colours and mosaic of windows to the physical environment of the user who may be listening to music, talking on the phone or engaged in exogenous conversations are also important to forming the whole IM experience". When the user personalises messages, very often they aim to call other users' attention, for example with humorous quotes or explaining in detail the reasons for being absent.

An element that differentiates IM from MIM is the notification of contacts entering the system. In the former, the user is given an alert message informing of contacts' connection to the program, which is normally absent in MIM. In the latter, users do have information about whether the user is online or not, which causes a lot of privacy issues and generates many misunderstandings concerning availability for conversation and willingness to reply to the user's message. This effect has been accentuated by additional sources of information, as in the polemic "blue double click" in *WhatsApp*, which informs the user that the addressee has not only received the message, but also read it. Actually, users often disable these "last time online" and "double click" options for privacy and to prevent unwanted inferences.

Besides, the management of multiple conversations is easier in IM than in MIM. In the former, the user can have multiple windows open with parallel conversations. In this case, the user has to monitor and follow, in a relevant manner, several conversational threads with different people and about different topics simultaneously, despite the effort-producing challenge that this involves. This multi-party activity is related to the social need to make it clear to other users (i.e. to obtain a mutual manifestness) that the user is connected and able to sustain several interactions, a signal of sociability and a source of prestige for other users. In fact, a third of the informants in Boneva et al. (2006) commented that one of the strong features of IM is, precisely, the possibility of carrying on multiple conversations simultaneously, what Garrett and Danziger (2007) call *polychronic communication*. This "strong feature" certainly demands extra cognitive resources and supplementary mental effort to maintain "interactive congruency" throughout all the conversations in these windows. By contrast, this kind of "multi-windows management" is more challenging in MIM. These applications do allow for multi-party conversations in groups, but in order to have multiple one-to-one conversations, the user has to return to the main chat area, where conversational partners are listed and resume conversations with the other users, which may turn out tiring and demanding, especially if the parallel interlocutors demand instant replies to their messages.

3 Basic Cyberpragmatic Research on MIM

In the same way that RT is interested in how addressees turn words into meaningful and contextualised interpretations that differ, to a greater or lesser extent, from the literal meaning encoded by these words, cyberpragmatics is also interested in how users make sense of the messages that they are sent through the Net.

One central interest within cyberpragmatics is to determine the extent to which the interfaces used for Internet-mediated communication favour sufficient contextualisation so as to convey the users' messages and their intended interpretations in a satisfactory (relevant) way. This entails analysing the texts themselves and whether (and how much) the interfaces allow for the communication of nonverbal information (in its vocal, visual or multimodal quality) which typically combines with verbal communication to guarantee a successful interpretive outcome. In parallel, it analyses why users tend to rely on cues-filtered, poorly contextualised forms of Internet communication when other more contextualised options are available even within the same app or program. Indeed, MIM users stick to plain text even though free phone calls or even video calls are also available from these apps. Apart from not willing to be intrusive when making a phone call, another reason why many MIM users shy away from direct face-to-face contact may be the challenge of controlling the interrelation of verbal and nonverbal information on the fly. The control that users have over other users' impressions and interpretations may lead to a preference for text-based virtual conversations. The new developments in this type of mobile-mediated interactions, for example the introduction of phone calls, add a new dimension because users have to assess to what extent they are willing to let other users perceive their vocal and visual nonverbal behaviour (intentional or exuded) and which impressions they want to convey. Nowadays, despite these developments in MIM applications, many users still resort to (more secure) plain-text-based communication, except when interacting with close friends and relatives.

Concerning the limitations imposed by the MIM interface upon effective communication and contextualisation, we can conclude that some of these are also found in chat rooms (Yus 2005, 2011a). Among others, the following can be listed:

1. In MIM, text-based conversational turns are subject to the sequencing imposed by the application that manages interactions. The imposed sequencing of utterances may have little to do with the intended sequence of turns, and this may lead to misunderstandings, especially in multi-party conversational groups. Besides, as Nilsen and Mäkitalo (2010: 92) comment, programs for text-based interactions -specifically chat rooms- are designed so that several persons can post messages simultaneously, which means that there is no competition for the floor since all messages sent off will be posted.
2. One of the most typical attributes of chat rooms is the juxtaposition of several conversational threads on the same screen. This may also be the found in MIM communication, but with variations. In chat rooms, unless the user is engaged in a private conversation with another user (in a different window), the norm is that all the messages arrive at the "central area" of the chat room, together with messages that the system creates automatically. By contrast, in MIM communication, one-to-one interactions are the norm, but there are also groups in which multiple threads of conversation may overlap without a clear linear arrangement. Even within the same conversation, the application may reproduce conversational threads in an unwanted order, and this quality might produce increased effort when following conversations that are mixed up without a clear arrangement, and affect the users' eventual estimation of relevance. Consider the following MIM conversation that took place on February 7th, 2016 through *WhatsApp* between a female (A) and a male (B) user.

(7) A: La voy a facturar en el aeropuerto [*I'm going to check her in at the airport*].
B: Eso [*That's it*].
A Egipto, que allí los idolatran [*To Egypt, since they idolise them there*].
A: Jaja
O a Marruecos pa q aprenda lo que vale un peine [*Or to Morocco, so that she learns the tough way*]
Q está muy mimadita [*because she's too spoiled*]
B: Yeah
A: Yastan aqui mis padres [*My parents are here already*]
B: Que vea que la vida no es solo hacer trastadas [*She has to realise that life is not all about playing tricks around*].
A: 😩
B: Ohhhh
Planazo [*Great plan*]
A: Total [*Totally*]
B: Yo iré al gym luego [*I'll go to the gym later*]

In this conversation, the initial topic is how angry A is with her naughty cat. Half-way through the conversation, A informs B that her parents have just arrived

(*Yastan aquí mis padres*), but B's next message is still related to the naughty cat, and the application has reproduced it in strict order of arrival to the system. Similarly, A's next message, an emoji of anguish which codes a whole proposition (roughly "my parents' visit depresses me"), does not refer to the cat either, but it follows B's cat-related message. These mixed-up threads in MIM conversations may be a potential source of misunderstanding or of increased processing effort.

Given the limitations that plain text messages exhibit when compared to face-to-face exchanges, one of the central areas of cyberpragmatic research focuses on the users' ability to connote their messages with different attributes of orality, typically found in the vocal (e.g. repetition of letters and creative use of punctuation marks) and the visual (e.g. emoticons) channels of oral interactions (see Yus 2005; Bays 2008; Maíz-Arévalo 2015, among others). Therefore, cyberpragmatics analyses the challenges that users face when they attempt to compensate for this lack of orality and nevertheless expect to communicate not only the right interpretation from verbal content, but also the whole range of feelings, emotions and impressions associated with this content that are also relevant and may alter drastically the eventual interpretation of the accompanying verbal input. Certainly, very often more effort has to be devoted to tracking down underlying intentions, feelings, and emotions conveyed by text-based utterances, and users rely on these connotative techniques of vocal and visual text deformation in order to lead the interlocutor in the right interpretive direction.

Emoticons, now turned into fully iconic emoji, usually accompany verbal texts providing additional and relevant non-propositional information, and have become an inherent element in MIM communication. As summarised in Luor et al. (2010: 890), these iconic signs are indeed similar to non-verbal cues in face-to-face interactions, since they also help to accentuate or emphasise a tone or meaning during message creation and interpretation. Furthermore, they help to communicate more clearly a current mood or mental state of the user, also providing additional social cues about this person. Thus, emoticons serve the function of clarifying textual messages, which is similar to non-verbal displays in physical scenarios. However, emoticons or emoji may also appear with no accompanying text, usually typed for the sake of brevity and typing economy. MIM users are now accustomed to inferring propositional interpretations from sequences of emoji, often without accompanying text.

In Yus (2011a), it was wrongly claimed that emoticons (and by extension emoji) mainly play the role of redundancy regarding the text to which they are attached, as in "I feel great today :-)", in which the emoticon seems to add no further meaning to what is said verbally. However, emoji signs are typed with an expectation of relevance. Their readers are pushed into supplementary mental effort to determine the feeling or emotion that underlies the emoji and to work out its relationship to what has been typed verbally. This extra effort has to be offset with additional interest (cognitive effects). In this sense, Lo (2008) and Luor et al. (2010: 891) comment that when Internet users are faced with text without emoticons, most of them cannot perceive the correct emotion, attitude, and intent of the sender. On the contrary, the combination of visual cues and text does create a more positive attitude than text alone. Therefore, both emoticons and evolved iconic emojis do perform a number of substantial functions that are crucial to get the right interpretation of the text typed on the mobile phone keyboard. Huang et al. (2008: 466) also noticed that users exhibit more "enjoyment, personal interaction, perceived information richness, and perceived usefulness" when interacting in emoticon-laden virtual conversations.

Several classifications of functions of emoticons have been proposed. For example, Xu et al. (2007) list three of them: to accentuate or emphasise a tone or meaning of the message, to establish the current mood or impression of the sender, and to make the otherwise completely textual conversation creative and visually salient. By contrast, in Yus (2014a) up to eight of these functions were isolated, all of which are present in MIM text-based interactions. These will be briefly described and illustrated below.

1. *To signal the propositional attitude that underlies the utterance and which would be difficult to identify without the aid of the emoji.* Propositional attitudes are important for successful interactions, since they introduce an additional metarepresentational layer of information beyond the explicit content of the utterance. Speakers rely on a number of verbal elements to convey attitudes, including that-clauses introduced by an attitudinal verb, as in (8a), parenthetical clauses (8b), verbal moods (8c), illocutionary adverbials (8d), and evidentials (8e), among others:

(8) a. I regret that you failed your exam.
b. It's time to go, I guess.
c. Come here right now!
d. Frankly, I am not surprised.
e. No doubt, he is the best candidate for the job.

Sometimes, though, the underlying attitude can only be derived from non-linguistic evidence, and this is where emojis may play a clarifying role. Consider (9):

(9) Yo no tengo tiempo de aburrirme, ni de leer :((
[*I have no time to get bored, nor to read :((*].
Que toquen en martes no nos facilita las cosas :,(
[*The fact that they are playing on a Tuesday, doesn't make things easier :,(*].
Aquí no hay fingers, y mira q los he buscado :-(
[*There are no fingers here, and I looked for them everywhere :-(*].

In all of these cases, the user "regrets that *p*" (*p* being time to read, etc.), but the identification of this attitude is made possible with the aid of the emoji, otherwise the utterances could have been considered mere assertions. This use is similar to the one found in face-to-face interactions, where certain aspects of the speaker's attitude are most often expressed through non-linguistic or paralinguistic cues.

2. *To communicate a higher intensity of a propositional attitude that has already been coded verbally.* In this case, the user does resort to a linguistic means to communicate the propositional attitude, and the emoji adds to the eventual relevance by adding an additional layer of intensity in the way this attitude is held, as in (10) below:

(10) Espero que siempre os acordéis de mis lecciones de español :-)
[*I hope you'll always remember my Spanish lessons :-)*].

3. *To strengthen/mitigate the illocutionary force of a speech act.* Emoji may also achieve relevance by enhancing or softening the illocutionary force of speech acts and thus communicate a more adequate extent of the impact that the user intends with his/her utterance. The mitigating function is usually more frequent than the strengthening one. Dresner and Herring (2010): 64–66) suggest these examples:

(11) a. I would like a non-circumventing solution;->
b. I am very sensitive and cry easily, and gets even worse when i feel awful :)

In (11a), the winking emoticon indicates that the message should not be taken as a request or a demand, as its form ("I would like") otherwise suggests. Instead, its function is to downgrade the utterance to a less face-threatening speech act, a simple assertion. In (11b), the emoticon mitigates what otherwise looks like a self-pitying list of complaints, suggesting that the interpretation is not that of complaining, but rather asserting or describing.

4. *To contradict the explicit content of the utterance (a): Joking.* An important role of emoji in MIM is to signal that the user should not be understood literally, that the underlying intention is to joke about some state of affairs, and therefore the propositional attitude is not that of endorsement but of humorous dissociation. The relevance of the emoji lies in its capability to direct the reader away from a literal interpretation of the utterance and, instead, to offer him/her interpretive reward in terms of generation of humorous effects. An example is (12):

(12) a. [Text commenting on a photo of a shop with the same name as the addressee user].
No sabía que tenías una tienda en Alicante :)))))) Besos…
[*I didn't know you had a shop in Alicante :)))))). Kisses…*].

5. *To contradict the explicit content of the utterance (b): Irony.* A similar case to joking, this time involving contradicting propositional content due to an ironic intention. The main difference with jokes is the explicit dissociative attitude that

irony exhibits. Spotting this attitude as dissociative is essential to differentiate irony from the incongruity found in jokes. An example is (13):

(13) Que vida mas dura xD
[*What a hard life you lead xD*].

6. *To add a feeling or emotion towards the propositional content of the utterance (affective attitude towards the utterance).* Emoji is very often used in MIM to convey feelings and emotions (and the affective attitudes attached to utterances), which are different from propositional attitudes, although the dividing line is often blurred (see Yus 2014a for examples of overlapping classifications). This sixth function refers to occurrences in which the user shows, with the aid of emojis, a certain feeling or emotion towards the content of the utterance. Examples include (14a–b):

(14) a. En Badajoz, nació sobrina :-) !!!
[*In Badajoz, my niece was born :-) !!!*]
b. El reencuentro se acercaaaaa :-)
[*The reunion is approaching :-)*].

7. *To add a feeling or emotion towards the communicative act (feeling or emotion in parallel to the communicative act).* Sometimes, nonverbal behaviour has a more social connotation (the typical quality of phatic exchanges), in which the speakers show what the act of communicating or interacting *as a whole* is making them feel, and hence the nonverbal behaviour is produced in parallel to the verbal content, thereby connoting the communicative act, rather than only qualifying the propositional content being typed. This function is illustrated in (15a–b) in Yus (ibid.):

(15) User 1: que guapa!!!peazo fiestas que te pegas, no paras!!!! :-)
[*How pretty!!! Some parties, uh! You never stop!!!! :-)*].
User 2: La próxima t aviso a ver si te animas!!! :-)
[*Next time, I'll give you the heads up in case you feel like coming!!! :-)*].

In (15), user 2 is not using the emoticon because she is happy to let user 1 know about a future party, or happy to ask whether user 1 will be willing to go. Instead, she is showing the kind of nonverbal behaviour that is aroused by the fact that she is communicating with user 2, by the prospect of getting user 1 to join her in the party, and in general by the emotions that she feels while she is typing that message for user 1 (including a feeling of bonding or enhanced friendship), rather than towards the content of the message itself. Besides, the message needs inferencing so as to be turned into a fully propositional and relevant explicature. The development of user 2's message would be as follows:

(16) a. Contextualised proposition (via inferential enrichment):
Next time [*that I go to a party*] I'll give you the heads up in case you feel like coming [*there with me*].
b. Proposition plus propositional attitude:
[*I inform you that/I promise you that*] Next time [*that I go to a party*] I'll give you the heads up in case you feel like coming [*there with me*].
c. Proposition plus propositional attitude plus affective attitude (towards the communicative act):
[*I am happy to tell you that**] [*I inform you that/I promise you that*] Next time [*that I go to a party*] I'll give you the heads up in case you feel like coming [*there with me*] [*and I insist on your coming with me***].
* Communicated by the emoticon.
** Communicated by the repetition of the exclamation mark.

8. *To communicate the intensity of a feeling or emotion that has been coded verbally*. Finally, emoji can also enhance the intensity of a feeling or emotion which has already been coded verbally in the message. Some examples are provided in (17), where the emotions conveyed by the words in italics are enhanced by the addition of an emoji (here replaced with a simpler emoticon for editing convenience):

(17) a. Esta va por mi hermana y por los bailes ochenteros, *nos encantan* :-)
[*This is on my sister and the dances of the 80s, we love them :-)*].
b. No me gusta, me rechifla! Me has *emocionado*, amiga :-)
[*I don't like it, I love it! You've really moved me, my friend :-)*].

4 Extended Cyberpragmatic Research

RT (and cyberpragmatics) analyses four types of communicated content. Firstly, explicit interpretations (*explicatures*), which differ, to a greater or lesser extent, from the meaning literally coded by the utterance. Secondly, implicated conclusions (*implicatures*), fully inferential and obtained from combining the explicature and further contextual information. Thirdly, feelings, emotions or impressions, of a non-propositional quality, but which the communicator intends the interlocutor to recover as part of the relevant interpretation of his/her communicative activity. An often cited example is provided in Sperber and Wilson (1995: 55), about a couple that has just arrived at the seaside. She opens the window overlooking the sea and sniffs appreciatively and ostensively. When Peter looks at her, there is no specific interpretation that comes to his attention: the air smells fresh, fresher than it did in town, it reminds him of their previous holidays, he can smell the sea, seaweed, ozone, fish; all sorts of pleasant things come to mind, and since her sniff was appreciative, he is bound to assume that she must have intended him to notice at least some of them, he is unlikely to be able to pin down her intentions any further. Finally, RT also addresses what they call *weak implicatures*, not overtly intended by the speaker and forming a continuum between those that the speaker strongly holds as part of his/her intentions, and others which are derived by the hearer's sole responsibility.

These four types of communicated content are obtained as part of the relevance-seeking interpretive procedure. However, the underlying assumption within RT is that information itself is relevant enough to be worth the hearer's interpretive activity. This claim clashes with today's tendency in Internet communication to base the relevance not on the objective value of the information transferred to other users, but on the effects that using this information -even if devoid of any informational value- produces on these users. Miller (2008) is right in pointing out that nowadays we are witnessing a shift from dialogue and communication between users on the Net, where the point of communication is to provide users with substantive content, to a situation where the maintenance of the network itself has become the primary focus, that is, communication and exchange of information subordinated to the maintenance of networks and to sustaining connected presence. This has resulted in a rise of what he calls *phatic media* in which communication without content has taken precedence. In other words, nowadays we witness a huge amount of Internet-mediated exchanges whose relevance does not lie in the content communicated, but in what the act of communication *as a whole* generates in users, providing non-propositional effects that compensate for the lack of relevance that the content inherently possesses. Indeed, we can find many instances of MIM interactions characterised by a phatic quality, filled with (apparently) irrelevant utterances if we analyse them from a purely informative point of view. But they do provide relevance in making mutually manifest assumptions such as awareness of co-presence inside the group or network of friends who are synchronously inter-connected, as well as relevance in the mutual manifestness of being present in the conversation, even if not actively participating. In MIM conversations, there is an interest in demonstrating that the user is part of the interaction, part of the collectivity, and very often, underlying the posting of photos, videos and recorded audios, there is a covert need to feel noticed and acknowledged by friends or collectivities (MIM groups).

Besides, Internet communication is affected by a number of interface-related and user-related qualities that may also alter the eventual estimation of the relevance of the act of communication in terms of cognitive effects and mental effort. These are mainly related to users' management of interface usability, the kind of relationship existing between interlocutors, etc.

As a consequence of the specificity of Internet-mediated communication, in previous research an extension of cyberpragmatic research (and, in parallel, of relevance-theoretic research) has been proposed by adding two elements that play a part in the eventual relevance of Internet-mediated communication, but which are not tied to the relevance of the content being communicated (Yus 2011b, 2014b, c, 2015a, b, c):

1. The term *contextual constraint*, restricted to aspects that underlie or "frame" communication and interaction (i.e. they exist prior to the interpretive activity) and constrain its eventual (un)successful outcome.
2. The term *non-intended non-propositional effect*, which refers to feelings, emotions, impressions, etc. which are not overtly intended, but are generated from the act of communication, and add (positively and negatively) to the cognitive effects derived from utterance interpretation or to the mental effort required for processing the utterance.

This pair of terms allows us to explain why users are glued to their mobile screens while they are exchanging utterly useless messages, why some users feel frustrated upon finding it extremely difficult to manage the mobile phone interface in order to achieve their communicative goals, etc. In a sense, these added elements operate at a different level from information-centred explicatures, implicatures, etc. The latter are constrained by the *communicative principle of relevance* and the expectation of informative reward. By contrast, these new terms are rather constrained by the *cognitive principle of relevance*, since they cover aspects not directly tied to the content of what is exchanged on the Net, but nevertheless alter the estimation of relevance of the act of communication as a whole. As a consequence, the aforementioned conditions of relevance, guided by optimal balances of cognitive effects and mental effort (repeated again below as clauses (a) and (b) for convenience) should be complemented with these new cognition-related terms, as defined in (a′) and (b′), respectively. Both (a–b) and (a′–b′) should be complemented if a more accurate description of what counts as "relevant" in Internet-mediated communication is intended:

Condition a — An assumption [*information*, in plain words] is relevant to an individual to the extent that the positive cognitive effects [its *interest*, in plain words] achieved when it is optimally processed are large.

Condition a′ — An assumption is relevant to an individual to the extent that the *non-intended non-propositional effects* add to the positive cognitive effects that the information produces in a specific context (to the extent that they make the act of communication relevant even if the actual content is itself irrelevant).

Condition b — An assumption is relevant to an individual to the extent that the [mental] effort required to achieve these positive cognitive effects is small.

Condition b′ — An assumption [*information*, in plain words] is relevant to an individual to the extent that the *contextual constraints* save (or at least do not add to) the addressee's mental effort devoted to the processing of the information in a specific context (to the extent that they threaten the eventual relevance of the act of communication).

In the specific context of MIM communication, we can list a number of constraints and non-propositional effects specifically affecting the eventual (ir)relevance of this kind of mobile phone-mediated interaction. A preliminary classification would yield two broad types depending on whether the constraints and non-propositional effects are interface-related (*user-to-system communication*), or user-centred (*user-to-user communication*). Some of them are briefly commented upon below. All of them are bound to alter the eventual estimation of the relevance of interactions carried out through MIM interfaces.

1. *Interface-related constraints.*

As pointed out above, these constraints, of a positive or negative quality, underlie or frame MIM communication, they exist prior to the actual act of communication, but affect the eventual relevance obtained by the user when attempting acts of communication through MIM applications. In this case, interface usability plays a major part in the eventual generation of (dis)satisfaction in the user. The mental effort will decrease if all the menus are clearly arranged, if the options for emoji use and typing conditions are satisfactory, etc. In this sense, Casaló et al. (2008) mention several factors that are related to usability, and which also apply to the use of MIM applications: (a) how easy it is to assimilate the structure of an interface, its functions, and the content; (b) how simple it is to use the interface at initial stages; (c) how fast users can find what they are searching for; (d) how easy the user feels it is to navigate the interface; and (e) to what extent can users control what they are doing and where they are at a particular stage of navigation. All of these factors have an influence in the eventual relevance of the content retrieved through the app and the kind of interactions sustained therein.

Besides usability, other constraints may be listed such as familiarity with the interface, user's task at hand and frequency of use.

2. *Interface-related non-propositional effects.*

The quality of the interface and the options for fulfilling the user's communicative needs generate a number of non-propositional effects. In general, the user may feel gratification if the interface serves all the communicative needs (positive effects) or impedes proper communication (negative effects). Satisfaction with the interface, feelings of enjoyment, opinion of reliability and usefulness towards the application, etc. count as possible non-propositional effects. Secondly, the user may feel that this kind of MIM-related communication is more appropriate and less "pushy" that traditional phone calls. Thirdly, if the interface allows for personalisation, the MIM user may feel isolated and special in the way the program addresses his/her preferences for communication.

Concerning negative outcomes, some of the already cited limitations of text-based communication may generate misunderstandings due to the way texts are sent and displayed on the mobile phone screen (an effect which users typically try to mitigate with the use of emoji that may produce better interpretations of plain text). Time is another constraint: if the application does not allow for a feeling of synchronicity in the way messages are displayed and replied to, the user may feel frustrated. Besides, the way notifications are personalised may generate effects regarding both privacy and interaction management. Users are often unable to process and reply to the barrage of notifications that remind the user of an in-coming message from a single user or from a group of users.

3. *User-to user constraints.*

Communication through MIM may be constrained by a number of user-centred non-propositional elements that influence the eventual (ir)relevant outcome of communication. Two of them involve (a) the kind of relationship held between the users and (b) the user's personality. The former may alter drastically which conversational topics are addressed, together with rules of politeness and the appropriateness of using emoji, among others. Concerning the latter, some users may shy away from interactions which exhibit too much information about themselves, for example rejecting the recording of voice messages because that level of contextualisation gives away too much information about their tone of voice or even indicates their lack of self-esteem.

4. *User-to-user non-propositional effects.*

A cyberpragmatics of MIM communication will me more interested in the kind of non-propositional effect that is generated out of users' interactions with other users and which adds, positively or negatively, to the (information-centred) cognitive effects, as predicted by RT.

On the positive side, users get an offset of non-propositional effects from the feeling of connectedness, of group membership, of being acknowledged within the network of friends and contacts. Users feel the capacity for non-stop inter-connection and interaction, and they build rewarding social capital in the process. This kind of sustained connectivity makes up for the loss of connections that physical scenarios exhibit nowadays (Yus 2007), but at the same time serves the purpose to manage and arrange actions and events that do take place offline. Besides, the continuous exchange of information generates a more fine-grained sense of mutuality between interactants, a sort of cumulative background knowledge that can be used as preliminary context for future interactions, both online and offline.

On the personal point of view, with MIM users are provided with an opportunity for self-expression and identity management, often through sustained acknowledgment from friends.

Some negative non-propositional effects may also be isolated. One major source of dissatisfaction has to do with the chronemics of MIM communication. Indeed, MIM users are under constant pressure to reply to messages, and failure to do so in as short time as possible leads to negative reactions, recrimination, and overall misunderstandings. An example is *WhatsApp*. Initially, the "person is online" status information on the user was already a source of misunderstandings, since a message sent to someone who was supposed to be online demanded immediate reply, which is not always possible (but the sender has no idea of this unavailability). Recently, the introduction of the famous "blue double click" has also triggered a number of misunderstandings. This double click is supposed to inform the user that the addressee has not only received the message, but has already read it. Then, an absent immediate reply often generates complaints from the "sender user", but the reality is that the addressee may have indeed read the message, but there may be a myriad of reasons why he/she was unable to reply to it, information which is not mutual to both interlocutors. In general, so-called "peer pressure" is a constant source of dissatisfaction because users feel overwhelmed by the pressure to reply to all messages and as soon as possible. Small wonder, many users disable both the "user online" status information and that "blue double click" from the system.

Finally, there are many unwanted non-propositional effects related to the management of feelings and emotions communicated through MIM. Even though users rely on galleries of emojis in order to try to get an interpretation not only of the propositional content but also of the feelings, emotions attached to this content, the reality is that many MIM users complain that their messages get misinterpreted, that their emotions are not clearly conveyed and that sometimes the text typed is not rich enough to manage their communicative needs effectively.

5 Concluding Remarks

Cyberpragmatics analyses how users get messages across to one another through the Net. MIM is an ideal area of research for cyberpragmatics, since the gap between what is typed and what is intended (and eventually interpreted) requires much contextualisation. However, in order to get a realistic picture of what is really at stake regarding sender users' communicative intentions and addressee users' interpretations we need to enlarge the framework of analysis. The introduction of the labels *contextual constraint* and *non-intended non-propositional effect* into the overall relevance-theoretic proposal of relevance in terms of cognitive effects and mental effort may be a sound step forward in this direction.

References

Ahad, A. D., & Lim, S. A. M. (2014). Convenience or nuisance?: The 'WhatsApp' dilemma. *Procedia, 155*, 189–196.

Awan, F., & Gauntlett, D. (2013). Young people's uses and understandings of online social networks in their everyday lives. *Young, 21*, 111–132.

Baym, N. K. (2010). *Personal connections in the digital age*. Cambridge: Polity Press.

Bays, H. (2008). Visual iconic patterns of instant messaging: Steps towards understanding visual conversations. In J. Hunsinger, L. Klastrup, & M. Allen (Eds.), *International handbook of internet research* (pp. 41–64). Dordrecht: Springer.

Boneva, B. S., Quinn, A., Kraut, R. E., Kiesler, S., & Shklovski, I. (2006). Teenage communication in the instant messaging era. In R. Kraut, M. Brynin, & S. Kiesler (Eds.), *Computers, phones, and the Internet: Domesticating information technology* (pp. 201–218). New York: Oxford University Press.

Casaló, L., Flavian, C., & Guinaliu, M. (2008). The role of perceived usability, reputation, satisfaction and consumer familiarity on the website loyalty formation process. *Computers in Human Behavior, 24*, 325–345.

Church, K., & de Oliveira, R. (2013, August 27–30). What's up with WhatsApp? Comparing mobile instant messaging behaviors with traditional SMS. In *Proceedings of MobileHCI' 2013* (pp. 352–361). Munich: ACM.

Dresner, E., & Herring, S. C. (2010). Functions of the non-verbal in CMC: Emoticons and illocutionary force. *Communication Theory, 20*, 249–268.

Garrett, R. K., & Danziger, J. N. (2007). IM=Interruption management? Instant messaging and disruption in the workplace. *Journal of Computer-Mediated Communication, 13*, 23–42.

Huang, A. H., Yen, D. C., & Zhang, X. (2008). Exploring the potential effects of emoticons. *Information & Management, 45*, 466–473.

Knop, K., Öncü, J. S., Penzel, J., Abele, T. S., Brunner, T., Vorderer, P., & Wessler, H. (2016). Offline time is quality time. Comparing within-group self-disclosure in mobile messaging applications and face-to-face interactions. *Computers in Human Behavior, 55*, 1076–1084.

Lo, S.-K. (2008). The nonverbal communication functions of emoticons in computer-mediated communication. *Cyberpsychology & Behavior, 11*, 595–597.

Luor, T., Wu, L., Lu, H.-P., & Tao, Y.-H. (2010). The effect of emoticons in simplex and complex task-oriented communication: An empirical study of instant messaging. *Computers in Human Behavior, 26*, 889–895.

Maíz-Arévalo, C. (2015). Typographic alteration in formal computer-mediated communication. *Procedia, 212*, 140–145.

Miller, V. (2008). New media, networking and phatic culture. *Convergence, 14*, 387–400.

Nilsen, M., & Mäkitalo, Å. (2010). Towards a conversational culture? How participants establish strategies for co-ordinating chat postings in the context of in-service training. *Discourse Studies, 12*, 90–105.

Park, K., & Sundar, S. S. (2015). Can synchronicity and visual modality enhance social presence in mobile messaging? *Computers in Human Behavior, 45*, 121–128.

Sperber, D., & Wilson, D. (1995). *Relevance: Communication and cognition* (2nd ed.). Oxford: Blackwell.

Xu, L., Yi, C., & Xu, Y. (2007). Emotional expression online: The impact of task, relationship and personality perception on emoticon usage in Instant Messenger. In *Proceedings of the 11th Pacific-Asia conference on information systems*, Auckland.

Yus, F. (2001). *Ciberpragmática. El uso del lenguaje en Internet*. Barcelona: Ariel.

Yus, F. (2005). Attitudes and emotions through written text: The case of textual deformation in Internet chat rooms. *Pragmalingüística, 13*, 147–174.

Yus, F. (2007). *Virtualidades reales. Nuevas formas de comunidad en la era de Internet*. Alicante: University of Alicante, Servicio de Publicaciones.

Yus, F. (2010). *Ciberpragmática 2.0. Nuevos usos del lenguaje en Internet*. Barcelona: Ariel.

Yus, F. (2011a). *Cyberpragmatics. Internet-mediated communication in context*. Amsterdam: John Benjamins.

Yus, F. (2011b). Relevance equations of effective internet communication. In B. Pennock & T. Suau (Eds.), *Interdisciplinarity and languages. Current issues in research, teaching, professional applications and ICT* (pp. 65–86). Frankfurt: Peter Lang.

Yus, F. (2013). Cyberpragmatics. In C. A. Chapelle (Ed.), *The encyclopedia of applied linguistics*. Chichester: Wiley-Blackwell.

Yus, F. (2014a). Not all emoticons are created equal. *Linguagem em (Dis)curso* (special issue on relevance theory), *14*, 511–529.

Yus, F. (2014b, April). Turismo móvil: Discurso, interactividad y usabilidad en las 'apps' de turismo. Paper delivered at *Discurso y Géneros del Turismo 2.0*. Valencia: University of Valencia and IULMA.

Yus, F. (2014c, October). La seducción de lo no codificado. Paper delivered at *Intermedialidad en la lengua y la literatura hispánicas*. Coloquio Internacional. Université de Lausanne.

Yus, F. (2015a). The role of cognition and relevance in new digital narratives. In E. Carpi (Ed.), *Prospettive multilingue e interdisciplinari nel discorso specialistico* (pp. 81–107). Pisa: Pisa University Press.

Yus, F. (2015b, September). Should relevance theory analyse what is non-propositional, non-intentional but yet affects the eventual relevance?. Paper delivered at *Relevance round table meeting 4*. Institute of English Studies, Jagiellonian University of Kraków.

Yus, F. (2015c, November). The discursive management of the phatic internet (and how to explain it pragmatically). Paper delivered at *Approaches to Digital Discourse Analysis* (ADDA). Valencia.

Connected Parents: Combining Online and Off-Line Parenthood in Vlogs and Blogs

Carmen Santamaría-García

Abstract This article explores evaluative discourse in a corpus sample of parents' vlogs (video blogs) and blogs (henceforth v/ blogs) dealing with family tasks and responsibilities, as a reflection of underlying values concerning parenthood. It pays special attention to the important role played by the expression of *attitude*, understood as "ways of feeling" and including the meanings of *affect*, *judgment* and *appreciation*, together with positive politeness in the social practices of the discursive construction of online and off-line parenthood. Analysis and description of the data show two main patterns in parents' practices, either aiming at perfection through juggling and multi-tasking or building resistance to the demands of families and society. Results show that parents frequently exploit the system of *affect* for building positive face and rapport, while indirectly expressing *judgment of social esteem* and *social sanction*, which construct their identities as mothers and fathers and those of the members of their communities of practice. The corpus for the study consists of a random sample of 400 evaluative units in posts and comments on v/ blogs dealing with family tasks and responsibilities (200 in English and 200 in Spanish, with half the sample being drawn from fathers' and the other half from mothers' v/ blogs). I will approach the analysis of the data from appraisal (Martin JR, White PRR, The language of evaluation. Appraisal in English. Palgrave Macmillan, New York, 2005; Bednarek M, Emotion talk across corpora. Palgrave Macmillan, Houndmills/New York, 2008) and politeness theory (Brown P, Levinson S, Politeness: Some universals in language usage. Cambridge University Press, Cambridge, 1987) in order to explore the features of evaluative discourse and the management of face. The methodology for processing the data borrows quantitative techniques from Corpus Linguistics, involving coding and statistical treatment of the sample with UAM Corpus Tools (O'Donnell M, UAM Corpus Tool 3.2. UAM, Madrid, 2011), together with Pragmatics and Discourse Analysis (DA), as done in some previous research (Santamaría-García C, Int J Corpus Linguistics, 16(3):346–371, 2011, Santamaría-García C, Evaluative discourse and politeness in university

C. Santamaría-García (✉)
Filología Moderna/Facultad de Filosofía Y Letras, Universidad de Alcalá, Alcalá de Henares, Madrid, Spain
e-mail: carmen.santamaria@uah.es

J. Romero-Trillo (ed.), *Yearbook of Corpus Linguistics and Pragmatics 2016*, Yearbook of Corpus Linguistics and Pragmatics 4,
DOI 10.1007/978-3-319-41733-2_3

students' communication through social networking sites. In: Thompson G, Alba-Juez L (eds) Evaluation in context John Benjamins, Amsterdam/Philadelphia, pp 387–411, 2014).

Keywords Digital discourse • Blogs • Vlogs • Social networking sites • Internet-mediated interaction • Pragmatics • Politeness • Appraisal • Evaluation

1 Introduction

Despite the many accomplishments in so-called Western societies towards gender equality we know there is still a long way ahead in order to achieve equal treatment in the various spheres of our everyday lives. New technologies reveal very different gender patterns of social practices regarding the reasons why men and women decide to get connected in their free time. A quick browse through v/ blog indexes shows the vast range of categories in which people can and do participate regardless of their sex or gender. A closer look to those dealing with family tasks and responsibilities shows they are mainly written by and oriented to women. "The stressed mom" blog or "*Madres estresadas*" for instance, do not seem to have equivalent v/ blogs for fathers. This does not mean that fathers do not become stressed with childcare and, in fact, there are webs with advice for them, but, to date, there are fewer fathers than mothers sharing their parental stress with other men in b/ vlog format. However the number of men who are v/ blogging from a father's perspective is increasing. Worth mentioning is a public campaign in Spain while writing this article, March 2016, by fathers who want to show their involvement in child care. The campaign "#padresigualitarios" ("fathers for equality") is supported, among others, by the "Asociación de Hombres por la Igualdad" ("*Association of men for equality*") and "Padres blogueros" ("*Blogger Fathers*"), who claim their part in childcare and want to show that they want to get involved in parenthood. "Padres blogueros" contains a list of 147 v/ blogs of men who are sharing their experiences as fathers in this format in Spain since 2011, as reported by Lantigua (2016) in *El Mundo* newspaper. "Madresfera", a site that keeps a register of b/ vloggers dealing with parenthood, lists more than three thousand in their directory, which includes mothers and fathers' sites. This shows that despite the growing development in father v/ blogs in the last 5 years, there are more mothers sharing through this medium.

Let's see what the situation is like in other countries. We can find lists of "top 10 daddy bloggers" in English from US and UK to Canada, Australia or Singapore. At "tots100", the site for parent blogs in UK, it is reported that "around 95 % of blogs are written by women", (November 2012). It seems that, although there are more blogger mothers than fathers, the number of dads who are discussing the tribulations and joys of parenting from a father's perspective is increasing. At the digital media website mashable.com, Walden (2015) observes that "more and more often, dads are joining in on the trend, developing online hubs where they can discuss everything from diaper rash to DIY tree houses".

In this article I will not be exploring gender discursive differences but treating genders under the roof of parenthood while looking for the dominant discourses v/ blogger fathers and mothers are giving their voices to.

My aim is to explore the use of evaluative discourse and politeness strategies in the situated social practices associated with the digitally mediated discourse of parents' v/ blogs when dealing with family tasks and responsibilities. I will focus on the evaluative expression of *attitude*, understood as "ways of feeling" and including the meanings of *affect*, *judgment* and *appreciation*, together with positive politeness strategies, namely, strategies for *claiming common ground*, *conveying cooperation* and *fulfilling the addresses' needs*.

My hypothesis, based on participant observation of v/ blogs, is that evaluative discourse and positive politeness strategies are exploited to reflect and negotiate the underlying values concerning parenthood in the construction of parents' identities and their social communities of practice. I expect a high frequency of attitudinal meanings of affect (i.e. happiness, security, satisfaction, inclination and surprise) and judgment (social esteem and social sanction) together with positive politeness strategies (claim common ground, conveying cooperation and fulfilling addressee's needs) to be used in order to build connection between speakers and addressees in the management of interpersonal rapport.

2 Theoretical Framework

In the following sections I review some relevant aspects regarding studies on personal and social identity, appraisal and politeness theories that shape the present study. Some of the specific features of parents' v/ blogs are also discussed, as they may explain the reasons underlying users' motivation for their choice of evaluation and politeness resources. Finally, some considerations regarding online and off-line social practices are included.

2.1 Studies on Personal and Social Identity

Studies of identity emerged with strength after the work of the neo-freudian Erik Erikson in the 1950s and 1960s, which "provided a psychological addition to earlier studies of 'groupness', an addition that stressed identity in context", as Edwards (2009: 15) observes, quoting Gleason's (1983) article on the historical development of identity. Worth mentioning from that period are the studies by Goffman (1959, 1967) on social self-presentation, which would lead to Brown and Levinson's (1978, 1987) formulation of *face* as "the public self-image that every member wants to claim for himself", (Brown and Levinson 1987: 61), and their distinction between *positive* and *negative faces* and *politeness theory* to be discussed in the following section.

Edwards (2009: 15) reports, following Joseph (2004), that "the early 1980s saw the appearance of important studies focusing on the linguistic aspects of identity", such as the collection of essays edited by Gumperz (1982) or Le Page and Tabouret-Keller's (1985), which were "quickly followed by work on a variety of aspects of social identity" such as language, history and identity (Kroskrity 1993) or history and identity (Calhoun 1994). A more recent contribution to the multiplicity of social identities, Edwards (2009: 17) mentions the collection edited by Taylor and Spencer (2004) with some discussion and updating of Goffman's original ideas on the social self-presentation.

As some of the main reasons underlying current salience of identity we could mention changes in family roles and other social challenges: "It seems clear enough that people need social anchors. If the older and smaller intimacies of family and village are eroded by the urbanizing pressures of the modern dystopia, then substitutes will have to be found", Edwards (2009: 22). I would also suggest the connection between social challenges, transitions and interest in identity observed in Edwards (2009: 16): "If it is true that our age is one in which social stresses and strains are particularly marked, and if we are faced with many sorts of social and political challenges and transitions, then it is entirely understandable that matters of identity –its definition, its negotiation, its re-negotiation –will seem particularly salient". In our time we are faced with high levels of parenting stress deriving from lack of social support, time pressure, need for multitasking, low incomes or a change in the expectations from parents' roles, among other factors. The journalist Bristow (2006) describes the current maternal crisis as follows:

> (…) a problem that is new: the identity shock experienced by a generation of women accustomed to being equal, having freedom and choices and careers and some semblance of control over their lives and emotions, upon the birth of a child. (…) Having reached the stage in their lives when finally, they feel grown-up and wanting to settle down, the birth of a child unsettles everything and everyone, Bristow (2006).

It seems that our mothers in the 1960s did not have so many options as we do now but there is still a lot to complain about. All the above mentioned factors could serve as triggers for the current need to build connection and groupness in parenthood through v/ blogs, which will eventually enhance the self-esteem of parents. We can find support for this idea in social identity theory, associated with Tajfel (1978, 1982) and scholarly descendants edited by Turner and Giles (1981) or Abrams and Hogg (1990). Edwards (2009: 27) explains the relationship between self-esteem and social affiliation derived from this approach: "The assumption here is that besides our uniquely personal sense of self, we also have social identities based upon the various groups to which we belong. Thus we can maintain and enhance self-esteem through valued social affiliations, as well as by purely personal activities and achievements." It seems reasonable to think that parenthood presents an important challenge to one's sense of worth, and sharing in parents groups would alleviate stress and strengthen self-esteem. This observation finds support in Edwards (2009: 27) when he observes that "us and them boundaries (…) can heighten feelings of individual worth. A corollary is that in-group solidarity should be expected to strengthen at times when one's sense of worth is threatened or tenuous". No wonder, then, that stressed parents use v/ blogs to share both their worries and achievements in an attempt to find solidarity and renewed strength to put up their heavy daily routines.

Observations regarding the use of language in the construction of parenthood will need references to the identity of individual fathers and mothers and the groups they belong to in an attempt to contextualize their discourse and link it to the bigger social picture in which it is produced. I will take Edwards' (2009: 1) cautionary note, delivered quoting Spolsky (2004), that "studies of the social life of language are often too 'language-centred'. Any investigation of language that considers only language will be deficient, and inappropriate limitations and restrictions can cripple insights". Therefore, my exploration of evaluative discourse dealing with family tasks and responsibilities will need the consideration of social factors, such as society's expectations on mothers and fathers in the construction of parenthood identity. Language and identity are "ultimately inseparable" (Joseph 2004:13) and thus, exploration of the use of evaluative language will show the individuals' own subjective sense of self and also their group membership(s).

Regarding the discursive construction of gendered identities, Litosseliti (2006: 48) explains how we draw on discourses about gender "that are recognizable by and meaningful for the language users (i.e. they pre-exist their users)" and gives "a 'female emotionality' discourse" or "a 'part-time father' discourse" as examples, (Litosseliti 2006: 48–49). Quoting Coates (1997), Litosseliti (2006: 49) describes two competing discourses of feminity: "a dominant maternal discourse, which involves mother's sharing of their pride and positive feelings about their children and a competing or 'subversive' maternal discourse, which includes expression of their negative feelings about their children". What seems most interesting for the present study is Litosseliti's (2006: 49) observation, in line with post-structuralist and social constructionist theories that "(...) discourses construct or give meaning to how we see the world" and "(...) at the same time, they articulate, maintain, constitute, re-constitute, negotiate, and even resist some of these ways. (...). In resisting and contesting dominant discourses and the assumptions embedded in them, we are part of a process of changing perceptions of experience, as well as roles and identities (see Weedon 1987; Fairclough 1992)". This observation helps to understand the importance of v/ blogs in the process of spreading views and hence, in shaping roles and identities.

2.2 *Studies on Evaluation and Politeness for Relational Work*

The discourse function of evaluation has been approached within the framework of Systemic Functional Linguistics (SFL) through the system of *appraisal*, the system for the expression of evaluation developed by Martin (2000) and Martin and White (2005). Appraisal resources include attitude, (for the expression of meanings of affect, judgment and appreciation), together with engagement and graduation

Table 1 Overview of appraisal resources

Appraisal		
Engagement	Monogloss	
	Heterogloss	
Attitude	Affect	Un/happiness, In/security, Dis/satisfaction, Dis/inclination, Surprise
	Judgment	Social esteem (normality, capacity, tenacity)
		Social sanction (veracity, propriety)
	Appreciation	Reaction, Composition, Valuation
Graduation	Force	Raise
		Lower
	Focus	Sharpen
		Soften

resources, which are used "for adopting a position with respect to propositions and for scaling intensity or degree of investment respectively", (Martin and White 2005: 39). See Table 1 for an overview of appraisal resources, adapted from Martin and White (2005: 38) and including surprise as a distinct category for affect (Bednarek 2008: 161).

This model shares many concomitances with the work on evaluation by Thompson and Hunston (2000: 6), who distinguished three main functions of evaluation: expressing opinion, maintaining relations and organizing the discourse. However, I will be following appraisal theory and for this study, specifically focusing on attitude (including meanings of affect, judgment, and appreciation), and leaving aside the study of engagement and graduation because the main interest is to explore the role played by the expression of attitude and its relationship with politeness strategies. The category of affect has been explored in the realizations of happiness/ unhappiness, security/ insecurity, satisfaction/ dissatisfaction, inclination/ disinclination and other feelings that can be associated with them and are included in the inventory by Martin and White (2005: 48–51) and in the modifications by Bednarek (2008: 142–182), who adds the meaning of surprise as a different category. I have followed Martin and White's (2005: 52–58) categories of judgment, including social esteem (normality, capacity, tenacity) or social sanction (veracity, propriety) and for the categories of appreciation (reaction, composition, valuation).

The need to connect evaluation with politeness was pinpointed by Channell (2000: 55): "The whole area of evaluative language seems to require tying up with the notion of 'facework' employed by Brown and Levinson (1987) in their explanation of politeness". I have explored this connection in previous studies (Santamaría-García 2013, 2014) for the analysis of the relationship between the expression of attitudinal meanings and the realization of politeness strategies. Politeness theory can account for various aspects underlying the evaluative function of language and its exploitation for the management of face and interpersonal rapport in terms of individuals' need to express attitude while saving face and doing relational work.

I will be using Brown and Levinson's (1987) concepts of positive and negative politeness in order to explore users' orientation to face while doing relational work. Speakers may choose to orient to the addressees' positive face, i.e. their "(…) desire that this self-image be appreciated and approved of" or to their negative face, redressing their need to be "free from imposition" (Brown and Levinson 1987: 61).

Politeness theory has provided a useful theoretical framework for the study of relational work, even when it has been severely criticized (e.g., Eelen 2001; Watts 2003; Mills 2003; Locher and Watts 2005) and further developed into a more discursive approach (Watts et al. 2005; Lakoff and Ide 2005 and Spencer-Oatey 2000). Critiques have not destroyed the model but triggered new trends of research in theoretical, descriptive, comparative and historical perspectives. As Locher and Watts (2005: 10) note, even when Brown and Levinson's framework has been challenged in different aspects, it can still be used "(…) if we look at the strategies they have proposed to be possible realizations of what we call relational work". Therefore, politeness strategies will not only be considered for mitigation of face-threatening acts but for "(…) the 'work' individuals invest in negotiating relationships with others", Locher and Watts (2005: 10).

Many authors suggest returning to Goffman (1967 [1955]: 5) for the original definition of face (Dippold 2009; Locher and Watts 2005; Riley 2006; Spencer-Oatey 2002 and Watts 2003) because "Brown and Levinson seem to be thinking of the self as a stable core of values lodged somewhere in the individual, whereas for Goffman self is far less 'real' and is constantly renegotiable", (Watts 2003: 105). Social interaction is essential for the negotiation of self and face: "Goffman implies that our knowledge of the world and the place we occupy in that world is gained entirely through social interaction", (Watts 2003: 123) and face is interpreted by others in interaction: "(…) face is dependent on the interpretation of the other participants more than ourselves", (Watts 2003: 124). Likewise, for Dippold (2009: 3), face is seen as the result of speakers' presentation and its construction by others: "face is a conglomerate of the self-image speakers want to present to the outside world and the image that is constructed of them by others".

In the context of parents' v/ blogs we can expect v/ bloggers and followers to preserve their needs for positive face in order to key into some commonality of experience amongst mothers of young children while building rapport and bonding in their social communities of practice. Therefore, we can expect a frequent use of positive politeness strategies, such as claiming common ground or conveying cooperation. Positive politeness will be, therefore, the focus of this study, including the strategies briefly summarised in Table 2.

Table 2 Positive politeness strategies according to Brown and Levinson (1987: 102)

Positive politeness strategies	
1. Claim common ground	Convey X is admirable, interesting
	1. Notice, attend to H (his interest, wants, needs, goods)
	2. Exaggerate interest, approval
	3. Intensify interest to H
	Claim in-group membership with H
	4. Use in-group identity markers
	Claim common point of view, opinions, attitudes, knowledge, empathy
	5. Seek agreement
	6. Avoid disagreement
	7. Presuppose/ raise/ assert common ground
	8. Joke
2. Convey that S and H are cooperators	Indicate S knows H's wants and is taking them into account
	9. Assert or presuppose S's knowledge of and concern for H's wants
	Claim reflexivity:
	10. Offer, promise
	11. Be optimistic
	12. Include both S and H in activity
	13. Give (ask for) reasons
	Claim reciprocity:
	14. Assume or assert reciprocity
3. Fulfill H's want (for some X)	15. Give gifts to H (goods, sympathy, understanding, cooperation)

2.3 Distinctive Features of Parents' v/ blogs That Shape the Production of Appraisal and Positive Politeness

The exploration of some of the distinctive features of parents' v/ blogs attempting at description of the genre, using Bhatia's (2004) approach, may lead to the definition of their main communicative purpose as sharing stance towards different aspects of parenthood. This purpose may be responsible for the frequent production of evaluation and positive politeness for the construction of v/ bloggers' communities of practice as groups of individuals sharing feelings and values. As distinctive features of this type of v/ blogs, I would stress their combination of (i) interactional and transactional functions of language, (ii) interpersonal and ideational meaning, and (iii), their dialogic orientation.

(i) Interactional and transactional functions of language

These v/ blogs provide a space for sharing parenthood stance and create a feeling of community and bonding. Thus, they can be seen to serve the interactional function described as "establish and maintain social relationships", (Brown and Yule

1983: 3), as well as conveying "factual or propositional information", that is, the transactional function, (Brown and Yule 1983: 2) about parenthood matters.

V/ bloggers can address a whole community of, usually, some hundreds or thousands of followers at once through their posts who, due to their condition of followers, will most probably feel linked by "positive affective involvement", using the terms referring to the dimensions of social identity in Eggins and Slade (1997: 52). Once they gain the status of followers, the expectation is that they provide support, which involves doing relational work by making use of appraisal and positive politeness resources. However, we may find followers who occasionally choose to challenge previous posts by expressing disapproval or disagreement on factual or propositional content but usually saving face (for them and addressees) in order to maintain their community feeling.

(ii) Interpersonal and ideational meaning.

Parent v/ bloggers' decision to open a v/ blog is usually driven by a strong desire to communicate ideational or propositional meaning with an essential interactive dimension as posts usually contain prompts that stimulate engagement of followers and their expression of attitude. A community of followers will usually provide support to the v/ bloggers they are following by making use of an extensive range of language resources for construing interpersonal meaning, as the manifestation of the purpose "to act on the others" (Halliday 2004: xiii). Interpersonal deals with "meaning about roles and relationships (e.g. status, intimacy, contact, sharedness between interactants)", (Eggins and Slade 1997: 49). Followers will tend to express their attitude in comments and invite other followers' contributions, building rapport and solidarity. This happens because "(...) when speakers/writers announce their own attitudinal positions they not only self-expressively 'speak their own mind', but simultaneously invite others to endorse and to share with them the feelings, tastes or normative assessments they are announcing." (Martin and White 2005: 95).

(iii) Dialogic frame.

One of the most significant features of parents' v/ blogs that also seems to be responsible for their increasing success is their implementation of a dialogic frame, which facilitates dialogue between v/ bloggers' and their followers, even when they are not engaged simultaneously in their dialogic activity. The comments show the contributions of the community, which create a "heteroglossic" framework of different voices. While writing has typically been an asynchronous communication mode with addressees out of sight, v/ blogs bridge the gap between writing and speech to some extent. The creation of a socially significant community of practice with common ground stimulates dialogue and facilitates engagement among users.

Thus, from this review of v/ blog features, it seems that their use for the interactional and interpersonal, together with a dialogic frame that allows for simultaneous communication with many addressees connected by positive affective involvement, can be held responsible for the expectation of the frequent use of evaluation and positive politeness, as resources for building rapport and solidarity in the community.

2.4 *Online and Off-Line Social Practices with Special Mention to Everyday Creativity*

The lines between online and off-line social practices are not clear cut, as online practices permeate through off-line contexts and vice-versa. As Jones et al. (2015: 9) note, "Digital technologies have altered our experience of the spatial and temporal aspects of context by creating complex 'layerings' of online and offline spaces". Both Carrington (2015) and Merchant (2015) show that digital technologies alter not only the ways people interact online but also the ways they do so in physical spaces. As a blogger father reports, he writes his blog and then talks to friends and family about his blog ("yanosoyunpadrenovato.blogspot.com.es" in "cajón de sastre" (*wastebasket*) section). The blogger mother at modern-moms-life.blogspot.com says "I definitely didn't know it [blogging] would totally take over my life at some points". The vlogger of Spanish "mimodemami.com" also reports (personal communication) that her activity in the vlog has had very positive consequences in her relationship with her twodaughters. She prepares tutorials of handicrafts with their help and the girls even act in some of the videos. This means they spend quality time together while planning scripts, collecting ideas and materials, video recording and discussing what could be improved next. Vlogging is improving their affective relationship by triggering the connection between creativity, emotion and motivation, with very positive effects in children upbringing and feelings of happy parenthood. The consideration of creativity, "as a quality of all human beings, which can be manifested in all types of discourses" and not only "associated with the innate talent of an individual, such as the gifted artist or scientist" is noted by Hidalgo Downing (2015: 108) who mentions Carter (2004), Gibbs (1999), Jones (2010, 2012), Lakoff and Johnson (1980) and Maybin and Swann (2006): "creativity is currently considered as much a feature of everyday language use and social practices as a feature of significant works of art, scientific discoveries or world-changing theories". She also observes the distinction in Cameron (2011) and Jones (2012) between "creativity with a small 'c' (everyday creativity) and creativity with a big 'C' (world changing creativity)". My impression is that everyday creativity also contributes to changing the world, though, and creative v/ blogging is an important tool for spreading and encouraging this type of creativity.

Mimodemami.com vlog would feature what Coates (1997) describes as "maternal discourse", involving mother's pride and positive feelings about her children. On the other end of the continuum, more resistant discourses would be represented by the Bad Mothers Club or workingmomsbreak.com, "For mums who can do it all but wonder why they should" in UK, or by "malasmadres.com" (*badmothers*) in Spain, where mothers complain that they do not have time for themselves, which most of the time means they cannot find the time for fashion or beauty care.

In fathers' blogs discourses could also range from paternal discourse, showing pride in children, to the more subversive expression of negative feelings regarding changes in life due to paternity. However I have not found any father v/ blogs fitting the latter category as openly as bad mothers do, although some fathers express their resistance to new situations through humour. Why is this so? It could be that fathers who are investing their energies in father v/ blogging want to show that they care for children, the family and home, that they want to get involved in all aspects of their children's lives and that they can manage. Otherwise they would not be v/ blogging on this. The blogger father on hangingwithdad.com says he is telling the story "of a stay at home dad who, with his son, is venturing into the world dominated by women". And he expresses how he feels challenged by this world: "We feel we are hitting out heads against a constant societal whispering that says, 'Men don't quite belong here.'"

3 Data and Method for Analysis

Data analysis has combined extensive reading of the top ten father and mother v/ blogs in English and Spanish with the collection of a corpus containing 400 evaluative units from posts and their manual annotation with UAM Corpus Tool (O'Donnell 2011) for automatic retrieval and statistical treatment of data.

Extensive reading has covered, approximately, 100 posts and comments to them from each of the following categories: 100 from father and 100 from mothers' v/ blogs in English and 100 from father and 100 from mothers' v/ blogs in Spanish. Extensive reading has served to identify dominant discourses in the genre. The sample has been collected during 2015–2016.

After extensive reading I have collected a corpus of a sample of 400 evaluative units (200 in English and 200 in Spanish) from posts and the comments to them. Total number of words is 6356. Selection has included 50 % of posts related to the philosophy of the v/ blog contained in the "about me" section, plus 50 % of posts in other sections dealing with time pressure in connection to parenthood.

Extensive reading has served to identify two main types of discourses. On the one hand, discourses showing good performance at time management for parental care while solving task-oriented everyday issues and, on the other side of the continuum, discourses resisting the temptation of perfection and declaring the parents' need of time for themselves apart from children and away for family duties, thus building some resistance to the demands of families and society.

In the case of mother v/ blogs, the first type is represented by craft-oriented v/ blogs, which encourage mothers' skills for DIY, and the second by, what I will call, the "bad-mother-club philosophy" or, as workingmomsbreak.com puts it: "mums who can do it all but wonder why they should". These two types will be identified as: "type 1, craft-oriented mother v/ blogs" and "type 2 mother v/ blogs", respectively.

In the case of father v/ blogs, the two types identified are: "type 1, craft-oriented father v/ blogs" and "type 2 joking-father v/ blogs". I did not find an equivalent to "bad-mother-club philosophy" featuring a "bad-father-club philosophy", most probably because, as noted in 2.4., it seems that fathers who are investing their energies in father v/ blogging want to show that they care and want to get involved in every aspect of their children's lives. What I found instead, was the use of humour to express how fathers manage to meet the fatherhood challenge. This type of joking father v/ blogs represents the other end of the continuum in father v/ blogs.

In order to have a balanced sample of the discursive types found, I collected half the amount of the data from the craft-oriented type 1 and the other half from type 2 "bad-mother" or "joking father" v/ blogs.

Analysis of the data has been approached from appraisal (Martin and White 2005; Bednarek 2008) and politeness theory (Brown and Levinson 1987), as discussed in the theoretical framework above, in order to explore the features of evaluative discourse and the construction of rapport. Therefore, pragmatics and discourse Analysis (DA) methodologies have been combined with quantitative techniques from Corpus Linguistics, including the coding and statistical treatment of the sample with UAM Corpus Tools (O'Donnell 2011), as done in previous research (Santamaría-García 2011, 2014).

The degree of delicacy of the analysis presented here has made it necessary to compile a "tailor-made corpus", as expressed by Romero-Trillo (2014: 2) in order to illustrate some very specific features of communication in the yet little researched discourse of v/ blogs. As Jones et al. (2015:1) observe discourse analysts need to "both draw upon the rich store of theories and methods developed over the years for the analysis of 'analogue' discourse, and to formulate new concepts and new methodologies to address the unique combinations of affordances and constraints introduced by digital media". And this is so because of the fast pace of new technologies and because digitally mediated discourse opens the scope for new social practices and forms of interaction, often including the production of multimodal texts, that challenge approaches that focus only on written or spoken language. My study is also in line with Jones et al. (2015) in its focus on the situated social practices that people use discourse to perform, with roots in Bourdieu's (1990) approach. Because of the rapid pace at which these social practices are being introduced, it is difficult for any single framework to meet the challenge of understanding all of the complex relationships between discourse and digital practices. In order to cope with the fast-changing landscape of digital media, discourse analysts need to both draw upon the rich store of theories and methods developed over the years for the analysis of 'analogue' discourse, and to formulate new concepts and new methodologies to address the unique combinations of affordances and constraints introduced by digital media.

Regarding codification, I want to discuss one of the most persistent difficulties for coding real data with the categories in the appraisal model, as noted in Santamaría-García (2014). It relates to indirectness and has also been discussed by Thompson (2011): "(…) an expression of one category of appraisal may function as a token (an indirect expression) of a different category; and that token may itself function as an indirect expression of yet another category, and so on." He argues for a coding system that includes information on the different component categories. For example, an expression of surprise that can be read as a token expressing judgment, can be coded as "t-judgment [surprise]." As a result from his observation, I decided to incorporate tags for indirect realizations of attitude in the coding system for the mark up of the data.

4 Data Analysis and Discussion of Results

The hypothesis of this study is that evaluative discourse and positive politeness strategies are exploited to both reflect and negotiate the underlying values concerning parenthood in the construction of parents' identities and their social communities of practice. I expect a high frequency of attitudinal meanings of affect and judgment together with positive politeness strategies to be used in order to build connection between speakers and addressees in the management of online interpersonal rapport.

4.1 Realizations of Appraisal as Types of Attitude

According to my expectations, I found a high frequency of attitudinal meanings of affect and judgment. Table 3 presents, in the first column, the overall frequencies of types of attitude while second and third columns show realizations of the same phenomena in mother and father v/ blogs, respectively.

As Table 3 shows, affect is present in 37 % (n = 148) of the total number of evaluative utterances and judgment features higher, 53.5 % (n = 214), while appreciation is only contained in 9.5 % (n = 38). Affect and judgment together represent 90.5 % (n = 362), which reveals they are more useful resources for v/ bloggers to connect with their followers than the expression of appreciation, which could also be used to express reactions to things but seems not to be favored, probably because it lacks the emotional content of affect and the potential to build social connection by communicating underlying values of parenthood through the expression of social esteem or social sanction. For instance, the blogger in the next fragment (type 2 blog) connects hairstyle and shoes with self-confidence while expressing judgment of social esteem, normality type (considered special and fashionable), social sanction, veracity type, (credible) and social sanction, propriety type (good behavior) instead of expressing mere appreciation for those hairstyle and shoes:

Fragment 1, mumsnet.com. (Type 2 blog)

10 ways to feel more confident Wonder woman

Confidence isn't a personality trait, it's a habit – and one you can easily get into. Mumsnetters recommend everyday things that can give you a real boost. *All you need to look good is to get your hair and shoes right. A haircut and a new pair of shoes does < sic > the trick for me.*

Table 3 Realisation of appraisal as types of attitude in the data

	Global results				Mothers' data				Fathers' data			
Feature	N		Percent		N		Percent		N		Percent	
Attitude type	N = 400				N = 200				N = 200			
Affect	148	362	37 %	90.5 %	66	186	33 %	93 %	82	176	41 %	88 %
Judgment	214		53.5 %		120		60 %		94		47 %	
Appreciation	38		9.5 %		14		7 %		24		12 %	

Table 4 Realizations of judgment including token judgments

	Global results		Mothers' data		Fathers' data	
Feature	N	Percent	N	Percent	N	Percent
Attitude-type	N = 400		N = 200		N = 200	
Affect	148	37 %	66	33 %	82	41 %
Judgment	214	53.5 %	120	60 %	94	47 %
Judgment including token judgments	266	66.5 %	158	79 %	108	54 %

"Get your hair and shoes right", contains expression of judgment of propriety, i.e. "behavior we praise", judgment (Martin and White 2005: 52), which will make you feel "special and fashionable", two categories for normality, social esteem, in Martin and White (2005: 52). Credibility is expressed in "does the trick for me" conveying the assumption that it will also work for us. Thus we find judgment of the three types of propriety, normality and veracity expressing the underlying value of the importance of the looks for the self confidence of mothers behind "wonder women".

Moreover, many of the realizations of affect include token judgments, which raises the number of expressions of judgment, as shown in Table 4.

In the mothers' data, consideration of token judgments expressed by categories of affect would raise total instances of judgment from n = 120 to n = 158, which is 79 % of attitudinal units. In the fathers' sample I only found n = 14 token judgments, raising the expression of judgment from 47 to 54 %. This makes judgment the overall most frequent attitudinal meaning (n = 266, 66.5 %), and shows that father v/ blogs contain fewer instances of judgment, which could suggest a possible gender difference, although more data would be necessary to draw conclusions.

The following example includes an instance of an indirect token judgment, realized through the expression of surprise:

Fragment 2, malasmadres.com. (Type 2 blog)

¿Y tú eres madre? Pues no lo parece.

(*And you are a mother? You don't look like one*).

The reported question both causes and expresses surprise in the blogger mother. It conveys judgment, propriety type, negative polarity, regarding the mother's behavior, a meaning also expressed by "No lo parece" (*You don't look like it*). It sounds as an accusation that something in her behavior causes surprise and is not adequate at the same time. And the sentence is further evaluated with affect-displeasure, as an annoying buzz in the brain, and an indirect judgment of the inconvenience of the question (propriety):

Fragment 3, malasmadres.com. (Type 2 blog)

Así que ahí se queda la frase retumbando en tu cerebro: "¡Ah! ¿Eres madre? No lo parece."

(*So the sentence keeps buzzing in your brain "Ah! You are a mother? You don't look like*).

Table 5 Realizations of positive politeness

	Global results		Mothers' data		Fathers' data	
Feature	N	Percent	N	Percent	N	Percent
Positive politeness	N = 400		N = 200		N = 200	
Claim common ground	272	68 %	126	63 %	146	73 %
Convey cooperation	100	25 %	57	28.5 %	43	21.5 %
Fulfill addressee's wants	18	4.5 %	12	6 %	6	3 %
No strategy coded	10	2.5 %	5	2.5 %	5	2.5 %

In the same vein, the question in the following fragment communicates affect, surprise type while conveying an indirect judgment of propriety, negative polarity, regarding the mother's behavior with distrust.

Fragment 4, workingmomsbreak.com. (Type 2 blog)

"How do you do it all?" I used to get that a lot. From other moms at my son's preschool. From parents at the Y where my daughter took swim lessons. From coworkers at the web consulting agency where I managed a team of designers. From the editor at the publishing company that offered me a contract to write a design book. Even from my husband.

As this mother admits in the following sentences of her blog, in fact she was "not being able to do it all and one day, [she] broke down". The contradiction between her real experience of being overwhelmed, not able to cope and the surprise mixed with distrust in the question by people who thought she was, increases the feeling of tension leading to her collapse. She shares her experience and her indirect negative judgment of people' s questioning attitude, while presupposing and raising common ground with readers, who may have had a similar experience. Her judgment is exploited, hence, to presuppose and raise common ground with readers.

4.2 *Realizations of Politeness*

Regarding realizations of politeness, my analysis has explored the different categories, presented in Table 5. The table shows the overall frequencies of realizations of positive politeness in the first column, while second and third columns contain results for mother and father v/ blogs, respectively.

The data show that meanings of affect and judgment are mainly used to realize positive politeness by claiming common ground, 68 % (n = 272), which is a more frequent mechanism than conveying cooperation, 25 % (n = 100), or fulfilling the addressee's needs, 4.5 % (n = 18) in the corpus. Claiming common ground indicates that "S and H belong to some set of persons who share specific wants, including goals and values", (Brown and Levinson 1987: 103) and the data reveal that it is the more frequently exploited mechanism to either convey that some want of the addressee is admirable or interesting to speaker too, or to claim common perspective.

Table 6 Realizations of types of claiming common ground politeness

	Global results		Mothers' data		Fathers' data	
Feature	N	Percent	N	Percent	N	Percent
Positive politeness Claim common ground types	N = 272		N = 126		N = 146	
Convey X is interesting by noticing, exaggerating, intensifying	110	40.44 %	52	41.26 %	58	39.72 %
Raise-assert-common-ground	62	22.79 %	54	42.85 %	8	5.47 %
Joke	83	30.51 %	8	6.34 %	75	51.36 %
Seek/avoid disagreement	11	4.04 %	7	5.5 %	4	2.73 %

4.2.1 Claiming Common Ground

When it comes to claiming common ground, there are some interesting features to be discussed, which are included in Table 6.

There is an even distribution among corpora of strategies conveying that something is interesting by noticing, exaggerating or intensifying such interest: 41.26 % (n = 52) for mothers and 39.72 % (n = 58) for fathers. However, when claiming point of view and attitudes, mothers seem to prefer to do so by presupposing, raising or asserting common ground, 42.85 % (n = 54), while joking features very low, with 6.34 % (n = 8), and strategies to seek/avoid disagreement even lower 5.5 %, (n = 7). Fathers, on the other hand, seem to show preference for joking 51.36 % (n = 75), with strategies for asserting or presupposing knowledge of and concern for the addressees' wants featuring lower, 5.47 % (n = 8), and strategies to seek/avoid disagreement even lower 2.73 % (n = 4).

Fragment 5 illustrates uses of claiming common ground, joke, and fragment 6, the strategy of raise, assert common ground.

Fragment 5, daddybloggers.com.au. (Type 2 blog)

A Dad's Diary #6 – "The nuggets are having kids and chips for dinner"

You know when you're so tired you can't English word speak goodly? "The nuggets are having kids and chips for dinner." I said this to my wife on the phone tonight. Then I told my son to "wash your teeth and brush your face." My daughter got, "have you fed the… thing*." Cracks are beginning to show, people – the kids are more emotional, I have less patience, we're all tired. So damn tired.

This fragment contains meanings of affect, dissatisfaction and displeasure with token judgment of incapacity of the narrator himself, who admits not being able to cope with the situation. But he makes use of humour as a way to connect with his audience. Humour stresses "shared background knowledge and values" according to Brown and Levinson (1987: 124) and the data reveal it is a common strategy for fathers in type 2 v/ blogs, 42.46 % (n = 62), out of 146.

In fragment 6 we find several instances of raise, assert common ground:

Fragment 6, doitonadimeblog.com. (Type 1 vlog)

It's easy to feel defeated and wish you were rich, perfectly organized, and had it all together. But you want to know what? Life isn't a picture on Pinterest. And that's where I come in. I'm a video blogger and frugal mommy.

Table 7 Realizations of conveying cooperation

	Global results		Mothers' data		Fathers' data	
Feature	N	Percent	N	Percent	N	Percent
Positive politeness Conveying cooperation types	N = 100		N = 57		N = 43	
Indicate S knows H's wants and is taking them into account	68	68 %	25	43.85 %	13	30.23 %
Claim reflexivity	45	45 %	25	43.85 %	20	46.51 %
Claim reciprocity	17	17 %	7	12.28 %	10	23.25 %

The vlogger indicates that she and the audience belong to a set of persons sharing specific wants, goals and values: "being rich, perfectly organized and had it all together" and claims common perspective and will to help "And that's where I come in. I'm a video blogger and frugal mommy" presupposing familiarity with the familiar term "mommy".

4.2.2 Conveying Cooperation

Conveying cooperation is also exploited by v/ bloggers in order to express that they share goals with addressees in some domain and can be cooperatively involved in an activity, thus redressing addressees' need for positive face.

The corpus of v/ blogger mothers contain more instances of this type of politeness, 28.5 % (n = 57), than the corpus of fathers, with 21.5 % (n = 43), as shown in Table 6 above. Table 7 presents different realizations for conveying cooperation.

The most frequent strategy for conveying cooperation is indicating the speaker knows the addressees' wants and is taking them into account by asserting or presupposing knowledge of and concern for addressee's wants. Mother v/ blogs show more instances of this strategy, 43.85 % (n = 25), than the corpus of fathers 30.23 % (n = 13). The other strategies, namely, claiming reflexivity and reciprocity are less frequent but occur mostly when the v/ bloggers indicate that they want what the addresses want for themselves (having quality family time, enjoying DIY, gaining self-confidence, etc.) and they can mutually help each other with reciprocity, for instance, the v/ blogger receives support through comments of friends and family and gives inspiration to the audience in return who may pay back with more inspiration, as this vlogger says:

Fragment 7, www.doitonadimeblog.com/ (Type 1 blog)

> With the support of my family and friends, I started this blog to simply test and challenge myself to start new projects, share my inspirations, and hopefully inspire a few others along the way.

Claiming reflexivity amounts to 43.85 % (n = 25) and reciprocity to 12.28 % (n = 7) in mother data, while the figures we find in fathers' are 46.51 %, (n = 20) and 23.25 %, (n = 10) respectively.

In example number 8, the vlogger who claimed to know the addressees' wants for organization and a tight budget (see fragment 5) indicates that she is taking such wants into account, which serves as illustration of the strategy "conveying cooperation, indicating that speaker knows the addressees' wants and takes them into account":

Fragment 8, doitonadimeblog.com. (Type 1 blog)

I'm a video blogger and frugal mommy: I share with you what organization and budget living is for a REAL person. Me, my video camera and real systems that work for me to make your life better and easier. Real life. Realistic ideas.

4.3 Appraisal and Politeness in the Definition of Type 1 and Type 2 v/ blogs

Extensive reading of the corpus and analysis of results have also revealed some interesting differences between type 1 and type 2 v/blogs. Table 8 presents differences regarding appraisal.

Type 1, craft-oriented v/ blogs communicate positive polarity of the affect types of happiness, satisfaction, security, inclination and surprise more often than negative polarity and they usually refer to the results of crafting and the use that could be made of crafts by the family. Affect of positive polarity is present in 82 % of the realizations of affect in type 1, English language v/ blogs and in 90 % in type 1, Spanish language ones. However, type 2 v/ blogs contain a higher percentage of unhappiness, dissatisfaction, insecurity, disinclination and surprise with a negative meaning and, consequently, positive polarity is less present, with the following figures: 50 % of the occurrences of affect in the English data contain positive polarity and 40 % in the Spanish sample. In the following example, the v/ blogger in mimodemami expresses happiness and satisfaction with her daugthers' performance:

Fragment 9, mimodemami.com. (Type 1 blog)

¡¡Ayúdales a hacer este invento y ni te imaginas lo bien que se lo pasan doblando todas las camisetas de la colada!!!

(*Help them to make this gadget and you cannot imagine how much they will enjoy while folding all the T-shirts*!!!)

Table 8 Differences in appraisal between type 1 and type 2 v/ blogs

	Type 1 English	Type 1 Spanish	Type 2 English	Type 2 Spanish
Features	Percent (%)	Percent (%)	Percent (%)	Percent (%)
Affect, positive polarity	82	90	50	40
Judgments, positive social esteem, capacity	80	92	45	46
Judgments, positive social sanction, propriety	88	94	49	48

(…) ¡Te enseño lo fácil que es hacerlo en el vídeo! Y por favor! Fijaos en lo bien que lo hace la niña y ¡no en mis michelines!

I show you how easy it is to make it on this video and please! See how good the girl is and ignore my spare tyre!

She jokes about her "spare tyres" and puts the focus on her daughter's performance and good behavior, expressing positive judgment of social esteem, capacity and social sanction, propriety. The production of judgments presents a difference between type 1 v/ blogs, mainly oriented towards increasing esteem of capacity and social sanction of propriety, and type 2 v/ containing a higher amount of judgments of negative polarity, social esteem, related to lack of capacity and of social sanction related to propriety in relation to wrong behavior or unfair and overwhelming situations like the following:

Fragment 10, workingmomsbreak.com. (Type 1 blog)

They suffered from panic attacks and depression, heart palpitations and hives, migraines and mysterious coughs that won't go away.

The blogger tells about the experience of several mothers and their lack of capacity to cope with their difficult situations. This connects with judgments of propriety claiming common ground: "At first, I thought there was something wrong with me!"

Regarding differences in politeness, type 1, craft-oriented v/ blogs show a preference to build common ground by calling attention to the interest of crafts and usually presuppose, raise or assert common ground on needs for DIY. Conveying cooperation is mainly realized by considering the addressees' needs and showing knowledge and concern for them. In type 2 v/ blogs mothers claim common ground by calling attention to different situations which frequently are problems, needs and possible solutions or advice to overcome them. When they convey cooperation they usually do so by giving reasons why addressees can fulfill their needs, usually acquiring goods and services. If knowledge and concern for addressees are shown, they usually refer to goods and services that can be acquired too. In relation to father type 2 v/ blogs, I observed more frequent use of humour and irony, as discussed above, in order to claim common ground and share their evaluation of different situations. This could hint at a possible gender difference but more data would be necessary to be conclusive.

Summarizing the analysis presented above, results show the following features of parent v/ blogs.

Affect and judgment are the most useful appraisal resources for v/ blogger parents to connect with their followers. The expression of judgment is the most frequent in the data, most probably because of its potential to build social connection by communicating underlying values of parenthood through the expression of social esteem or social sanction. Results show that mother v/ blogs contain more judgment than fathers'. Regarding politeness, the data show that meanings of affect and judgment are mainly used to realize positive politenesss by claiming common ground, which is more frequent than conveying cooperation or fulfilling the addressee's needs. Mother v/ blogs show a tendency to claim common ground by presupposing, raising or asserting common ground, showing concern for the addressees' wants, while father v/ blogs contain more instances of joking strategies in an attempt to connect with the audience. Conveying cooperation is also exploited by v/ bloggers in order to express that they share goals with addressees in some domain and can be cooperatively involved in an activity, thus redressing addressees' need for positive face. The corpus of mother v/ bloggers contains more instances of this type of politeness than the corpus of fathers.

Analysis of appraisal and politeness has also revealed some interesting differences between type 1 and type 2 v/blogs. Type 1, craft-oriented v/ blogs show a more frequent expression of positive polarity for the expression of affect (happiness, satisfaction, security, inclination and surprise), usually referring to crafting abilities and their use by the family. Type 2 v/ blogs contain a higher percentage of unhappiness, dissatisfaction, insecurity, disinclination and surprise with a negative meaning instead. The production of judgments also presents a difference between type 1 v/ blogs, mainly oriented towards increasing esteem of capacity and social sanction of propriety, and type 2 v/ containing a higher amount of judgments of negative polarity, social esteem, related to lack of capacity and of social sanction related to propriety in relation to inadequate behavior or unfair and overwhelming situations. Regarding politeness, type 1, craft-oriented v/ blogs show a preference to build common ground by calling attention to the interest of crafts, usually presupposing, raising or asserting common ground on needs for DIY. Conveying cooperation is mainly realized by showing knowledge and concern for the addressees' needs. In type 2 v/ blogs mothers claim common ground by calling attention to different situations (problems, needs and possible solutions or advice to overcome them) and convey cooperation by giving reasons why addressees can fulfill their needs, usually involving acquisition of goods and services. When knowledge and concern for addressees are shown, they usually refer to goods and services that can be acquired too. Type 2 father v/ blogs make a more frequent use of humour and irony in order to claim common ground and share evaluation of different situations.

5 Conclusions and Suggestions for Further Research

Analysis of the data has provided evidence supporting the hypothesis of this study that evaluative discourse and positive politeness strategies are exploited to both reflect and negotiate the underlying values concerning parenthood in the construction of parents' identities and their social communities of practice, featuring a high frequency of attitudinal meanings of affect and judgment together with positive politeness strategies used to build connection between speakers and addressees in the management of interpersonal rapport. Extensive reading and data analysis have revealed interesting patterns in the frequencies of the different categories of affect (i.e. happiness, security, satisfaction, inclination and surprise), judgment (social esteem and social sanction) and their distribution along with positive politeness strategies (claim common ground, conveying cooperation and fulfilling the addressee's needs) that can be summarised as follows.

Affect, and especially judgment, are the most frequent categories of appraisal realized in the corpus of parent v/ blogs analyzed. The high frequency of judgment is attributed to its potential to build social connection through communication of underlying values of parenthood through the expression of both social esteem and social sanction. Craft-oriented, type 1 v/ blogs, contribute to build positive social esteem of capacity and social sanction of propriety, while type 2 v/ blogs contain a higher amount of judgments of negative polarity for social esteem related to lack of capacity and for social sanction related to propriety in relation to wrong behavior or unfair and overwhelming situations. The appraisal categories of affect favored by type 1 are of positive polarity while type 2 contains negative polarity to express negative feelings related to parenthood. Regarding politeness, the most striking difference has to do with a higher use of humour by men in type 2 v/ blogs for claiming common ground, while women show preference to claim common point of view by presupposing, raising or asserting common ground.

Type 1 communicates a discourse of "doing it all and doing it yourself" (DIA and DIY), encouraging parents to cope with many different situations and finding resources in DIY to succeed, while type 2 challenges expectations for good parents with a discourse of "Even if we could, why should we do it all?", which often derives in the "spend time on yourself" philosophy, resulting in acquiring goods and services.

Although the modest size of the sample used is in line with the "somewhat critical attitude towards large-scale corpus analysis" (Bednarek 2008: 142) due to the qualitative character of appraisal theory, the findings reported here may be worth of further exploration with more data. I hope this study serves to illustrate the most salient behavior among parent v/ bloggers. My aim was not to collect a representative sample of parent v/ blogs but to explore particular individuals' discourse on them in an attempt to find out common patterns in the use of appraisal and politeness resources. After all, it is the actions of individual members which contribute to the actions of groups. As Eelen (2001: 145) points out: "(…) groups as such do not act, only their individual members do. So, in the end even the most extremely 'socio'-oriented framework needs to say something about individual behavior." As individuals, we are all responsible for social processes and the discourse choices we make everyday play their role in shaping society. The growing popularity and dissemination of v/ blogs portrays them as an emerging means of mass communication with social potential for either change or continuity. The values communicated through posts and comments will have an important share in shaping discourses of parenthood -and other topic fields- and time will say which will be the dominant types of parenthood discourses that give meaning to the world.

Acknowledgments This paper has been written while doing research for the project "EMO-FUNDETT: EMOtion and language 'at work': The discursive emotive/evaluative FUNction in DiffErent Texts and contexts within corporaTe and institutional work", I + D FFI2013-47792-C2-1-P, sponsored by the Spanish Ministry of Science and Innovation and directed by Dr. Laura Alba Juez (UNED, Spain) http://www2.uned.es/proyectofundett.

I also want to thank all the v/ bloggers who contributed to the corpus.

References

Abrams, D., & Hogg, M. (1990). *Social identity theory*. London: Harvester Wheatsheaf.

Bednarek, M. (2008). *Emotion talk across Corpora*. Houndmills/New York: Palgrave Macmillan.

Bhatia, V. K. (2004). *Worlds of written discourse: A genre-based view*. London: Continuum.

Bourdieu, P. (1990). *The logic of practice*. Cambridge: Polity.

Bristow, J. (2006). Why I won't be joining the 'Bad Mothers Club'. Accessed 31 March at http://www.spiked-online.com/newsite/article/2666#.VwBQMY9OKyJ

Brown, P., & Levinson, S. (1978). Universals in language usage: Politeness phenomena. In E. N. Goody (Ed.), *Questions and politeness: Strategies in social interaction* (pp. 56–311). Cambridge: Cambridge University Press.

Brown, P., & Levinson, S. (1987). *Politeness: Some universals in language usage*. Cambridge: Cambridge University Press.

Brown, G., & Yule, G. (1983). *Discourse analysis*. Cambridge: Cambridge University Press.

Calhoun, C. (1994). *Social theory and the politics of identity*. Oxford: Blackwell.

Cameron, F. R. (2011). From mitigation to creativity: The agency of museums and science centres and the means to govern climate change. *Museum and Society, 9*(2), 90–106.

Carrington, V. (2015). Digital discourse@public space: Flows of language online and offline. In R. Jones, A. Christoph, & A. Hafner (Eds.), *Discourse and digital practices* (pp. 144–157). London: Routledge.

Carter, R. (2004). *Language and creativity: The art of common talk*. London/New York: Routledge.

Channell, J. (2000). Corpus analysis of evaluative lexis. In S. Hunston & G. Thompson (Eds.), *Evaluation in text: Authorial stance and the construction of discourse* (pp. 38–56). Oxford: Oxford University Press.

Coates, J. (1997). Competing discourses of feminity. In H. Kothoff & R. Wodak (Eds.), *Communicating gender in context* (pp. 285–313). Amsterdam/Philadelphia: John Benjamins.

Dippold, D. (2009). Face and self-presentation in spoken L2 discourse: Renewing the research agenda in interlanguage pragmatics. *Intercultural Pragmatics, 6–1*, 1–28.

Edwards, J. (2009). *Language and identity*. Cambridge: Cambridge University Press.

Eelen, G. (2001). *A critique of politenesss theories*. Manchester: St Jerome.

Eggins, S., & Slade, D. (1997). *Analysing casual conversation*. London: Cassell.

Fairclough, N. (1992). *Discourse and social change*. Cambridge: Polity Press.

Gibbs, R. (1999). Researching metaphor. In L. Cameron & G. D. Low (Eds.), *Researching and applying metaphor* (pp. 29–47). Cambridge: Cambridge University Press.

Gleason, P. (1983). Identifying identity: A semantic history. *Journal of American History, 69*, 910–31.

Goffman, E. (1959). *The presentation of self in everyday life*. Garden City: Doubleday.

Goffman, E. (1967). *Interaction ritual: Essays on face to face behavior*. Garden City: Doubleday.

Gumperz, J. (Ed.). (1982). *Language and social identity*. Cambridge: Cambridge University Press.

Halliday, M. A. K. (2004) [1994/1985]. *An introduction to functional grammar.* London: Edward Arnold. (Third edition revised by Matthiessen).

Hidalgo Downing, L. (2015). Linguistic creativity: Metaphor and metonymy. In R. Jones (Ed.), *The Routledge handbook of language and creativity* (pp. 107–128). London: Routledge.

Jones, R. (2010). Creativity and discourse. *World Englishes, 29*(4), 467–480.

Jones, R. (Ed.). (2012). *Discourse and creativity*. Harlow: Pearson Education.

Jones, R., Christoph, A., & Hafner, A. (Eds.). (2015). *Discourse and digital practices. Doing discourse analysis in the digital age*. London: Routledge.

Joseph, J. (2004). *Language and identity: National, ethnic, religious*. Basingtoke: Palgrave Macmillan.

Kroskrity, P. (1993). *Language, history and identity*. Tucson: University of Arizona Press.

Lakoff, R., & Ide, S. (2005). *Broadening the horizons of linguistic politeness*. Amsterdam/Philadelphia: John Benjamins.

Lakoff, G., & Johnson, M. (1980). *Metaphors we live by*. Chicago: University of Chicago Press.

Lantigua, I. F. (2016). La rebelión de los #padrazos. *El Mundo*. Accessed 15 Mar 2016 at http://www.elmundo.es/sociedad/2016/03/12/56e326c9268e3eb6508b4642.html

Le Page, R., & Tabouret-Keller, A. (1985). *Acts of identity*. Cambridge: Cambridge University Press.

Litosseliti, L. (2006). *Gender and language. Theory and practice*. London: Hodder Education.

Locher, M., & Watts, R. J. (2005). Politeness theory and relational work. *Journal of Politeness Research, 1*(1), 9–33.

Martin, J. R. (2000). Beyond exchange: APPRAISAL systems in English. In S. Hunston & G. Thompson (Eds.), *Evaluation in text: Authorial stance and the construction of disourse* (pp. 142–175). Oxford: Oxford University Press.

Martin, J. R., & White, P. R. R. (2005). *The language of evaluation. Appraisal in English*. New York: Palgrave Macmillan.

Maybin, J., & Swann, J. (Eds.). (2006). *The art of English: Everyday creativity*. Basingstoke: Palgrave Macmillan.

Merchant, G. (2015). 'It's changed my life': iPhone as technological artefact. In R. Jones, A. Christoph, & A. Hafner (Eds.), *Discourse and digital practices* (pp. 158–174). London: Routledge.

Mills, S. (2003). *Gender and politeness*. Cambridge: Cambridge University Press.

O'Donnell, M. (2011). *UAM Corpus Tool 3.2.*. Madrid: UAM.

Riley, P. (2006). Self-expression and the negotiation of identity in a foreign language. *International Journal of Applied Linguistics, 16*(3), 295–318.

Romero-Trillo, J. (2014). New empirical and theoretical paradigms in Corpus pragmatics, an introduction. In *Yearbook of Corpus linguistics and pragmatics*. New York: Springer.

Santamaría-García, C. (2011). Bricolage assembling: *CL, CA and DA* to explore the negotiation of agreement in English and Spanish conversation. *International Journal of Corpus Linguistics, 16*(3), 346–371.

Santamaría-García, C. (2013). A compelling need to evaluate: Social networking sites as tools for the expression of affect, judgment and appreciation. In I. Kecskes & J. Romero-Trillo (Eds.), *Intercultural pragmatics* (pp. 459–478). Berlin: Mouton de Gruyter.

Santamaría García, C. (2014). Evaluative discourse and politeness in university students' communication through social networking sites. In G. Thompson & L. Alba-Juez (Eds.), *Evaluation in context* (pp. 387–411). Amsterdam/Philadelphia: John Benjamins.

Spencer-Oatey, H. (2000). *Culturally speaking*. London/New York: Continuum.

Spencer-Oatey, H. (2002). Rapport management: A framework for analysis. In H. Spencer-Oatey (Ed.), *Culturally speaking: Managing rapport through talk across cultures* (pp. 11–45). London: Continuum.

Spolsky, B. (2004). *Language policy*. Cambridge: Cambridge University Press.

Tajfel, H. (Ed.). (1978). *Differentiation between social groups*. London: Academic.

Tajfel, H. (Ed.). (1982). *Social identity and intergroup relations*. Cambridge: Cambridge University Press.

Taylor, G., & Spencer, S. (Eds.). (2004). *Social identities: Multidisciplinary approaches*. London: Routledge.

Thompson, G. (2011). Russian dolls, target-VALUE mismatches, and evaluation. In Plenary at Int-eval, *International workshop on the evaluative function of language: Evaluation across text-types and cultures*. Madrid: UNED.

Thompson, G., & Hunston, S. (2000). Evaluation: An introduction. In S. Hunston & G. Thompson (Eds.), *Evaluation in text: Authorial stance and the construction of disourse* (pp. 1–28). Oxford: Oxford University Press.

Turner, J., & Giles, H. (Eds.). (1981). *Intergroup behaviour*. Oxford: Blackwell.

Walden, S. (2015) Six of the best dad blogs on the Internet Accessed Mar 2016 at: http://mashable.com/2015/06/15/best-dad-blogs/#T.arvDuMzmq2

Watts, R. (2003). *Politeness*. Cambridge: Cambridge University Press.

Watts, R., Ide, S., & Ehlich, K. (2005). *Politeness in language*. Berlin: Mouton de Gruyter.

Weedon, C. (1987). *Feminist practice and poststructuralist theory*. Oxford: Blackwell.

Vlogs and Blogs Mentioned

Dad street http://www.dadstreet.com
Dadand https://dadand.com
Madres estresadas http://madresestresadas.com
Madresfera http://www.madresfera.com/
Malas madres http://www.malasmadres.com
Mumsnet http://www.mumsnet.com
Tots 100 http://www.tots100.co.uk/
Working Mom's Break http://www.workingmomsbreak.com/

Healing and Comfort on the Net: Gender and Emotions in Violent Domestic Environments

Eva M. Mestre-Mestre

Abstract The present article analyses the online expression of emotions in environments of extreme distress. In a Computer Mediated Communication environment, support communities are created worldwide, also to help in cases of violence against women. The role that gender plays in virtual communication and the language used by women in these contexts has been analysed to determine its particularities. These women express their pain and their support towards each other by means of common and not so commonly used adjectives, both positive and negative. Likewise, they tend to use greater amount of social words, and few self-references.

Keywords CMC • Discussion boards • Gender • Domestic violence • Emotions

As technology and Internet are increasingly becoming part of our daily lives, they are also transforming our reality (Mey 2009). In return, the adaptation to Computer Mediated Communication (henceforth CMC) environments is changing both the form and the content of our communication and, as a consequence, our meanings. Therefore, CMC is now also reaching the realm of privacy, and virtual communities (Sardar 1996; Fox and Roberts 1999) are being created as interactive forums in different settings: teaching (Benigno and Trentin 2000; Burstall 2000); business (Vance Wilson and Lu 2008; Litvin et al. 2006; Zehrer et al. 2011); politics (Wojcieszak and Mutz 2009; Blader and Tyler 2003), and also more personal interactions (Mestre and Romero-Trillo forthcoming).

One of the intimate situations in which real life seeks virtual support communities is domestic or intimate partner violence (henceforth IPV). Victims (survivors) of abuse search consolation and support in such forums, where they are allowed to express their feelings and look for sympathy or advice. Such extreme circumstances allow us to reflect upon the role of gender in CMC. Although Dalampan (2006) identified minor differences between genders in online academic environments, Fox et al. (2007) concluded after a 3 week study of gender on instant messaging that

E.M. Mestre-Mestre (✉)
Lingüística Aplicada/Escola Politècnica Superior de Gandia, Universitat Politècnica de València, Camí Vera s/n, València, Spain
e-mail: evamestre@upvnet.upv.es

J. Romero-Trillo (ed.), *Yearbook of Corpus Linguistics and Pragmatics 2016*, Yearbook of Corpus Linguistics and Pragmatics 4,
DOI 10.1007/978-3-319-41733-2_4

some differences appear in relation to the degrees of expressivity. Also Kapidzic and Herring (2011) pointed to teenage changes in behaviour in chatrooms in terms of self-presentation, while Li (2005) directly faces the issue of conflict and harassment online. In fact, violence on the net is increasingly worrying and needs a deeper analysis from a linguistic perspective (Herring 2002; Shalom et al. 2015).

Taking as a starting point the universal consideration of emotions (Wierzbicka 1993), this research will analyse the online expression of sentiments related to domestic and IPV, based on a corpus of forums and will focus on the identification of the adjectives that help to describe the feelings and emotions of the users, and the responses they obtain from their companions. In this sense, the study of emotions has been quite prolific in CMC contexts as, for instance, Birkley and Eckhardt (2015) who have looked into online ways to express anger and negative emotions; Pierotti (2013) who has focused on worldwide reactions (rejections) towards violence, or Shalom et al. (2015) who have analysed anxiety and arousal during CMC.

Four basic aspects provide the context for the present research: (1) computer mediated communication, and in particular discussion boards, (2) gender, (3) contexts of violence towards women and (4) the emotions communicated in such settings.

1 Computer Mediated Communication (CMC) and Discussion Boards

Access to technology in general, and to Internet in particular, is altering the way we communicate. This fact is acknowledged by numerous authors who have explained its development in recent years. Some focus on the new particularities that can be found in online texts, which are lacking in offline texts (Herring 1996; Crystal 2001; Yus Ramos 2010). Other authors are more interested in identifying discourse features that can link them to one or another specific genre and describe it as "hybrid", pointing to its significance as a language half way between written and oral (Murray 1995; Kling 1996; Kolko and Reid 1998; Herring et al. 2004; Herring 2007, 2010; Ho and Swan 2007). In this sense, previous studies (Mestre and Romero Trillo forthcoming) have identified three different defining aspects that function synergically in CMC: the textual: the particular text under construction; the social-situational: the real-life environment of the person who is typing, reading or interacting with a message; and the medium: the particular communication channel used. In other words, three types of elements condition CMC: first, they are texts; second, they can produce different types of interactions; and third, regarding the textual tradition, they are online.

Herring (2007) has widely described the factors that influence the 'textuality' of CMC: she points to the different elements which interact in order to shape communication differently than in other environments: (1) synchronicity, i.e., a type of communication that takes place at the same time, in real time, in different moments in time; when message is transmitted (immediately or not), (2) persistence of transcript (how long is that message going to be readable), (3) size of the message buffer (is there a size limit), (4) channels of communication (is it just written texts, or is it a multimodal type of communication permitted) and (5) message format (is it anonymous, private, public). Complementarily medium-related factors, that is to say, channels used for communication, are also determining in the characterisation of language.

As compared to face-to-face (henceforth FTF) communication, CMC seems to be more persuasive (Wilson 2003), offers empowering tools for the user (Blau et al. 2009; Blood 2002; Hall and Davison 2007; Herring 2010), and motivates in certain environments, such as education (Efimova and de Moor 2005; Langellier and Peterson 2004;). However, in some cases, it seems that CMC also helps perpetuate some real life roles by reproducing status differences based on real-world ranks (Kolko and Reid 1998; Mackinnon 1995), or gender, as will be discussed below (Eubanks 2000; Fox et al. 2007; Herring 2000).

Finally, the social-situational aspect of CMC determines the type of interaction (private, public, one-to-one or group), the possibility of exchangeability (being at the same time sender and audience of the message) and the purpose, tone or form of communication (debate, support, information exchange).

Specifically, discussion boards are proving especially beneficial in the provision of social support by means of virtual communities (Wright 2002; Wright and Bell 2003). Only in the US, for instance, it appears that more than 35 million people were members of support groups in 2010 (Pew Internet and American Life Project 2010). A reason for their success, as Pfeil and Zaphiris (2009) point out, is the emphatic bonds created between the members who take part in the same discussion board. Some features that help in the proliferation and usefulness of these tools are, for instance, their asynchronicity, anonymity and thematic distribution (ranging from very public and general to very private and specific issues), and that they share the interactive aspects found in face-to-face (FTF) interaction. Also crucial is that they are unique and self-ruled because "their dynamic nature as self-organizing communities in which individual and group identities as well as communicative norms are displayed and negotiated" (Kleinke and Bös 2015).

2 Gender: Women Online

Although I will not deepen in the study of gender from the dichotomy of traditional cultural vs. difference standpoints or its view as a performative social construct, it is important to offer a general description of gender in this context, since the study delves into the ways in which women, under very specific stress conditions, communicate their emotions online.

In fact, gender seems to have called many a researcher's attention in the study of CMC, mainly in order to find out whether it is possible to identify male or female writers through their writings, and whether or not authorship can be identified. For instance, some authors have aimed at characterising women discourse used online, as compared to that used offline, based on oral or written communication, as for example Dalampan (2006:60) who reproduces some of the most outstanding characteristics of Lakoff's well-known "Women's Language". Here follow some of the features that have been traditionally identified as defining women's discourse:

> (1) Women use more variety of intonational contours and intonation patterns that "resembles questions, indicating uncertainty or need for approval," 2) Women use more of adjectives that express emotion (e.g., adorable, divine), 3) Women use better grammar and fewer colloquialisms. (4) Women are more polite (would you please, I'd really appreciate it if…) and 5) Women use forms that express vagueness (so, such). (Lakoff 1990:204)

Mulac and Lundell (1994) used these features to assess academic essays and coded the following female language variables (as compared to their male counterparts): references to emotion, intensive adverbs, dependent clauses, sentence-initial adverbials, uncertainty verbs, hedges, and long mean length sentences. Baron (2003:9), after having looked into male and female characteristics in oral communication, conclude that:

> […] women tend to use more affective markers (e.g., I know how you feel), more diminutives (e.g., little bitty insect), more hedge words (e.g., perhaps, sort of), more politeness markers (e.g., I hate to bother you), and more tag questions (e.g., We're leaving at 8:00 pm, aren't we?) than do men.

Nevertheless, this issue is controversial as, for instance, Herschel et al. (1994) did not find significantly different linguistic styles in his studies about how gender affected group brainstorming performance in a group support system, nor did Dalampan (2006) when looking at discussion posting made by male and female students. It seems that both context and topic play a key role in the differentiation on genre on communication.

Herring (2000) carries out a similar analysis in CMC contexts to identify whether there exist features that signal gender in anonymous settings and looks into two different sets of communicative contexts. The first is in synchronous contexts in which there seems to be greater gender equality and less differentiation of discourse; the second in asynchronous contexts in which the patterns of interaction are similar to those used in FTF communication: verbosity, assertiveness, use of profanity, politeness (and rudeness), typed representations of smiling and laughter, and degree of interactive engagement. In particular, in discussion boards or newsgroups women

> […] tend to post relatively short messages, and are more likely to qualify and justify their assertions, apologize, express support of others, and in general, manifest an "aligned" orientation towards their interlocutors

Selfe and Meyer (1991) support this finding and state that offline status and gender are reproduced in discussion boards and that males or participants with higher offline status dominate interactions, whereas women reported to prefer anonymity. On the same wavelength, Graddy (2004:3) agreed on differences in discussion boards and identified female messages as "qualifying, apologetic, supportive, and polite."

Pursuing in the comparison between FTF and CMC, it is also important to investigate the way gender is represented in online contexts. Indeed, the way women choose to present themselves as women is of interest in the literature as some authors imply that their self-portrayal affects the way women interact in a group (Cassell and Tversky 2005; Graddy 2004). From a different perspective, Koch et al. (2005:39) study gender in chat groups and are able to identify some particularities related to gender. For instance, they refer to "men's cooperatives and support" to be rated as lower as that of women, or that women's "quality of argumentation" was rated higher, using the Pragmatic Gender-in-Context Model (Deaux and LaFrance 1998; Deaux and Major 1987). This model describes how gender is communicated by using three elements: the specific situation, the target person, and the actor. And, although they conclude that gender expectations play an important role in CMC, they found no significant differences between gender salient and non-salient conditions, which, suggests that gender as a category is omnirelevant and automatically assessed in the process of each interaction, and that there exists significant conversational relevance of gender-stereotypic syntactic, semantic, and pragmatic cues, for inferring gender.

3 Intimate Partner Violence (IPV) and Gender Violence

The discussion boards that have been analysed for this study have in common the specific subject they address: they offer support to women who have suffered abuse and violence. In order to describe the specificity of this type of contexts, I will look at the online representation of violence. As mentioned above, the existence of online support groups is proliferating, due to the fact that they seem to have a positive impact on individuals with different kinds of difficulties (Andersson et al. 2005; Owen et al. 2010). I include in this section both IPV cases and gender violence cases in which the women describe what happened to them (whether they were abused by a relative, their partner, or an unknown person).

According to Breiding et al. (2015), the term Intimate Partner Violence describes physical violence, sexual violence, stalking and psychological aggression (including coercive acts) by a current or former intimate partner. In turn, an intimate partner is defined as a person with whom one has a close personal relationship that can be characterized by (1) emotional connectedness, (2) regular contact, (3) on-going physical contact and sexual behaviour, (4) identity as a couple, and (5) familiarity and knowledge about each other's lives.

This misconduct, although not new, is increasingly gaining visibility in today's policies and prevention programmes. Of great concern for the World Health Organisation (henceforth WHO), it claims in the preface of its 2013 report *Global and regional estimates of violence against women: prevalence and health effects of intimate partner violence and nonpartner sexual violence*, that, "acts of violence against women are not isolated events but rather form a pattern of behaviour that violates the rights of women and girls, limits their participation in society, and damages their health and well-being", (WHO 2013:1).

The numbers are overwhelmingly disturbing in the WHO (2013:2) report: "overall, 35 % of women worldwide have experienced either physical and/or sexual intimate partner violence or non-partner sexual violence". If we look at the countries that host the particular forums of the present investigation, United States and Canada, according to The Centers for Disease Control and Prevention nearly 25 % of women experience at least one physical assault during adulthood by a partner in the United States, and in Canada it is reported that "There were just under 88,000 victims of family violence in Canada in 2013, [...]. This represented more than one-quarter of all violent crimes reported to police".[1]

According to several medical and psychological reports, there appear to be several stages in the overcoming of abuse by women (Cluss et al. 2006; Chang et al. 2005; Hendy et al. 2003; Merritt-Gray and Wuest 1995). A useful diagram of the process would be that proposed by Chang et al. (2005: 264): "Their stages were labelled counteracting abuse, breaking free, not going back, and moving on". The participation in a discussion board can probably be situated in the stages where women are aware of their situation and either have taken action, or are thinking of doing so.

The first step is never making public this situation (although anonymously, or under a pseudonym or nickname). Abuse is usually first involved in silence and some of the forums analysed refer to that silence as of something to be freed from either in their names (aftersilence), or in their internal subcategories (breaking the silence). According to Tonsing (2016), who studies cases of abuse in Hong Kong, silence is a matter of culture as most women are "pressured not to disclose the abuse outside of their family due to the shame it would bring to their family, fear of being ostracised from their communities [...]". However, Rodriguez et al. (1996:155) point to other factors as the reason for that silence, such as self-esteem, or gender roles, including a sense to responsibility towards the family:

> The participants identified their psychological vulnerability (e.g., low self-esteem) as one of the underlying reasons for not disclosing their abuse. [...]. Many women felt pressure to fulfil their traditional gender roles within the family [...].

Here again we find reference to two of the aspects that I am considering in this study: the transfer of vulnerability from the real world to the online reality (Kolko and Reid 1998; Mackinnon 1995), and the strong genderdization of this type of discourse. In the study of cyber-harassment Herring (2002:188) seems to support this claim when she states that violence is related to gender and that violent attitudes offline are reproduced online:

> Research has shown that men are disproportionately the perpetrators, and women disproportionately the victims, of violence in the physical world (Cyber-stalking.net, 2002). Cyber violence shows a similar pattern. Women were the victims in 84 % of online harassment cases, and men the perpetrators in 64 % of cases reported to the organization

[1] (Family violence in Canada: A statistical profile, 2013).

In the post-silence stage, women search in these forums understanding, support and respect in a way that they cannot probably do in FTF communication, as they explain in some of the posts. This is in line with Shalom et al.'s (2015:202) findings about interlocutors dealing with social anxiety. It appears that in this struggle CMC can play a crucial role, as it offers "more ease of control of personal information and less openness to scrutiny, [...] the experience and effects of CMC interactions for those with high social anxiety may differ from their experience in FTF".

In this distressing contact-free context women communicate their feelings and emotions, in a free and –in some cases- anonymous way through language. In this regard, the paper aligns with other studies that propose the universal value of emotions and of their linguistic realisation, as in Romero-Trillo and Espigares (2012) who discuss the emotions enacted by the contemplation of nature. The types of positive and negative adjectives used by the interlocutors will be analysed following Gladkova and Romero-Trillo (2014) model in the realization of personal vs. social reference, of positive and negative emotions in language, and of the use of cognitive elements.

4 Data Collection and Analysis

For the present study a corpus of online comments have been collected with the common topical thread of gender violence, including rape, sexual assault, and relationship violence. All the texts have been obtained from three different discussion boards from those endorsed by the organisation Domestic Shelters (https://www.domesticshelters.org/). According to their own definition, they are "the first and largest online and mobile searchable directory of domestic violence programs and shelters in the U.S. and Canada". Their aim is to "make more people aware of the services available for those experiencing domestic violence." It is, therefore, a reliable site that recommends resources directly to the victims of abuse or their families.

Within the list proposed, three forums were selected for the study, after disregarding the ones which only offered services related to phone call support or private chatting, and also those directed exclusively at teenager relationships.

The three selected websites with their online descriptions are the following:

AfterSilence.org (AS)	After Silence aims to help victims become survivors and to communicate in the recovery of domestic and sexual violence. It offers an active message board and chat room for rape, sexual assault, sexual abuse, incest and molestation survivors. There are over 31,000 members and about 1,000,000 posts, including recent posts and many useful posts from days and months past

Fort Refuge (FR)	A clever, grassroots site run by survivors for fellow survivors as a safe place to come together and discuss their struggles and victories in healing from various types of abuse. Though the forum and chat do not boast the same numbers as some of the larger organizations, they are one of the more active conversation places on the Internet currently. Also adds new content to its site regularly
Pandora's Aquarium (PA)	An online forum with around 2,000,000 posts and over 70,000 members run by Pandora's Project that provides information, support, and resources to rape and sexual abuse survivors and their friends and family. Includes healing retreat weekends, an articles database and guest speaker chats

The three websites offered the opportunity for users to visit a public chat. Also, there were private forums for those people who preferred more intimate environments. The websites also warned about the need to protect the names and accesses of the discussers, recommending them to use safe connections to ensure their personal well-being. The access to the public chatroom was not similar in all the cases. While in two (Aftersilence.org (AS), and Pandora's Aquarium (PA)), a user was required to identify herself, and to provide a nickname in order to be able to comment on the site. In the third website (Fort Refuge (FR)), no identification was necessary. Significant differences could also be found in the display of the comments, since FR uses either the tag "guest" or the nickname of the user, whereas PA uses the nickname or "member" in all the cases. Also, next to the user comes some information about the relation of the user to the site, i.e., the number of posts that person has written. This offers sufficient information to know whether the user is new to the site or a veteran member, and also the degree of involvement with the site. A different type of approach is used by AS, which offers greater degree of information about its users. In this site, the nicknames of the users, together with the number of entries posted, their gender and location can be found next to their post. Also, apart from this, members have the opportunity to add some more personal information; they choose between different categories of membership: *survivor* or *secondary survivor*, also, between *contributing member*, *member* or *guest*. All this data is compulsory and related to their connexion to the site. Additionally, users can include personal information, also displayed on the site, like their personal interests: "Writing, Scrapbooking, Reading, Spending time with my kids, Volunteering at school, Teaching classes at the Red Cross, Listening to music" (AS).

Apart from the site managers, all the participants in the threads are either victims of violence or supporters of those victims (typically relatives helping in the process). They are women in their immense majority (there are other forums specialised in men), and, although we cannot know for certain, their age ranges from very young girls to adults and even elderly women.

The forums are organised in Threads, proposing a subject matter for conversation, opinion or comment. Often, the site managers propose the threads, although sometimes the members themselves propose a new topic for conversation. Examples of these are, for instance:

Five threads were selected from each website, taking into account that all had been answered by a significant amount of users, and that they were fairly recent. The posts published in AS date 2005–2016, in FR date 2014–2016 and PA date 2008–2016. Both, the number of words in each Thread, and the total number of words per site, are displayed in Table 1. In two cases, when the thread was too long and went very far back in time, only a sample of the entries was selected and analysed. In each case, this information is also provided in parenthesis.

As can be seen in the table, a total of 1615 posts were selected for analysis. They were distributed in two big groups: AS and PA, of 88,057 and 99,936 words respectively, and a significantly smaller one, FR, which accounts for 23,451 words of the entire corpus. The difference in the number of words is due to the nature of the

Table 1 Threads, posts and words selected per site

Site and dates	Thread	Posts	Words	Totals
AfterSilence (AS) 2005–2016	5 words to your perpetrator (10/35 pages)	250/872	3660	88,057
	Empathy, Sympathy Or Directive When Supporting You Choose	63	9410	
	Invalidation. Words Can Hurt! (5/31)	120/729	14,412	
	Did You Regret Reporting It? Where You Glad?	82	12,672	
	The inner child thread	460	47,903	
Fort Refuge (FR) 2014–2016	Understanding my fiancée's previous domestic abuse	27	10,632	26,451
	Life after integration	33	7924	
	Have any of you ever self harmed in the past?	18	1667	
	How can you tell if memories of abuse are real?	13	3242	
	How do I tell people about abuse/cutting/thoughts of suicide	13	2986	
Pandora's Aquarium (PA) 2008–2016	Who deserves to be here (all)	235	36,861	99,936
	Identifying unhealthy coping mechanisms	89	17,481	
	For those who didn't call it rape	92	17,285	
	You're lying	98	23,876	
	Alternative remedies – Share your thoughts	22	4433	
				214,444

forum threads, which determines the type of posts published. In the case of FR, posts were published by the users directly and obtained fewer responses that were much shorter in comparison with the other two. However, since we are not aiming to compare the different sites, but considering them as a big corpus, this was just considered one more characteristic of the data.

Then, once the threads were selected, the posts were downloaded and pre-processed for analysis. Below can be seen some examples which can help understand the type of comments posted on the forums, although there exists great variation on the length and degree of intimacy of the comments[2]:

AS-02 Hi Karen,
"I think I am probably the sympathetic with (I hope)
a dash of empathic!!
Another question could be 'who of the * would the trapped
survivor like to come along and help?' At the moment
I would like the sympathetic one!!"
Then you are in the right place Karen… :o)

FR-02 Me again. Was hoping to get replies here.
I have been searching online for info but there's not really
much out there. It is easy to find books,websites.support forums,
studies,etc.abiut DID but not about life after integration.
Even my therapist doesn't have experience with this, he has worked
with DID clients before, but I am the firsr for this.
I feel alone in this.

PA-02 Geez, you gals are hitting 'em all right on the nose! Lou,
a few days ago you mentioned how you fear dragging others
down by asking for their support; essentially fearing that they'll
see you as whining, when really you have a legitimate, honest,
very Real need which deserves attention. It is exactly that fear
which causes me to isolate myself. […]

As can be seen in the examples, both emoticons and asterisks to avoid bad language in the comments are often used. In the present study, this issue has not been analysed, since it focuses on the specific language used to express emotions. This would be, no doubt a line for future work.

Next, a first analysis was carried out in order to identify social and self-reference in the texts, together with the positive and negative emotions that could be found in the posts. For this purpose, the Linguistic Inquiry and Emotions (LWIC) analysis tool (Tausczik and Pennebaker 2010)[3] was used. This tool uses a reference database composed of almost 4500 words and word stems that defines one or more of the word categories used to analyse the input text, using multiple variables (e.g., total word count, words per sentence), 22 standard linguistic dimensions (e.g., percent-

[2] I have kept original spelling in all examples.

[3] http://www.liwc.net

age of pronouns words in the text), 32 word categories based psychological constructs (e.g., affect, cognition), 7 categories related to personal concern (e.g. leisure activities), or 12 punctuation categories (e.g. commas, etc.).

LWIC is based on psycholinguistic studies that evidence how individuals who benefit most from writing use high percentages of words related to positive emotion, as well as a modest number of negative emotion words, and an increasing number of thinking words from the first to last days of writing (Pennebaker et al. 2001; Tausczik and Pennebaker 2010).

Of the different categories analysed in LWIC, three were chosen as of interest in the present analysis: social processes, affective processes, both positive and negative, and cognitive processes. These were expected to shed light on the type of processes and the particular expressions materialised to communicate emotion in the forums. The idea was twofold: first, to see the texts in the context of a broader corpus, of general or formal texts, and second, to identify the type of emotion that was characteristic of the texts, for a second, more in-depth analysis. In Table 2 can be seen the categorisation of processes as used by LIWC in the processes chosen for the study.

Once this first part was completed, a second study was carried out focusing exclusively on the type of adjectives related to feelings used in the corpus. For this, the inventory of feelings provided online by The Center for Nonviolent

Table 2 LIWC categories for social, affective and cognitive processes

Category	Examples
Social processes	*Mate, talk, they, child*
Family	Daughter, husband, aunt
Friends	Buddy, friend, neighbor
Humans	Adult, baby, boy
Affective processes	*Happy, cried, abandon*
Positive emotion	Love, nice, sweet
Negative emotion	Hurt, ugly, nasty
Anxiety	Worried, fearful, nervous
Anger	Hate, kill, annoyed
Sadness	Crying, grief, sad
Cognitive processes	*cause, know, ought*
Insight	think, know, consider
Causation	because, effect, hence
Discrepancy	should, would, could
Tentative	maybe, perhaps, guess
Certainty	always, never
Inhibition	block, constrain, stop
Inclusive	And, with, include
Exclusive	But, without, exclude

Table 3 List of words to express positive emotion. Center for Nonviolent Communication(c) 2005

Affectionate	Engaged	Exhilarated	Peaceful	Excited	Grateful
compassionate	absorbed	blissful	calm	amazed	appreciative
friendly	alert	ecstatic	clear headed	animated	moved
loving	curious	elated	comfortable	ardent	thankful
open hearted	engrossed	enthralled	centered	aroused	touched
sympathetic	enchanted	exuberant	content	astonished	INSPIRED
tender	entranced	radiant	equanimous	dazzled	amazed
warm	fascinated	rapturous	fulfilled	eager	awed
JOYFUL	interested	thrilled	mellow	energetic	wonder
amused	intrigued	REFRESHED	quiet	enthusiastic	CONFIDENT
delighted	involved	enlivened	relaxed	giddy	empowered
glad	spellbound	rejuvenated	relieved	invigorated	open
happy	stimulated	renewed	satisfied	lively	proud
jubilant	HOPEFUL	rested	serene	passionate	safe
pleased	expectant	restored	still	surprised	secure
tickled	encouraged	revived	tranquil	vibrant	
	optimistic		trusting		

Communication (CNVC)[4] was used. According to its website, this US organisation supports the "the learning and sharing of Nonviolent Communication (NVC), and helps people peacefully and effectively resolve conflicts in personal, organizational, and political settings". A word list is one of the several resources made available to the possible users, who are encouraged to a greater self-understanding and deeper self-discovery. The list combines adjectives, verbs and nouns used to express a combination of emotional states and physical sensations. Obviously, it is a limited list, but it ambitions to inventor the most common words used. The list is made of two different sections: (1) "feelings we may have when our needs are being met" and (2) "feelings we may have when our needs are not being met." The lists contain some hyperonyms (in capital letters), and other adjectives. The entire list is reproduced below, divided into its two constituent parts:

Table 3 shows the 92 words chosen to best reproduce positive emotion.

Table 4 collects the 162 words chosen by CNCV to express negative feelings and emotions. It can be seen that the number of words in this list is considerably higher. A reason for this could be the will to help people with emotional dissatisfaction increase their awareness about it and the way they can express it.

These lists were contrasted with the corpus to identify which were the most used adjectives in our particular context. Specifically, the aim was to study the language of women who use CMC to talk about situations of real life violence, and who are undergoing a process of talking about it (self-discovery and self-understanding), for healing and recovery. From this purpose, I wanted to analyse two sets of data; on the one hand, the adjectives that appeared both, on the lists, and on the corpus. On the

[4] http://www.cnvc.org/

Table 4 List of words to express negative emotion. Center for Nonviolent Communication(c) 2005

Afraid	Annoyed	Disquiet	Tense	Aversion	Sad
apprehensive	aggravated	agitated	anxious	animosity	depressed
dread	dismayed	alarmed	cranky	appalled	dejected
foreboding	disgruntled	discombobulated	distressed	contempt	despair
frightened	displeased	disconcerted	distraught	disgusted	despondent
mistrustful	exasperated	disturbed	edgy	dislike	disappointed
panicked	frustrated	perturbed	fidgety	hate	discouraged
petrified	impatient	rattled	frazzled	horrified	disheartened
scared	irritated	restless	irritable	hostile	forlorn
suspicious	irked	shocked	jittery	repulsed	gloomy
terrified	ANGRY	startled	PAIN	FATIGUE	heavy hearted
wary	enraged	surprised	agony	beat	hopeless
worried	furious	troubled	anguished	burnt out	melancholy
DISCONNECTED	incensed	turbulent	bereaved	depleted	unhappy
alienated	indignant	turmoil	devastated	exhausted	wretched
aloof	irate	uncomfortable	grief	lethargic	nervous
apathetic	livid	uneasy	heartbroken	listless	overwhelmed
bored	outraged	unnerved	hurt	sleepy	restless
cold	resentful	unsettled	lonely	tired	stressed out
detached	CONFUSED	upset	miserable	weary	VULNERABLE
distant	ambivalent	YEARNING	regretful	worn out	fragile
distracted	baffled	envious	remorseful	EMBARRASSED	guarded
indifferent	bewildered	jealous		ashamed	helpless
numb	dazed	longing		chagrined	insecure
removed	hesitant	nostalgic		flustered	leery
uninterested	lost	pining		guilty	reserved
withdrawn	mystified	wistful		mortified	sensitive
	perplexed			self-conscious	shaky
	puzzled				
	torn				

other, those that did not, in order to establish their frequencies of use, and to be able to establish a comparison.

The initial tagging of the corpus was carried out by TagAnt (Anthony 2016),[5] which is able to tag the texts according to 58 Part of Speech (POS) categories. Those selected for the study were words tagged as JJ (adjective), JJR (adjective, comparative), and JJS (adjective, superlative). A total of 1601 adjectives were identified, disregarding their meaning. A sample of the adjectives identified can be seen below:

> abandoned; able; abnormal; above; absent; absolute; absurd; abused; abusive; academic; acceptable; accountable; accurate; acting; active; actual; ACCUSED; adamant; additional; adjoining; adolescent; adorable; adult;; affectionate; afraid; afraid; aggressive; awkward; alarmed; alarming; alcoholic; alcohol-induced;

In parallel, Mike Scott's Wordsmith Corpus Tools (2009) Concordancer[6] was used to identify the words on the corpus, both positive and negative, which appeared on the lists provided. Also, a wordlist was made of all the adjectives that appeared on the list but not on the corpus, in order to explore whether the adjectives used by these women in their conversation were among those considered "most used" to identify feelings.

5 Analysis and Results

5.1 Personal vs. Social Reference, Positive and Negative Emotions, Cognitive Elements

The results shed some light on the type of discourse used by these women, with some particular distinctive features. I will first discuss the results obtained after the LWIC analysis, which show the frequency of words that appear on the texts for each category in percentages. Table 5 displays the results calculated by LIWC, in percentages, for all three categories: in the first column, I show the results for the corpus under analysis (including all three discussion boards), in the second the average obtained for personal texts, written in informal contexts, and in the third the average for formal texts:

If we contrast the columns for the corpus analysed and the standard outcome for personal tests, it is clear in the table that, although they are contexts in which the main topic of conversation is the personal experience, personal references (I, me, my) in the corpus are 9.47, below the result of 11.4, representative of this category in standard personal texts. Also the number of articles and long words are slightly lower than the standard obtained for personal texts (4.29 vs. 5.0, and 12.93 vs. 13.1). A reason for this could be the high degree of informality expressed in the online exchanges, which reproduce sometimes some sort of stream of consciousness, having the interlocutors just write words as they come to their mind.

[5] http://www.laurenceanthony.net/software/tagant/

[6] Published by Lexical Analysis Software and Oxford University Press.

Table 5 Comparison of the texts with the general and formal texts

LIWC dimension	Corpus	Personal texts	Formal texts
Self-references (I, me, my)	9.47	11.4	4.2
Social words	10.66	9.5	8.0
Positive emotions	2.73	2.7	2.6
Negative emotions	3.29	2.6	1.6
Overall cognitive words	8.44	7.8	5.4
Articles (a, an, the)	4.29	5.0	7.2
Big words (>6 letters)	12.93	13.1	19.6

It is also important to highlight the great amount of social words that appear in the texts referring to family contexts or relations, referring to the offline setting of the interlocutor and the reason why she is participating on the forum (10.66 in the Corpus, vs. 9.5 average in personal texts, and 8.0 average in formal texts). As explained by Pennebaker et al. (2007:5), the words taken into consideration to identify this kind of category are: "Mate, Talk, They, Child, Family; Daughter, Husband, Aunt, Friends; Buddy, Friend, Neighbor, Humans; Adult, Baby, Boy". Below can be found examples of these words in the corpus:

Category	Word	Freq. %	Example	Text
Social processes	Talk, talking,	0.1475	are very safe things around us that can help you to **talk**. if you don't want to talk, we can wait because we love you very much, and we won't pressure you to do	AS-05
	They	0.3439	of the truth You are not forgiven…period. I noticed many people noted that **they** were not at the forgiving point yet – I'm sorry, but I have no need or	AS-01
	Child	0.2422	You did not know. You were only, only, only a **child**. Forgive yourself dear child. Deep forgiveness. Forgive your body. Let go. I love you Dear Young one,	AS-05

Category	Word	Freq. %	Example	Text
Family	Family	0.0742	That all those things REALLY were done to me by my **family** of origin. Sometimes I feel so much anger and rage towards them and	FR-02
	Sister	0.0369	Those who abused me were their brother/ **sister**, son/daughter, fellow church member, coworker, friend, etc. So I can sort of imagine it was hard for them to	FR-01
	Husband	0.0205	adopted daughter at all. i'm afraid that if i can't figure it out i'll lose my **husband**, wrecked a young girl's life, and dismantled my own. i feel intense	PA-01
Friends	Friend	0.111	sister, until I came up behind her 1 day as she was cruelly mocking me to her **friends**. Even so, half of the things they said in public weren't nearly as bad	PA-01

Category	Word	Freq. %	Example	Text
Humans	Adult	0.022	are so much stronger than this. You as the **adult** *, have a family now, a loving husband, a wonderful son, a caring brother, lean on them, don't shut them out. T	AS-05
	Baby	0.0126	Then when she was 22, she found out she was pregnant again. This time she chose to keep the **baby**. But she wasn't sure who the father was because she'd	PA-01
	Boy	0.0131	"(…)(he was adoloescent not pre-school and certainly capable of things a little **boy** isn't.) So that doesn't make it ok. After i told my friend i was raped"	AS-03

It is also important to mention that the appearance of words that express cognitive processes in the corpus is higher 8.44 %, whereas in personal texts the average obtained is 7.8 %.

Finally, if we look at the type of adjectives that are used, it can be seen that the expression of both positive and negative emotions are above the average. Whereas positive emotions are barely higher than the average for what is found in informal texts (2.73 vs. 2.7), negative emotions are expressed in the corpus in a much higher degree (3.29 vs. 2.6). The topic of the forums justifies this, as women write precisely to express their emotions and feelings. We can also see these results in Graph 1, which can help us identify the most relevant issues at first sight.

5.2 *Adjectives in The Corpus*

Once identified the different social, cognitive and general positive and negative results for the corpus, an in-depth study was carried out in order to identify the specific positive and negative adjectives that were used in the interlocutions. A total of

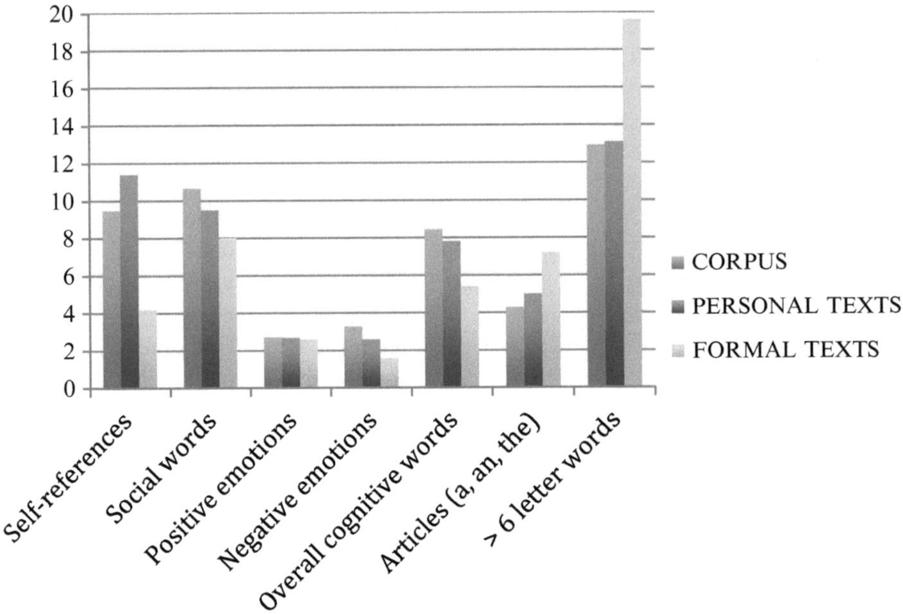

Graph 1 LWIC results for the corpus, personal and formal texts

1160 adjectives (referred to emotions, as well as other adjectives) were identified in the corpus, with 38,616 appearances and a frequency of 0.18 % in the total number of words.

Then, I contrasted the list of positive adjectives provided by the CNVC with the adjectives in the corpus, and 52 (0.56 %) of the 92 words proposed by the list could be found in the posts.

Table 6 displays the totals for the 15 most used positive adjectives that also appeared in the CNVC list, with the number of tokens in the corpus and their frequencies.

As can be seen, *safe* is by far the most used adjective used to express positive emotion in the corpus, with a frequency of 0.06 % and 131 tokens, followed by *quiet*, *loving*, and *proud,* which account for 0.01 % each, with 26 and 24 tokens in the corpus respectively., and very low frequencies for these adjectives. Graph 2 shows the distribution of the adjectives in a way that it is easily noticeable the enormous contrast between the use of *safe*, and the use of the rest of adjectives.

Examples of the use of these adjectives can be found below, as well as their texts of reference.

Table 6 Tokens and frequencies of the first 15 positive adjectives

Positive	Tokens	Frequency
safe	131	0.061121844
quiet	26	0.012131053
loving	24	0.011197895
proud	24	0.011197895
warm	21	0
sympathetic	18	0
calm	17	0
comfortable	17	0
involved	16	0
grateful	11	0
confident	10	0
trusting	10	0
friendly	8	0
happy	4	0
glad	1	0

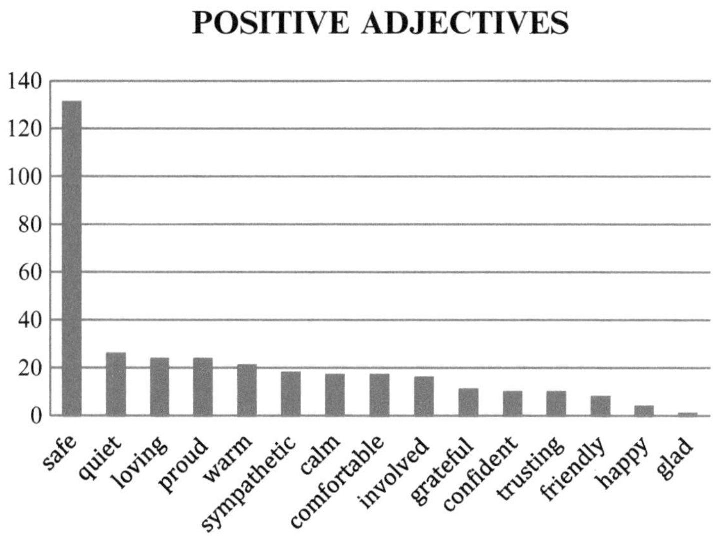

Graph 2 Distribution of the first 15 positive adjectives in the corpus

Word	**Example**	**Text**
calm	As if I wanted that piece of sh*t touching me. I've got to stay **calm** and be okay. I'm gonna go to his place…smoke some pot. That always clears m	AS-05

Word	Example	Text
comfortable	for tee ball and I'm trying to make friends with other moms so I can feel more **comfortable** letting him go places without me. I'm working through it with my	PA-01
confident	myself that much more. I want to move forward to where I can feel more whole and **confident** in myself. Maybe it would be different if my memories were	PA-01
friendly	not agree to that. Hope you will explore the Fort – People here are very **friendly** and accepting and it's a very supportive place regardless of where you	FR-02
glad	I was doing it. -Lis Firstly, Lis, I love you for that first paragraph. I'm **glad** I'm not the only one who is so bad about this! And yes, I beat myself up	PA-02
grateful	Hey, your thoughts are excellent and make me search myself for answers…so **grateful** for them# Brian dodo * before the end * * Contributing Member	AS-02
happy	us dance and they smiled. And when they smiled we smiled, because we were **happy** and we were dancing. Well little one, I saw you there today. I saw	AS-05
involved	family supports incesturous ideas, y'know? Even if the parents weren't directly **involved**, they often supported the abuser in some way. : (My CSA wasn't family	PA-04
loving	they are reluctant to end the situation. The abuser might genuinely be a **loving** person other than their abusive behavior. Nobody is 100 % good or 100 %	FR-01
proud	left for paying my health insurance and paying other basic bills. Actually, I'm **PROUD** that I wrote this list. At least I'm aware of the problem. Denial will not	PA-02
quiet	cousins were really close to us so they were around a lot. My sister was shy and **quiet**, and I'm sure it made her an easy target. I believe my cousin was probably	PA-01
safe	gotta hide or let people touch. i dont like the touching. i just want to feel **safe**. it makes me angry when people are nasty like that. people been lots nasty	AS-05

Word	Example	Text
sympathetic	Being sympathetic comes easily to me (mostly) because i am a **sympathetic** person although in the scenario given above offering sympathy is c	AS-02
trusting	sometimes i wonder whose fault it was, if only you hadn't been so **trusting** of grandad, if only you hadn't been so quiet, if only you'd have told	AS-05
warm	PRESSIVE Rest in my arms precious child; cradled and **warm**. You are safe. The war is over.	FR-05

If we look at the negative adjectives, 91 of the 162 proposed by CNVC appear in the corpus, i.e., 0.56 %, which is about the exact same proportion of those found in the list for positive adjectives. However, not only are the negative adjectives used to express emotion much more abundant in the corpus, they also appear to be much more used. In other words, there is greater coincidence in the choice of words and the number of tokens of the top fifteen negative adjectives is in general twice the number found for the positive adjectives, as can be seen in Table 7.

As the table shows, he most recurrent adjectives are *hurt*, *scared* and *angry*. In a separate analysis, I have considered nouns such as *hate* or *pain* because they are among the most used words to express emotion in the corpus, and were also included in the CNVC list. Only *hurt* adds up more tokens than the entire list of positive adjectives (271 tokens, and a frequency of 0.13 %). *Scared* is the second most used adjective, with 163 tokens (0.07 %), followed by angry, with 120 tokens (0.05 %)

Table 7 Tokens and frequencies of the first 15 negative adjectives

Negative	Tokens	Frequency
hurt	271	0.126442894
scared	163	0.076052368
hate	142	0.066254213
pain	132	0.061588421
angry	120	0.055989474
sad	108	0.050390527
afraid	93	0.043391842
lost	70	0.032660525
upset	49	0.022862369
guilty	43	0.020062895
ashamed	35	0.016330263
confused	35	0.016330263
lonely	34	0.015863685
tired	34	0.015863685
vulnerable	24	0.011197895

Word	Example	text
afraid	should just completely say NO, but I was saying no to myself, just cause I was too **afraid** to throw them out anywhere else. * Back to	PA-02
angry	it being a 'healing touch' he was giving me it was 'demons'. I was pretty **angry** and disgusted but since my Aunt lived 45 min	AS-04
ashamed	. i suck my thumb when i am sad but '*' dont let us suck our thumb. shes **ashamed** of us. she dont want there to be someone	AS-05
confused	kinda **confused** as I have feelings for this guy that are growing- but am soooooo terrified in general	AS-04
guilty	feel **guilty** about sex. Perhaps I was raped and someone else should be feeling guilty. Just a thought.) From some adults who got word of my molestation by the	AS-03
hurt	MY INNER CHILD FINALLY SPEAKING OUT. TRIGGER!!!!!!!! Read with caution. I hate being. Its hard. I'm scared. Dirty. I just **hurt**, don't know how to make it	AS-05
lonely	on the bus, in front of everyone. I was crying for you, because you are so hurt and lost and **lonely** and sad, but you were once so beautiful and innocent	AS-05
lost	naughty me. I want to sleep – i want to hide – hiding good. Im too tired. Confused, hurt, tired, **lost**.... Everything gonna go wrong…punishment is used	AS-05
pain	About the idea of losing our mothers, and the extraordinary **pain** and grief I feel, regularly, at the loss it is to have a living mother who is, rea	AS-05
sad	Been **sad** a lot lately. Maybe the phobia will lessen, now that I know WHY she's afraid – or at least, I'll be able to work through it, with her help. Twiggy is	AS-05
scared	with you?"-"Something is terribly wrong with you, what do you mean you were **scared** and	AS-03
tired	lot of mixed emotions for me....sad, happy, **tired**, guilt, frustrated, scared, angry.... I regret reporting it, If my daughter was to be raped in future I wo	AS-04
upset	That was as far as I got and it just hit me why the hell I was so **upset** and angry over my husband not believing me about something quite small. It also hi	AS-05
vulnerable	(I never gave consent, he knew that I was already extremely emotionally fragile and **vulnerable**) it seems like rape. But when I think about everything el	PA-04

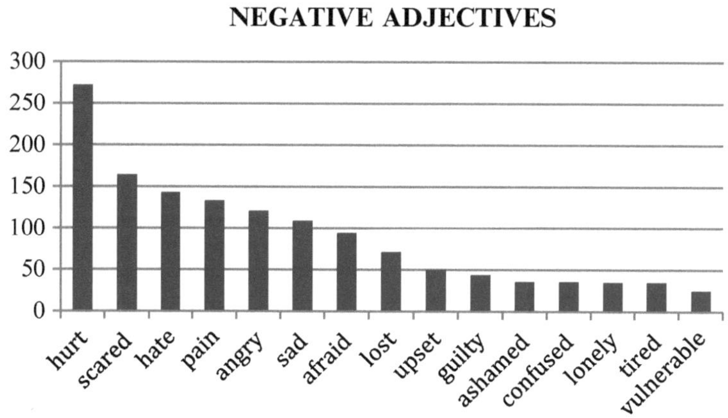

Graph 3 Distribution of the first 15 negative words in the corpus

The distribution of negative adjectives on the corpus, ordered by number of tokens, can be seen in Graph 3.

Hate has been studied separately, as it appears as Noun and Verb, with 142 tokens accounting for 0.06 % of all words in the text, and has been compared with *love*, with a significantly higher number of tokens, 294, accounting for 0.137 % of all words. Also, very high in the ranking of words comes pain, with 132 tokens, and a frequency of 0.061 %. Not even these two frequent words account for love, which is, by far, the most used word to express emotion and, interestingly enough does not appear in the list for positive emotions provided by CNVC. Examples of these are shown below:

Word	**Example**	**text**
love	are songs that can be seen as romantic and if you take the romance out of them and just listen to the promise of **love**, they can fit differently. So, I sang to my Inner	AS-05
hate	I've only just seen this thread but I need to say this somewhere. I **hate** little M. I'm terrified of her. I think she has a power over me	AS-05
pain	i hate and wish death to you after a long long life of **pain**. Lastly there is nothing I could say do or hear to take away the memory of what	AS-01

Due to the nature of the corpus, a fourth analysis was carried out to see whether these women were finding "out of the conventional" ways to express their emotions. The idea was to identify possible adjectives used by them to express emotion in the corpus that did not appear on the lists provided to help identify feelings of comfort and discomfort proposed by the CNVC to help users be aware of their emotions in order to be able to change them. Maybe some more awareness on the way emotion is expressed was necessary in these cases, and these women were expressing

Table 8 Tokens and frequencies for the first 15 first adjectives not on the lists

Negative	Tokens	Frequency
Hard	246	0.114778422
Sorry	237	0.110579208
Bad	224	0.104513682
Unhealthy	131	0.061121844
Needed	96	0.044791579
Mad	48	0.02239579
Horrible	46	0.021462632
Sick	45	0.020996053
Trapped	42	0.019596316
Crazy	42	0.019596316
Dead	36	0.016796842
Negative	32	0.014930527
Healthy	31	0.014463947
Honest	30	0.013997369
Brave	29	0.01353079

emotions differently. Maybe their emotions were different from the ones expected. A surprising amount of such adjectives was found. The top 15 most used adjectives which fall in this category can be found on Table 8:

It can be seen that *hard* and *sorry* are at the top of the list, with frequencies of 0.11 %, and number of tokens of 246 and 237, followed by bad, with 224 tokens, and a frequency of 0.10 %. It can also be seen that only three positive adjectives appear on this list, right at the bottom of the rank; *healthy* (31 tokens, 0.01 %), *honest* (30 tokens, 0.01 %), and *brave*, (29 tokens, 0.01 %). A few examples of the use of these adjectives on the corpus are shown below, together with the context in which they appear.

Negative adjectives used to express emotion		**Text**
hard	to me that you are so non-judge mental and open to trying to understand. It is **hard** for many of us to explain it, not an easy subject to talk about, however	AS-02
	was wrong. I didn't understand the magnitude of what happened. This may be very **hard** to comprehend and to be honest I still can't wrap my head around it.	FR-01
sorry	kind. I have silver sparkles in my wings and the tips shine like diamonds. I am **sorry** you are sad today. I know that Angel will take very good care of you. I'll	AS-05
	me just 'cause I'm a grown up. Or does all this just sound utterly daft? I'm **sorry** your husband doesn't understand the inner child. My husband is having trouble	AS-05

bad	from knowing that I am not alone. I have someone who wont judge me, when I feel **bad** they will give me a hug and listen to me and these things bring a level of	AS-02
	when I come HERE? "Someday, I'll forgive you all." you hurt me so **bad**… you will be caught.. soon You're not in control anymore! I am strong	AS-01
unhealthy	I know this is very **unhealthy** and I'm trying to change for his sake. I can't live in fear his whole life and keep him from experiencing normal childhood	PA-01
	belief system surrounding it, to compensate for the pain, leading myself to alienation and some **unhealthy** coping mechanisms. Mostly I just feel bewilderment and pain.	PA-01
needed	take Care xxx (((Hannah))) hello thanx alot for that!!i desperately **needed** to hear that.as a child sexual abuse survivor it feels really good to kno	AS-05
	again Thanks for posting this. It's amazing how you hit so many things that I **needed** to hear specifically. I have had people tell me that I made the choice to	PA-01
mad	to hold me and say it was going to be ok. She refused to hug me even. She was **mad** I didn't go running to her right after it happened. Why would I if you make	AS-02
	on my breast thats why he touched it all the time. All this makes me so damn **mad**. I honestly wish I could appeal. Try and charge him on those charges that	AS-04
horrible	K (drug) in my drink without me knowing. when i tried to tell people, it was **horrible**. when i told a couple friends (who i thought were, anyway), they said	PA-05
	little kid again. With sorrow in her voice she said "No you don't. You had such a **horrible** childhood." For her to admit that stunned me. I don't shut up easily,	PA-04
sick	son that he could not be your daddy. I'm sorry that mommy was such a frightened **sick** person that she could not help you. It was not your fault. You deserved so	AS-05
	is so crap she can never keep hold of you. And even just writing that I feel **sick** because it sounds so like mother, doesn't it? The way she |would try and man	AS-05

	but also to help me avoid my thoughts and feelings I pick at my skin which has a **negative** effect on my self esteem, I think its a SI thing too, but despite	PA-02

Positive adjectives used to express emotion

healthy	he did 'other things' and I cannot conceive. I'm, been trying for over a year, **healthy**, have regular periods etc. and nothing. I track my ovulation so I know t	AS-04
	Denial will not get me anywhere, acknowledging there is a problem is actually a **healthy** step. And I do have healthy coping mechanisms. Negativity seems to win o	PA-02
honest	and of course he laughed about the whole thing. HE knew I wasn't crazy. To be **honest**, all that was almost worse than the rape. But I really believe that	PA-04
	the magnitude of what happened. This may be very hard to comprehend and to be **honest** I still can't wrap my head around it. Basically, it took about three or f	FR-01
brave	opportunity. I can't imagine surviving that on top of my own feelings. You are a **brave** woman -- or should I say women, all of you who told. Elle ---------------	PA-04
	[y]ou need to. Just you tell me when you're ready, okay? Lots of love, you **brave brave** girl, of course you can *.... i feel im in for a long stay in the corner.	AS-05

Also, the distribution of these adjectives can be seen in Graph 4, which shows a clear predominance of three words over the rest, with a similar number of tokens (a much greater amount of tokens for *hard*, 246, *sorry* 237 and *bad* 224, and the next is *unhealthy* with 131).

If we now compare the results for all these words on the corpus, in order to see the distribution of the 15 most commonly used adjectives in all three lists, the results can be seen in Graph 5.

It is clearly noticeable that the most commonly used adjective is *hurt*, with a clear preponderance over the rest of adjectives, and that negative adjectives are used much more profusely than positive adjectives (let us recall that from the adjectives that were used on the corpus but not on the CNVC lists, only the last three were positive). Similarly, it can also be seen, that there is a significant use of the three first words on the list for specific adjectives on the corpus (*hard*, *sorry*, *bad*), which clearly outstands over other uses. In general can be seen a preponderance of use of negative adjectives, and of adjectives not proposed on the CNVC lists. It can be interesting to look at some examples of hard, sorry and bad, as they can help us glance the type of language used, both by the survivors, and their supporters.

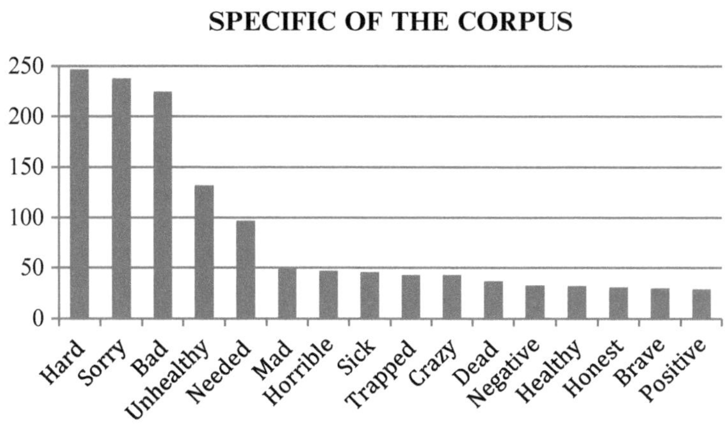

Graph 4 Distribution of adjectives specific of the corpus

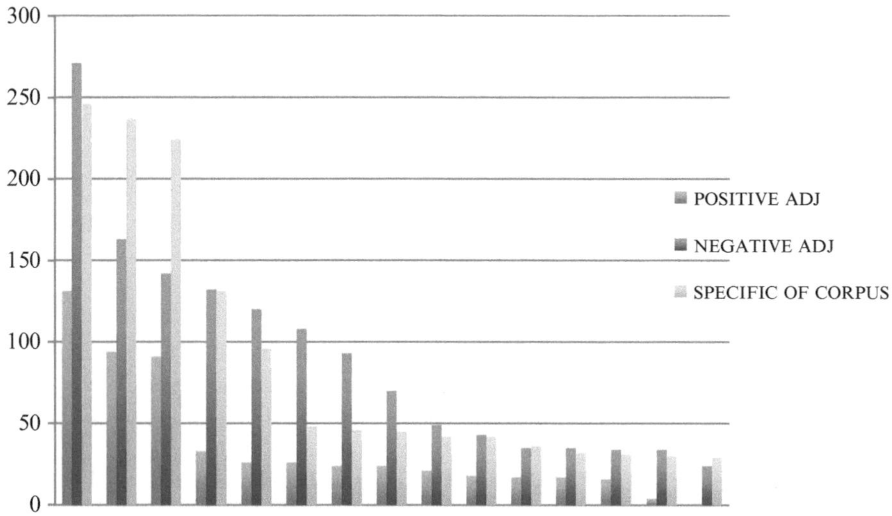

Graph 5 Distribution of emotion adjectives in the corpus

Word	Example	text
Hard	(survivor)WHY would ANYONE lie or make up a story about something as HORRID as sexual abuse? Its **hard** enough for us to tell our story because it is TRUE!	PA-04
	(supporter)(((((Christine))))) I am so sorry that you are having a **hard** time right now. Like you, I simply cannot cry for myself. I can cry for just	PA-04
Sorry	(survivor) in the book i could. i couldnt believe what she had done. it made me sick. **sorry**. my dad was out in the Med somewhere (he was on sea duty for the navy) and	PA-04

Word	Example	text
	(supporter) I agree! I'm **sorry** if your friend of so many years questioned you. I'd say that person wasn't much of a friend. We don't do that	PA-04
Bad	(survivor) makes me cringe when I hear that because not only does it make me feel **bad**, it just reinforces those myths in the minds of those who believe them	PA-04
	(supporter) I want to help my step-sister so **bad**, but she hides behind things too, and I can see she is just making things worse on herself than they have to be	PA-02

Finally, we will look into the most commonly used patterns in the text for the verb *to feel*, to see what are the words they most directly associate with their feelings, expressed as such. After the analysis, it can be seen that the most commonly used adjectives are *guilty,* and *bad,* for negative feelings, and *safe* and *good* for positive.

	Adjective	Tokens	Example	text
Feel*	Guilty	19	I gave up. I didn't know what to do, I was scared, I liked him. He made me **feel guilty**. I don't know how to cope with this…	PA-03
	Safe	19	and not cry. Just to remind me NOT to tell he burned the one place down that i **felt safe**. Put all my toys in there (a fort) and	PA-04
	Bad	18	Calls, laundry – you name it, I don't do it until I'm forced to. I do, however, **feel bad** about not doing it the entire time. Healthy. I	PA-02
	Good	14	nearly lost me). I punched walls and other hard surfaces, mostly because it **felt good** to 'crack the knuckles' not because I really	FR-03
	Alone	11	abandoned me, that was almost as bad a being raped. I was crushed, disappointed, **felt alone** abandoned, awful. I guess	PA-03
	Sad	11	sluts to justify their own abusive behavior. Ludditesunited, it makes me **feel sad** that your family was so mean and cruel to	PA-02
	Free	9	O.K… I think I was just venting. **Feel free** to disregard my comments. I am embarrased that I actually sent that	AS-02

Adjective	Tokens	Example	text
Lonely	6	hurt you any more. I hear you when you call to me, when you are sad, when you **feel lonely**, when you are hungry. I promise to	AS-05
Sick	6	Have random, aggressive/violent sex with strangers. * Chain smoke til I **felt sick**. And then smoke some more. * Ignore	PA-02
Weird	5	and we made plans to hang out, even though I didn't actually want to. I woke up **feeling weird**, and glad that I was next to my	PA-01

You need a summary after the examples

6 Conclusions

Several conclusions can be drawn from the present study. First, regarding the analysis of the emotional and cognitive lexical load of texts based on the psychological analysis of the words I expected that these discussion boards in which women seek support would have more self-reference than in other text types. However, the results of the analyses have shown that in the corpus there appears to be very little reference to the self on the texts. Also, women seem to express their thoughts and feelings avoiding articles and long words (for the LWIC analysis, words longer than six letters are long), seeming to write just what comes to their mind, without paying attention to the appropriateness, or correctness of their speech. In contrast, words referring to the social environment (most likely the family) are very common (10.66 %), as well as words that express cognitive processes (8.44 %), representing the women's individual processes of coming of awareness and overcoming very difficult personal situations.

Focusing on the use of adjectives and emotion words used, it can be observed in the LWIC results, that both positive and negative words are above the average in personal writings (2.76 and 3.29 respectively, as compared to 2.70 and 2.60). In the corpus, the most commonly used adjectives are *hurt* (271 tokens), *scared* (163 tokens), *angry* (120 tokens), and *sad* (108 tokens). However, these adjectives are used similarly in the corpus when women explain their personal circumstances (as survivors), and when they try to support others (as supporters), even if they are negative adjectives. This can imply that the women use empathetic language, also that many of them are both survivors and supporters, but mainly that the language used in the texts is almost a sort of sociolect.

As regards the use of positive adjectives in the corpus the most significant are *safe* (131 tokens), *quiet* (26 tokens) and *loving* (24 tokens). Also, this can be complemented with the list of adjectives that they use in collocation with the verb *to feel* in which we find coincidence in the adjectives *guilty* (19 tokens), *safe* (19 tokens), *bad* (18 tokens), *and good* (14 tokens).

However, if we take a closer look and analyse the type/token ratio of the adjectives most commonly used, we can observe that a significant amount of the words chosen by the women to express their feelings in the forum are different from those proposed by the CNVC to help take consciousness and identify one's feelings and emotions. This does not seem to indicate that the lists are not useful, since the emotions described within can also be found on the corpus, but rather that emotions caused by extreme circumstances are expressed in a different manner, as has been seen in the text; by the use of adjectives that express negative emotions, such as *hard* (246 tokens), *sorry* (237 tokens), *bad* (224 tokens), *or unhealthy* (131 tokens), but also to express positive emotions, such as *healthy* (31 tokens), *honest* (30 tokens), or *brave* (29 tokens). To support this fact, it is important to highlight the great coincidence of women in the use of these other adjectives, which help them better to express how they are feeling, instead of the standard adjectives proposed. Indeed, it has been seen in the analysis that, although women also use the adjectives that are commonly used by psychologists and other professionals, to identify feelings (in order to increase awareness and start personal changing processes), the majority of these women use other type of adjectives, both to express how they feel and to express support towards others showing that their personal awareness processes follow different paths. They do not use the ones proposed by the standard lists, but there is great coincidence in the choice of adjectives by these women *hurt*, *hard*, *sorry*, *bad*.

To sum up, I think that this study has shed light on the type of feelings expressed by women who write in domestic violence forums when they find themselves in free, supportive, sheltering spaces, where they feel understood and cared for. This study also helps to improve the understanding on how these women express their feelings through language. I believe that knowing the language patterns of the different phases they go through can help in their healing processes by mean of the coincidental feelings they express. Also, this study can help to understand the language used by women online when they give support to others and can opens avenues for research into the language of negative emotions and the linguistic strategies to offer comfort, sympathy and social support.

References

Andersson, G., Bergstrom, J., Hollandare, F., Carlbring, P., Kaldo, V., & Ekselius, L. (2005). Internet-based self-help for depression: Randomized controlled clinical trial. *British Journal of Psychiatry, 187*, 456–461.

Anthony, L. (2016). TagAnt (Windows 64 Bit, 1.2.1) [Computer Software]. Tokyo, Japan: Waseda University. Available from http://www.laurenceanthony.net/

Baron, N. S. (2003). *See you online: Gender issues in college student use of instant messaging.* Retrieved March 27, 2006, from http://www.american.edu/tesol/BaronSeeYouOnlineCorrected64.pdf

Benigno, V., & Trentin, G. (2000). The evaluation of online courses. *International Journal of Computer Assisted Learning, 16*(3), 259–270.

Birkley, E. L., & Eckhardt, C. I. (2015). Anger, hostility, internalizing negative emotions, and intimate partner violence perpetration: A meta-analytic review. *Clinical Psychology Review, 37*, 40–56. http://doi.org/10.1016/j.cpr.2015.01.002

Blader, S. L., & Tyler, T. R. (2003). A four-component model of procedural justice: Defining the meaning of a "fair" process. *Personality and Social Psychology Bulletin, 29*, 747–758.

Blau, I., Mor, N., & Neuthal, T. (2009). Open the windows of communication: Promoting interpersonal and group inteactions using blogs in higher education. *Interdisciplinary Journal of E-Learning and Learning Objects, 5*, 233–246.

Blood, R. (2002). *The Weblog handbook: Practical advice on creating and maintaining your blog.* Cambridge, MA: Perseus Publishing.

Breiding, M. J., Basile, K. C., Smith, S. G., Black, M. C., & Mahendra, R. (2015). *Intimate partner violence surveillance uniform definitions and recommended data elements.* Georgia: Centers for Disease Control and Prevention National Center for Injury Prevention and Control Atlanta.

Burstall, J. (2000). Learning communities for social change in forums on the web. *Australian Journal of Adult Learning, 40*(1), 33–52.

Cassell, J., & Tversky, D. (2005). The language of online intercultural community formation [electronic version]. *Journal of Computer-Mediated Communication, 10*(2). Retrieved March 27, 2006, from http://jcmc.indiana.edu/vol/10/issue2/cassell.html

Chang, J. C., Decker, M. R., Moracco, K. E., Martin, S. L., Petersen, R., & Frasier, P. Y. (2005). Asking about intimate partner violence : Advice from female survivors to health care providers. *Patient Education and Counseling, 59*, 141–147. http://doi.org/10.1016/j.pec.2004.10.008

Cluss, P. A., Chang, J. C., Hawker, L., Hudson, S., Dado, D., & Buranosky, R. (2006). The process of change for victims of intimate partner violence : Support for a Psychosocial Readiness Model. *Women's Health Issues, 16*, 262–274. http://doi.org/10.1016/j.whi.2006.06.006

Crystal, D. (2001). *Language and the internet.* Cambridge: Cambridge University Press.

Dalampan, A. E. (2006). 59 Gender issues in computer-mediated communications. *TESOL Working Paper Series, 4*(2), 59–66.

Deaux, K., & LaFrance, M. (1998). Gender. In D. Gilbert, S. Fiske, & G. Lindzey (Eds.), *The handbook of social psychology* (pp. 788–827). Boston: McGraw-Hill.

Deaux, K., & Major, B. (1987). Putting gender into context. An interactive model of gender-related behavior. *Psychological Review, 94*, 369–389.

Efimova, L., & de Moor, A. (2005). Beyond personal Webpublishing: An exploratory study of conversational blogging practices. In *Proceedings of the 38th annual Hawaii international conference on system sciences*, (January), 3–6. http://doi.org/10.1109/HICSS.2005.118

Eubanks, V. (2000). Paradigms and perversions: A women's place in Cyberspace. *The CPSR Newsletter*, pp. 1–18.

Fox, N., & Roberts, C. (1999). GPs in cyberspace: The sociology of a "virtual community." *The Sociological Review, 47*, 643–671. http://doi.org/10.1111/1467-954X.00190

Fox, A. B., Bukatko, D., Hallahan, M., & Crawford, M. (2007). The medium makes a difference: Gender similarities and differences in instant messaging. *Journal of Language and Social Psychology, 26*(4), 389–397. http://doi.org/10.1177/0261927X07306982

Gladkova, A., & Romero-Trillo, J. (2014). Ain't it beautiful? The conceptualization of beauty from an ethnopragmatic perspective. *Journal of Pragmatics, 60*, 140–159.

Graddy, D. B. (2004). Gender and online discourse in the principles of economics [Electronic version]. *Journal of Asynchronous Learning Networks, 8*(4). Retrieved March 27, 2006, from http://www.sloan-c.org/publications/aln/v8n4/v8n4_graddy.asp

Hall, H., & Davison, B. (2007). Social software as support in hybrid learning environments: The value of the blog as a tool for reflective learning and peer support. *Library and Information Science Research, 29*, 163–187.

Hendy, H. M., Eggen, D., Gustitus, C., McLeod, K. C., & Ng, P. (2003). Decision to leave scale: Perceived reasons to stay in or leave violent relationships. *Psychology of Women Quarterly, 27*, 162–173.

Herring, S. C. (1996). Two variants of an electronic message schema. In S. C. Herring (Ed.), *Computer-mediated communication: Linguistic, social, and cross-cultural perspectives* (pp. 81–106). Amsterdam: Benjamins.

Herring, S. C. (2000). Gender differences in CMC: Findings and implications. *Computer Professionals for Social Responsibility Journal, 18*(1). Retrieved January 7, 2016 from http://cpsr.org/issues/womenintech/herring/.

Herring, S. C. (2002). Computer-mediated communication on the internet. *Annual Review of Information Science and Technology, 36*(1), 109–168. http://doi.org/10.1002/aris.1440360104

Herring, S. C. (2007). *A faceted classification scheme for computer-mediated discourse.* Language@Internet 4: Retrieved October 15, 2014, from http://www.languageatinternet.org/articles/2007/761

Herring, S. C. (2010). Who's got the floor in computer-mediated conversation? Edelsky's gender patterns revisited. Language@Internet, 7 Retrieved November 2, 2014, from http://www.languageatinternet.org/articles/2010/2857

Herring, S. C., Scheidt, L. A., Bonus, S., & Wright, E. (2004). Bridging the gap: A genre analysis of weblogs. In *Proceedings of the 37th Hawai'i international conference on system sciences (HICSS-37)*. Los Alamitos: IEEE Computer Society Press. Retrieved June 21, 2014, from http://ella.slis.indiana.edu/~herring/herring.scheidt.2004.pdf

Herschel, R. T. (1994). The impact of varying gender composition on group brainstorming performance in a GSS Environment. *Computers in Human Behavior, 10*, 209–222.

Herschel, R. T., Cooper, T. R., Smith, L. F., & Arrington, L. (1994). Exploring numerical proportions in a unique context: The group support systems meeting environment. *Sex Roles, 31*, 99–123.

Ho, C., & Swan, K. (2007). Evaluating online conversation in an asynchronous learning environment: An application of Grice's cooperative principle. *The Internet and Higher Education, 10*, 3–14.

Kapidzic, S., & Herring, S. C. (2011). Gender, communication, and self-presentation in teen chatrooms revisited: Have patterns changed? *Journal of Computer-Mediated Communication, 17*(1), 39–59. http://doi.org/10.1111/j.1083-6101.2011.01561.x

Kleinke, S., & Bös, B. (2015). Intergroup rudeness and the metapragmatics of its negotiation in online discussion fora. *Pragmatics, 25*(1), 47–71.

Kling, R. (1996). Synergies and competition between life in cyberspace and face-to-face communities. *Social Science Computer Review, 14*(1), 50–54.

Koch, S. C., Mueller, B., Kruse, L., & Zumbach, J. (2005). Constructing gender in chat groups. *Sex Roles, 53*(1–2), 29–41. http://doi.org/10.1007/s11199-005-4276-7

Kolko, B., & Reid, E. (1998). Dissolution and fragmentation: Problems in on-line communities. In S. G. Jones (Ed.), *Cybersociety 2.0* (pp. 212–229). London: Sage.

Lakoff, R. (1990). *Talking power: The politics of language*. New York: HarperCollins.

Langellier, K. M., & Peterson, E. E. (2004). *Storytelling in daily life: Performing narrative.* Lanigan/Philadelphia: Temple University Press.

Li, Q. (2005). Gender and CMC: A review on. *Australasian Journal of Educational Technology, 21*(3), 382–406.

Litvin, S. W., Goldsmith, R. E., & Pan, B. (2006). Electronic word-of-mouth in hospitality and tourism management. *Tourism Management, 29*(3), 458–468. http://doi.org/10.1016/j.tourman.2007.05.011

MacKinnon, R. C. (1995). Searching for the Leviathan in usenet. In S. Jones (Ed.), *Cybersociety: Computer-mediated communication and community* (pp. 112–137). Thousand Oaks: Sage.

Merritt-Gray, M., & Wuest, J. (1995). Counteracting abuse and breaking free: The process of leaving revealed through women's voices. *Health Care for Women International, 16*, 399–412.

Mestre, E., & Romero-Trillo, J. (Forthcoming). Expressing opinions and emotions while travelling. In J. May & D. Silva (Eds.), *The pragmatics of adaptability*. Amsterdam: John Benjamins.
Mey, J. L. (2009). Adaptability in human-computer interaction. In *Concise encyclopedia of pragmatics* (2nd ed., pp. 7–13). Oxford: Elsevier.
Mulac, A., & Lundell, T. L. (1994). Effects of gender-linked language differences in adults' written discourse: Multivariate tests of language effects. *Language and Communication, 14*, 299–309.
Murray, D. E. (1995). *Knowledge machine: Language and information in a technological society*. New York: Longman.
Owen, J. E., Boxley, L., Goldstein, M. S., Lee, J. H., Breen, N., & Rowland, J. H. (2010). Use of health-related online support groups: Population data from the California health interview survey complementary and alternative medicine study. *Journal of Computer-Mediated Communication, 15*, 427–446. Pew.
Pennebaker, J. W., Francis, M. E., & Booth, R. J. (2001). *Linguistic inquiry and word count*. Mahwah: Erlbaum Publishers.
Pennebaker, J. W., Chung, C. K., Ireland, M., Gonzales, A., & Booth, R. J. (2007). *The development and psychometric properties of LIWC2007* (pp. 1–22). Austin: The University of Texas.
Pew Internet & American Life Project (2010). Retrieved February 11, 2016 from http://www.pewinternet.org/2010/08/11/home-broadband-2010/
Pfeil, U., & Zaphiris, P. (2009). Investigating social network patterns within an empathic online community for older people. *Computers in Human Behavior, 25*(5), 1139–1155. http://doi.org/10.1016/j.chb.2009.05.001
Pierotti, R. S. (2013). Increasing rejection of intimate partner violence: Evidence of global cultural diffusion. *American Sociological Review, 78*(2), 240–265. http://doi.org/10.1177/0003122413480363
Rodriguez, M. A., Szkupinski, S., & Bauer, H. M. (1996). Breaking the silence. Battered women's perspectives on medical care. *Archives of Family Medicine, 5*,153–158.
Romero-Trillo, J., & Espigares, T. (2012). The cognitive representation of natural landscapes in language. *Pragmatics and Cognition, 20*, 168–185.
Sardar, Z. (1996). Cyberspace as the darker side of the west. In Z. Sarda & J. R. Ravetz (Eds.), *Cyberfutures. Culture and politics on the information superhighway*. London: Pluto Press.
Selfe, C. L., & Meyer, P. R. (1991). Testing claims for on-line conferences. *Written Communication, 8*(2), 163–192.
Shalom, J. G., Israeli, H., Markovitzky, O., & Lipsitz, J. D. (2015). Social anxiety and physiological arousal during computer mediated vs. face to face communication. *Computers in Human Behavior, 44*, 202–208. http://doi.org/10.1016/j.chb.2014.11.056
Tausczik, Y. R., & Pennebaker, J. W. (2010). The psychological meaning of words: LIWC and computerized text analysis methods. *Journal of Language and Social Psychology, 29*(1), 24–54. http://doi.org/10.1177/0261927X09351676
Tonsing, J. C. (2016). Domestic violence : Intersection of culture, gender and context. *Journal of Immigrant and Minority Health, 18*, 442–446. http://doi.org/10.1007/s10903-015-0193-1
Vance Wilson, E., & Lu, Y. (2008). Communication goals and online persuasion: An empirical examination. *Computers in Human Behavior, 24*, 2554–2577. http://doi.org/10.1016/j.chb.2008.02.021
Wierzbicka, A. (1993). Reading human faces: Emotion components and universal semantics. *Pragmatics and Cognition, 1*(1), 1–23.
Wilson, E. V. (2003). Perceived effectiveness of interpersonal persuasion strategies in computer-mediated communication. *Computers in Human Behavior, 19*, 537–552.
Wojcieszak, M. E., & Mutz, D. C. (2009). Online groups and political discourse : Do online discussion spaces facilitate exposure to political disagreement ? *Journal of Communication, 59*, 40–56. http://doi.org/10.1111/j.1460-2466.2008.01403.x
World Health Organization. (2013). Global and regional estimates of violence against women: Prevalence and health effects of intimate partner violence and nonpartner sexual violence. (Online Report).

Wright, K. B. (2002). Social support within an on-line cancer community: An assessment of emotional support, perceptions of advantages and disadvantages, and motives for using the community. *Journal of Applied Communication Research, 30*, 195–209.

Wright, K. B., & Bell, S. B. (2003). Health-related support groups on the internet: Linking empirical findings to social support and computer-mediated communication theory. *Journal of Health Psychology, 8*, 39–54. Wright.

Yus Ramos, F. (2010). *Ciberpragmática 2.0. Nuevos usos del lenguaje en Internet*. Barcelona: Ariel.

Zehrer, A., Crotts, J. C., & Magnini, V. P. (2011). The perceived usefulness of blog postings: An extension of the expectancy-disconfirmation paradigm. *Tourism Management, 32*(1), 106–113. http://doi.org/10.1016/j.tourman.2010.06.013

"The More Please [Places] I See the More I Think of Home": On Gendered Discourse of Irishness and Migration Experiences

Nancy E. Avila-Ledesma and Carolina P. Amador-Moreno

Abstract One of the main challenges faced by Irish emigrants was the negotiation of diasporic identities and new community forms. This paper sets out to explore the notions of gender and the conceptualization of *Irishness* in post-famine emigrants' personal correspondence (1880–1930). Specifically, the study proposes an in-depth analysis of identity nouns such as *home* and *country* in order to elucidate the various ways in which the concepts of identity and mobility are interpreted and constructed within male and female discourses. The data for this chapter come from CORIECOR, the Corpus of Irish English Correspondence (McCafferty K, Amador-Moreno CP. In preparation. CORIECOR. The corpus of Irish English correspondence. University of Bergen and University of Extremadura, Bergen and Cáceres). This paper takes an interdisciplinary approach that combines sociolinguistics (Chamber JK, Sociolinguistic theory. Revised edition. Wiley-Blackwell, Malden, 2009) and corpus pragmatics (Romero-Trillo J, (ed), Pragmatics and corpus linguistics: a mutualistic entente. Mouton de Gruyter, Berlin, 2008; The yearbook of corpus linguistics and pragmatics 2013: new domains and methodologies. Springer, Dordrecht: http://dx.doi.org/10.1007/978-94-007-6250-3, 2013; The yearbook of corpus linguistics and pragmatics 2014: new empirical and theoretical paradigms. Springer, Dordrecht). Methodologically, our study relies on corpus linguistics techniques, namely keyness analysis and concordance lines, to identify the most common collocations and contextual uses of the nouns under study. In the second part of the analysis, the emotional load of these terms is examined from a sociopragmatic perspective in order to explain the way in which letter writers exploit language "to generate particular meanings, to take up particular social positioning" (Culpeper J, Historical sociopragmatics. John Benjamins, Amsterdam. 135 pp, 2011:2).

N.E. Avila-Ledesma (✉)
Filología Inglesa/Facultad de Filosofía, Universidad Autónoma de Madrid, Madrid, Spain
e-mail: nancy.avila@uam.es

C.P. Amador-Moreno
Filología Inglesa/Facultad De Filosofía, Universidad de Extremadura, Cáceres, Spain
e-mail: camador@unex.es

J. Romero-Trillo (ed.), *Yearbook of Corpus Linguistics and Pragmatics 2016*,
Yearbook of Corpus Linguistics and Pragmatics 4,
DOI 10.1007/978-3-319-41733-2_5

Keywords Irishness • Home • Country • Emigrants' letters • Gender • Corpus pragmatics

1 Introduction

> *Dear brother William,*
> *I received your welcome and kind letter by last mail. It is refreshing to*
> *get news from (Home) I still call it Home yet although I have lived longer*
> *here than in old Ireland, but I believe if we lived here for a century would*
> *still call the place of our birth Home.*
> *– James L. McIlrath, Lakeside, Canterbury, New Zealand to William McIlrath, Killinchy, Co. Down, Northern Ireland*
> *24 February 1891*

Early March 1861. A young boy arriving in New Zealand from Killinchy, co. Down, Northern Ireland. The promise of a better future. Personal correspondence to keep in touch with family. Ireland as an idealized place of attachment. Never coming back again. The story of James L. McIlrath is the story of more than 4 million Irish emigrants who – making the decision to escape post-famine Ireland – sailed from their homeland to different destinations (e.g. to New Zealand, Australia, the United States, Canada and Argentina) in search of a brighter future.

One of the main challenges faced by these emigrants was the negotiation of diasporic identities and new community forms. Home, then, became "a moveable concept, a psychological space, a community created within the changing links between here and there" (Al-Ali and Koser 2002:6). In this regard, diasporic communities played a crucial role provinding the emigrants with a specific place where they could not only "reinvent traditions and cultures associated with home, but also a sense of self, of one's identity" (ibid). Although most Irish emigrants made their everyday lives in the host countries "establishing careers, personal relationships, even families there" (Wiles 2008:133), the notion of *Irishness* was kept and enhanced within diasporic communities where the Irish "constructed their sense of identity around the idea of a shared collective imaginary of home" (ibid).

Although the construction of *Irishness* has elicited scholarly attention in the fields of migration history (cf. e.g. Miller 1985, 2008; Fitzpatrick 1994; Moreton 2012), and recent CORIECOR-based studies have provided interesting results in terms of morphosyntactic features (McCafferty 2014; McCafferty and Amador-Moreno 2014; Bonness forthcoming), pragmatics (Amador-Moreno and McCafferty 2015a, b), and phonological features (De Rijke 2016), there is still a dearth of academic studies focusing on the emotional component of personal correspondence in order to gain a better understanding of social mentalities, and consequently, individual and collective interpretations of emigration and home (but see Murray 2006:24–25). In an attempt to provide new insights into the emotional background of Irish migrations, the present chapter aims to explore the notions of gender and the conceptualization of *Irishness* in post-famine emigrants' personal correspondence. In doing so, we propose a corpus-based examination of *home* and *country* in order to elucidate the various ways in which the concepts of identity and belonging are linguistically and pragmatically constructed within male and female discourses.

This chapter is structured as follows. In Sect. 2, we will highlight some theoretical remarks about emotions, pragmatics and migration studies, and how such triangulation can be approached in a corpus-based study of Irish emigrants' personal correspondence. Section 3 will introduce the data and methodology used in the analyses. In Sects. 4 and 5, the linguistic and pragmatic uses of the identity terms under analysis will be presented and discussed. Finally, Sect. 6 presents the conclusions and the main ideas of the essay will be reviewed for the sake of future research.

2 Emotions, Personal Correspondence and Migration Studies

The examination of emotions in personal correspondence has traditionally been a neglected area in the field of migration studies. According to Cancian (2010:105) scholars "have shown limited interest in exploring the plethora of feelings that have been intrinsic to the experience of migration", probably because of the inaccessibility of such documents or, as William Reddy (2001:316) puts it, as a result of "our common sense supporting a certain division of labor among the disciplines that assigned emotions to the sphere of pshychology" (in Cancian 2010:166).

Regarded as "a treasure trove of all sorts of information" (Harper 2010:4), emigrants' letters have been extensively searched for historical and linguistic purposes in the research tradition (cf. e.g. Elspaß 2002; Dossena 2007; McLelland 2007; Fitzgerald and Lambkin 2008; Miller 2008). In the context of the Irish emigration, private letters have been used to trace the emergence and development of linguistic features of Irish English (cf. e.g. McCafferty and Amador-Moreno 2012a, b, 2014). The work of Amador-Moreno and McCafferty (2015a), for instance, has shown how such documents can offer valuable insights into the historical provenance and usage patterns of pragmatic markers in this variety. In the field of historical linguistics, de Rijke (2016) has searched emigrants' epistolary remittances to provide in-depth accounts of Northern Irish English phonology. By the same token, Moreton's (2012) and Amador-Moreno's (forthcoming) linguistic analyses of female speech have demonstrated the validity of emigrants' letters for sociolinguistic and gender studies.

In the field of migration history, Fitzpatrick's (1994) examination of nineteenth-century Irish migration to Australia has highlighted the importance of personal correspondence to unveil "the essence of Irish popular culture and even the very nature of Irishness" (Richards 2010:2). Here, Fitzpatrick explored the notions of home, emigration and homesickness as conceptualized in the letters of the Irish emigrants that travelled to the Australian colonies, concluding that – in the Australian-Irish context – home and emigration were not dichotomous but interdependent (see Ahmed et al. 2003), since he could not identify in the data any sign of "the anguished cry of a victim driven from home" (Fitzpatrick 1994:617). In the British context, Gerber's (2006) analysis of British personal correspondence has defended the emotional value of the private letters, arguing that emigrant letter-writing "was part of the 'post-emigration formation of personal identity', an epistolary reconstruction of the self in the 'immigrant's identity narrative" (Richards 2010:3). Focusing on the intersection of history and emotions, Cancian's (2010) furthermore provides a new framework for the examination of migration experiences and the emotional responses expressed in the Italian postwar personal correspondence.

More recently, the works of Moreton (2016) and Romero-Trillo and Avila-Ledesma (in press) have demonstrated the validity of personal correspondence for emotion studies. The former sets out to combine traditional historical sciences methods with digital humanities to address the conceptualization of recollections in a corpus of female Irish emigrant correspondence. The latter examines the ethno-pragmatic conceptualization of happiness and sadness in nineteenth-century Irish emigrants' private correspondence. In this regard, the study investigates the pragmatic uses of key emotion terms, namely, *happy, glad, unhappy* and *sad*, in order to unveil the linguistic specificities embedded in the conceptualization of such emotion terms in the letters. Building on the existing research, the present chapter aims to contribute to the now growing field of emotions and migration studies by analyzing the notions of home and *Irishness* as conceptualized in male and female emigrants' discourses.

3 Data and Methodology

The data for this chapter come from CORIECOR, the Corpus of Irish English Correspondence (McCafferty and Amador-Moreno in preparation). At the time of writing (May 2016), CORIECOR contains over 6000 private letters (approx. 3.5 million words) written by and to Irish emigrants of both sexes, with different social, religious and geographical backgrounds and sent from and to Ireland between 1600 and 1940 (see McCafferty and Amador-Moreno 2012a for further details).

In order to be able to explore the notions of gender and the conceptualization of *Irishness* in post-famine emigrants' personal correspondence, two sub-corpora: a 74,331-word female sub-corpus and a 121,525-word male sub-corpus dating from 1880 to 1930 (see Table 1), were investigated using Sketch Engine (Kilgarriff et al. 2004). The rationale behind timespan selection was to focus on the revolutionary generation of 1880–1930 in order to analyze the linguistic dimensions of the Irish Revolution of 1913–1923, i.e. how ordinary men and women, not only those leaving the island, but also the ones making the conscious decision to stand up for their rights (Gillis 2014), conceptualized *Irishness* in their private correspondence.

Table 1 Word counts for female and male sub-corpora (1880–1930)

Gender	Argentina	Australia & N. Zealand	Canada	Great Britain	USA	Total
Female	908	13,893	10,404	10,389	38,737	74,331
Male	2873	81,193	19,047	10,797	7615	121,525

The female sub-corpus consists of 152 letters by 28 different writers with a total of 74,331 words; 146 of these letters were written by 22 female emigrants (to Argentina, Australia and New Zealand, Canada, Great Britain and the United States, etc.), while only six letters were signed by women at home in Ireland and sent to their significant others in North America (i.e. the United States and Canada). The largest part of this sub-corpus was selected from the McIlrath letters (Australia & New Zealand), the New Brunswick collections (Canada), the Reynolds letters (Great Britain) and Your Fondest Annie letters (US). The Argentina component only includes two letters belonging to the Murphy collection. On the other hand, the male sub-corpus is comprised of 203 epistolary reflections by 32 authors. A total of 182 letters were written by 28 different letter writers who – involved in the process of migration or settlement in a new country – sent back home detailed accounts of their new lives and occupations. The remaining 21 letters were exchanged between Robert Fife, William Seymour and Michael Coogan in Ireland, and their families in Australia, Canada and the United States respectively. Most letters in this sub-corpus come from the Patrick McMahon Glynn collection (Australia & New Zealand). Letters belonging to the New Brunswick collections (Canada), the Reynolds letters (Great Britain) and the Carlow Coogan collection (US) are also part of the study.

Methodologically, this study places itself at the interception of emotions, pragmatics and migration studies, arguing that emigrants' personal correspondence, as texts of "sense-making and existential accounting" (Gerber 2006:5), provides a solid empirical base for the pragmatic study of emotions (cf. Cancian 2010; Moreton 2016). In an attempt to better understand how Irish emigrants navigated the pragmatic waters of geographical mobility and diasporic identities, the present investigation proposes an in-depth analysis of the terms *home* and *country* in order to explore the various ways in which the concept of *Irishness* is constructed within male and female discourses in the context of the Irish Revolution. In doing so, the study takes an interdisciplinary approach that combines sociolinguistics (Chamber 2009) and corpus pragmatics (Romero-Trillo 2008) methodologies. The value of corpus and computational tools to carry out pragmatic analysis has been highlighted in Luzky (2012) and Romero-Trillo (2013, 2014).

To evaluate the emotional dimensions of the terms under study, a two-stage analysis of the data was performed combining quantitative and qualitative methods in a corpus-based examination of identity nouns. The first stage involved obtaining keyword and word lists and examining differences between male and female sub-corpora. The analysis focused on *home* and *country* as "the most frequent and highly salient terms" (Baker et al. 2008:284) in the sphere of emigrants' conceptualization of *Irishness*. In the identification phase, all instances of *home* and *country* and its

Table 2 Most frequent collocates of *home* in female and male sub-corpora (1880–1930)

74,331-word female sub-corpus		
Pattern	**Freq.**	**Examples**
Verbs with "home" as object	97	come (20)/go (20)/get (19)/be (10)/leave (5)/arrive (3)/have (3)/write (3)/return (2)/call (2)/bring (2)/keep (2)/stay (1)/haul (1)/miss (1)/make (1)/send (1)/do (1)
Prepositional Phrases (PP+home)	51	at home (18)/from home (11)/of home (5)/in home (5)/for home (3)/to home (2)/on home (1)/about home (1)/without home (1)/as home (1)/like home (1)/over home (1)/towards home (1)
Prepositional Phrases (home+PP)	30	home from (9)/home to (6)/home in (5)/home of (3)/home for (2)/home with (2)/home at (2)/home on (1)
Modifiers of "home"	23	old (7)/way (3)/dear (3)/near (2)/nice (2)/little (2)/new (1)/this (1)/welcome (1)/comfortable (1)
121,525-word male sub-corpus		
Pattern	**Freq.**	**Examples**
Prepositional Phrases (PP+home)	68	at home (44)/from home (10)/to home (5)/of home (4)/as home (2)/in home (1)/about home (1)/by home (1)
Verbs with "home" as object	62	go (7)/remain (7)/be (7)/come (6)/leave (6)/send (7)/get (4)/ make (2)/stay (2)/return (2)/enjoy (2)/call (2)/write (2)/ accompany (1)/arrive (1)/suggest (1)/walk (1)/pass (1)/pay (1)/
Prepositional Phrases (home+PP)	34	home in (7)/home with (6)/home of (4)/home at (3)/home to (3)/home on (3)/home for (2)/home till (2)/home from (2)/ home by (1)/home after (1)
Verbs with "home" as subject	11	be (4)/have (2)/assist (1)/conclude (1)/deserve (1)/attend (1)/ work (1)

plurals in the data were extracted using Sketch Engine.[1] Here, concordance lines were manually examined to assess the validity of the samples collected. In the particular case of *home*, and due to the fact that the search terms were not case sensitive, a number of 'Home Rule' instances were retrieved from the data. These examples were excluded from the analysis as well as those occurrences where the search terms were used as modifiers as in *home letters* and *country people*. Having collected all instances of the two nouns in the sub-corpora, the next stage involved obtaining a word sketch of *home* and *country* in order to identify the most frequent collocates, contextual uses and lexical specificities embedded in the realization of such concepts. As Tables 2 and 3 show, the word sketch tool "aims to present a full and complete account of a word's grammatical and collocational behavior" (Kilgarriff et al. 2010).[2] Although it "identifies both collocates and their grammati-

[1] More information about Sketch Engine is available at the website: https://www.sketchengine.co.uk

[2] See Baker et al. (2008, 2013) and Pearce (2008) for detailed descriptions of Word Sketch functions.

Table 3 Most frequent collocates of *country* in female and male sub-corpora (1880–1930)

74,331-word female sub-corpus		
Pattern	**Freq.**	**Examples**
Modifiers of "country"	19	this (7)/fine (2)/that (1)/civilized (1)/foreign (1)/any (1)/ delightful (1)/grand (1)/old (1)/beautiful (1)/very (1)/good (1)
Prepositional Phrases (PP+country)	18	in country (9)/of country (5) for country (1)/to country (1)/with country (1)/from country (1)
121,525-word male sub-corpus		
Pattern	**Freq.**	**Examples**
Prepositional Phrases (PP+country)	52	of country (21)/in country (18)/up country (4)/from country (3)/ to country (2)/through country (2)/for country (1)/with country (1)
Modifiers of "country"	48	this (15)/old (8)/great (3)/good (2)/surrounding (2)/that (1)/hilly (1)/hunting (1)/stiff (1)/misfortune (1)/copper (1)/blessed (1)/ unfortunate (1)/ballarat (1)/religious (1)/rough (1)/hot (1)/high (1)/nice (1)/poor (1)/young (1)/other (1) /manufacturing (1)
Prepositional Phrases (country+PP)	23	country for (4)/country in (3)/country as (3)/country at (2)/ country of (2)/country than (2)/country about (1)/country by (1)/country on (1)/country under (1)/country from (1)/country like (1)/country without (1)
Verbs with "country" as object	17	be (10)/swamp (1)/cripple (1)/wither (1)/ruin (1)/describe (1)/ stop (1)/visit (1)
Verbs with "country" as subject	17	be (10)/have (2)/seem (2)/look (1)/support (1)/call (1)

cal relation to the headword" (ibid), a more qualitative assessment of collocates was conducted in order to amend those "non-standard spellings without a preceding 'correctable' word" (de Rijke 2016:56) identified in illiterate letter writers' correspondence. Following Moreton's (2016:13) research procedures for the compilation and examination of linguistic patterns, we concentrated on the collocations that occurred 10 or more times in the corpus data.

In addition to examining the quantitative distribution of *home* and *country*, the present study proposes a pragmatic examination of the emotional load of the search terms in order to explain the precise way in which specific letter writers exploit language "to generate particular meanings, to take up particular social positioning" (Culpeper 2011:2). The following sections provide a detailed account of the quantitative and qualitative analyses and findings.

4 Quantitative Analysis

4.1 Home

Considering the above-mentioned criteria, a total of 196 examples of *home(s)* were registered in the female data and 204 in the male discourse. Following Baker's (2010) principles for the corpus linguistic examination of sociolinguistic data, a log-likelihood test of *home* was carried out in order to investigate the statistical significance of differences between the two sub-corpora (Table 4).[3] The log-likelihood value obtained, 20.15, was very significant, meaning that the probability of the result happening by chance was less than 1 % (Baker 2010:62). Normalized frequencies of *home(s)* in the male and female data were calculated per thousand words and also included in Table 4.

Quantitatively, the word sketch of *home* in the female sub-corpus revealed that it collocated most frequently with a range of verbs that indicated directed motion. More specifically, a total of 97 instances of the pattern '*verbs with "home" as object*' were identified with 18 different verbs such as *come*, *go*, *get*, *be*, *leave, arrive, have* and *write*, which coincides with other authors' interpretations (cf. e.g. Rosen 1984, Levin and Rappaport Hovav 1992). An interesting observation here is that there was a strong tendency for certain collocates to trigger a specific directional reference, i.e. Ireland or the host country as *home*. To illustrate this assertion, let us consider the verbs *come*, *leave* and *write*. In the particular case of *come* home*, in 19 out of 20 occurrences the collocate was used to describe directional movements taking place in the United States as in examples (1) and (2).[4]

(1) I hope you will excuse this hurried letter as we have been quite busy since we **came home**. (Annie O'Donnell, 27.09.1901)

(2) Your letter reached me yesterday just as I **had come home** from Church. In my last letter I told you we were going to St. Augustine, but we are not. (Annie O'Donnell, 28.03.1904)

Table 4 Identity term *home* in female and male emigrants' letters

Home	Female letters	Male letters	LL
Rf	196	204	20.15
Wpm	74.331	121.525	
Nf (pthw)	2.6	1.8	

Abbreviations in this table: *Rf* raw frequency, *Wpm* word per million and *Nf* normalized frequency

[3] Log likelihood (LL) scores were calculated using UCREL tool at: http://ucrel.lancs.ac.uk/llwizard.html

[4] The letters in the corpus are referred to as follows: (Author, date).

In this regard, it is important to mention that most of the examples come from Your Fondest Annie collection, the personal correspondence of a well-educated Irish emigrant who went to work as a children's nurse for a wealthy American family. Her positive migration experience, then, may have influenced the way Annie O'Donnell perceived and conceptualized the new country, a fact that was linguistically constructed in her private correspondence through the use of *come* home*. On the other hand, *leave* and *write* were fundamentally used to refer to the Emerald island, with 7 out of 8 examples describing directed motion in Ireland as in (3) and (4).[5]

(3) Jim, do you mind that night when you told us of your **leaving home**, how I cried, yes, fit to break my heart, for I know then, as I do now, what parting with a Mother meant. (Annie O'Donnell, 25.08.1901)

(4) I Hope You will send me Her adress in the next Letter John & if Mary Lenighan does **wright** [write] **home** will you remember me to her. (Burke Biddy, 19.06.1882)

The directionality of motion was also expressed by means of prepositional phrases such as *at, from, to, in*, etc. A total of 51 examples of the linguistic pattern *'prepositional phrase + home'* were registered with 13 different types. The word sketch of *home* also identified the presence of the structure *'home + prepositional phrase'* with 30 tokens and 8 different types. As examples below show, this pattern was largely used to describe either a motion taking place in the receptor country (8–9) or a metaphorical place as in the case of *home to heaven* (10). Interestingly enough, explicit references to Ireland were frequently constructed using *'prepositional phrases + home'*. Consider the following examples illustrating the principal linguistic realizations of the noun in the corpus data:

(5) Dear parents I am nearly 2 years landed in this country and I never yet meet with anybody that I knew **at home** but Brine Conner from Oranmore. (Biddy Burke, 19.06.1882)

(6) I should very much like to know if you have yet learned to like Uncle Sam. I am sure I don't and never will like it as well as dear old Galway. I hear **from home** quite often. (Annie O'Donnell, 02.08.1901)

(7) Dear father it is a heart broken case that we cannot go and see you but I hope in God that you will live to see the day that we will all meet together **in the old home** again for I can see nothing that takes the memory of it out of my head. (Biddy Burke, 02.02.1882)

(8) I guess I must close as they are coming **home from** Sunday School. (Nina Robinson, 06.05.1883)

(9) I had an awful time going to and coming from church so I decided to stay **home for** the rest of the day. (Annie O'Donnell, 28.12.1903)

(10) She seemed anxious to go **home to** heaven. (Margaret Good, 04.04.1894)

[5] The authors have kept the original spellings of the extracts collected and provided in the study.

By the same token, the collocate '*modifiers of home*' provided valuable insights into the female interpretation and conceptualization of *home* in the letters. A total of 23 occurrences were collected and grouped into 10 different types, namely, *old, way, dear, near, nice, little, new, this, welcome* and *comfortable*. The dichotomy old world (Ireland) vs. new world (North America) was fairly represented in the letter as in (11) and (15). Apart from *old* and *dear*, the modifier *comfortable* (12) was also used to refer to Ireland. In contrast, the modifiers *nice* and *little* were identified as adjectives describing *home* in the host country (13–14):

(11) He is forced to leave perhaps never again to see those dear ones and would give anything in after years for one hour of that innocent happy fun known only in their **dear old homes**. (Annie O'Donnell, 03.05.1902)
(12) Dear John it is hard lines to have served and waited on anybody and to think of a **comfortable home** and of a father and mother. (Biddy Burke, 19.06.1882)
(13) I know you will miss the **nice home** you have had and its pleasant surroundings, Mrs. B[rennan] especially, but then you could go back some times and see them all. (Annie O'Donnell, 19.02.1904)
(14) I have to try to live and keep **a little home**. (Bridget Liptrot, 12.02.1905)
(15) We had quite a pleasant 4th in our **new home**. (Annie O'Donnell, 17.07.1903)

The word sketch of *home* in the male sub-corpus revealed an interesting fact that will be the focus of the qualitative analysis in this chapter (Sect. 5). In this regard, while female letter writers used *home* to refer to both Ireland and the adopted country, male emigrants generally associated *home* with the native land. In terms of collocates, '*prepositional phrases*' stands as the most frequent and highly salient collocation in male speech with a total of 102 examples. More specifically, 68 instances of '*prepositional phrase + home*' were identified with 8 different prepositions and 34 occurrences of '*home + prepositional phrases*' with 11 types. Linguistically, both patterns were commonly used to either establish comparisons between Ireland and the new country as in (16) or signal motion in the homeland (17). Regarding external references, a total of 6 out of 102 examples were identified describing the receptor country (18–19):

(16) They are working hard from the rising of the Sun to the going down of the Same for a living in a burning hot climate far different **to Home** and after all we find we are the poorest of the different nationalities in Australia. (Philip Mahoney, 18.09.1882)
(17) Please remember me to her in the best manner you are able and say that the prolonged period which has elapsed since my departure **from home** has but increased for her my most tender regards. (Michael Coogan, 08.11.1881)

(18) He is quite at **home in** Kapunda now. (Patrick McMahon Glynn, 21.11.1893)
(19) During the next engagement at the front, this MacMervie was wounded and badly shell shocked, was sent **home to** Scotland. (Jack Walker, 12.01.1922)

Ultimately, *home* also collocated with a wide variety of verbs in subject and object positions in the male data. In the case of *'verbs with "home" as object'*, a total of 62 occurrences were registered with 19 different types. Here, it could be noted that the most frequent verbs, i.e. *go, leave, remain, write* and *send*, were fundamentally used to describe a directional motion oriented towards the old country. Regarding *'verbs with "home" as subject'*, a total of 11 instances with 7 different verbs were identified in the data. Excluding the metaphorical use of *home* in (23), all occurrences of *home as subject* linked the identity noun to Ireland:

(20) Uncle Pat is thinking of **going Home** soon. (Philip Mahoney, 18.09.1882)
(21) When the time comes for **leaving home** you will Send us all particulars and we will meet him at Liverpool. (William Reynolds, 27.02.1894)
(22) My private correspondence has swollen to such a size that I cannot **write home** often. (Patrick McMahon Glynn, 14.06.1886)
(23) And wherever a true wife comes, this **home is** always round her. (Patrick McMahon Glynn, 20.10.1884)
(24) Sir R. Barry and a solicitor I met told me that a man from **home has** very little chance. (Patrick McMahon Glynn, 11.11.1880)

4.2 Country

For the purpose of consistency and uniformity, *country(s)* was also explored using the same procedures. As a result, a total of 33 examples were retrieved from the female data and 97 from the male sub-corpus. Although the term under analysis is less frequent and collocates with a lower p-value than *home*, the log-likelihood value 9.24 still reveals gender differences which are statistically significant. Normalized frequencies of *country(s)* in the male and female data were also calculated per thousand words and included in Table 5.

Table 5 Identity term *country* in female and male emigrants' letters

Country	Female letters	Male letters	LL
Rf	33	97	9.24
Wpm	74.331	121.525	
Nf (pthw)	0.4	0.8	

In the female data, the word sketch of *country* revealed that it collocated most frequently and saliently with three main types of modifiers: demonstrative pronouns, adjectives and quantifiers. In particular, a total of 19 instances were registered in the data with 12 different types, namely, *this, fine, that, old, civilized, foreign, any, delightful, beautiful, good, very* and *grand*. The qualitative analysis of the concordance lines revealed that, in 17 out of 19 occurrences, the aforementioned modifiers were used to define the host country. As expected, *old* and *that* were exclusively used to refer to Ireland as in (26):

(25) [We] looked as though we had been seasick for a week, but a good wash and a little rest fixed us all up and are now enjoying the balmy breezes of **this delightful country**. (Annie O'Donnell, 05.02.1904)

(26) I feel young again in the **Old Country**. (Delia Fitzgerald, 19.08.1896)

(27) But Jim, friends are not always the ones who help you along, and if you take notice, this is the **very country** they help you least in. (Annie O'Donnell, 13.08.1901)

Prepositional phrases + country stands as the second most frequent collocate with 18 occurrences and 6 different prepositions. In this respect, a closer examination showed that, in 16 out of 18 examples, the search term was used to refer to the adopted country as in (28–29), while only two examples included references to Ireland as (30):

(28) She has been **in this country** for years and now talks of going back. (Annie O'Donnell, 25.08.1901)

(29) I went home to my father's house and it was soon decided that I should sail **for this country**. (Mary Ann Harley, 07.02.1898)

(30) […] there is great distress in parts **of the country** the people are very badly off there is a lot of money sent from foreign countries to help them. (Susan Seymour, 16.02.1880)

The word sketch of *country* in the male data showed that '*prepositional phrases*' preceded or followed by the term under analysis occurred much more frequently in male than female discourse, with 75 tokens and 21 different types. In line with the findings in the female letters, '*prepositional phrases*' also appeared to trigger external references. Consider the following examples:

(31) As regards all friends **in this country** they were all in very good health when last I heard from them. (William Seymour, 26.01.1881)

(32) There is nobody that I Know of more Suitable **for this country** than Servants at home. (Philip Mahoney, 18.09.1882)

(33) […] but in the present stage of their development, the produce of the soil, which, except in the case of a really manufacturing **country like** England, constitutes real wealth, is too small for the number of distributers. (Patrick McMahon Glynn, 25.04.1881)

Similarly, a total of 48 tokens of '*modifiers of country*' were registered with 23 different types. The demonstrative pronoun *this* was the most numerous modifier in the data with 15 instances. Although most structures containing *this* usually referred to the new country, the qualitative analysis also identified 5 examples where the male letter-writer in Ireland used the demonstrative pronoun to point to a particular situation in the homeland as in (35–36). The demonstrative pronoun was then followed by *old* and *great* with 8 and 3 examples respectively. It has to be noted here that while positive adjectives such as *young, blessed, good* and *nice* were used to refer to the host country as in (38–39), a number of adjectives with negative connotation like *misfortune*, *unfortunate* and *rough* were used to portray the economic, political and social situation prevailing in nineteenth-century Ireland as in examples (34) and (35) below:

(34) Ireland is certainly an **unfortunate country**; the country of patriots, quacks, grandiloquent bombast, & real and poetical grievances. (Patrick McMahon Glynn, 02.12.1890)

(35) The poor natives of **this misfortunate country** are being led astray more & more every day, and its thought that ere long we will have a civil war, there is not a day passes without an outrage of some sort being committed either a Murder, Cattle Houghed, Houses burned [...] (William Seymour, 26.11.1880)

(36) You may feel assured that I would have done so only I have been knocked about a great deal this time past. on account of the disturbed state of **this Country** which I must say is nearly gone beyond cure [...] (William Seymour, 26.01.1881)

(37) We have difficult times here, though probably not as acute as you are experiencing in the **Old Country**. (Patrick McMahon Glynn, 25.07.1917)

(38) It is a **nice country**. (William Reynolds, 01.01.1898)

(39) [...] and come home in the Sumer you Will be able to Nowe what you think about The States and which is **the Best country** for you to live In? (John Sullivan, 02.02.1903)

In addition to the patterns mentioned above, the analysis showed that *country* also collocated with a wide variety of verbs in object and subject positions. More specifically, a total of 17 tokens of *'verbs with "country" as object'* were identified with 8 types, namely, *be, swamp, cripple, wither, ruin, describe, stop* and *visit*. On the other hand, 17 instances of *'verbs with "country" as subject'* were registered with 6 different verbs such as *seem, support, have, look* etc. Excluding *ruin, stop, visit, seem* and *support* which were particularly used to refer to Ireland, the remaining verbs were used to describe the receptor country:

(40) All the governments in the past have done all thay possiable Could **to stop** the Country from been devaloped and done all in thair power **to ruin** the **Country**, but once Ireland gets Home Rule the Country will advance rapid ley in Trade and everything. (William Reynolds, 16.09.1890)

(41) But in another letter I will **describe** the **country** –I have to be off to travel again in half an I canvassed from house to house at Egerton for 3 weeks but had bad luck. (Patrick McMahon Glynn, 13.03.1882)

(42) This **country is looking** beautiful at present the crops are doing better, so far, than they were for a great many years past, please God we will have a bountiful Harvest […] (William Seymour, 05.06.1880)

(43) Sheep that sold last year for 18/= are fetching at present about eight or nine shillings but after all I don't think there **is** any better **country** than N. Zealand. (Hamilton McIlrath 02.05.1886)

Overall, and based on the corpus evidence reviewed, the examination of *home* and *country* reveals gender-related variation in terms of linguistic realization. In the particular case of *home*, it should be noted that while men exclusively relied on two main collocates, i.e. *'verbs with "home" as object/subject'* and *'prepositional phrases'* to conceptualize their notions of *home*, women also employed a wide range of *'modifiers of home'* to produce identity enactments. Conversely, the linguistic realization of *country* in the female data appears to be rather limited. Here, *'modifiers of country'* and *'prepositional phrases + country'* stood as the most frequent collocates with a relatively small number of occurrences per category. In contrast to the female findings, the conceptualization of *country* was lexically rich in the male data. As can be seen in the examples above, the term frequently collocated with the five categories described in the study.

5 Home and Country: A Qualitative Approach

Before turning to the pragmatic examination of *home* and *country* in the corpus data, let us first consider the prevailing current academic literature on the subject. In recent years, the study of transnationalism, international migration, receptor country and home has enjoyed an upsurge of academic interest, both theoretically and empirically, as illustrated by the number of works which highlight such concepts (cf. e.g. Al-Ali and Koser 2002; Ahmed et al. 2003; Burman and Chantler 2004; Nowicka 2007; Wiles 2008).

Based on empirically driven research, Al-Ali and Koser's (2002), for instance, provided a renewed vision of the transformation of transnational migrants and the different meanings of *home*, i.e. *home* as a physical place, a symbolic space, an abstract ideal and habitual social interaction (cf. e.g. Rapport and Dawson 1998). On this wavelength, Ahmed et al. (2003) examined the interdependence of mobility and belonging by focusing on how home and attachment are formed in relationship to migration. More recently, Wiles (2008) explored the idea of 'New Zealandness' and the way New Zealanders living in London discursively constructed and identified with home. Building on the existing research, the final part of our analysis, then, involved reading through all concordance lines in order to identify and group those emotional meanings embedded in the realization of *home* and *country* in the two sub-corpora.

5.1 Home, Country and the Irish Female Discourse

In the case of the female speech, their conceptualizations of *home* and host country are of paramount importance to understand female migration experiences and the process of diasporic identity making. With regard to *home*, women defined it in diverse ways, i.e., *home* as a particular place in Ireland or the receptor country, as a symbolic space built upon interpersonal relationships and as a metaphorical place.

In terms of space, the pragmatic examination of the collocate *'verbs with "home" as object'* did not only confirm our initial hypothesis about the existence of a verb-reference relationship, but it also offered crucial information about the female emigrants' directional enactment of *home*. Pragmatically, four verbs, *send, write, go* and *leave*, were used to refer to a physical place in Ireland as in the examples:

(44) he has got his photograph taken to **send home** and he dosent like to send it without mine and I cannot delay the letter now but yea will have them the nex mail. (Biddy Burke, 19.06.1882)

(45) I hope you will send me Her adress in the next Letter John and if Mary Lenighan does **write home** will you remember me to her. (Biddy Burke, 19.06.1882)

(46) I have two sisters here, both married long before I dreamt of **leaving home**. (Annie O'Donnell, 18.10.1901)

(47) He was a government surveyor and wanted me to come over to him as soon as possible, as he had a young handsome and wealthy husband waiting for me over there. I **went home** to my father's house and it was soon decided that I should sail for this country.

Conversely, *home* thought as a physical place in the host country was constructed through the use of *come, get, be* and *arrive*, as in:

(48) Mary Doyle **is home from** Boston Ned Wonders if she will go to see the Saddler, They are putting the rafters on the mil today. (Katie McCarthy, 25.12.1903)

(49) I had my pictures taken about 18 months ago, haven't any with me but will send you one when I **get home to** Pittsburgh which will not be before the end of September. (Annie O'Donnell, 13.08.1901)

A finer analysis of the collocate *'prepositional phrase + home'* unveiled the symbolic meaning of this term in the female data. Here, it was consistenly used to link *home* to Ireland, family and "personal relations, to familiarity with a place and with local ways of doing things" (Wiles 2008:134) as in the examples:

(50) His nice pleasant manner **made me feel at home** with him right away, and how it pleased me to hear him talk so well of you, Jim. (Annie O'Donnell, 01.02.1903)

(51) You like Indianapolis better I am sure than any other city, and therefore, you would feel better contented than here with twice as much and you know my liking for it, so that will not put you back as I can **make myself at home** anywhere you are. (Annie O'Donnell, 25.06.1904)

Finally, the metaphorical meaning of *home* was also identified in the realization of the collocate *call home*. As examples (52) and (53) show, the identity noun was used interchangeably with heaven to refer to death:

(52) And that little one was myself and her prayer was answered for when she was **called home** I was long passed my babyhood. (Eva McIlrath, 24.07.1907)

(53) Is it not blessed to know if we love and serve our Father here below He will in His own good time **call** us all **Home**. And what a meeting. Yes, like the Hymn "We will all meet at Home in the morning". (Eva McIlrath, 24.07.1907)

On the other hand, the pragmatic conceptualizations of *country* as either Ireland or the receptor country in the female data suggest tentatively that women gradually assimilated to the culture and work environment of the host place "recreating and negotiating a sense of national identity rather than signalling its demise (Wiles 2008:124). This is consonant with Ní Laoire's argument that Irish women tended "to interpret their own migrations in less polarized ways than the men, emphasizing the excitement and opportunity over escape and exile; yet showing a strong attachment to home, the need for family, community and a sense of belonging" (2005: 193–4).

5.2 *The Conceptualization of Home and Country in the Male Data*

In the case of the male discourse, male letter-writers emphatically referred to Ireland as *home*. Spacially, the term is synonymous with nation and region as in examples (54) and (55). In addition, we identified instances of *home* as a physical place in Ireland as in (56) and (57). Here, *home* is constructed as "a place either to escape from, or to return to, associated with the migrant-as-hero image" (Ní Laoire 2005:193) prevailing in the male migration discourse:

(54) I can't see how the middle classes are better off than **at home** [...] The Upper classes, but who are they, perhaps bankers, squatters, book makers, and some doctors, are some very rich, some not, but they are rich because they came here early. (Patrick McMahon Glynn, 02.01.1881)

(55) It is refreshing to get news from (Home) I still **call it Home** yet although I have lived longer here than in old Ireland, but I believe if we lived here for a century we would still **call the place of our birth home**. (James L. McIlrath, 24.02.1891)

(56) When the time comes for **leaving home** you will send usa ll perticulers and we will meet him at Liverpool. (William Reynolds, 27.02.1894)

(57) Uncle Pat is thinking of **going Home** soon. (Philip Mahony,18.09.1882)

Symbolically, the identity term was also associated with intimacy, familiarity and interpersonal relationships as in examples (58) and (59):

(58) He found me out after a long search, and we **felt at home with each other** at once. (Patrick McMahon Glynn, 10.09.1880)

(59) Uncle Mike and Mrs was to see us also so we had one good meeting and the only time I **felt myself at Home** while in the Country. (Philip Mahony,18.09.1882)

According to Wiles (2008:128–129), this feeling of being on a similar wavelength enabled [emigrants] to feel comfortable and validated as individuals, a fact that triggered a sense of community and belonging. Furthermore, Irish diasporic identity was also constructed through the practice of social activities and familiar rutines as in (60):

(60) [...] she generally gets over to the store every day after dinner and sits in the office most of her time as she **feels more at home** in the store talking to old friends than sitting in the house. (Dennis McGaffigan, 24.01.1912)

Finally, the structure *to see him pass triumphant home to glory* unveiled the metaphorical meaning of *home* in the male data. As observed in the female discourse, *home* is also used interchangeably with heaven and glory to refer to death:

(61) We have every right to be thankful to God when It was his will to take him too see him pass triumphant **home to Glory** And our friends and Neighbours told us that we had no right to be sorry. (Robert Fife, 21.01.1881)

Regarding *country*, male emigrants' categorical use of this term to refer to the host nation supports the gendered views of emigration, i.e. the male 'migration-as-exile' and the female 'migration-as-opportunity' discourses described by Ní Laoire (2005). In this regard, what we observed was that while female emigrants promoted a renewed image of emigration based on individual and economic liberation, men strongly emphasized the Irish traditional values of family, community and belonging.

6 Conclusions and Further Directions

Our aim in this paper was to explore the notions of gender and the conceptualization of *Irishness* in post-famine emigrants' personal correspondence. In doing so, we proposed an in-depth analysis of *home* and *country* in order to elucidate the various ways in which the concepts of identity and belonging were constructed within male and female discourses in the context of the Irish Revolution of 1913–1923. The results can be summarized as follows:

From a corpus linguistic point of view, *home* and *country* stand as the most frequent and highly salient terms for men and women in the sphere of diasporic identity making. In the case of *home*, the picture that emerges from the quantitative analysis shows that while men mostly relied on prepositional phrases and verbs to conceptualize their notions of *home*, women also used a wide variety of modifiers to produce identity enactments. Here, the lexical richness of '*modifiers of home*' does not only offer a panoramic view of the traditional old vs. new world dichotomy, but also provides detailed accounts of the changing relationship between female emigrants and their homes (Al-Ali and Koser 2002:1).

From a ideological perspective, there are also significant differences in the way women and men show and conceptualize their emotional interpretations of emigration and identity. The analysis of the female data demonstrated the fuzzy boundaries that exist between *home* and *country* in the female discourse where women use both to refer to either their homeland or receptor country. Conversely, the *home* (Ireland) vs. *country* (host nation) distinction has been cleary identified in the male data, a fact that emphasizes the gendered discourses of emigration, i.e. emigration as opportunity or exile, prevailing in the Irish context.

From a historical sociopragmatic viewpoint, we believe that the changing economic and social structure of post-famine Ireland reinforcing impartible inheritance, arranged marriages and the subordination of women together with the national sentiments triggered by the Irish Revolution of 1913–1923, might have influenced the way male and female emigrants regarded their emigration, and consequently, conceptualized *home* and *country*. However, we believe that more research is needed in order to better explain the way in which letter writers exploit language to convey particular meanings. In this regard, we acknowledge that the narrow focus of our study – concentrating on a particular period of time and two identity concepts – might have limited the scope of the investigation. Future research might also investigate other pragmatic elements such as adjectives, verbs and adverbs in a variety of settings and incorporate other sociolinguistic variables like age and religious backgrounds.

References

Ahmed, S., Castañeda, C., Fortier, A. M., & Sheller, M. (2003). *Uprootings/regroundings: Questions of home and migration*. Oxford: Berg.

Al-Ali, N., & Koser, K. (2002). *New approaches to migration? Transnational communities and the transformation of home*. London: Routledge.

Amador-Moreno, C. P., & McCafferty, K. (2015a). "Sure this is a great country for drink and rowing at elections": Discourse markers in the *Corpus of Irish English Correspondence*, 1750–1940. In C. P. Amador-Moreno, K. McCafftery, & E. Vaughan (Eds.), *Pragmatic markers in Irish English* (pp. 270–291). Amsterdam: John Benjamins.

Amador-Moreno, C. P., & McCafferty, K. (2015b). '[B]ut *sure* its only a penny after all': Irish English discourse marker *sure*. In M. Dossena (Ed.), *Transatlantic perspectives in late modern English* (Advances in historical sociolinguistics, pp. 179–198). Amsterdam/Philadelphia: John Benjamins.

Baker, P. (2010). *Sociolinguistics and corpus linguistics*. Edinburgh: Edinburgh University Press.

Baker, P., Gabrielatos, C., Khosravinik, M., Krzyzanowski, M., McEnery, T., & Wodak, R. (2008). 'A useful methodological synergy? Combining critical discourse analysis and corpus linguistics to examine discourses of refugees and asylum seekers in the UK Press,' *Discourse and Society, 19*/3, 273–306.

Baker, P., Gabrielatos, C., & McEnery, T. (2013). Sketching Muslims: A Corpus Driven Analysis of Representations Around the Word 'Muslims' in the British Press 1998–2009. *Applied Linguistics, 34*(3), 255–278.

Bonness, D. (Forthcoming). NEG/AUX contraction in eighteenth-century Irish English emigrant letters. In D. Villanueva-Romero, C. P. Amador-Moreno, & M. Sánchez García (Eds.), *Voice and discourse in the Irish context*. Basingstoke: Palgrave Macmillan.

Burman, E., & Chantler, K. (2004). There's no-place like home: Emotional geographies of researching "race" and refuge provision in Britain'. *Gender, Place and Culture, 11*, 375–397.

Cancian, S. (2010). *Families, lovers, and their letters: Italian postwar migration to Canada*. Winnipeg: University of Manitoba Press.

Chamber, J. K. (2009). *Sociolinguistic theory* (Rev. ed.). Malden: Wiley-Blackwell.

Culpeper, J. (2011). *Historical sociopragmatics*. Amsterdam: John Benjamins. 135 pp.

de Rijke, P. M. (2016). *'[S]ince we came across the Atalantic'. An empirical diachronic study of Northern Irish English phonology.* Unpublished PhD thesis, University of Bergen. Date of *Disputas*: 22.04.2016.

Dossena, M. (2007). "As this leaves me at present" – Formulaic usage, politeness and social proximity in nineteenth-century Scottish Emigrants' Letters'. In S. Elspaß, N. Langer, J. Scharloth, & W. Vandenbussche (Eds.), *Germanic language histories from below* (pp. 1–30). Berlin: Walter de Gruyter.

Elspaß, S. (2002). Standard German in the 19th-century? (Counter-) evidence from the private correspondence of "ordinary people". In A. R. Linn & N. McLelland (Eds.), *Standardization: Studies from the Germanic languages* (pp. 43–65). Amsterdam: Benjamins.

Fitzgerald, P., & Lambkin, B. (2008). *Migration in Irish history, 1607–2007*. London: Palgrave Macmillan.

Fitzpatrick, D. (1994). *Oceans of consolation: Personal accounts of Irish migration to Australia*. Cork: Cork University Press.

Gerber, D. A. (2006). *Authors of their lives: The personal correspondence of British immigrants to North America in the nineteenth century*. New York: New York University Press.

Gillis, L. (2014). *Women of the Irish revolution*. Cork: Ireland. The Mercier Press Ltd.

Harper, M. (2010). Opportunity and exile: Snapshots of Scottish emigration to Australia. *Australian Studies, 2*, 1–21.

Kilgarriff, A., Rychly, P., Smrz, P., & Tugwell, D. (2004). *The sketch engine*. Proceedings from EURALEX (pp 105–116), France: Lorient.

Kilgarriff, A., Kovár, V., Krek, S., Srdanovic, I., & Tiberius, C. (2010). *A quantitative evaluation of word sketches*. Available at https://www.sketchengine.co.uk/wp-content/uploads/Quantitative_Evaluation_2010.pdf. Date accessed 12 May 2016.

Levin, B., & Rappaport, H. M. (1992). The lexical semantics of verbs of motion: The perspective from unaccusativity. In I. M. Roca (Ed.), *Thematic structure: Its role in grammar* (pp. 247–269). Berlin/New York: Foris Publications.

Luzky, U. (2012). *Discourse markers in early modern English*. Amsterdam: John Benjamins Publishing Company.

McCafferty, K. (2014). "I dont ca re one cent what [Ø] goy in g on in great britten": Be -deletion in Irish English. *American Speech, 89*(4), 441–469.

McCafferty, K., & Amador-Moreno, C. P. (2012a). A Corpus of Irish English Correspondence (CORIECOR): A tool for studying the history and evolution of Irish English. In B. Migge & M. Ní Chiosáin (Eds.), *New perspectives on Irish English* (pp. 265–287). Amsterdam: John Benjamins.

McCafferty, K., & Amador-Moreno, C. P. (2012b). 'I will be expecting a letter from you before this reaches you'. Studying the evolution of a new-dialect using a Corpus of Irish English Correspondence (CORIECOR). In M. Dossena & G. Del Lungo Camiciotti (Eds.), *Letter writing in late modern Europe* (pp. 179–204). Amsterdam: John Benjamins.

McCafferty, K., & Amador-Moreno, C. P. (2014). 'If you write soon I shall get it & will reply at once' The spread of first-person future *will* in Irish English. *English Language and Linguistics, 18*, 407–429. doi:10.1017/S1360674314000100.

McCafferty, K., & Amador-Moreno, C. P. (In preparation). *CORIECOR. The corpus of Irish English correspondence*. Bergen and Cáceres: University of Bergen and University of Extremadura.

McLelland, N. (2007). "Doch mein Mann möchte doch mal wissen ..." A discourse analysis of 19th-century emigrant men and women's private correspondence. In S. Elspaß, N. Langer, J. Scharloth, & W. Vandenbussche (Eds.), *Germanic language histories from below (1700–2000)* (pp. 45–68). Berlin: De Gruyter.

Miller, K. A. (1985). *Emigrants and exiles. Ireland and the Irish exodus to North America*. Oxford: Oxford University Press.

Miller, K. A. (2008). *Ireland and Irish America. Culture, class, and transatlantic migration*. Dublin: Field Day.

Moreton, E. (2012). Profiling the female emigrant: A method of linguistic inquiry for examining correspondence collections. *Gender & History, 24*(3), 617–646.

Moreton, E. (2016). 'I never could forget my darling mother': The language of recollection in a corpus of female Irish emigrants correspondence. *The History of the Family*. doi:10.1080/1081602X.2016.1155469.

Murray, E. (2006). *Becoming Irlandes, private narratives of the Irish emigration to Argentina (1844–1912)*. Buenos Aires: L.O.L.A.

Ní laoire, C. (2005). Gender issues in Irish rural out-migration. In P. Boyle & K. Halfacree (Eds.), *Migration and gender in the developed world*, (pp. 184–195). Taylor and Francis e-Library.

Nowicka, M. (2007). Mobile locations: Construction of home in a group of mobile transnational professionals. *Global Networks, 7*, 69–86.

Pearce, M. (2008). Investigating the collocational behaviour of MAN and WOMAN in the British National Corpus using Sketch Engine. *Corpora, 3*(1), 1–29.

Rapport, N., & Dawson, A. (1998). The topic and the book. In N. Rapport & A. Dawson (Eds.), *Migrants of Identity: Perceptions of home in a world of movement* (pp. 3–17). Oxford/New York: Berg.

Reddy, W. M. (2001). The Navigation of Feeling. *A Framework for the History of Emotions*. New York: Cambridge University Press.

Richards, E. S. (2010). Australian colonial mentality in emigrant letters. *Australian Studies, 2*, 1–17.

Romero-Trillo, J. (Ed.). (2008). *Pragmatics and corpus linguistics: A mutualistic entente*. Berlin: Mouton de Gruyter.

Romero-Trillo, J. (Ed.). (2013). *The yearbook of corpus linguistics and pragmatics 2013: New domains and methodologies*. Dordrecht: Springer. http://dx.doi.org/10.1007/978-94-007-6250-3

Romero-Trillo, J. (Ed.). (2014). *The yearbook of corpus linguistics and pragmatics 2014: New empirical and theoretical paradigms*. Dordrecht: Springer.

Romero-Trillo, J., & Avila-Ledesma, N. E. (In press). The ethnopragmatic representation of positive and negative emotions in Irish immigrants' letters. In K. Allan, A. Capone, & I. Kecskes (Eds.), *Pragmemes and theories of language* use. Dordrecht: Springer.

Rosen, C. (1984). The interface between semantic roles and initial grammatical relations. In D. M. Perlmutte & C. Rosen (Eds.), *Studies in relational grammar 2* (pp. 38–77). Chicago: University of Chicago Press.

Wiles, J. (2008). Sence of home in a transnational social space: New Zealanders in London. *Global Networks, 8*(1), 116–137.

A Cross-Linguistic Study of Conceptual Metaphors in Financial Discourse

María Muelas Gil

Abstract This study analyses the explanatory strength of conceptual metaphors (Lakoff and Johnson, Metaphors we live by. The University of Chicago Press, Chicago, 1980; Lakoff, Cogn Linguist 1(1):39–75, 1990; McGlone, Lang Commun 27:109–126, 2007; Kövecses, Metaphor: a practical introduction, 2nd edn. Oxford University Press, New York, 2010) in the field of economics and financial reporting. This type of discourse is, in particular, "heavily metaphorical" (McCloskey, J Econ Lit 21:481–517, 1983), for its complicated and specific terms that are difficult to decode by a non-expert eye. The work analyses the most salient metaphorical expressions within this field, showing how experts conceptualize financial constructs and how non-experts are able to process and understand them through specific metaphorical projections in English and Spanish. As a parallel goal, the results might be used as a tool to enhance the teaching and learning of Lakoffian Conceptual Metaphor Theory in ESP programmes (Charteris-Black, Engl Specif Purp 19:149–165, 2000; Charteris-Black and Ennis, Engl Specif Purp 20:249–266, 2001).

To this aim, concepts such as '*situationally, topically and culturally triggered metaphors*' coming from recent work within metaphors in real discourse (Semino, Metaphor in discourse. Cambridge University Press, Cambridge, 2008; Kövecses, Annu Rev Cogn Linguist 6:168–184, 2008, Iberica 17:11–24, 2009, Metaphor: a practical introduction, 2nd edn. Oxford University Press, New York,2010; Semino, Deignan and Littlemore, Metaphor Symb 28:1–19, 2013) helped to understand how these financial notions are conceptualized. The corpus consists of texts from six financial newspapers (*Expansión, Cinco días, El Economista, The Economist, The Guardian* and *The Financial Times).* Following Stefanowitsch's (Corpus-based approaches to metaphor and metonymy. In: Stefanowitsch A, Gries ST (eds) Corpus-based approaches to metaphor and metonymy. Mouton de Gruyter, Berlin/NewYork, pp 1–16, 2006) 'metaphorical pattern analysis', all the expressions referring to five selected target areas were searched for in the corpus. Moreover, Moreno Lara's taxonomy, used by scholars studying metaphor in economics discourse (Silva, Rev

M. Muelas Gil (✉)
Universidad Autónoma de Madrid, Madrid, Spain

Departamento de Filología Moderna/Facultad de Educación, Universidad de Castilla-La Mancha, Cuenca, Spain
e-mail: Maria.Muelas@uclm.es

J. Romero-Trillo (ed.), *Yearbook of Corpus Linguistics and Pragmatics 2016*, Yearbook of Corpus Linguistics and Pragmatics 4,
DOI 10.1007/978-3-319-41733-2_6

Media Jornalismo 23(1):11–34, 2013a, Obese bodies, indebted families and good students: metaphors of austerity in the Portuguese press. In: Philip G, Barnden J, Lee M, Moon R, Wallington A, Shank C (eds) Corpus-based approaches to figurative language: metaphor and austerity. The University of Birmingham, Birmingham, pp 29–32, 2013b, The persuasive power of metaphor in 'austerity' discourse: embodied and moral metaphors of austerity in the Portuguese press. Paper delivered at the 47th annual meeting of Societas Linguistica Europaea, Adam Mickiewicz University Poznan, Poland, 11–14 Sept, 2014; Rojo López and Orts, J Pragmat 42:3300–3313, 2010) was applied to divide the metaphors according to three generic groups: the Great Chain of Being, the Image-Schema and the Events metaphor.

In sum, the results show similar mappings at a generic level but different at more specific ones and in the inner distribution of each group. This work contributes to studies on the pervasiveness of metaphors in real specific discourse, and supports the belief that cross-linguistic studies of metaphor-in-use should help raise translators' and L2 teachers' awareness of the relevance of such intrinsic linguistic component in finance discourse.

Keywords Conceptual metaphor • Finance discourse • Corpus studies • Comparative studies

1 Introduction

The present chapter presents a study of metaphor as a pervasive discursive element in the field of economics and of the stock market through the analysis of a cross-linguistic corpus of financial reports from English and Spanish newspapers. The grounding of the study comes from the field of Cognitive Linguistics (Geeraerts and Cuyckens 2007), since it focuses on metaphor, combined with corpus studies and pragmatics. In addition, it observes the effect of the use of this element in the communication-interpretation process.

Metaphor has been regarded as a phenomenon of language since Aristotle and the ancient Greek. Over the centuries it has been seen as a linguistic element in literature and in more recent decades it started to be observed as not just a mere decorative component but as a pervasive element in the language that humans use every day. Lakoff and Johnson (1980) coined the term *Conceptual Metaphor*, which focuses on concepts rather than expressions and is defined as a mapping between two domains (a target and a source domain). Since then, many scholars have studied conceptual metaphors (Semino 2008; Kövecses 2008, 2009, 2010; Semino et al. 2013) as an element of discourse and as an element of thought (Steen 1999; Charteris-Black 2004; Deignan 2005, Stefanowistch and Gries 2006; Pragglejaz Group 2007; Kövecses 2008, Rojo López and Orts 2010; Silva 2013a, b). Studies of metaphor in specialized discourse are also extensive (Deignan 1999; Cameron 2003; Charteris-Black 2004; Koller 2008; Musolff 2004, 2006; Semino 2008; among others) but the field of economics in general and, more precisely, the language used in and referring to the stock market, has not been largely addressed

(Henderson 1986; Mason 1990; White 1996, 2004; Fuertes Olivera 1998; Charteris Black and Ennis 2001; Charteris-Black and Musolff 2003; White 2003; Charteris-Black 2004; Herrera Soler 2009). Some scholars have contrasted metaphors in different languages (Charteris-Black and Ennis 2001; Charteris-Black and Musolff 2003; Rojo López and Orts 2008, 2010) but most of them started from one or a few conceptual metaphors and analysed them within the corpus in question. If compared to other fields such as medicine or politics we can say that there is still a lot to cover in corpus studies of metaphors in financial discourse.

The results presented in this chapter are part of an on-going project that takes a much larger corpus in both languages and investigates mainly the use of conceptual metaphors depending on the political stance of the newspaper during the election period of each country. The present focuses on a corpus made of twelve reports: six of them were retrieved from the online version of three Spanish newspapers (*El Economista, Cinco Días* and *Expansión*); the other six belong to the online version of three English newspapers (*The Economist, the Telegraph and Financial Times*). The timeframe goes from November to December 2014 and the total amount of words reaches 7499 words: 4285 in the English corpus and 3214 in the Spanish one. It can be argued that amount of words is too small to consider this study a corpus one. However, as Vaughan and Clancy (2013) defend, "small corpora are eminently suitable for investigating phenomena in context given the constant interpretative dialectic between features of texts and the contexts in which they are produced". As my study analyses texts coming from two different languages, and is aimed at investigating specicif differences in a very definite context, I think that my study can be included in the category of small-corpora.

The purpose of the present study was threefold: (1) to find and compare metaphors in texts of similar nature but written in different languages and, therefore, contexts; (2) to apply the results to two different fields in which metaphors are more and more pervasive and need to draw the attention of scholars, namely English for Specific Purposes and Translation; and (3) to try to justify the strong explanatory value of metaphor, as it serves as a vehicle that allows the non-expert reader of financial discourse to understand the message of a very complex domain.

In the next section, previous studies of metaphors in corpus will be discussed; then, the methodology will be presented, starting with how the data was selected and retrieved and continuing with the method of classification of metaphors used in this paper. The analysis will differentiate between generic-level and specific-level metaphors. The results and conclusions obtained will indicate future paths of research in this area.

2 Metaphor and Corpus Studies

Corpus studies of metaphor have been extensively approached, above all during the last decade (Steen 1999; Charteris-Black 2004, 2005; Deignan 2005; Stefanowistch 2006; Stefanowistch and Gries 2006; Pragglejaz Group 2007; Kövecses 2008; Rojo

López and Orts 2008, 2010; Orts and Rojo López 2009; Silva 2013a, b). As Veronika Koller (2006) claims, all studies of metaphor will need to observe the contextual factors and implications. She also defends that corpus approaches serve as a meaningful and reliable tool for studying metaphor in real discourse as they are more representative than other studies of isolated samples of metaphorical language. This opinion is in line with Steens' arguments (1999) who claimed that

> corpus research can yield realistic materials for rating studies of metaphors, offering an opportunity to establish the desirable connection between analytic metaphor properties produced un linguistic research on the one hand, and informants' judgment of metaphor on the other (Steen 1999: 81)

There seems to be a general agreement that corpus studies are a representative and useful tool for metaphor observation. However, it also appears to be the case that the most representative or useful method of extraction of metaphors is not that extensively agreed upon between metaphor scholars (Stefanowitsch 2006). In 1999, Lynne Cameron and Graham Low edited a pioneering volume where they collected the work of several scholars dealing with metaphor identification and research on metaphor in general. More recent approaches to corpus studies of metaphor have been introduced during the last decade (Stefanowitsch 2004, 2006; Stefanowitsch and Gries 2006; Steen 2008; Pragglejaz group 2007- which seems to enjoy the greatest agreement and most applications among scholars).

The Pragglejaz's group introduced the Metaphorical Identification Procedure (MIP) in 2007 and extended this into the renewed and redefined version in 2010, which they called MIPVU (VU stands for *Vrije Universiteit*, in Amsterdam). MIPVU focuses on the linguistic analysis of metaphorically used words, or lexical units, in discourse, and follows several established steps to decide whether a given word is used metaphorically or not (Steen et al. 2010: 5).

Concurrently to MIP, Stefanowitsch and Gries (2006) edited a book where they collected articles by several scholars performing corpus-based studies of metaphor in different types of discourse (Semino 2006 and Koller 2006, among others). In this volume, Stefanowitsch summarized three main strategies for extracting metaphors from non-annotated corpora: (1) manual searching, (2) searching for source domain vocabulary, and (3) searching for target domain vocabulary. Other methods summarized in the same chapter are (4) searching for sentences containing lexical items from both the source domain and the target domain (which combines the two last methods above) and (5) searching for metaphors based on markers of metaphor (Goatly 1997).

As for the types of annotation, Stefanowitsch distinguishes two types: (1) extraction from a corpus annotated for semantic fields/domains and (2) extraction from a corpus annotated for conceptual mappings. Finally, in a different chapter of the same volume, he introduces the term 'metaphorical pattern' and defines it as

> a multi-word expression from a given source domain (SD) into which one or more specific items from a given target domain (TD) have been inserted (2006: 66).

In other words, he recognizes those sentences or expressions in the text where there is a reference to both domains in proximity. For example sentences like A and B would be analysed as metaphorical patterns:

A. *Your claims are indefensible*
B. *His criticisms were right on target*

The conceptual metaphor they instantiate is the well-known ARGUMENT IS WAR (Lakoff and Johnson 1980:4), and both expressions contain lexical items from the SD "war" ("indefensible, target) and from the TD "argument" ("claims", "criticisms"). Stefanowistch coined this approach 'Metaphorical Pattern Analysis', as it focuses on these metaphorical patterns within the corpus. One of the positive aspects of this approach is that it does not only provide us with the general mapping or conceptual metaphor, but also with specific relations between elements of the target domain and elements of the source domain. In the very same example of ARGUMENT IS WAR, the metaphorical expression does not only give us this generic metaphor, but also the more specific mapping between the "claim" and "attack" in example A (as if saying that CLAIMS ARE ATTACKS) and between "criticisms" and "missiles" in example B (as if implying that CRITICISMS ARE MISSILES). This enables us "to investigate the correspondences between source and target domain at a level of detail not usually found in studies of metaphor" (Stefanowistch 2006: 67).

3 Methodology

This section will discuss the different steps followed in the analysis. First the methods applied to retrieve the metaphors from the corpus will be explained in Sect. 3.1. Then, Sect. 3.2 will cover the procedure to classify and divide all the metaphors following Moreno Lara's taxonomy (2008).

3.1 Data Sets and Collection

Upon several analyses of a sub-sample using different methods of extraction, a combination of Stefanowistch's methods has been used to retrieve the metaphors from the corpus, which are explained in turn below. First, I set a list of five common domains in the field of economics and I looked for them in the corpus, retrieved all the expressions that contained and item of the list. Consequently, I applied Metaphorical Pattern Analysis, to retrieve not only the generic but also the specific metaphorical expressions of the texts. Finally, I performed a manual search to find any potential metaphor that could have been missed with the other two methods.

3.1.1 Searching for Vocabulary Related to the Five Domains

First, I selected five fields that are conventional in the world of finance and banking: MARKET, MONEY, ECONOMY, COMPANIES and INVESTORS, and PRODUCTS. 'Companies' and 'investors' go under the same category as they are the 'human' component of the market. I composed this list out of some general knowledge that we all share and that allows us to easily recognize these terms and link them more or less quickly and directly to the stock market and the world of finance.

3.1.2 Metaphorical Pattern Analysis

Once the list was settled, I continued by reading each text and using Stefanowitch's MPA, retrieving all the metaphorical expressions where I found a word (or more than one) that belonged to the familiar scope of the original five targets, or even the very same word. For example:

1. *"London Stock Exchange Group (LSEG) proved to be one of the best performers on its own market."*
2. *"The FTSE 100 finished down 153.74 points or 2.35 % at 6388.46"*

Both sentences were selected for the analysis as they contain a word that refers to one of the five target domains ("market"), even if one of them is not exactly in the list but falls within the familiar scope of one of the five ("The FTSE 100" is an index of reference, and indexes are the indicators of the state of the economy in the market, and "market" is one of the five target items). Something similar would occur with the next sentence. It was also taken for analysis because even if it does not contain the word "product", it is talking about one of the products that are part of the stock market and banking industry.

3. *"Copper touched its lowest in more than 4 years before rebounding to close 1.5 % higher in London."*

3.1.3 Manual Search

As explained above, this third method was also used last as a complementary method to try to find any potential conceptual metaphor that the other two had missed. It was one of the search methods introduced by Stefanowitch in 2006 and it proves useful when the corpus under analysis is not too large, as it consists in reading the texts word by word several times as a whole.

3.2 *Classification and Division*

Once all the metaphors were retrieved from both corpora, they were classified in two different categories. First, I made a distinction between more specific and more generic metaphors. Then, they were classified according to a taxonomy that had been previously used in studies of not equal but somehow similar nature (see below).

3.2.1 Generic and Specific Metaphors

This distinction was introduced by Lakoff and Turner (1989) and, in sum, it states that generic-level metaphors are those that can be filled with many instantiations or metaphorical expressions. For example, in our corpus, ACTIONS ARE EVENTS would be a generic-level metaphor, as it can be filled with many different instances and in many different contexts; however, if we say that THE MARKET IS A RACE, it would be a specific-level metaphor that belongs to the generic one; the latter cannot be filled with as many metaphorical expressions as the former.

One of the positive aspects of using Stefanowistch's MPA is that it allows the researcher to extract the specific and the generic conceptual metaphor, making it easier to organize both lists. As an example of this:

4. "LSEG is not the only exchange group with big ambitions"
5. "…el selectivo (Ibex 35) ha subido en los últimos treinta días del año en torno a un 3 % (destacando de forma individual, 2010 sería el ganador con un repunte del 6,39 %)."
   Eng.: *the Ibex 35 has gone up in the last 30 days of the year about 3 % (standing out individually, 2010 would be the winner with an upturn of 6,39 %)*

In example 4 we can observe that human attributes are given to a company (having ambitions is something specific to humans), so this metaphorical expression is an instance of the conceptual metaphor "COMPANIES ARE PEOPLE". As for example 5, both the generic metaphor and a specific relation are found. First, this expression is talking about an index (*IBEX 35*), and indexes were placed within the domain of "market". Second, it also belongs to the generic conceptual metaphor THE MARKET IS A RACE, as there are references to going up and being the winner. However, in this case we also have the specific relation within the generic one, or INDEXES ARE RACERS, since they are portrayed as the competitors within a race between all the indexes.

3.2.2 Division Criteria

The division criteria applied in the study was first introduced by Moreno Lara (2008), albeit in the context of political discourse, and has been then applied in the field of economics by Soares da Silva (2014) or Rojo López and Orts (2008, 2010), Orts and Rojo López (2009). This taxonomy divides the conceptual metaphors into three different categories:

- THE GREAT CHAIN OF BEING (Lakoff and Turner 1989; Musolff 2005). It parts from the basis of the next chain of natural beings: humans, animals, plants and complex and natural objects; and it accounts for those metaphorical expressions that attribute natural beings characteristics and behaviour to other animate or inanimate elements.
- The IMAGE SCHEMA and the more specific PATH SCHEMA (Lakoff 1987; Johnson 1987). These metaphors have a skeletal structure and derive from our experience and interaction in the world (Kövecses 2010: 43). Some examples are "in-out", "front-back" or "up-down". Our experience and interaction with the world make our conceptual system conceptualize what we perceive in relation to those structural elements. The more concrete PATH SCHEMA conceptualizes the target as a path with a final destination and includes all the components in that path.
- ACTIONS ARE EVENTS (Lakoff 1990, 1993), which maps a given activity, in this case financial activities, as a certain kind of event, such as a race or a game.

Once they were divided according to this taxonomy, the next step was to decide whether they are specific to the language of finance or have at least a given conventionality.

4 Research Questions

The research questions I propose for my study are the following:

- Will this selection of five domains prove significant in the case of metaphorical meanings? If the five domains are found, which one(s) will be the most frequently instantiated in each corpus?
- Which generic conceptual metaphors will be found in each language? Will all conceptual metaphors be the same in the two languages, and with the same frequency of occurrence?
- Will the study allow us to classify the conceptual metaphors into conventional of the economic discourse or non-conventional?
- To what extent will the use of conceptual metaphor mean the comprehension of the text for a non-expert reader?
- Will different non-expert readers conceptualize this abstract language and field equally? Will their background have an effect on this conceptualization?

5 Quantitative Analysis

This section presents the results obtained from the analysis in three different subsections. First, all the retrieved metaphors were classified according to their level of specificity. Section 5.1 summarizes the generic-level metaphors belonging to each one of the three categories within our taxonomy. The specific-level metaphors of the study are presented in Sect. 5.2 in turn and separately, depending on the generic level they belong to. Finally, Sect. 5.3 collects and compares all the specific level metaphors that belong to each corpus (English and Spanish).

5.1 Generic-Level Metaphors

The metaphorical expressions found in the corpus were included in different tables, exactly three per language, each one corresponding to a newspaper (these tables have not been included in this chapter for reasons of length). The next step was to divide all the generic metaphors according to the threefold division of the Great Chain of Being, Image Schemas or Path schema, and the Actions are Events metaphor.

Table 2 summarizes all the instances found for each of category. Some examples from the corpus are first gathered in Table 1. Italics have added to highlight the word or part of the expressions that make each of them belong to one category or another (i.e. "liking" is a humanlike property attributed to markets).:

I calculated the percentages for each corpus so that the distribution of the three parts of the taxonomy could be better observed and compared. These percentages are depicted in Figs. 1 and 2.

The highest percentage of metaphors in the English corpus belongs to The Great Chain of Being (39 %), followed by the Image Schema (32 %). The opposite occurs in the Spanish corpus, since the highest percentage belongs to the Image Schema (40 %) and the second highest to the Great Chain. In order to see the statistical significance of these results we carried out a chi-squared test, which resulted in $p=0.6$, therefore non-relevant statistically speaking.

Table 1 Examples from our corpus

	English corpus	Spanish corpus
The Great Chain of Being	The uptick in volatility on commodity and foreign exchange markets is not something that markets *like*	Mejor *se ha comportado* el mercado de deuda, con la rentabilidad del bono español a diez años en el 1.84 % y la prima de riesgo cerca de los 110 puntos básicos
Image Schemas-Path Schema	Italy and Spain, however, were an exception, ending the day slightly *lower*.	En la *subida* acompañaron otras materias primas, lo que permitió que muchos mercados asiáticos, muy vinculados a las materias primas, cerrasen al alza
Actions are Events	Europe's big stock-exchange groups have different *strategies* for growth	…el selectivo ha subido en los últimos treinta días del año en torno a un 3 % (destacando de forma individual, 2010 sería el *ganador* con un repunte del 6.39 %).

Table 2 Summary of results of ML's division

	English corpus	Spanish corpus
The Great Chain of Being	36	22
Image Schema – Path	29	25
Actions are Events	26	16
Total	91	63

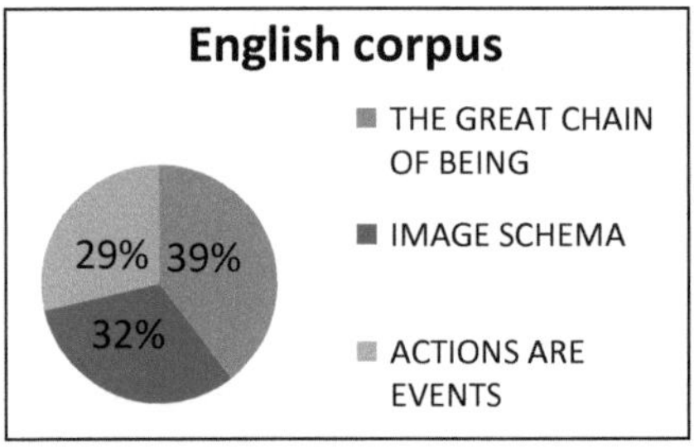

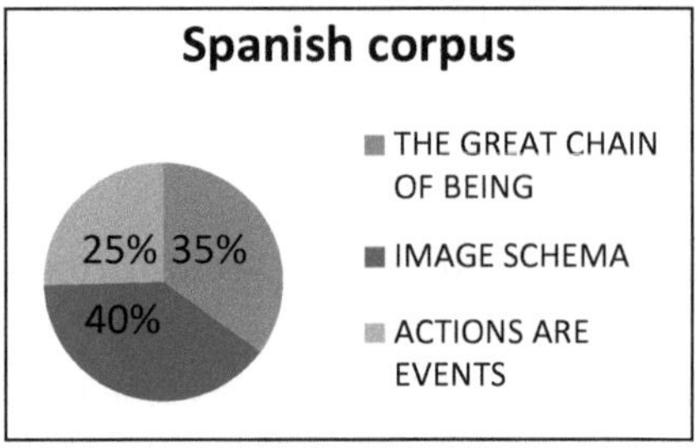

Figs. 1 and 2 Percentage of instances belonging to each group in ML's taxonomy

5.2 Specific-Level Metaphor

5.2.1 The Great Chain of Being

To start with the first generic level, the total number of each specific relations belonging to The Great Chain of Being are summarized in Table 3. Some examples are also provided after it.

- English examples:
  - The uptick in volatility on commodity and foreign exchange *markets* is not something that markets *like*
  - Fresh evidence of the *fragile state* of the region's economy [...]
- Spanish examples:
  - Mejor se ha comportado el mercado de deuda [...]
  - Entre *miedo* a la desaceleración y estímulos monetarios, las Bolsas europeas *se mantienen cautas.*

As seen in Figs. 3 and 4, the distribution or percentages of each specific conceptual metaphor is different. While in the English corpus there is greater variation, the Spanish corpus has fewer types of specific-level metaphors but a greater predominance of one of them over the rest (MARKETS ARE PEOPLE). However, the statistical results of the *chi-square* test applied to this part of the analysis was non-significant ($p=0.51$)

Table 3 Summary of specific relations of The Great Chain of Being

Specific relation	English	Spanish
Markets are people	9	11
The economy is a body	5	3
Money is a person	8	2
Companies are people	10	5
Companies are animals	1	0
Products are people	1	0
The market is a natural force	2	1
Total	**36**	**22**

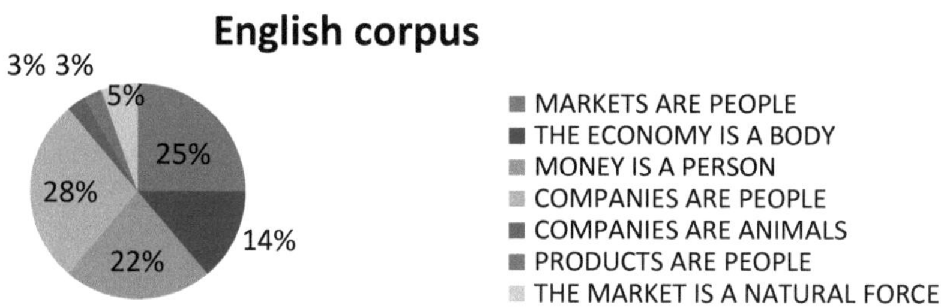

Fig. 3 Specific relations in The Great Chain of Being, English corpus

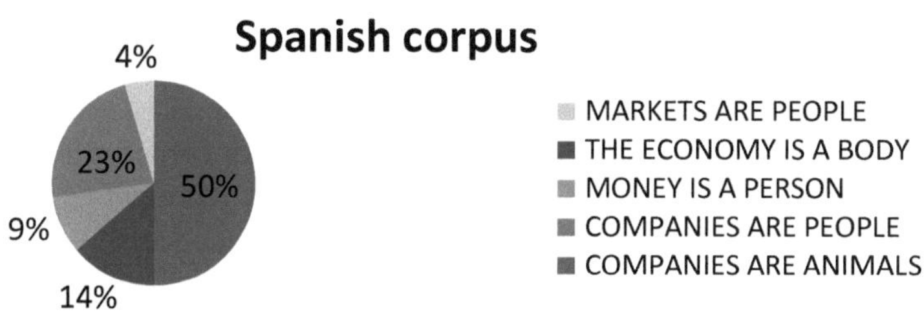

Fig. 4 Specific relations in The Great Chain of Being, Spanish corpus

5.2.2 Image-Schema

Table 4 shows the total number of specific metaphors that belong to the second category in our taxonomy. There are fewer instances of this type in the English corpus than in the previous one (32 % of the cases belong to this category, while 39 % of them represented the Great Chain), in spite of the fact that it is the most instantiated in the Spanish corpus and the second in the English one. It also shows a subdomain of the path schema where the path is not earthlike but aquatic.

To exemplify this group better:

- English examples:
  - Italy and Spain, however, were an exception, *ending the day slightly lower.*
  - But the broader FTSE Eurofirst 300 *remains up* 0.5 % as the oil and gas production sub-index *climbs* 2.6 %

Table 4 Summary of specific relations of the Image schema – Path

Specific relation	English	Spanish
The market is a vertical path	20	20
The market is a path with obstacles	7	5
The market is a voyage	2	0
Total	**29**	**25**

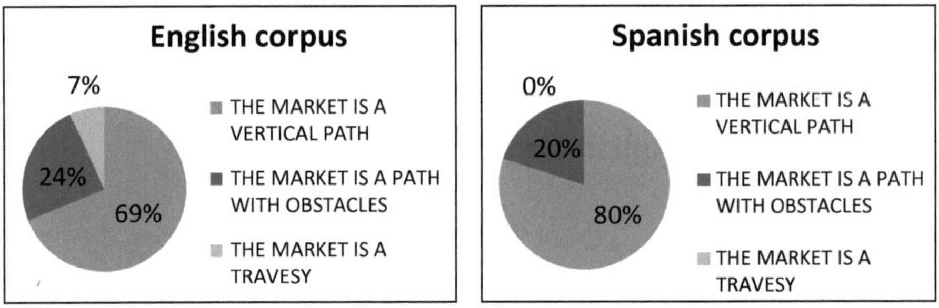

Figs. 5 and 6 Specific relations in the Image schema – Path metaphor. Spanish and English corpus

- Spanish examples:
  - *En la subida* acompañaron otras materias primas, lo que permitió que […]
  - Las principales Bolsas habían terminado la jornada con *leves retrocesos*

Figures 5 and 6 represent the percentages of these three specific metaphors within the Image-Path Schema group. As observed, both corpora show a notable preference for the Market is a Vertical Path metaphor, representing 69 % in the English texts and 80 % in the Spanish ones.

Finally, in line with the procedure applied to all steps and all categories, the statistical analysis applied to this part using a chi-square test resulted non-significant, with a value of $p = 0.35$.

5.2.3 Actions Are Events

To finish, Table 5 and Figs. 7 and 8 summarize the specific relation of the Events metaphor. It is also observed that all the events used as a source in this category are of a similar nature, which is a competitive event or a warlike one. The statistical value of the chi-square test is, again, non-significant ($p = 0.09$).

Some examples from both corpora are:

- English examples:
  - Europe's big stock-exchange groups have *different strategies* for growth.
  - On Wall Street, the S&P 500 is *adding 8 points* to 2061 following a broadly *upbeat Asian session*

Table 5 Summary of specific relations of the Actions are Events metaphor

Specific relation	English	Spanish
The market is a competition	8	6
The market is a show	3	0
The market is a fight	11	6
The market is a strategy game	4	1
The market is a race	0	2
The market is a war	0	1
Total	**26**	**16**

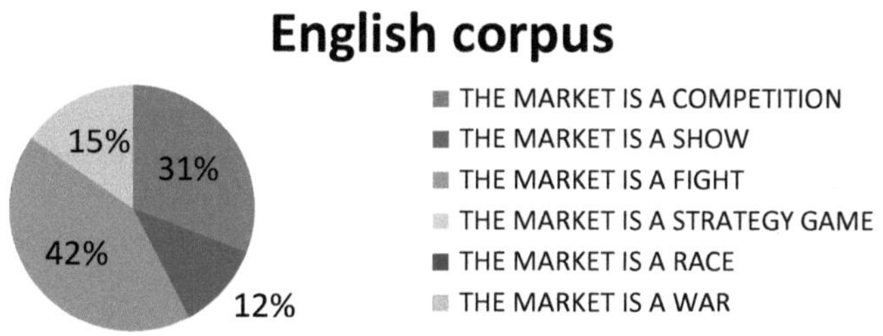

Fig. 7 Specific relations in The Actions are Events metaphor, English corpus

Fig. 8 Specific relations in The Actions are Events metaphor, Spanish corpus

- Spanish examples:
  - Mejor se ha comportado el mercado de deuda [...]
  - Hay nuevos síntomas de *desaceleración* en China.

Finally, even if statistical analyses have proved to be non-significant in all cases, this factor does not need to be a drawback or negative aspect, since the original purpose of this study was of a quantitative nature.

5.3 Summary of the Most Specific Metaphors

Table 6 collects all the specific-level metaphors that were retrieved upon analysis. They have been divided according to the generic metaphor they belong to. For reasons of length, examples of each one of them could not be included, but reference to all the texts of both corpora is included later.

As observed in Tables 2 and 3 and in the complete table in the Appendix, most of the generic-level metaphors were retrieved together with the most specific ones. Table 6 collects all of them, dividing them according to the corpus they belong to and to the most generic level. It can be seen that most of them use the same sources as the generic ones, although they were selected as specific-level metaphors for they can be filled with fewer instantiations.

Table 6 summary of specific-level metaphors

English corpus	Spanish corpus
The Great Chain of Being	**The Great Chain of Being**
Indexes are people	Indexes are people
Activity downward is economy sickness	Activity downward is economy sickness
Banks are people	
Companies are food	
Devaluation is an ill body	
Image schema – Path	**Image schema – Path**
Indexes are climbers	Indexes are climbers
Products are climbers	Products are climbers
Products are vehicles (boat)	Markets are climbers
Money is a vehicle (spaceship)	Companies are climbers
Economic difficiculties are obstacles in the path	Currencies are climbers
The economy is a path with shelters	Companies are walkers on a path with obstacles
Currencies are walkers in a path with obstacles	
Actions are Events	**Actions are Events**
Markets are competitors	Markets are competitors
Companies are competitors	Companies are competitors
Investors are fighters	Indexes are fighters
Currencies are fighters	Markets are fighters
Countries are performers of the show	Investors are fighters
Currencies are people	Currencies are fighters
Banks are strategy players	Markets are racers
Investors are players	The economy is a vehicle
Companies are players	Indexes are vehicles
Companies are vehicles	Indexes are competitors
The Market Is A Vehicle	

6 Discussion

6.1 Generic-Level Metaphors

To start with, the distribution of metaphors in each corpus varies: while the most common one in the English corpus is The Great Chain of Being, it occupies the second place in the Spanish corpus. Equally, the Image Schema is the most instantiated one in the Spanish and the second most instantiated in the English group. In both cases, then, the least frequent generic-group in Moreno Lara's taxonomy is the Actions are Events metaphor. In other words, the English texts of our study tend to have a preference for attributing human and animal characteristics to inanimate entities (39 % of the cases), being in most cases the markets, money and companies. This could be a strategy of the writer to bring the texts closer to the reader. Meanwhile, the Spanish corpus has a tendency to use the structural schema of a path with a final goal and a vertical path with obstacles (in 40 % of the cases).

6.1.1 The Great Chain of Being

In both languages we have found five CMs that can be considered relatively conventional: MARKETS ARE PEOPLE, THE ECONOMY IS A BODY, MONEY IS A PERSON, COMPANIES ARE PEOPLE and, albeit only found once or twice, THE MARKET IS A NATURAL FORCE.

The English corpus has resulted more creative or varied in this category, although we must always keep in mind this is a small-scale study. They both agree, however, in the representation of CMs that are conventional in the economics discourse.

6.1.2 Image Schema – Path

The Path Schema portrays markets as a path where there is a final goal. This is, to me, a very explicative and reflective metaphor as most humans will be familiar with the Black screen in markets, full of lines going up and down. This line is portrayed metaphorically as a path, and the abstract activities that motivate the ups and downs of such line are conceived as obstacles or inclinations of the path. Such vertical path is the most common source in both English and Spanish reports, representing 69 % of the cases in the English corpus and 80 % in the Spanish one, followed by THE MARKET IS A PATH WITH OBSTACLES. The critical reader could argue that both cases use the same source, the path, and could be taken as the same conceptual metaphor; however, those cases of the path with obstacles where there was no specific reference in the expression to verticality were considered different and representative of a different source domain. After all, the "path" is the common element of this generic group.

6.1.3 Actions Are Events

Finally, the least represented group is the Events metaphor, where the inner structure of a given activity or action (such as investing money or using one investing strategy or another) is compared to an event because of the similarities in the inner structure. Consequently, the mapping is created and used to conceptualize the latter in terms of the former. In this case, the reverse case to that observed in the Great Chain is seen. In general, six types of conceptual (generic) metaphors are found within the category of the Events metaphor; however, they are distinctively found in each language. Out of this six, only four of them are instantiated in the English corpus, while the Spanish texts prove to be more varied in what this CM is concerned, contrary to what occurred with the Great Chain. It turns out curious that none represents the six of them, and that one of the four found in the English reports (THE MARKET IS A SHOW) is not present in the Spanish one.

Thus, the results show that both corpora are similar in terms of typology at the most generic level, since the Events metaphor is the least frequent in both. However, there is higher variety in this group than in the rest.

Aside from the variety, the most frequent CM of this category in both languages is THE MARKET IS A FIGHT (42 % of the cases in the English corpus and 38 % in the Spanish), together with THE MARKET IS A COMPETITION (31 % and 37 % respectively), so we find again similarity in the most instantiated CM, which has proved to be conventional if contrasted with previous studies of similar nature.

6.2 Degree of Conventionality

The study has proved to be in line with previous research on the field of metaphor in finance and economics discourse. The vast majority of conceptual metaphors (at the generic level at least), with the exception of two of them, have the exact same or similar nature than those found in these reference works. Therefore, this seems to suggest that there is in fact a clear list of conventional CM in finance discourse and they should be consequently an intrinsic part of translations and programmes of ESP and Business English. If rooted in one specific type of language, any scholar or student working with that language should be aware of them, for it can definitely suppose a time saving tool that will at the same time pave the road for both writers and readers of this discourse when creating or reading it.

6.3 Answers to Research Questions

Concerning the research questions of the study, we can state that all five items were helpful when finding metaphorical patterns, as they all have been instantiated and have drawn the attention of the reader at first sight, independently of which conceptual metaphor they were encapsulating. The most common in all texts was "market", followed by "companies" and "investors" (where "companies" was much more frequent). The other three are also found but less frequently and not in the same order. Moreover, the three generic level metaphors included in the divisor taxonomy were found in both corpora, so the typology is the same but the preference is not.

As for similarities between corpora in terms of which CMs are instantiated, most of them coincide in both languages (except for a few cases). Concerning the frequency of all, this has turned out negatively answered in the case of the Great Chain and the Events metaphor, and positively in the case of the Image schema, where the distribution within corpus was very similar in both.

In terms of the degree of conventionality of the metaphors in our corpus, practically all of them have also been found in studies analysing larger corpora and in different languages, so it seems to be justifiable enough to say that the conceptual metaphors found are conventional in the finance discourse.

Non-expert reader's comprehension is a very relevant point of the study. One of the original purposes and motivations was to observe if and how a non-expert reader of finance discourse could understand what these texts were saying. Due to the high metaphorical load of the texts and to the metaphorical construction of our cognitive system, non-expert readers manage to disintegrate the meaning within the text and the abstract reality it is talking about. This has been proved by the researcher's own experience with the texts and by the observation of other non-expert's reactions and interpretation of the texts. Even if this was a small study, it seems to be a very interesting aspect to investigate more deeply, observing the reaction of a considerably large number of non-expert readers.

Finally, concerning the potential application of Conceptual Metaphor Theory in programmes of ESP or Translation, I believe that an organized corpus of common/conventional metaphors in each language could be of much help in ESP programs. With such corpus, the students would familiarize with abstract target domains in the target language through source domains that are familiar to them. In case they do not do it because of potential influence of cultural factors, it should be the role of the teacher then to provide examples of the source domain in the target language until the students are familiar with it. As for translation studies, this study also supports other scholars' claims that awareness is needed in this sphere if more reliable outcomes are desired. Giving the case that the translator knows deeply the metaphorical constructions of the language, this will inherently help them to translate a given expression. If the conceptual metaphor is similar in both languages, the task will be easier, and if it is not, the task of finding the equivalent might be tough in some cases, but using annotated corpora formed from studies like the present one might be a very useful tool.

7 Conclusion

Drawing from Lakoff and Johnson's Conceptual Metaphor Theory and further studies in Metaphor in Discourse (Semino 2008; Kövecses 2008, 2009, 2010), as well as theories within the field of economics and financial discourse, this study shows a corpus-based approach and a comparative study of English and Spanish texts. Apart from observing and comparing two different corpora, another aim was to support awareness of conceptual metaphor in Translation and Business English programmes.

The results have shown that the metaphors retrieved from our corpus are conventional in the discourse of finance. The study also suggests that both languages (Spanish and English) tend to use the same conceptual metaphors, mainly at a more generic level. Inside each category under analysis there is more variation in some cases, but the highest degree of deviation occurs at the most specific levels of CMs. Our study agrees with others pointing to a high occurrence of metaphorical language in this type of discourse and I believe that the methodology used with the combination of Metaphorical Pattern Analysis and Manual Search, is convenient for the size of a corpus of a length like ours. This methodology allowed me to retrieve all the metaphorical expressions manually and to organize them for a subsequent analysis. I think that this study could be a starting point for further analyses with a larger corpus, which would obviously require adjusting the methodology to maintain the same level of detailed analysis.

References

Cameron, L. (2003). *Metaphor in educational discourse*. London: Continuum.

Cameron, L., & Low, G. (1999). *Researching and applying metaphor*. Cambridge: Cambridge University Press.

Charteris-Black, J. (2000). Metaphor and vocabulary teaching in ESP economics. *English for Specific Purposes, 19*(2), 149–165.

Charteris-Black, J. (2004). *Corpus approaches to critical metaphor analysis*. Basingstoke: Palgrave.

Charteris-Black, J. (2005). *Politicians and Rhetoric. The persuasive power of metaphor*. Basingstoke: Palgrave.

Charteris-Black, J., & Ennis, T. (2001). A comparative study of metaphor in Spanish and English financial reporting. *English for Specific Purposes, 20*, 249–266.

Charteris-Black, J., & Musolff, A. (2003). 'Battered hero' or 'innocent victim'? A comparative study of metaphors for euro trading in British and German financial reporting. *English for Specific Purposes, 22*(2), 153–176.

Deignan, A. (1999). Corpus-based research in metaphor. In L. Cameron & G. Low (Eds.), *Researching and applying metaphor* (pp. 177–199). Cambridge: Cambridge University Press.

Deignan, A. (2005). *Metaphor and corpus linguistics*. Amsterdam: John Benjamins.

Fuertes Olivera, P. A. (1998). Metaphor and translation: A case study in the field of economics. In P. Fernández Nistal & J. M. Bravo Gozalo (Eds.), *La Traducción: Orientaciones Lingüísticas y Culturales* (pp. 79–95). Valladolid: Servicio de Apoyo a la Enseñanza.

Geeraerts, D., & Cuyckens, H. (Eds.). (2007). *The Oxford handbook of cognitive linguistics*. Oxford/New York: Oxford University Press.
Goatly, A. (1997). *Critical reading and writing*. London: Routledge.
Henderson, W. (1986). Metaphor in economics. In M. Coulthard (Ed.), *Talking about text* (Discourse Monograph No 13, pp. 109–127). Birmingham: University of Birmingham English Language Research.
Herrera Soler, H. (2009). A metaphor corpus in business press headlines. *Iberica, 15*, 51–70.
Johnson, M. (1987). *The body in the mind: The bodily basis of meaning, imagination, and reason*. Chicago: The University of Chicago Press.
Koller, V. (2004/2008). *Metaphor and gender in business media discourse: A critical cognitive study*. Basingstoke/New York: Palgrave.
Koller, V. (2006). Of critical importance: Using electronic text corpora to study metaphor in business media discourse. In A. Stefanowitsch & S. T. Gries (Eds.), *Corpus-based approaches to metaphor and metonymy* (pp. 237–266). Berlin/NewYork: Mouton de Gruyter.
Kövecses, Z. (2008). Conceptual metaphor theory: Some criticisms and some alternative proposals. *Annual Review of Cognitive Linguistics, 6*, 168–184.
Kövecses, Z. (2009). The effect of context on the use of metaphor in discourse. *Iberica, 17*, 11–24.
Kövecses, Z. (2010). *Metaphor: A practical introduction* (2nd ed.). New York: Oxford University Press.
Lakoff, G. (1987). *Women, fire and dangerous things*. Chicago: University of Chicago Press.
Lakoff, G. (1990). The invariance hypothesis: Is abstract reason based on image-schemas? *Cognitive Linguistics, 1*(1), 39–75.
Lakoff, G. (1993). The contemporary theory of metaphor. In A. Ortony (Ed.), *Metaphor and thought* (2nd ed., pp. 202–251). Cambridge: Cambridge University Press.
Lakoff, G., & Johnson, M. (1980). *Metaphors we live by*. Chicago: The University of Chicago Press.
Lakoff, G., & Turner, M. (1989). *More than cool reason. A field guide to poetic metaphor*. Chicago: University of Chicago Press.
Mason, M. (1990). Dancing on air: An analysis of a passage from an economics text book. In A. Dudley-Evans & T. Henderson (Eds.), *The language of economics: The analysis of economics discourse* (pp. 16–28). London: Modern English Publications in Association with the British Council.
McCloskey, D. (1983). The rhetoric of economics. *Journal of Economic Literature, 21*, 481–517.
McGlone, M. (2007). What is the explanatory value of a conceptual metaphor? *Language and Communication, 27*, 109–126.
Moreno Lara, M. A. (2008). *La Metáfora en el Lenguaje Político de la Prensa Americana. Modelos cognitivos y formación de significado*. Granada: Comares.
Musolff, A. (2004). *Metaphor and political discourse: Analogical reasoning and debates in Europe*. Hampshire: Palgrave Macmillan.
Musolff, A. (2005). Cross-language metaphors: Parents and children, love, marriage and divorce in the European family. In J. Cotterill & A. Ife (Eds.), *Language across boundaries* (pp. 119–134). London: Continuum.
Musolff, A. (2006). Metaphor scenarios in public discourse. *Metaphor and Symbol, 21*(1), 23–28.
Orts Llopis, M. A., & Rojo López, A. M. (2009). *Metaphor framing in Spanish economic discourse: a corpus-based approach to metaphor analysis in the Global Systemic Crisis*. Paper Delivered at the First International Conference of AELINCO (Corpus Linguistics Spanish Association). University of Murcia, 7–9 May.
Pragglejaz Group. (2007). MIP: A method for identifying metaphorical used words in discourse. *Metaphor and Symbol, 22*, 1–39.
Rojo López, A. M., & Orts Llopis, M. A. (2008). Conceptual metaphors and translation: A comparative study of metaphors in English and Spanish financial reports. In P. Sánchez-Hernandez, P. Pérez-Paredes, P. Aguado Jiimenez, & R. Criado Sanchez (Eds.), *Researching and teaching specialized languages: New contexts, new challenges* (pp. 424–434). Murcia: Editum.

Rojo López, A. M., & Orts Llopis, M. A. (2010). Metaphorical pattern analysis in financial texts: Framing the crisis in positive or negative metaphorical terms. *Journal of Pragmatics, 42*, 3300–3313.

Semino, E. (2006). A corpus-based study of metaphors for speech activity in British English. In S. Anatol & T. Stephan (Eds.), *Corpus-based approaches to metaphor and metonymy* (pp. 36–62). Berlin/NewYork: Mouton de Gruyter.

Semino, E. (2008). *Metaphor in discourse*. Cambridge: Cambridge University Press.

Semino, E., Deignan, A., & Littlemore, J. (2013). Metaphor, genre, and recontextualization. *Metaphor and Symbol, 28*, 1–19.

Soares da Silva, A. (2013a). O que sabemos sobre a crise económica, pela metáfora. Conceptualizações metafóricas da crise na imprensa Portuguesa. *Revista Media & Jornalismo, 23*(1), 11–34.

Soares da Silva, A. (2013b). Obese bodies, indebted families and good students: Metaphors of austerity in the Portuguese press. In G. Philip, J. Barnden, M. Lee, R. Moon, A. Wallington, & C. Shank (Eds.), *Corpus-based approaches to figurative language: Metaphor and austerity* (pp. 29–32). Birmingham: The University of Birmingham.

Soares da Silva, A. (2014). *The persuasive power of metaphor in 'austerity' discourse: Embodied and moral metaphors of austerity in the Portuguese Press*. Paper delivered at the 47th annual meeting of *Societas Linguistica Europaea*, Adam Mickiewicz University Poznan, Poland, 11–14 September.

Steen, G. J. (1999). From linguistic to conceptual metaphor in five steps. In R. Gibbs Jr. & G. J. Steen (Eds.), *Metaphor in cognitive linguistics* (pp. 57–77). Amsterdam: John Benjamins.

Steen, G. J. (2008). *Finding metaphor in grammar and usage: A metaphorical analysis of theory and research*. Amsterdam: John Benjamins.

Steen, G., Dorst, A., Herrmann, B., Kaal, A., Krennmayr, T., & Pasma, T. (2010). *A method for linguistic metaphor identification*. Amsterdam: John Benjamins.

Stefanowitsch, A. (2004). Happiness in English and German: A metaphorical-pattern analysis. In M. Achard & S. Kemmer (Eds.), *Language, culture and mind* (pp. 37–149). Standford: CSLI.

Stefanowitsch, A. (2006). Corpus based approaches to metaphor and metonymy. In A. Stefanowitsch & S. T. Gries (Eds.), *Corpus-based approaches to metaphor and metonymy* (pp. 1–16). Berlin/NewYork: Mouton de Gruyter.

Stefanowitsch, A., & Gries, S. T. (2006). *Corpus-based approaches to metaphor and metonymy*. Berlin/New York: Mouton de Gruyter.

Vaughan, E., & CLancy, B. (2013). Small corpora and pragmatics. In J. Romero-Trillo (Ed.), *Yearbook of corpus linguistics and pragmatics 2013: New domains and methodologies* (pp. 53–73). Berlin: Springer.

White, M. (1996). *La metáfora en el tratamiento de la crisis monetaria en la prensa británica*. Madrid: Universidad Complutense. Servicio de Publicaciones de la UCM, CDRom.

White, M. (2003). Metaphor and economics: The case of *growth*. *English for Specific Purposes, 22*(2), 131–151.

White, M. (2004). *Turbulence* and *turmoil* in the market or the language of a financial crisis. *Ibérica, 7*, 71–86.

Part II
Linguistic and Educational Implications of Corpus Pragmatics

Teaching Pragmatics with Corpus Data: The Development of a Corpus-Referred Website for the Instruction of Routine Formulas in Russian

Edie Furniss

Abstract While there has been an increasing number of studies incorporating the use of computer-assisted language learning (CALL) applications in pragmatics instruction over the past decade, these applications have yet to harness the explanatory and illustrative power of corpus data. The current chapter documents the process of developing a corpus-based online instructional website for the teaching of routine formulas in Russian, including a description of the process of selecting routine formulas using corpus methodologies and of designing the online modules using excerpts from the oral subcorpus of the Russian National Corpus. Recommendations based on this experience are provided for others interested in creating similar resources. Learner feedback on the site itself, with particular focus on the comprehensibility and usefulness of the corpus excerpts, is presented to demonstrate the effects of corpus-referred instructional materials. This project promotes the case for the utilization of corpus methodologies in pragmatics-focused CALL applications as it provides insight into developmental processes, benefits, and potential future avenues of exploration.

Keywords Routine formulas • Russian • Interlanguage pragmatics • CALL • Materials development

1 Introduction

The current chapter reports on a project in which learners of Russian received instruction in a particular area of language with pragmatic functions crucial to conversation: *routine formulas*. Coulmas (1979) first used *routine formulae* to refer to "expressions whose occurrence is closely tied to types of recurrent social

E. Furniss (✉)
Department of Hispanic Studies and Modern and Classical Languages,
University of Houston, Houston, TX, USA
e-mail: eafurniss@uh.edu

J. Romero-Trillo (ed.), *Yearbook of Corpus Linguistics and Pragmatics 2016*,
Yearbook of Corpus Linguistics and Pragmatics 4,
DOI 10.1007/978-3-319-41733-2_7

situations" (p. 239). They function to maintain the "orderliness" of communication by providing social support; they "represent petrified forms of typical behavior for handling certain types of situations" (Coulmas 1979: 251). Bardovi-Harlig and Vellenga (2012) called them *conventional expressions*, noting that they are also known as *pragmatic routines* and *formulaic sequences*. There exists within interlanguage pragmatics research—that is, research on pragmatic use and acquisition in language learners—a variety of terms that vary subtly. Here, the term *routine formula* is used to refer to any recurring word or phrase that conveys pragmatic meaning in interaction (for a comprehensive review of all the various terms used to describe formulaic language generally, see Wray 2002). Such language shares three key characteristics: "the form as a recurrent sequence, its occurrence in specific social contexts, and the idea of the social contract which extends to members of a particular speech community" (Bardovi-Harlig 2012: 207). These criteria are sufficiently flexible to account for the range of formulaic language in interaction that is context-dependent, frequent, and pragmatically productive.

2 Noticing Hypothesis

Schmidt's (1990, 1993, 2001) noticing hypothesis is the most common theoretical framework used in interlanguage pragmatics research (Alcón Soler and Martínez-Flor 2008; Kasper 2001; Taguchi 2011). The noticing hypothesis states that "what must be attended to and noticed is not just the input in a global sense but whatever features of the input are relevant for the target system" (Schmidt 1993: 209). One of the central issues in instructional pragmatics is whether instruction should be explicit or implicit—that is, with or without the provision of metapragmatic information. Takahashi (2010), in a review of studies examining the teachability of pragmatics, found that explicit methods were superior to implicit ones, and argued that this supported Schmidt's (1990, 1993, 2001) noticing hypothesis.

An awareness-raising approach to instruction is a hallmark of studies in interlanguage pragmatics that test the noticing hypothesis. Such an approach "is designed to facilitate learners' noticing and understanding of the form–context relationship" (Ishihara and Cohen 2010: 113). Ishihara and Cohen's (2010) proposed awareness-raising tasks include the analysis and practice of relevant pragmalinguistic forms, and the identification and analysis of sociopragmatic norms. This supports Schmidt's (2001) proposal that "in order to acquire pragmatics, one must attend to both the linguistic form of utterances and the relevant social and contextual features with which they are associated" (p. 30).

Bardovi-Harlig and Vellenga (2012) examined the effectiveness of teaching conventional expressions with pragmatic functions through the use of contextualized tasks that encouraged metapragmatic awareness. Learners improved on assessments of receptive and productive ability, despite the fact that they did not engage in output-focused tasks during the instructional period. In a study of knowledge of conventional expressions among EFL learners, Rafieyan et al. (2014) found that awareness of these expressions was correlated with appropriate comprehension and production. Narita (2012) investigated the effects of pragmatic consciousness-raising activities on the acquisition of hearsay evidential markers in Japanese, finding that learners in the treatment group outperformed those in the control group on both metapragmatic knowledge and production of the markers. These studies provide evidence to support the noticing hypothesis for the acquisition of pragmatics, including the instruction of formulaic language with pragmatic functions.

Formulaic language features heavily in the oral mode; thus, guidelines for teaching speaking are particularly relevant. However, all too often textbooks and reference materials generally represent spoken language inadequately. Bao (2013) argued that materials for teaching speaking should equip learners with concrete strategies and linguistic devices to participate fully in target language conversation. Instead, as Hughes (2010) pointed out, materials for improving speaking are primarily developed in service of the goal of increasing proficiency in general through "prompts for talk, and pronunciation/fluency work" (p. 221) rather than creating activities that allow for "pragmatic or affective skills building" (p. 209). Thornbury and Slade (2006) presented an extensive list of approaches to teaching speaking based on a review of the treatment of formulaic language, fillers, discourse markers, and other hallmarks of conversational language in textbooks and in classroom research. The authors presented excerpts from English Language Teaching (ELT) materials that address this language in detail, such as a textbook by Dörnyei and Thurrell (1992) that provides instruction on various elements of conversation (interrupting, fillers, enhancing fluency, and functions, among others) separated into short units full of exercises for the classroom. This type of functional approach to teaching the mechanics of conversation is rare, perhaps due to the fact that grammar and lexis have historically been separated. The pragmatic markers and formulaic sequences needed for speaking proficiency typically straddle both categories. Thus, control of both grammar and lexis is necessary for functional, and, by extension, pragmatic competence (Sinclair 2004). Presenting these elements in isolation neglects to illustrate how they work together to create pragmatic meaning. This problem can be remedied through the implementation of real-world examples of usage.

Russian language teaching materials also suffer from a lack of high-quality coverage and activities focused on the formulaic language necessary for conversation. Nearly three decades ago, Agastein (1988) criticized the poor treatment of conversational language in textbooks of Russian. However, the situation improved somewhat in the 1990s as a result of a "new generation" of textbooks that incorporated findings from SLA research (Rifkin 1997). While Rifkin praised that wave of textbooks for the inclusion of roleplays and other activities focused on the speaking skill, the pragmatic elements of conversation (beyond basic speech acts, or functions) were unrepresented. More recently, after examining popular textbooks for advanced learners of Russian, Pavlenko (2006) advocated for more explicit activities that focus on cohesive devices (a type of discourse marker) and that incorporate cross-linguistic comparisons. Promoting noticing of this type of language can lead to gains in pragmatic competence.

3 CALL for Pragmatics Instruction

CALL applications are popular within language pedagogy, as a variety of technologies and online environments have been widely used in language instruction (see Garrett 2009, for an overview of the history of technology and foreign language teaching). Encouragingly, there has been an increasing number of studies over the past decade incorporating the use of technology in pragmatics instruction in particular. The growing prevalence of mobile apps, social networking, digital games, and other technological resources has multiplied the avenues for exploring pragmatics, both for teachers and learners. These materials can provide access to an enormous supply of authentic language from a variety of contexts and speakers and can be used to structure instruction according to research findings and pedagogical theories. CALL applications can utilize the latest findings in pragmatics research, serving as a theoretically grounded resource for instructors who may lack knowledge of this area, and who do not have the time to address pragmatic issues in the classroom. These materials can enable learners, at their own pace, to engage in noticing features of language they might not otherwise be exposed to. Technological tools can be flexibly designed to accommodate a range of learners through the provision of diverse exercise types with feedback. According to Taguchi and Sykes (2013), technology-mediated teaching has potential benefits beyond the facilitation of noticing:

> [it] provides systematic work with focused aspects of language; affords opportunities for input, output, and interaction; offers individualized help through feedback, dictionaries, and search tools; promotes autonomous learning and strategy training; enhances learners' motivation and interest in learning; facilitates cooperative learning; and expands learners' participation in authentic discourse communities. (p. 8)

One type of technological tool that has been harnessed in the teaching of pragmatics is the web-based interactive instructional module. Ishihara and Cohen (2010) listed the following characteristics of these tools: "self-study exercises, learner-directed feedback, optional tasks, and linguistic and cultural scaffolding" (p. 249). They may "contain examples of multimodal [native speaker] pragmatic performance and explicit discussions of pragmatic competence" (Belz 2007: 63). These modules have been developed for English (Waugh 2013), Spanish (Sykes and Cohen 2008; Russell and Vasquez 2011) and Japanese (Ishihara 2007), and guidelines for their development were published by the Center for Advanced Research on Language Acquisition (2006). Clearly there is room for innovative technological applications for the instruction of a variety of topics in pragmatics in all languages.

4 Corpus Linguistics for Pragmatics Instruction

Adolphs (2008), in her study of patterns of speech act expressions in English through the analysis of spoken corpora, made a case for harnessing the explanatory power of corpus analysis in pragmatics research. Norrick (2015) proposed the use of corpus methodologies in the study of interjections—a linguistic category that often overlaps with routine formulas—in order to "reveal their distribution and range of functions" (p. 249). Because pragmatic categories are rarely tagged in corpora, Norrick (2015) called for research that triangulates the results of large quantitative and small qualitative studies. Quantitative studies are needed "to discover the multifarious contexts and functions of interjections" (as well as other pragmatic markers) while qualitative research is necessary "to determine particular functions" (Norrick 2015: 271). These explorations are particularly relevant to pragmatics instruction, as learners can potentially benefit from exposure to accurate linguistic descriptions based on real data. Corpus linguistics also provides tools for determining whether or not a phrase is formulaic. This is useful in studies of language with pragmatic functions, as these functions are often codified in the language in predictable—and thus formulaic—ways. Cross-linguistic research, which can aid educators in discovering learners' potential deficiencies and thus in planning instruction, can also be enhanced through the use of corpus data. For example, Belz and Vyatkina (2005) detailed an approach to teaching German modal particles (language with pragmatic functions) that included activities based on contrastive analyses of learner and native speaker corpus data. The intervention increased learner usage of the modal particles as well as their metapragmatic awareness. Unfortunately, there is thus far no published corpus-based research on routine formulas or related phenomena in Russian learner language. However, there is a crop of scholars doing exciting research on Russian learner corpora; see Alsufieva et al. (2012).

The appeal of corpus applications to instruction lies in the ability of corpora to provide access to the patterns of language frequently used in particular contexts, and thus to facilitate the noticing of form–function mappings—mappings that may take years to notice in naturalistic environments. While corpora can only provide a (hopefully representative) sample of natural language occurring in the world, they can still act as a model of typical language use. They "can provide language learners with increased exposure to authentic language examples and invaluable information about the distribution and frequency of different linguistic features in different contexts" (Vyatkina 2013: 45) and thereby provide insight into the web of language in use. Insights from corpus linguistics and the employment of texts that reflect actual usage (such as corpus excerpts), can be an invaluable tool in instructional pragmatics as they can raise awareness, facilitate noticing, increase exposure, and provide opportunities for practice of target features.

5 Corpus, Pragmatics, and Materials Development

While the field of corpus linguistics has grown significantly over the past several decades, pedagogical applications of corpus methodologies and data are still infrequent (see Römer 2011, for an overview). Tan (2002) explained that materials based on corpus data can help learners:

> a) be consciously aware of the unfamiliar usages of language they have heard or read in native speaker contexts, b) investigate how these unfamiliar usages are employed in natural authentic communication, and finally, c) experiment with these usages in spoken or written communication, so that they become familiar. (pp. 5–6)

This philosophy is grounded in Schmidt's (1993, 2001) noticing hypothesis. In addition to furnishing opportunities for learners to notice how language is used in context, corpus research enables authors to make more informed decisions about the language they choose to include in textbooks. Biber and Conrad (2010) advocated for the use of corpus data in developing materials for teaching grammar, noting that textbook writers do not have access to any kind of reference that will tell them what should be included in their materials. Instead, "authors' intuition, anecdotal evidence, and traditions" are the source of such decisions (Biber and Conrad 2010: 1). While that can provide effective guidance to developers to some extent, relying on such subjective information can result in textbooks that do not reflect language in use and therefore do not prepare learners to interact in the world outside of the classroom.

McCarten and McCarthy (2010) listed three approaches to the application of corpus data to language teaching materials: *corpus-driven* (corpus data drive linguistic descriptions), *corpus-based* (pre-existing linguistic descriptions are supported by corpus data), and *corpus-informed* (corpus data inform all choices made in the construction of a syllabus, including selection not only of grammar and vocabulary, but also of topics and methodology). Timmis (2013) proposed a fourth approach, *corpus-referred*, which "explicitly allows an honourable place for intuition, experience, local need, cultural appropriacy and pedagogic convenience in determining syllabus content and the order in which items are taught" (p. 470). This approach combines the principles of effective materials design with the explanatory power of corpora and privileges the role of the expert, who is charged with making pedagogically sound choices grounded in usage data. As McCarten (2007) reminded, a corpus is merely a tool, and therefore it "cannot tell us exactly what to teach or how to teach, and it has nothing to tell us with respect to how students learn best" (p. 3). Experts in pedagogy are needed to sort through raw corpus data and determine the topics and excerpts that will be most useful and effective in instructional contexts. According to Sinclair (2004), "[a] good pedagogical description of a language will organise the variation and prioritise the variants for language teaching purposes" (p. 275). However, in this process of selecting and editing corpus data, contextual information may be lost. This exacerbates one of the chief criticisms of the use of corpus methodologies in pragmatics instruction—"communicative intent and sociocultural purpose are lost to the corpus, which cannot tell us why or how something was said, or how it was received" (Mishan 2004: 220). In other words, corpus excerpts lack the background information on speakers and setting that is crucial for interpreting pragmatic meaning. Ishihara and Cohen (2010) recommended that authors, when employing authentic corpus data in their materials, include the following information about the text: its context, background information on its interlocutors and their relationships, its purpose(s), its source, and its author or proprietor. These details can assist teachers and learners in better understanding the context of excerpts of authentic speech. However, the full context can never truly be preserved. Even corpora with extremely detailed metapragmatic information can only approximate the contextual variables present during a given usage event.

Corpus methodologies have influenced the developers of ELT materials over the past few decades (see McCarten and McCarthy 2010, for an overview). Diepenbroek and Derwing (2014) advocated for the adoption of materials driven by corpus research, noting that the corpus-based textbook series *Touchstone* (McCarthy et al. 2005, 2006), "provided more consistent coverage on pragmatic themes" than any of the other textbooks they analyzed for presentation of pragmatic information (p. 17). Unfortunately, the use of corpus methodologies by authors of materials for the teaching of other languages has been minimal. Furniss (2013) recommended that Russian textbook authors follow the lead of ELT materials developers, even though there are fewer corpora of Russian. However, since developers have access to a large, sophisticated, user-friendly corpus of Russian—the Russian National Corpus (RNC) located at http://www.ruscorpora.ru/—and since compiling one's own corpus is increasingly straightforward, utilizing corpus methodologies to inform Russian material design is entirely feasible.

In order to apply corpus research on the pragmatics of conversational language to materials and classroom instruction, corpora of spoken language are needed for investigating the meaning and range of usage of poorly understood phrases like routine formulas. Moreover, spoken corpora can effectively illuminate the patterns and linguistic elements that characterize speech, as "it is helpful to be able to freeze a large number of instances for observation, since it may be very difficult to pay attention to such recurrences in ongoing interaction" (Mauranen 2004: 103). Learning the details of spoken language can be overwhelming due to the fact that speech (other than in audio and video recordings) is ephemeral. If the learner has a limited vocabulary, even frequently used chunks of language will pass by unnoticed in the flood of input. Oral corpus data can be used to inform the design of highly accurate materials that can assist learners in acquiring conversational language efficiently, in a systematic and deliberate way.

McCarten and McCarthy (2010) listed the following steps in creating a syllabus for developing a textbook of conversational language using spoken corpus data: identify the most frequent words and phrases; analyze these items in context in order to classify their functions in conversation; organize these functions into a coherent syllabus. Thus, the linguistic material presented to learners will be based on the most frequent language of conversation, with reference to their actual functions in speech. There is a need for effective materials that address the formulaic language necessary for pragmatically appropriate communication. The use of corpus methodologies can assist materials developers in finding authentic examples of usage, and in selecting the formulas that will be most relevant and useful to learners. Research on corpus applications in materials development, as well as recommendations for the design of materials focused on speaking and pragmatics, are relevant not only to the creation of physical textbooks and references, but also to technological applications, like the one described in the current study.

6 Methodology: Research Design

This chapter reports on the qualitative results of a larger study in which a pre-/post-/delayed post-test design was used to compare the acquisition of nine routine formulas, selected with reference to spoken corpus data, in experimental ($n = 18$) and control group ($n = 16$) participants. Participants were American learners of Russian at the intermediate and advanced levels who received gift cards in small denominations for their participation. The experimental group completed a set of interactive online instructional modules that contained excerpts from the RNC illustrating authentic usage of the selected formulas. Participants completed an oral proficiency assessment, a background questionnaire, and pre-/post-/delayed post-tests. Additionally, experimental group participants submitted an online feedback form and underwent an oral retrospective interview, and control group participants completed a final questionnaire on the routine formulas selected for the project. The quantitative results indicated that the intervention led to gains in learners' awareness of the instructed routine formulas (Furniss 2016). This chapter reports on the design of the website and experimental group participants' feedback form and interview responses, with particular emphasis on their reactions to the corpus excerpts. The feedback form completed by the experimental group participants is located at http://nadozhe.weebly.com/feedback.html and the responses are summarized in the results section. The retrospective interviews took place over Skype and were recorded and transcribed. The interview consisted of eight questions, but the interviewee was told that s/he could interject at any time with comments, even if they were off-topic. The researcher asked all interviewees the same eight open-ended questions (Appendix A), as well as supplementary questions in order to clarify responses or solicit deeper feedback. This was done in order to avoid restricting interviewees to providing feedback only related to the questions asked. The retrospective interview has been used previously to collect feedback from learners on their experience using a CALL application (Sykes and Cohen 2008). The retrospective interview was included in the current study in order to gain more detailed feedback than the online written form might elicit. All participant names used when reporting results from the retrospective interviews are pseudonyms.

6.1 *Methodology: Routine Formula Selection*

Selection of formulas for instruction was informed by a previous, unpublished study of Russian conversation carried out by the researcher using a small corpus of subtitle files from Soviet and Russian films. The purpose of that study was to determine what words and phrases are used most frequently in Russian conversational language. A homemade corpus, rather than the RNC, was used because the latter's raw texts are not available for manipulation. The Russian film corpus consists of subtitle files for 21 classic films commonly watched and studied by learners of Russian. Of course, these texts serve as a representation of authentic Russian conversation, as they are scripted and therefore not as naturalistic as private speech samples. However, the raw film subtitle texts were readily available, and film scripts are endowed with context (both background information on the characters and the situational context of the action at any given time during the film), which is generally not available in authentic speech samples. The total word types in the corpus is 16,250; total word tokens is 89,357.

Word frequency and N-gram lists of formulaic sequences of two to five words in length (minimum frequency of five) were compiled using Antconc (Anthony 2014). The N-gram lists were examined for the current study, and chunks that could be classified as routine formulas were extracted. The definition of routine formula used in the study at hand guided this process: eligible strings were "recurrent sequence[s]" that occur in "specific social contexts" and have a role in upholding "the social contract" within a community (e.g., that had function(s) in conversation) (Bardovi-Harlig 2012: 207). Furthermore, they are lexically opaque expressions whose pragmatic meaning cannot be determined based solely on the definitions of their constituent words. The researcher relied on personal experience as a teacher and learner of Russian to supplement this list with routine formulas that occur frequently in Russian conversation but are difficult for learners to understand and use. Formulas to be targeted for instruction were then chosen according to the principles of a corpus-referred approach (Timmis 2013). In this approach, corpus data as well as intuition, learner needs, and pedagogical principles guide the selection of language for instructional purposes. Only nine formulas, each with one or two main functions, were selected in order to provide learners with a manageable amount of new language to acquire. Table 1 contains the list of the nine selected formulas along with rough idiomatic English translations.

An evaluation (not reported on here due to space limitations) of eight of the most commonly used beginning and intermediate Russian as a foreign language textbooks was undertaken in order to investigate how (if at all) instructional materials address the selected routine formulas. This was done in order to ensure that study participants were minimally exposed to the targeted phrases. Each textbook was analyzed page-by-page for inclusion of routine formulas of any kind. The results of the analysis demonstrated that textbooks generally include the routine formulas targeted for the current study infrequently and then only incidentally, almost always without any explanation of usage or opportunities for practice. As Kasper and Schmidt (1996) and Bardovi-Harlig (2001) summarized, pragmatic information in textbooks may be defective and inauthentic; Utashiro and Kawai (2009) noticed the same for reactive tokens in Japanese. Clearly, there is a place for in-depth, focused, and explicit instruction of these phrases. The instructional website developed for the current study used corpus excerpts (oral language transcripts and video clips) as input sources in order to ensure that the materials reflected real-life usage.

Table 1 Targeted routine formulas with translations

Routine formula	English translation
V chem delo?	What's the problem?
Da net!	Nah!
Da ty chto!	You're kidding!
Nado zhe!	You don't say!
Nichego sebe!	Wow!
Nichego strashnogo.	No big deal.
Nu i kak?	So how was it?
Nu i chto?	So what?
...chto li?	...is it?

6.2 Methodology: Instructional Website Design

Several website platforms were evaluated for selection. Weebly (http://www.weebly.com/) was chosen due to its attractive and user-friendly interface, and the fact that it allows embedded video and forms. A paid plan was chosen as it provided access to more editing features and website support. Forms were needed to collect and store user input in the form of exercises and feedback on the website itself. Each form required users to input their participant code in order to keep track of individual user data. The data from submitted forms were automatically stored in a spreadsheet on the Weebly administrative page, accessible only to the researcher. The goals of the open education movement (Blyth 2012) drove the design of the instructional modules: they were developed using a low-cost, easy-to-use website builder in order to model the creation of a CALL application for other educators who may not have the necessary programming skills or institutional support to build interactive websites. Additionally, they utilized a modular format that allows for adaptation by users in any context.

The landing page of the instructional site (http://nadozhe.weebly.com/) includes the title of the website, *Nado zhe!*, and instructions on its use. A navigational bar at the top of each page contains the following sections: Home, Modules, Review, Feedback, and Contact. From the Modules button, users can access the nine modules (each focusing on a different routine formula). The Review page (located at http://nadozhe.weebly.com/review.html) is a nine question test targeting the routine formulas addressed on the website, intended to be taken upon completion of all modules. At top of the page, a message informs participants that they may refer back to individual modules for guidance. Each question consists of an excerpt from the corpus (not used in the module or in the pre-/post-/delayed post-test) with the targeted formula removed. For the first five questions, test-takers must select from one of four multiple choice options in order to complete the dialogue. Multiple choice distractors were routine formulas from the website that could not be used to fulfill the function needed in the given dialogue. The final four questions were open-ended cloze tasks in which users produced the missing routine formula by typing it into a text box. Finally, the Feedback page (located at http://nadozhe.weebly.com/feedback.html) consists of a form that solicited information from participants on their experience using the website.

A corpus-referred approach was used to integrate corpus data into the instructional modules. The researcher extracted excerpts featuring the targeted formulas from the oral and multimedia subcorpora of the RNC. While there were plenty of instances of usage to choose from, those which were more conventional and easier to parse were chosen for inclusion. Popular Russian and Soviet film clips excerpts were selected from the multimedia subcorpus to provide users with interesting and engaging authentic material. The corpus excerpts presented in the website were minimally edited in order to preserve their authenticity. However, decisions were made from a pedagogical standpoint on their selection and the extent to which their contexts were preserved (e.g., where to place the boundaries of the excerpts, and information about the speakers themselves). The excerpts were reformatted to resemble instructional dialogues, as the raw excerpts may be difficult for learners to read:

Excerpt 1

[Поля, жен] А девочка на самом деле молодец/я тоже считаю/что переспать на первом свидании не очень хорошо. Тебе она хотя бы нравится/или Юлька моя тебя окончательно покорила? [Саша, муж] Ну так/средненько я бы сказал. [Поля, жен] Я вчера тоже в кино ходила. Ходила на «Мглу». [Саша, муж] Ну и как? Я анонсы видел еще давно. [Поля, жен] Сначала мне вообще не понравилось/очень все страшно/запутанно/и даже мерзко. Но потом я поняла/что очень классный фильм. [Саша, муж] Чей фильм? [Молодежные разговоры// Из коллекции НКРЯ, 2007]	*[Polia, fem] But good for the girl actually/I also think/that sleeping with someone on the first date isn't very good. You like her at least/or has my Iul'ka conquered you for good? [Sasha, male] Well/I'd say partially. [Polia, fem] I also went to the movies yesterday. I went to see "The Mist." [Sasha, male] Well how was it? I've been seeing the ads for a while. [Polia, female] At first I didn't like it at all/it was really scary/and confusing/disgusting even. But then I realized/that it's a really cool movie. [Sasha, male] Who made it? [Youth conversations// From the RNC collection, 2007]*

Non-essential turns were removed, turns were formatted to be more distinct, and speaker information was deleted:

Excerpt 2

— Я вчера тоже в кино ходила. Ходила на «Мглу».	*— I also went to the movies yesterday. I went to see "The Mist."*
*— **Ну и как** ? Я анонсы видел еще давно.*	*— **Nu i kak** ? I've been seeing the ads for a while.*
— Сначала мне вообще не понравилось, очень все страшно, запутанно, и даже мерзко. Но потом я поняла, что очень классный фильм.	*— At first I didn't like it at all, it was really scary and confusing, disgusting even. But then I realized that it's a really cool movie.*

Молодежные разговоры//Из коллекции НКРЯ, 2007	*Youth conversations//From the RNC collection, 2007*

Following the guidelines listed on the RNC website, source information for each excerpt was included in the modules. Furthermore, at the bottom of each module, the following disclaimer was included:

> *All film clips and excerpts from written and oral texts presented on this site (unless otherwise noted) have been taken from the Russian National Corpus for non-commercial educational use.*

The corpus excerpts featured in the instructional presentations as well as the interactive exercises. The website was designed to include the components of Judd's (1999) model for teaching speech acts (it can also be used for the instruction of pragmatic competence more generally): "(1) teacher analysis of speech acts, (2) cognitive awareness skills, (3) receptive/integrative skills, (4) controlled productive skills, and (5) free, integrated practice" (p. 162). Additionally, it fulfills the five functions of materials listed by Tomlinson (2012): it is informative, instructional, experiential, eliciting, and exploratory. Table 2 presents the general module structure; however, not every module contained all elements (see the website, located at http://www.nadozhe.weebly.com/, for the organization of each module). Study participants were required to complete every exercise by inputting their responses into forms embedded in the module pages.

Dictionary and reference materials were included in the modules primarily to exploit all available resources for understanding these formulas. The researcher queried physical references and an online repository of Russian dictionaries and encyclopedias (http://dic.academic.ru/) including specialized linguistic references, for any mention of the targeted formulas. Reference materials additionally provide legitimacy; in their study of folk linguistic theories of language learning among students of Russian, Miller and Ginsberg (1995) found that there is "a strong suspicion that those words not legitimatized through inclusion in dictionaries are unsuitable or incorrect" (p. 299).

Exercises requiring the use of Twitter as a "live" corpus of colloquial Russian were included in order to expose participants to unedited, current usage examples, and to potentially empower them to use Twitter and similar resources to address the pragmatic functions of language in use. However, by having learners explore raw authentic language, there is necessarily potential for exposure to taboo language, which instructors may not condone depending on their own pedagogical philosophy and on the learners themselves.

Table 2 Instructional website module structure

Component	Example	
Activating background knowledge	Have you heard the phrase *Nu i kak*? before?	
	–Yes	
	–No	
	–Not sure	
	What do you think is the function of *Nu i kak*?	
Dictionary definitions	Возглас, выражающий удивление, недовольство или недоверие. [An exclamation, expressing surprise, dissatisfaction, or disbelief.]	
	Толковый словарь Ефремовой. Т. Ф. Ефремова. 2000.	
Reference materials	**—Всё в порядке?**	**—Is everything in order?**
	— Да нет , о чём вы говорите?! Какой порядок?!	**— *Da net* , what are you talking about?! Nothing's in order!**
	В зависимости от контекста [этот оборот может] выражать или мягкое, вежливое, "успокаивающее" возражение (а), или "горячее", решительное (эмоционально окрашенное) возражение (б). [Depending on the context, [this phrase can] express either mild, polite, "reassuring" objection (a), or "impassioned," emphatic (emotionally colored) objection (б)]	
	G. I. Volodina, A kak ob etom skazat'?(2008)	
Summarizing information in dictionary definitions and reference materials	According to the dictionary definitions, what emotion does *Nichego sebe*! primarily express?	
	dissatisfaction	
	indignation	
	surprise	
	excitement	
Idiomatic translation	What English expressions would you use to perform the same functions as those described above?	
Data-driven learning with Twitter	Click here to look at the latest tweets on Twitter featuring the phrase ***Nichego sebe*** **!** Find a tweet you understand and think about what emotion is being expressed. Copy and paste the tweet and the emotion being expressed in the box below.	
Uses of the phrase	***… chto li*** occurs frequently at the end of a question as a tag that the speaker uses to emphasize that s/he is asking a question:	
	О магнитофоне	*About a tape player*
	—Дай посмотреть!	**—Let me see it!**
	—Только не выключай!	**—Just don't turn it off!**
	—Записываешь что ли?	**—You're recording *chto li* ?**
	—Да.	**—Yes.**
	Праздный разговор молодых людей, Московская область// практиканты, 2005	*Holiday conversation between young people, Moscow region// trainees, 2005*
	— Билеты купила, что ли?	**— You bought tickets, *chto li* ?**
	— Купила.	**— I bought them.**
	Короткие телефонные разговоры// Из коллекции Ульяновского университета, 2007	*Short telephone conversations// From the Ul'ianovskii University collection, 2007*

(continued)

Table 2 (continued)

Component	Example	
Cloze	Read the following dialogues. Uses of ***chto li*** have been removed; indicate in the blank where it should be.	
	— Как же он назывался? Не могу вспомнить. «Надежда»?	— What was it called? I can't remember. "Hope"?
	— «Романтик».	— "The Romantic."
	— «Романтик», да.	— "The Romantic," yeah.
	[Разговор на рынке о Дальнегорске в прошлом и настоящем // Дальневосточный ГУ, База данных «Живая речь дальневосточников», 2009]	[Conversation at the market about Dal'negorsk in the past and present // Dal'nevostochnii GU, Database "Live speech of Dal'nevostochniks," 2009]
Dialogue turn matching	In the box below, match the turns (left column) with the appropriate response (right column):	
	1. Это собаки! Всё, я сюда на роликах больше не поеду кататься…	1. Those are dogs! That's it, I'm not coming here to roller-skate any more…
	2. Так прикольно! Такое сочетание прикольное, даа? Маша Малиновская	2. So cool! Such a cool combination, yeah? Masha Malinovskaia
	....	....
	a. Ничего себе! Их там так много! Пошли кругом обойдем… *[Разговоры на прогулке // Из коллекции НКРЯ, 2006]*	a. *Nichego sebe*! There's so many of them! Let's go around… *[Conversations on a walk // From the NKRIA collection, 2006]*
	b. Ничего себе! Фамилия шикарная! *[Праздные разговоры // Из материалов Ульяновского университета, 2006]*	b. *Nichego sebe*! What a grand last name! *[Holiday conversations // From the Ul'ianovskii University collection, 2006]*
	…	…
Film excerpts with partial transcript	Watch the following short film clips containing the phrase ***Nichego sebe***. Pay close attention to the intonation, as well as the function and meaning of this phrase. Watch the clips several times and practice repeating ***Nichego sebe*** with the same intonation as the actors.	
Dialogue creation	Write a short dialogue that incorporates the phrase ***Da ty chto*** **!**	

Other exercise types were selected on the basis of the Center for Advanced Research on Language Acquisition's (2006) third research-based guideline on the development of CALL applications for the instruction of pragmatics: "Tasks will be learner-oriented, varied, and lend themselves to the use of learning strategies and self-discovery."

Each module contains functional descriptions of the routine formulas, based on the researcher's analysis of corpus excerpts. For example, here is the description of *da ty chto* used in the module:

Da ty chto: used to express strong surprise at something someone has said
It can stand alone:
— So the cat bit the surgeon's finger, spontaneously.
— What happened?
— It tensed its muscles then just pierced his finger.
— Da ty chto!
— Yeah, I mean you can get seriously injured.
Conversation about veterinary practice// from the RNC collection, 2005

Or it can be followed by a confirmation check:
— And so he started to say, oh, everyone's such a romantic, hahaha...
— Da ty chto? He said that?
Conversations at home // from the RNC collection, 2006

It can also be followed by a question, in order to get more information:
— I was surprised myself, he calls and says that he's just hit someone with his car.
— Da ty chto, how?
— He was just driving along with a friend and suddenly a drunk guy runs out into the road, he didn't notice him, starts to break, and the car skids.
Conversations among female students about bad things // from the Ul'ianovskij university collection, 2007

Sometimes the speaker gives an explanation for his/her surprise:
— Who's he?
— Max.
— Da ty chto? I thought you couldn't stand each other!
— It's a thin line between love and hate!
Conversations among Ul'ianov women// from the Ul'ianovskij university collection, 2007

Finally, it can also be used ironically, when responding to something that is not very surprising:
— Where are you?
— I'm at the university. I'm about to head over to your place.
— Da ty chto!
— Yeah!
Telephone conversations between mothers and their student daughters// from the Ul'ianovskij university collection, 2009

The modules include both implicit and explicit activities in order to give learners varied opportunities to acquire the routine formulas.

7 Results: Participant Response to Instructional Website

A post-intervention feedback form (http://nadozhe.weebly.com/feedback.html) was completed by 17 of the 18 experimental group participants. All of them responded that the module increased their awareness of the ways the presented phrases are used in conversation (Yes – 59 %; Somewhat – 41 %). They described the website as Useful (88 %), Informative (76 %), Engaging (71 %), and Fun (53 %). Forty-seven percent of respondents found the language of the corpus excerpts (both from the oral conversation transcripts and films) easy to understand, while 35 % found it somewhat difficult, and 18 % found it difficult. The majority of participants indicated that the most helpful parts of the modules were the excerpts from authentic conversations (71 %), the explanations of usage (59 %), and the film clips (59 %). This demonstrates that students responded positively to the corpus excerpts and corpus-based explanations.

According to retrospective interview results, the learners who had heard and used the targeted routine formulas before the study said that the instructional website helped them gain confidence in using the phrases and increased their awareness of a wider range of the expressions' functions and appropriate contexts of use. This empowered some users to use them more frequently, like Arthur, who started using *Nu i kak* after learning more about it on the website.

According to Joseph, the website helped him understand more functions of the routine formulas than he had been aware of before. Stephanie and Arthur (Excerpt 3) both noted that the website helped refine their understanding of the routine formulas:

Excerpt 3 Arthur

1 I had a general understanding of it but then like seeing it, like on paper, explained, on the
2 website, um, I think helped clarify

Additionally, the website appeared to have an effect on the automatization of the targeted routine formulas. Nicole said she was able to recognize the phrases more quickly, "because they were presented as kind of like a set phrase," while Claudia mentioned that she uses them more readily since "they're a little bit more integrated into my vocabulary."

For participants with lower proficiency or who have spent limited or no time in a country where Russian is spoken, the website appeared to increase awareness of the targeted routine formulas. Several participants started noticing the phrases in use after using the website. This could be due to the phenomenon that Amber mentioned: "once you learn a word you see it everywhere." Without this awareness, learners may have been exposed to routine formulas in use but these occurrences went by unnoticed. Terry suggested that, before gaining awareness of the routine formulas and their contexts of use, he ignored the phrases in films because he did not understand them, and assumed they were unimportant.

By far the most popular element of the website was the inclusion of Russian and Soviet film excerpts drawn from the RNC. The clips were useful because they provided an opportunity to hear natural language in use; Susan suggested that film clips might be useful as a replacement for exposure to "everyday people talking" for learners who are not in frequent contact with the language. Another respondent, Claudia, spoke to their role in expanding her knowledge of appropriate usage contexts, as the clips provided "an idea of different scenarios that I might not have encountered in my own interactions in which those expressions would be used." Additionally, Amber pointed out that the video format allowed for users to be exposed to paralinguistic information such as tone.

Improving listening skills through watching the clips served as a means to recognize the formulas in the real world; Andrew said that he was able to pick them up while listening to the radio after hearing them in the film clips. By presenting the formulas in writing, or in video clips that can be played multiple times, learners have the opportunity to "catch" and analyze them. The overwhelming speed and ephemeral nature of speech can keep learners from noticing these phrases.

Several participants appreciated the variety of activity types included on the website, including Claudia (Excerpt 4):

Excerpt 4 Claudia

1 I thought that was a really… rich way to, um, familiarize yourself with new vocabulary.

According to Craig, the different parts of the website complemented each other and provided many opportunities to consolidate information on the functions of the routine formulas in context. Many interviewees were in favor of addressing conversational language in pedagogical materials. David (Excerpt 5) wished that he had been familiar with this type of conversational language before spending time abroad. He saw the website as a useful tool to prepare learners for the phrases they would be hearing abroad:

Excerpt 5 David

1 I honestly wish I had, you know, been introduced to this website, for example, before I
2 left for Russia, meaning, as part of my introductory Russian classes. So when I knew I
3 was going to Russia, and I heard someone say *Nichego sebe* over and over and over again
4 I would actually know, like, kinda what he meant by it.

While instructional materials might prepare learners for hearing routine formulas and increase their confidence in using these phrases, interviewees nonetheless emphasized the importance of interaction in mastering this language. The use of pedagogical materials and real interaction with L1 Russian speakers in tandem was attractive to most participants; the most effective approach to teaching routine formulas might be a combination of these two elements. Samantha's comment (Excerpt 6) is representative:

Excerpt 6 Samantha

1 I think it'd be helpful if it was kinda taught in a textbook setting but at the same time, I
2 mean it's also helpful if you speak with native Russians and they use it because they can
3 like tell you when to use it, what it means, and like what settings and everything.

However, proficiency may be a mitigating factor in the effectiveness of the website, even as a preparatory tool. Two users with more limited Russian learning experience, Adam and Shelly, felt that the website was slightly beyond their level of proficiency. Adam felt that he first needed a solid foundation in grammar and vocabulary, saying his speech was too "clunky" and "disjointed" to use any of the phrases. Shelly said she had to look up vocabulary in order to understand the dialogues; Grace also mentioned that the vocabulary was too difficult for lower proficiency learners. This was a particular challenge in the Twitter activity, where learners had to find and explain an instance of a particular routine formula found by using the Twitter search function. Amber suggested that a materials developer could choose a handful of clear uses of the phrase in tweets in order to exclude "sarcastic" or otherwise atypical uses. Natural language extracted from a corpus is likely to be incomprehensible to learners without a certain level of proficiency.

One interviewee, Craig (Excerpt 7), suggested that the website include more fine-grained information on the differences between routine formulas with overlapping functions:

Excerpt 7 Craig

1 maybe a comparative summary of those particular issues, um, because it, I wasn't entirely
2 sure if the expressions of surprise were, like is this a question of personal taste, you just
3 pick one and go with it, um, are, like, are there particular situations where one is more
4 appropriate than another

This addresses the crux of the matter of nativelike selection. In an oft-cited article, Pawley and Syder (1983) stated that the critical issue in linguistic theory is understanding two "puzzles": *nativelike selection* and *nativelike fluency*. That is, how do we make sense of the fact that, firstly, native speakers of a language are able to choose, amongst a range of possible expressions, those that are idiomatic and best express their intended meaning and that, secondly, native speakers are able to produce coherent, fluent discourse even though human planning and processing capabilities appear to be insufficiently suited to this task? The use of formulaic language is essential to nativelike selection and fluency. While the website provided a range of expressions to acquire for use in speech, Craig (Excerpt 7) lacked the skill of selection needed to choose the appropriate routine formula, based on a nativelike knowledge of its connotations and the contexts in which it is appropriate.

Instructional materials have the potential to fill this gap; the website in the current study, however, was perhaps not sufficiently detailed to do this. Even though the corpus excerpts appeared to be useful for illustrative purposes, learners may require more extensive exposure to the phrases in real life contexts.

Experimental group participants had unique experiences with the website, which appears to be a function of level of familiarity with the targeted routine formulas, proficiency, learning styles, overall proficiency, and other factors. For learners with advanced proficiency and extensive in-country experience, like Keith, the website may have only been useful as a review; for low proficiency learners, like Adam, it may have only been effective as a means of gaining awareness of previously unfamiliar phrases. However, participants agreed that the language contained in the website was important; it seems to be most amenable to instruction at the intermediate and advanced levels.

8 Discussion

This chapter has documented the procedure of using corpus methodologies in the development of materials for the instruction of pragmatics. Results of the current study lend support to the claim that a corpus-referred instructional intervention, in this case a CALL application, can aid in the acquisition of routine formulas, both by raising awareness of these phrases and by strengthening and expanding users' knowledge of their form–function–context mappings. Materials that draw from corpus findings and integrate corpus data can be motivating, engaging, and useful to language learners. Corpus research can aid materials developers and instructors in describing the pragmatics of conversation, and corpus excerpts can be utilized to illustrate usage in pedagogical materials. The excerpts in this project served as sample usage events (albeit decontextualized ones) that increased learners' exposure to routine formulas in use (Vyatkina 2013). Film clips performed a similar function. Increased comprehension can lead to production, as it builds learners' confidence that they can understand and use the routine formulas appropriately, which in turn empowers them to practice integrating them into their speech.

Based on the experience developing and implementing this pedagogical intervention, I recommend the following procedure when developing a corpus-referred instructional website:

- Decide on the linguistic forms/pragmatic features/etc. that you would like to focus on. This selection process can be informed by your intuition as a language teacher/learner, by corpus research, and/or by a particular text (e.g., speech acts performed in a film used in your language course).
- Select an appropriate corpus to extract examples from (e.g., a corpus of oral language if spoken language is the focus), or create your own corpus.
- Query the language under study in the corpus. The results of your search will inform your analysis of the targeted linguistic feature.

- Analyze the corpus data. This is where your expertise as a linguist and/or language teacher comes into play. Document and categorize excerpts by function; highlight words, phrases, and/or grammatical constructions that tend to occur with the language you queried; organize them by speaker type (gender, age, etc.). If possible, use previous research on your targeted linguistic feature to inform your analysis, and solicit the perspectives of other experts.
- Design a module based on your analysis. Think about how you want to present the material–in what order, according to what kind of format. Use clear corpus samples and excerpts from other sources (e.g., media, literature, etc.) to illustrate functions and to be used in module exercises based on real language. Decide if and how you want to edit authentic data to make it more accessible to learners. Cite the source of any data you use.
- Choose a website builder with the necessary functionality (e.g., ability to embed audio/video, forms for collecting student responses, etc.). Or, if you have access to web programmers who can create a website to your specifications, provide them with a list of the exact features you would like to have.
- Create the module and develop a variety of exercises in the website builder. These exercises should be designed to appeal to a range of user preferences and should be diverse enough to keep learners interested. Keep in mind any technological limitations of the website.
- After you have built your website, check all links, media, and exercises for functionality. Ask others–language instructors/researchers, students, instructional designers–to go through the website as well, looking closely for inaccuracies and technical issues on a range of browsers and operating systems.

9 Limitations and Future Directions

The results of this study are necessarily tentative, given the small sample size and limited duration and intensity of the pedagogical intervention. Additionally, the sample is unique since it is composed of learners who voluntarily participated, receiving minimal financial compensation. The intervention may have been positively received by participants because they were highly self-directed, motivated, or otherwise atypical learners of Russian. Larger and more representative samples would be needed to confirm the benefits of this and similar corpus-referred CALL applications for pragmatics instruction.

The website itself suffers from limitations as well: the tasks did not require spoken responses, and, as indicated by some of the participants' feedback, the functional descriptions were possibly inadequate. Also, the provision of detailed feedback would likely increase the pedagogical value of the website, particularly for independent learners. Additionally, although participants reported that the website was useful in their acquisition of the targeted formulas, observation and analysis of actual performance in real or simulated conversational contexts would be needed to support their claims and to confirm the validity of their scores on the testing instrument.

Further research is needed on the effectiveness of corpus-referred materials in the instruction of pragmatics. Corpus methodologies have begun to be implemented in ELT, but their use and evaluations of their value should be explored in instructional applications and materials for other L2s as well. Additionally, there is dire need for an empirically validated, accessible framework for the development of materials (both physical and digital) that use corpus methodologies and data. Such a framework would enable teachers, researchers, and materials developers to make use of the ever-increasing wealth of corpora and corpus tools in the creation of technological applications and textbooks that reflect usage and aid in language acquisition.

10 Conclusion

While this study is only a first step into the exploration of the benefits of corpus data for pragmatics instruction, it nonetheless demonstrates the great potential in this area. As corpus methodologies become increasingly accessible to a general audience, and as corpus tools become more user-friendly, the possibility for taking advantage of the insights into language from corpus research becomes more and more realistic. Sophisticated linguistic analyses have been made possible thanks to the continuing development of well-constructed corpora; the more accurately we as pedagogues and researchers can document the behavior of language in use, the more useful instruction will be to our students. This is particularly true for pragmatics, which is completely dependent on the context(s) that corpus data can readily provide.

Appendix A

1. Did you encounter the expressions presented in the module in other contexts, such as in conversation or in Russian texts (e.g., movies, songs, writing)? If so, where did you encounter them?
2. Did you find that you were better able to understand the expressions presented in the module when you encountered them in Russian conversation/texts?
3. Did you ever use the expressions presented in the module in your spoken Russian? If so, when and with whom? Please give concrete examples if you remember them.
4. If you used the expressions presented in the module, how did using them make you feel (*e.g., more fluent; awkward because I wasn't quite sure how/when to use them; etc.*)?

5. Please comment on any other aspect of the web-based module or the expressions presented in it that you feel would be useful to the researcher.
6. Which phrases were less common/less used?
7. Do you find a self-study module effective?
8. Do you think conversational language is better used in conversation or from a textbook/website?

References

Adolphs, S. (2008). *Corpus and context: Investigating pragmatic functions in spoken discourse*. Amsterdam: John Benjamins.

Agastein, D. (1988). Colloquial Russian in the classroom. *Russian Language Journal, 141–143*, 41–49.

Alcón Soler, E., & Martínez-Flor, A. (2008). Pragmatics in foreign language contexts. In E. Alcón Soler & A. Martínez-Flor (Eds.), *Investigating pragmatics in foreign language learning, teaching and testing* (pp. 3–21). Bristol: Multilingual Matters.

Alsufieva, A., Kisselev, O., & Freels, S. (2012). Results 2012: Using flagship data to develop a Russian learner corpus of academic writing. *Russian Language Journal, 62*, 79–105.

Anthony, L. (2014). *AntConc (Version 3.4.3) [Computer Software]*. Tokyo: Waseda University. Available from http://www.laurenceanthony.net/

Bao, D. (2013). Developing materials for the speaking skill. In B. Tomlinson (Ed.), *Developing materials for language teaching* (pp. 407–428). London: Bloomsbury.

Bardovi-Harlig, K. (2001). Evaluating the empirical evidence: Grounds for instruction in pragmatics? In K. R. Rose & G. Kasper (Eds.), *Pragmatics in language teaching* (pp. 13–32). Cambridge: Cambridge University Press.

Bardovi-Harlig, K. (2012). Formulas, routines, and conversational expressions in pragmatics research. *Annual Review of Applied Linguistics, 32*, 206–227.

Bardovi-Harlig, K., & Vellenga, H. E. (2012). The effect of instruction on conventional expressions in L2 pragmatics. *System, 40*(1), 77–89.

Belz, J. A. (2007). The role of computer mediation in the instruction and development of L2 pragmatic competence. *Annual Review of Applied Linguistics, 27*, 45–75.

Belz, J. A., & Vyatkina, N. (2005). Learner corpus analysis and the development of L2 pragmatic competence in networked intercultural language study: The case of German modal particles. *Canadian Modern Language Review/La Revue canadienne des langues vivantes, 62*(1), 17–48.

Biber, D., & Conrad, S. (2010). *Corpus linguistics and grammar teaching*. White Plains: Pearson Education.

Blyth, C. (2012). Opening up foreign language education with open educational resources. In F. Rubio & J. J. Thoms (Eds.), *Hybrid language teaching and learning: Exploring theoretical, pedagogical and curricular issues* (pp. 196–218). Boston: Heinle Thomson.

Center for Advanced Research on Language Acquisition. (2006). *Dancing with words: Strategies for learning pragmatics in Spanish. Important information for researchers*. Retrieved from http://www.carla.umn.edu/speechacts/sp_pragmatics/for_researchers.html

Coulmas, F. (1979). On the sociolinguistic relevance of routine formulae. *Journal of Pragmatics, 3*, 239–266.

Diepenbroek, L. G., & Derwing, T. M. (2014). To what extent do popular ESL textbooks incorporate oral fluency and pragmatic development. *TESL Canada Journal, 30*(7), 1–20.

Dörnyei, Z., & Thurrell, S. (1992). *Conversation and dialogues in action*. New York: Prentice Hall.

Furniss, E. (2013). Using a corpus-based approach to Russian as a foreign language materials development. *Russian Language Journal, 63*, 195–212.
Furniss, E. A. (2016). Teaching the pragmatics of Russian conversation using a corpus-referred website. *Language Learning & Technology, 20*(2), 38–60.
Garrett, N. (2009). Computer-assisted language learning trends and issues revisited: Integrating innovation. *The Modern Language Journal, 93*, 719–740.
Hughes, R. (2010). Materials to develop the speaking skill. In N. Harwood (Ed.), *English language teaching materials: Theory and practice* (pp. 207–224). Cambridge: Cambridge University Press.
Ishihara, N. (2007). Web-based curriculum for pragmatics instruction in Japanese as a foreign language: An explicit awareness-raising approach. *Language Awareness, 16*(1), 21–40.
Ishihara, N., & Cohen, A. D. (2010). *Teaching and learning pragmatics: Where language and culture meet*. Harlow: Pearson Longman.
Judd, E. L. (1999). Some issues in the teaching of pragmatic competence. In E. Hinkel (Ed.), *Culture in second language teaching and learning* (pp. 152–166). Cambridge: Cambridge University Press.
Kasper, G. (2001). Four perspectives on L2 pragmatic development. *Applied Linguistics, 22*(4), 502–530.
Kasper, G., & Schmidt, R. (1996). Developmental issues in interlanguage pragmatics. *Studies in Second Language Acquisition, 18*(2), 149–169.
Mauranen, A. (2004). Spoken corpus for an ordinary learner. In J. M. Sinclair (Ed.), *How to use corpora in language teaching* (pp. 89–105). Amsterdam: John Benjamins.
McCarten, J. (2007). *Teaching vocabulary: Lessons from the corpus, lessons for the classroom*. Cambridge: Cambridge University Press.
McCarten, J., & McCarthy, M. (2010). Bridging the gap between corpus and course book: The case of conversation strategies. In F. Mishan & A. Chambers (Eds.), *Perspectives on language learning materials development* (pp. 11–32). Bern: Peter Lang.
McCarthy, M., McCarten, J., & Sandiford, H. (2005). *Touchstone 1 & 2*. Cambridge: Cambridge University Press.
McCarthy, M., McCarten, J., & Sandiford, H. (2006). *Touchstone 3 & 4*. Cambridge: Cambridge University Press.
Miller, L., & Ginsberg, R. (1995). Folklinguistic theories of language learning. In B. F. Freed (Ed.), *Second language acquisition in a study abroad context* (pp. 293–315). Amsterdam/ Philadelphia: John Benjamins.
Mishan, F. (2004). Authenticating corpora for language learning: A problem and its resolution. *ELT Journal, 58*(3), 219–227.
Narita, R. (2012). The effects of pragmatic consciousness-raising activity on the development of pragmatic awareness and use of hearsay evidential markers for learners of Japanese as a foreign language. *Journal of Pragmatics, 44*(1), 1–29.
Norrick, N. R. (2015). Interjections. In K. Aijmer & C. Rühlemann (Eds.), *Corpus pragmatics: A handbook* (pp. 249–275). Cambridge: Cambridge University Press.
Pavlenko, A. (2006). *Rationale and research basis for teaching materials on narrative and conceptual proficiency in advanced-level Russian* (CALPER Report). University Park, PA: Center for Advanced Language Proficiency Education and Research Report. Retrieved from http://calper.la.psu.edu/docs/pdfs/studiesreports/Teaching_Russian_for_Advanced_Proficiency_USDOED.pdf
Pawley, A., & Syder, F. H. (1983). Two puzzles for linguistic theory: Nativelike selection and nativelike fluency. In J. C. Richards & R. W. Schmidt (Eds.), *Language and communication* (pp. 191–226). New York: Longman.
Rafieyan, V., Sharafi-Nejad, M., & Eng, L. S. (2014). Effect of pragmatic awareness on comprehension and production of conventional expressions. *Theory and Practice in Language Studies, 4*(7), 1352–1358.

Rifkin, B. (1997). Review article: Second language acquisition theory and the new generation of Russian language textbooks. *The Slavic and East European Journal, 41*(2), 330–340.
Römer, U. (2011). Corpus research applications in second language teaching. *Annual Review of Applied Linguistics, 31*, 205–225.
Russell, V., & Vasquez, C. (2011). A web-based tutorial for the instruction of Spanish pragmatics. *IALLT Journal of Language Learning Technologies, 41*(2), 27–55.
Schmidt, R. W. (1990). The role of consciousness in second language learning. *Applied Linguistics, 11*(2), 129–158.
Schmidt, R. W. (1993). Awareness and second language acquisition. *Annual Review of Applied Linguistics, 13*(1), 206–226.
Schmidt, R. W. (2001). Attention. In P. Robinson (Ed.), *Cognition and second language instruction* (pp. 3–32). Cambridge: Cambridge University Press.
Sinclair, J. M. (2004). New evidence, new priorities, new attitudes. In J. M. Sinclair (Ed.), *How to use corpora in language teaching* (pp. 271–299). Amsterdam: John Benjamins.
Sykes, J. M., & Cohen, A. D. (2008). Observed learner behavior, reported use, and evaluation of a website for learning Spanish pragmatics. In M. Bowles, R. Foote, & S. Perpiñán (Eds.), *Second language acquisition and research: Focus on form and function* (pp. 144–157). Somerville: Cascadilla.
Taguchi, N. (2011). Teaching pragmatics: Trends and issues. *Annual Review of Applied Linguistics, 31*, 289–310.
Taguchi, N., & Sykes, J. M. (Eds.). (2013). *Technology in interlanguage pragmatics research and teaching*. Amsterdam: John Benjamins.
Takahashi, S. (2010). Assessing learnability in second language pragmatics. In A. Trosborg (Ed.), *Pragmatics across languages and cultures* (pp. 391–422). Berlin: De Gruyter.
Tan, M. (2002). Introduction. In M. Tan (Ed.), *Corpus studies in language education* (pp. 1–12). Bangkok: IELE Press.
Thornbury, S., & Slade, D. (2006). *Conversation: From description to pedagogy*. Cambridge: Cambridge University Press.
Timmis, I. (2013). Corpora and materials: Towards a working relationship. In B. Tomlinson (Ed.), *Developing materials for language teaching* (pp. 461–474). London: Bloomsbury.
Tomlinson, B. (2012). Materials development for language learning and teaching. *Language Teaching, 45*(2), 143–179.
Utashiro, T., & Kawai, G. (2009). Blended learning for Japanese reactive tokens: Effects of computer-led, instructor-led, and peer-based instruction. In N. Taguchi (Ed.), *Pragmatic competence* (pp. 275–300). Berlin: Mouton de Gruyter.
Vyatkina, N. (2013). Discovery learning and teaching with electronic corpora in an advanced German grammar course. *Die Unterrichtspraxis/Teaching German, 46*(1), 44–61.
Waugh, E. (2013). Teaching pragmatics and intercultural communication online. *TESL Canada Journal/Revue TESL du Canada, 30*(7), 98–107.
Wray, A. (2002). *Formulaic language and the lexicon*. Cambridge: Cambridge University Press.

Beyond Engaged Listenership: Assessing Spanish Undergraduates' Active Participation in Academic Mentoring Sessions in English as Academic Lingua Franca

Fiona MacArthur

Abstract The academic mentoring of undergraduate students has been a focus of interest in educational research, with attention being drawn to the role of individual mentoring for students' overall academic achievement. However, the quality of the interaction in mentoring sessions is an important aspect of this kind of communicative event: how successful the dyads are in communicating with each other may very well affect the academic outcomes pursued. This article contributes to this research by examining a corpus of 27 conversations recorded at five different European universities in which Spanish Erasmus students sought advice from their lecturers at the host university about various aspects of their academic work. The quantitative and qualitative analysis of these conversations shows that the student responses to the advice given by their mentors varied considerably, ranging for a preference for minimal response tokens such as *yeah* or *uhu* to more engaged replies, consisting of utterances which built on and contributed to developing the topic at hand. These different "response-styles" were not found to be related to the student's mastery of English, as assessed on the current Common European Framework of Reference for Languages (CEFR) scales, and therefore cannot be solely attributed to the linguistic disadvantage that may oblige a speaker to consistently adopt the role of secondary speaker in such conversations. Rather, it appears to relate more closely to how the individual student enacts his/her role in this type of interaction. I point out some pedagogical implications of these findings and suggest the need for further research.

Keywords Listenership • Understanding • Office hours' consultation • Erasmus

F. MacArthur (✉)
Filología Inglesa/Facultad de Filosofía y Letras, Universidad de Extremadura, Cáceres, Spain
e-mail: fionamac@unex.es

J. Romero-Trillo (ed.), *Yearbook of Corpus Linguistics and Pragmatics 2016*,
Yearbook of Corpus Linguistics and Pragmatics 4,
DOI 10.1007/978-3-319-41733-2_8

1 Introduction

Listenership – or the verbal and non-verbal behaviour of a person who, in the course of an interaction, adopts the role of secondary speaker – has long been a topic of great interest to conversation analysts, with a number of recent studies adding to the already extense literature on the role of different response tokens in conversational interaction (e.g. Gardner 2005, 2007; McCarthy 2003; Norrick 2012). Understanding, in contrast, is a much more tricky aspect to investigate. What is going on in a listener's mind as he or she responds to a conversational partner's words is not accessible through the analysis of a transcript of a recorded conversation. It is true, however, that the conversational behaviour of the participants may nevertheless provide insights into the coordination of meanings and understandings in that conversation. Sacks (1992) claimed, for example, that the way people display understanding is "not to say, e.g., 'I understand,' or to say 'What you said was…' but to produce an action that fits there" (Vol. II, p. 112), and described some of the ways that listeners may show that they are experiencing difficulty in following another's talk.

The coordination of meanings and understandings between speakers in intercultural communication – specifically, uncovering the problems that may arise in the course of conversational interactions between people with different mother tongues (L1) or cultural backgrounds – has been the subject of numerous studies. Some of these have focused on communication in academic settings involving international students enrolled at English-speaking universities (e.g. Chiang 2011; Farr 2003; House 2013; Skyrme 2010; Waring 2002a, b; Willemyns et al. 2006, or Young 2013), drawing attention to diverse features of the interactions that take place between international students and their lecturers or supervisors in seminars or supervisions. The present study explores another kind of intercultural interaction in an academic setting – an office hours' consultation – involving Spanish Erasmus students at five different European universities. This particular study was motivated by the results of the analysis of a questionnaire administered to the participants in 27 face-to-face conversations (between Spanish undergraduate students and their lecturers) after they had been recorded in conversation with each other. This revealed that, while there was broad agreement on other aspects of these conversations, there was significant divergence between the responses of lecturers and students regarding the degree of understanding achieved. The students were much more optimistic about how much they had understood than the lecturers.

The purpose of this article is to explore the question of why the lecturers might have judged the conversations with the students as relatively unsuccessful in some cases, relating this to the verbal behaviour of the Spanish students in response to the advice and information they were being given. As will be seen, the response styles of the students varied considerably, ranging from a relatively passive participation in these academic mentoring sessions to displays of what has been termed "substantive recipiency" (Waring 2002a). The ability to show much more than "engaged listenership" (Farr 2003) is, I suggest, fundamental to the outcomes of such academic conversations, where lecturers may assess and negatively evaluate learners' understanding as a consequence of their verbal behaviour in this type of dyadic interaction.

In the next section, I describe the background that informed the present study generally, before moving on to describe the conversational data focused on, how it was gathered and subsequently analysed. I then provide an overview of the most significant results as regards the variation in response styles among the student cohort, quantitatively speaking, before zooming in on some extracts of these conversations to examine how students variously enacted their roles as participants in an academic conversation. Given the limits of an article such as this, the conclusions offered can only be tentative, but the findings suggest that further investigation of the phenomena under discussion is needed.

2 Background

At the risk of over-simplifying the complexity of the various systems of assessment used in Centres of Higher Education (HEs), it can nevertheless be suggested that, at the heart of the various means used (written assignments, projects of various kinds, exams, tests or classroom observations, among others) is the general aim of gathering evidence or feedback on advances in undergraduate students' understanding or "epistemic store" (Gardner 2007) or progress in the knowledge and skills which are relevant to their particular discipline or the degree in which they are enrolled. Some of this feedback is delayed, in that in an exam, for example, the interplay between two kinds of monologic communication may be compared and contrasted: the written and spoken texts that they have been exposed to in lecture halls or libraries, for example, are interpreted in written and/or spoken texts produced by the students, to be later assessed by those responsible for ensuring that learning outcomes are commensurate with the standards set by the local institutions or educational authorities. However, teaching and learning activities in HEs are not composed entirely (nor even mostly) of these monologic acts of communication. On the contrary, seminars, tutorials, supervisions or office hours' consultations comprise everyday dialogic acts of communication taking place in universities, in which learning can be monitored and co-constructed by the various participants in these communicative exchanges: both teaching staff (henceforth, lecturers) and students. These less visible genres of academic communication have received a growing amount of research interest from applied linguists generally and, most especially, by conversation analysts (Chiang 2011; Farr 2003; House 2013; Skyrme 2010; Waring 2002a, b) to discover how knowledge is shared, meanings negotiated or how participant roles are enacted in the processes of disciplinary enculturation that take place in HEs.

This area of research is of particular importance in an age of growing internationalization of HEs in Europe. For example, in 2013 the Erasmus programme reached its goal of enabling the exchange of three million students among European universities. This means that a very large number of undergraduate and graduate students enrolled at a university in one European country spent a period of time (normally between 5 and 9 months) studying at another European HE, where academic communication is most often not carried out in the students' mother tongue (L1) but, increasingly, in English, which is the language adopted by many institutions as academic lingua franca. The challenges posed to students by these linguistic circumstances have been met in various ways, ranging from minimum proficiency levels required by the host university to research efforts aimed at describing the characteristics of spoken and written academic discourse that may then inform the teaching programmes designed to enable students to participate fully in academic communication in their second language (L2). However, research into academic discourse in English has been dominated by attention to the major genres of academic communication –lectures, textbooks or essay writing – but have paid less attention to the less visible ones mentioned earlier. In particular, an area which has received relatively little research attention is that of the interactional skills that will enable Erasmus (and other international) students to participate fully in the kind of dialogic communication that they will engage in with their peers and staff at the host university.

In contrast, in the field of teaching English as a second or foreign language (TES/FL), there has been growing interest in identifying the interactional behaviour that characterizes "confluence" (McCarthy 2009) as opposed to "fluency" in conversation. Fluency, as McCarthy points out (2009:13), is a monologic achievement, a notion often irrelevant to two-party interactions where confluence more accurately describes how the flow across turns reflects "the jointly produced phenomenon which constitutes a successful interaction" (McCarthy 2009: 17–18). Analysis of smaller and larger amounts of spoken data has enabled a number of scholars (e.g. Buysse 2014, Müller 2005 or Romero-Trillo 2002), to describe the differences between the ways that native and non native speakers of English behave in conversational interaction. Furthermore, McCarthy and his colleagues (McCarthy 2002, 2003, 2009; O'Keeffe et al. 2007) have contributed to the already extensive literature on listenership behaviour (which has often focused on what are most usually termed "minimal response tokens" such as *uhu*, *yeah*, or *okay*, for example) by describing the roles and functions of lexical items such as *right*, *really*, *perfect* or *absolutely* as "non-minimal" responses. A similar division between minimal and non-minimal response tokens was used by Farr (2003) in her study of the recordings of meetings between students and tutors involved in an MA in English Language Teaching programme, which, like the work by McCarthy and colleagues cited earlier, was also particularly concerned with how good –or "engaged" – listenership may be displayed, in this case focusing specifically on academic communication. As Farr asserted (2003: 71) "[i]n an academic environment it is paramount that even if a learner does not attend to pragmatic conventions, s/he must have the necessary resources to operate interactionally and transactionally through the use of response signals" and further argued that the ability to participate effectively in the co-construction of discourse is vital because "education is achieved through discovery, reflection and insight" (p. 73).

The attention paid to listenership in these studies is of great interest, if only because the unequal status of interlocutors in academic interactions may give rise to asymmetric conversations in which the expert (the lecturer or tutor) may frequently adopt the role of primary speaker in the course of a mentoring session, with the student playing a supporting role primarily as listener or secondary speaker. Nevertheless, it can be pointed out that, in academic dialogue, being a good listener may well not be sufficient: students will also be expected to participate more actively in the co-construction of an academic mentoring session, taking longer turns at talk and, in general, contributing actively to their own learning by showing that they are understanding (or not) what they are being told. This will be particularly the case when students have specifically sought out their tutor or lecturer in order to get advice or information about specific issues that are of concern to them. In such cases, they may take advantage of the office hours when lecturers may be available to answer questions students may have about course contents or written assignments, among others.

Office hours' consultations have received attention from some scholars (e.g. Limberg 2007, 2010; Reinhardt 2010, or Skyrme 2010) and, while these interactions have been characterized as somewhat asymmetrical (with the lecturer controlling to a large extent the course of the interaction and the student adopting the role of secondary speaker [Limberg 2010]), nevertheless, in these interactions students may need to display not only "engaged listenership" (Farr 2003) but also more "substantive recipiency" (Waring 2002a) in the form of utterances that indicate that s/he understands – or is attempting to understand – what a tutor is telling them. The notion of "substantive recipiency" is, as Waring acknowledges (2002a: 454), a somewhat slippery concept, but may nevertheless serve to describe the kind of verbal behaviour at the heart of academic discussion, because "[i]t is in substantive recipiency that knowledge is constructed collaboratively" (Waring 2002a: 456). In her exploration of seminar discussions, Waring identified three ways that this may be displayed – through reformulating, extending and jargonizing – thus providing a useful framework for further investigation of how students show that they have (or have not) understood the concepts discussed in an academic encounter.

The studies briefly reviewed here have aimed to describe listenership behaviour in general by examining students' use of minimal or non-minimal response tokens in academic interactions (e.g. Farr 2003), or how they may display that they are fully understanding what their tutor is telling them by more substantial contributions to an academic conversation (e.g. Waring 2002a).

The focus of the present study is somewhat different in that it aims to show how the kind of verbal behaviour of students may be quite different from each other in academic interaction: response styles were found to vary greatly among an otherwise fairly homogeneous cohort of Spanish undergraduate students spending between 5 and 9 months at a university in another European country. A total of 27 Erasmus students participated in a semi-guided conversation with a lecturer who was responsible for a course they were taking, which was video-recorded and subsequently transcribed. Closer analysis of what I will term their "response styles" was largely motivated by the results of a questionnaire administered to the students and lecturers after they had talked together, which showed that there was a mismatch between the students' and lecturers' perceptions of how well they had managed to understand each other. While the students appeared confident that the conversation had resulted in successful communication, the lecturers reported feeling less persuaded that the students had fully understood what they were being told. This appeared to be due, at least in part, to how the students displayed their understanding in the course of the conversation through the use of minimal and non-minimal response tokens as well as displays of substantive recipiency.

In the next section, I describe the data and how it was collected, transcribed and analysed, before presenting the overall findings that emerged from this analysis in Sect. 4.

3 The Data

The primary purpose of the research resulting in the compilation of the European Corpus of Academic Talk (EuroCoAT) referred to here was to describe the use of metaphor in intercultural academic conversations in English. Full details of the research project, the research team involved, the methodology employed, as well as access to the corpus itself, can be found at www.eurocoat.es. Here, I limit myself to describing the procedure used to gather the conversational data, its transcription, and how the response behaviour of the student participants was analysed.

The EuroCoAT corpus consists of the transcripts of 27 conversations between lecturers and Spanish undergraduate students that were video-recorded at five different European universities between April and November 2012. This yielded a total of 5 h, 47 min and 33 s of conversational data (consisting of conversations lasting between 6 min 32 s [the shortest] and 22 min 22 s [the longest]).

3.1 Participants and Procedure

The 27 student participants (11 male and 16 female) were all Spanish undergraduates spending between 5 and 9 months at universities in Ireland, England, the Netherlands and Sweden within the Erasmus programme, which makes it possible for students from universities participating in this programme to complete part of their degree at another university in Europe. All the undergraduate degree courses that these students were enrolled in were taught in English, an increasingly common phenomenon in HEs across Europe (Coleman 2006).

A total of 21 lecturers were involved in these conversations (five participated in more than one session recorded). Fourteen of the lecturers were L1 speakers of English; the remaining seven had different L1s: Greek (1), Spanish (1), Dutch (2), Chinese (1), Swedish (1) and German (1). This means that only in one of these conversations, where Spanish was the first language of both participants, did there exist a shared language background. In all cases, the conversations were in English.

The data being sought were to resemble, as far as possible, the kinds of interactions that may take place in office hours' consultations, when lecturers are available for individual consultations with students. To this end, we sought volunteers among Erasmus students at the five different universities involved, asking those willing to participate in the study to suggest the name of a lecturer they were currently being taught by in order to engage in a semi-guided academic consultation with him/her that would be video-recorded, transcribed and later analysed. Once agreement had been reached with the lecturer, timetables for the recordings were set up.

All participants in this research (students and lecturers) were fully informed of the purpose of this research and their role in it, and signed a form declaring that they fully understood the nature of their participation and their right to request that the recording equipment be turned off if they felt uncomfortable being recorded. They likewise gave their consent to the data gathered being used for research purposes. This included both the linguistic data gathered and their responses to two questionnaires administered before and after the recording.

In order to ensure that the conversations would deal with academic topics (rather than others that might arise, such as personal problems the students were experiencing), the students were asked to prepare two or three questions for their lecturers on one of three topics: written or other assignments that they had completed or were in the process of completing; the systems of assessment used at the host university for that particular course; and/or difficulties being experienced in understanding the course contents. The lecturers were not informed in advance of the content of the questions, although they were made aware of the general areas that the students would wish to discuss.

The conversations took place in the lecturer's office and were video-recorded. After the equipment had been set up, the researcher responsible for the recording left the room and did not enter again until invited to do so by the participants, although after 9 min s/he knocked on the door to warn them that the 10 min foreseen for the conversations to last were almost up. This procedure meant that participants were free to continue talking for as long as they liked, resulting in conversations of unequal length, as might be the case of "real" conversations of this kind.

3.2 *Transcription*

The video-recorded conversations were transcribed, using a slightly modified version of the conventions used for the Vienna-Oxford International Corpus of English (VOICE 2013). For full details of the spelling and mark-up systems used, readers are referred to the research project website: http://www.eurocoat.es/web_sections_1/the_corpus_12. The transcription of each conversation underwent four stages to ensure, as far as possible, the accuracy and homogeneity of the 27 transcripts: the first version of each transcript was the result of the work of one research assistant; this was then checked for accuracy by two other researchers independently. Any disagreements about the way elements of the conversation had been transcribed were discussed and resolved by the three researchers involved. Finally, all transcripts were proof-read and corrected by one person to ensure that the spelling and mark-up conventions had been consistently applied across the corpus. Each transcript was assigned a place identification (UE, UI, UNL and US, refer to recording made in England, Ireland, the Netherlands and Sweden, respectively) followed by a number, referring to the order in which the recordings were made. For example, UNL2 is the transcript of the second recording made at a university in The Netherlands.

3.3 *Data Analysis*

The corpus as a whole comprises 55,718 words,[1] of which 38,384 were uttered by the lecturers and 17,280 by the students. Lexical profiles of the two groups of speakers were generated by dividing the corpus into two sub-corpora (lecturers and students) and subsequently using WordSmith 5.0 to analyse the words used by each group. One interesting finding of this initial investigation of the vocabulary used by the students was that *yeah* and *okay* were, respectively, the third and fourth most frequently used words. A more detailed analysis of the transcripts showed that *yeah* and *okay* were most frequently used as stand-alone items or minimal responses in these conversations. Subsequently, searches of the corpus were undertaken for other minimal response tokens, namely *uhu*, *mhm*, *oh* and *ah*, and also some lexical response tokens (or non-minimal response tokens), namely *right*, *all right* and *perfect*. As in previous studies, the occurrence of each of these items was considered to be a response token only when it occurred in utterance initial position and did not extend into a fuller turn. Instances of repetitions – *yeah yeah* or *okay okay* – were counted as one instance as they constituted a single response to their interlocutor's words.

In the analysis of the use of these tokens as responses to the lecturers' talk, I have made no effort to distinguish between their use as backchannels or as speaker turns. As Tottie (1991) pointed out, it is often very difficult to establish the boundaries of backchannels, because what to the analyst might look like a backchannel may in fact be responded to by an interlocutor, lending it the status of a turn in the context of the interaction in which it was uttered.

In order to investigate substantive recipiency (Waring 2002a), a somewhat different procedure was followed. This sought to explore only two of Waring's three categories – reformulating and jargonizing. The search for instances of reformulating and jargonizing was done, in the first instance, by a close reading of all the transcripts. However, as *so* is a discourse particle that may introduce a reformulation, instances could be automatically retrieved in the same way as the response tokens previously described. Nevertheless, as the focus was not on the use of *so* as

[1] These were the tokens used for generating word lists, and did not include items not found in dictionaries.

a minimal response token (although it could function as one, as will be seen in Sect. 4.2) all instances occurring in utterance initial position were taken into account. As regards jargonizing, Waring defines this as "a means through which prior talk is crystallized in discipline-specific terminology" (2002a, p. 474) and regards it as a particular kind of extending, which

> is motivated by the possibility that there is a technical way of expressing a certain idea within a field, and one [that] supplies that ingroup characterization to invoke the shared context that defines the group... It tends to be brief in length and structurally uncomplicated (e.g., a simple sentence or a phrase) (p. 472).

As Waring found in her study of seminar discussions, such canonical expressions are often metaphors. Thus, because all metaphorical language uses had been tagged in the corpus and studies of their systematic use the subject of a separate study (MacArthur 2016), examples of this particular type of extending can be provided here to illustrate how they were used by some of the student participants.

4 Results

Obvious disfluencies or misunderstandings were extremely rare in these conversations, and, when they did occur, were quickly cleared up. Nevertheless, the lecturers did not appear to think that they had been well understood by the student interlocutors. The mismatch between the subjective impressions of students and lecturers about the success of their conversations was revealed by their responses to a questionnaire administered to all participants after the recording of their conversation – specifically, to statements relating to the ease or difficulty with which the participants had understood each other and others about how natural they thought the conversation had been – on a Likert scale from "completely incorrect" to "completely correct". Two paired-sample t-tests were conducted to discover whether there was any difference of opinion between the lecturers and the students participating in the 27 sessions regarding the naturalness of the conversation and the degree of understanding between them. The results indicate that students (mean=4.39, sd=0.52) seemed to consider the conversation to be more natural than lecturers (mean=4.19, sd=0.79), although the difference was not found to be significant (t=−1.190, p=0.245, df=26). However, students' perception of their level of understanding (mean=4.64, sd=0.506) was much higher than that of lecturers (mean=4.07, sd=0.56), and in this case was statistically significant (t=−3.794, p=0.001, df=26).

4.1 *Minimal Response Tokens in the Student Corpus: An Overview*

Table 1 shows how frequently the students used the different minimal response tokens in their conversations with the lecturers. If the number of uses of minimal response tokens is related to the total number of words uttered by each student in these interactions, it can appreciated that reliance on this kind of response to the lecturer's speech varied among the students. These figures can thus provide some indication of the symmetry or asymmetry of the office hours' consultations recorded, because the adoption of the role of secondary speaker may be revealed by the frequency of use of minimal response tokens by the student participants. Limberg's

Table 1 Use of minimal response tokens in relation to the total number of words uttered by the students in each conversation

Transcript	Total number of words uttered	Total number of minimal response tokens	Percentage (%)
UE1	547	169	30.89
UE2	694	49	7.06
UE3	937	77	8.21
UE4	387	42	10.85
UE5	752	49	6.51
UE6	394	34	8.63
UE7	511	15	0.03
UE8	463	28	6.04
UI1	456	27	5.92
UI2	809	23	2.84
UI3	1409	37	2.62
UI4	846	55	6.50
UI5	1140	113	9.91
UI6	399	108	27.06
UI7	602	65	10.79
UI8	430	43	10.00
UI9	774	35	4.52
UI10	820	81	9.87
UNL1	470	31	6.59
UNL2	462	34	7.35
UNL3	472	54	11.44
UNL4	246	22	8.94
US1	657	36	5.47
US2	706	60	8.49
US3	261	19	7.27
US4	1245	47	3.77
US5	392	71	18.11
TOTALS	**17,281**	**1424**	**8.24**

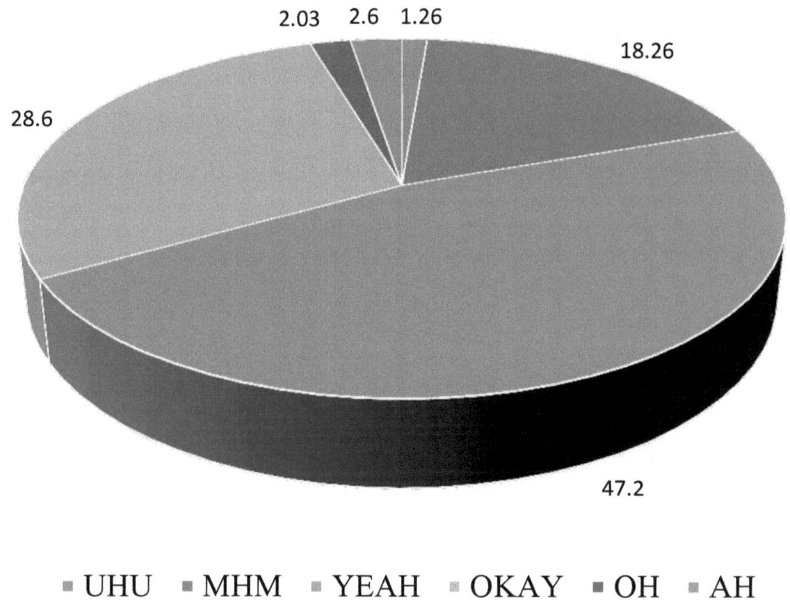

Fig. 1 Overall preference for different minimal response tokens across the student sub-corpus (percentages)

(2010) observation that these kind of conversations tend to be quite asymmetrical is not completely confirmed by the present study because, as can be seen, the adoption of the role of secondary speaker throughout any one conversation was quite variable: the student participating in the conversation labelled UI1 appears to have engaged in a far less symmetrical conversation than the student who participated in the conversation labelled UI7, for example. However, the contrast between these findings and those of Limberg (2010) could very well be the consequence of the fact that the conversations analysed here were not spontaneous office hours' consultations and they were controlled for topic, while Limberg's were not.

Figure 1 shows how the students generally showed a preference for the minimal response tokens *yeah*, *okay* and *mhm*.

More specifically, the use of the tokens *yeah* and *okay* accounted for just over 28 % of the total number of words uttered by the student involved in the conversation labelled UE1, for example. Likewise, the student participating in the conversation labelled UI6 similarly used a relatively high number of these same tokens, which comprised 19.7 % of the total number words she uttered. In contrast, a far lower use was made of *yeah* and *okay* by the students participating in the conversations labelled UI5 and UI2, registering only 2.8 % or a bare 1.7 % respectively in relation to the overall word count.

As can be appreciated in Fig. 2, the tendency for one particular kind of token to be used by the individual students rather than another in the context of the conversation they had with their lecturer may also be discerned. For example, the student in

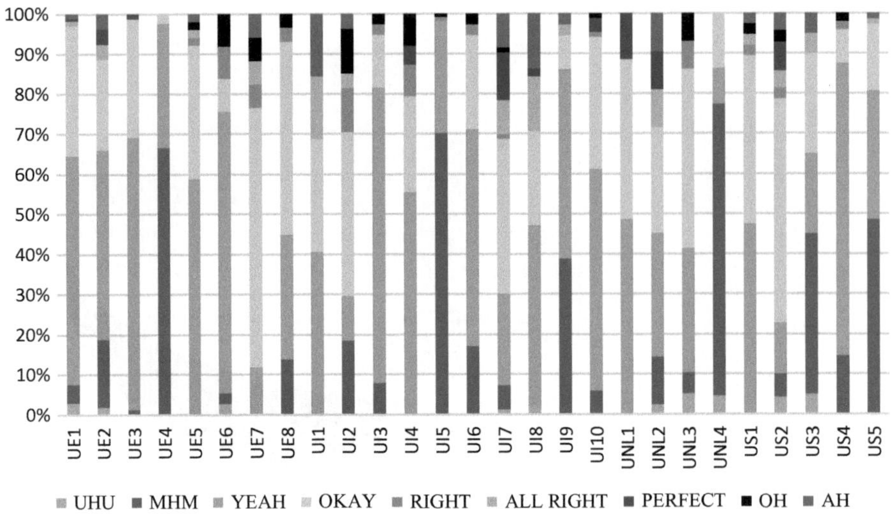

Fig. 2 Use of different minimal response tokens by the students individually

UE4 produced *uhu* a total of 28 times in the course of her conversation with her lecturer, accounting for 66.6 % of her uses of minimal response tokens, but used *yeah* and *okay* relatively infrequently (39 % and 2.3 % respectively), and the student participating in the conversation labelled UI5 produced *mhm* 80 times (70.7 % of the total number of response tokens she used), which is not very significant in terms of the overall number of words she uttered, but contrasts with the absence of any uses of *okay* and a relatively small number of uses of *yeah* (28.3 %) in the same conversation. Similarly, the complete absence of certain tokens in several transcripts (for example, *oh*, *ah*, and even *uhu* or *mhm*) points to a degree of variation in these transcripts which is interesting, in the light of the fact that the conversations were controlled for topic and participants. Further study of these conversations from a qualitative point of view might shed light on the significance of the presence or absence of these tokens in the different mentoring sessions and contribute to efforts made by researchers such as Bernier et al. (2005) or Poteat et al. (2009), which have looked at the optimal pairing of tutors and mentees in similar kinds of interactions. Here it will suffice to point out this variation before moving to consider each of these items in turn.

4.1.1 Minimal Response Tokens. Continuers and Acknowledgers: *YEAH, OKAY, UHU* and *MHM*

As was pointed out in Sect. 3.3, *yeah* and *okay* comprised the third and fourth most frequently used words in the student corpus, which makes them of particular interest to this study. The main difference between those two tokens, according to previous studies, is that *yeah* is typically an acknowledging and aligning token, with high speaker incipiency (Jefferson 1993) whereas *okay* not only signals acknowledgement but also functions as a "change-of-activity" token, inviting the primary speaker to move on to some new topic (Beach 1993). Beach (1993) further associated *okay* not only with simple acknowledgement of what has been said before but also with signalling affiliation. That is, the two tokens have slightly different functions and their judicious use in talk by the secondary speaker may have consequences for the interaction. However, in the case of the Spanish students, they were often used interchangeably and their use, as Farr (2003) also found in her study, were rarely used to signal alignment or agreement, but rather were used – and interpreted by the lecturers – as simple continuers, functioning in similar ways to *uhu* or *mhm.* That is, as Jefferson (1984, p.200) pointed out in relation to *mm hm*, these were used as signals of passive recipiency, and effectively functioned to hand the floor back to the lecturer as primary speaker. The over-use of some of these tokens appears to be far from unusual among L2 speakers of English. Gardner, for example, found that *yeah* was used more frequently by L2 speakers than L1 speakers at a ratio of 5:4 (Gardner 1998, p.207), a high frequency which is reflected also in the EuroCoAT corpus. Romero-Trillo (2002, 2015) likewise remarks on the fossilization of what he terms "pragmatic markers" such as these in L2 speaker discourse, and further holds that many such markers are functionally equivalent to each other, allowing for substitution in different contexts. While this is not a position all analysts would agree with, the evidence from the EuroCoAT corpus points to this possibility, at least as far as the students recorded are concerned. It is difficult to discern much difference in the way students employed *yeah*, *okay* or indeed continuers like *uhu* or *mhm.*

The following extract from a transcript that displayed very frequent uses of *yeah* and *okay* (UE1) shows the use by the student (DI) both as turn slots and backchannels. In all cases, these are interpreted by the lecturer (JW) as simple acknowledgements, with no change of activity or topic initiated by the use of *okay*:

47 JW this is whe- this is where we (.) we put erm
48 DI yeah okay
49 JW all sorts of fo:rms erm (.) er useful web pages (.) study
skills documents
50 DI okay
51 JW erm our module descriptions (.) erm er handbook materials er erm
er exam dates
52 DI yeah
53 JW er so on th- that are relevant to all students regardless
54 DI yeah okay
55 JW of the modules they (.) they're on and erm (.) er so there are some
study skills (.) notes on here (.) and erm i ought to be able to find
it but it's (.) it's probably true that it's not (1) obvious (1) in er (.) er
it'll be in the handbook hh

The combined uses of the two tokens (*yeah okay*) appear to have had no special interactional effects, but were interpreted by the lecturer as the kind of acknowledgement ("I heard what you said"), functioning in much the same way as *uhu* in the academic writing tutorials studied by Thonus (2007, p. 137). Another extract from the same conversation (occurring only a little later in the conversation) confirms this iterative use of these tokens as acknowledgers:

63	JW	on this one (.) erm (1) er (.) this is the erm er (.) year one handbook on here and the
64	DI	okay
65	JW	and the module criteria are within that but it is obviously (.) not as (.) as visible as it could be (.) erm (.) and (.) er this is the handbook (.) for er for year four (.) erm (1) er (.) so (.) erm (1) er yes the (.) the criteria (23) are here (1)
66	DI	okay
67	JW	erm (.) and erm (.) these are the (.) the the college's (.) criteria that
68	DI	yeah yeah yeah
69	JW	th- they're the same across college so the ones you have for english should should be
70	DI	okay
71	JW	identical to this
72	DI	yeah (.) okay (.) good
73	JW	erm (.) er er and erm there is an (.) an extra cri- criterion (.) placed in here to do with language proficiency

Schegloff (1982: 85) observed that the use of the same response in sequence may signal "incipient disinterest", suggesting that repeating the same token in four or five consecutive slots would be the upper limit for creating this effect. In the case of DI, this limit is not reached by one token (*yeah* or *okay*) and the alternation of the two may have prevented this unintended effect. This was not always the case in these conversations, however, as can be observed in the following extract from a conversation (US5) in which a student (DE) has specifically requested that his lecturer (SB) help him understand better the meanings of "amplification attack and control" and "reflection" in Computer Security:

68	SB	i can try to explain and then if we need it we can go back to it
69	DE	mhm
70	SB	hh so the reflecting is erm (1) that you play it off of someone else so you don't go directly (.) to the target?
71	DE	mhm
72	SB	but erm (.) like for example don't you play (.) er pool do you play billiard (.)
73	DE	uhu
74	SB	yes
75	DE	mhm
76	SB	so instead of going directly to the ball you would er then (.) er go to a corner first and then it would reflect and

77	DE	mhm
78	SB	hit it at a different angle
79	DE	yeah
80	SB	and here it's er similar so you don't go to the: target directly but you er use another (.) erm machine to
81	DE	mhm
82	SB	er send the attack there and it can hit it differently and then you can also have hh erm (.) erm an interaction between the two of them that you don't have to worry about so it saves you resources
83	DE	uhu
84	SB	and for amplification (.) you try to (.) exploit some mechanism so that when (.) the input you give in (.) er is multiplied (.) and erm you can do this (.) i:n the number of messages (.) so if you send something to a broadcast address and everyone
85	DE	yeah
86	SB	responds then you get many more messages
87	DE	hm (.)
88	SB	or it could be erm in terms of size so if you send something (.) a query to er (.) erm d n s domain name system
89	DE	mhm

A very simple observation can be made about this part of the conversation between the lecturer and the student: the lecturer is obliged to do all the work, with insufficient response from her interlocutor that lets her know that her explanation is proving useful. His repeated uses of the continuers *uhu* and *mhm*, as well as two uses of *yeah* appears to spur the lecturer to ever greater efforts to reformulate and expand her explanations in order to ensure the student's understanding. The impression of disengagement or lack of interest created by the student's repeated use of these minimal response tokens may have been no reflection of what was actually going on in the his mind (he may very well have found the explanation very illuminating), but would have been likely to contribute to the lecturer's impression that she was failing to make herself understood.

4.1.2 Minimal Response Tokens: Change-of-State Indicators *OH* and *AH*

In the context of an office hours' consultation, where students are specifically seeking advice and information relating to their academic work, it would seem that response tokens that indicate that information previously known to only one of the speakers (in this case, the lecturer) has become shared or common ground would be used with a certain frequency by the student participants. Two minimal response tokens that are often associated with this function are *oh* and *ah*. Heritage (1984, p. 305), for example, described *oh* as indicating a change of state, strongly signalling that "the producer has been informed as a result of a prior turn's talk". In this regard, the very low numbers of uses of *oh* (as well as of *ah*, which may fulfill a similar function) in the student corpus (see Fig. 1) is arresting. In four of the transcripts, no uses of either token were found, and even the largest number of occurrences (5 in UI4) were extremely small in comparison with *yeah* and *okay*. In fact, *oh* regularly co-occurred with *yeah* in this conversation, and in others also with *okay*, and was used by the students in response to very specific (critical) feedback on their work. The following extract from UI4 illustrates this use:

89 AM erm don't forget to sk- spell john elliott's name right (.) it's amazing the number of people hh who (.) just have elliott with one t (.) erm
90 PP oh yeah
91 AM er
92 PP i don't know
93 AM did you buy his book
94 PP yeah (.) i've got it
95 AM erm (2) hh i think most of my comments here were just linguistic (.) er (2) i mean they're typographical errors i think fifteen-seventy rather than si- sixteen-seventy there (.) erm <reading aloud> fortune has stripped you of your splendour </reading aloud> you s- you wrote striped (.) so there's two ps in
96 PP oh yeah

Norrick (2012: p. 571) has suggested that *oh* may indicate some difficulty in accepting or assimilating new information and may thus elicit continuation by the prior speaker. In the conversations analysed here, it did not appear to function in this way. Rather, when coupled with the acknowledgement tokens *yeah* and *okay*, *oh* signals that the correction or information offered has been understood and accepted.

Uses of *ah* by the students was virtually identical to that of *oh*, often co-occurring with *yeah* or *okay*. In the following extract, the reception of the specific advice that the lecturer (OL) is offering a Business Studies student (JR) on an assignment he is preparing seems to have been interpreted by the lecturer as successfully completed, as signaled by her use of "good okay" in 74, which preceded a transition to another topic:

58 OL this is going to tie (.) this ratio (.) is going to tie into what they have (.) and you're going to be able to see that they will have analysed the loss (.) and why
59 JR okay
60 OL there is a loss (.) and you need to relate your discussion of this ratio (.) into
61 JR ah
62 OL their work
63 JR ah okay
64 OL and that's that's how you work as the group

65 JR yeah
66 OL so you can look at this individually (.) they will look at their section individually but then you need to come toGEther
67 JR xx
68 OL and you look at their insights and you get you can understand more this ratio
69 JR o:h
70 OL there (.) so that will be good when when your colleague has completed the profitability ratios you look at
71 JR ah
72 OL look at them and you tie that back (.) okay? (.)
73 JR okay
74 OL good (.) okay

Norrick's finding (2012, p. 571) that *oh* "disrupt[s] the primary speaker's turn in progress" is not replicated in the data examined here. Rather, both *oh* and *ah* are reacted to by the primary speaker as supportive tokens that function (as turn slots or backchannels) to indicate that the listener has understood the information s/he is hearing.

4.2 Non-Minimal Response Tokens: Right, All Right *and* Perfect

Following McCarthy (2003) or Farr (2003), the present analysis distinguishes between minimal and non-minimal response tokens. The latter consist of lexical items or phrases that occurred in the corpus as single utterances used to respond to the lecturers' talk or alongside other tokens, such as those considered in the previous section. The list of possible non-minimal response tokens in conversation is a long one (see McCarthy 2003 or O'Keeffe et al. 2007, pp. 140–155 for examples), and may include a number of different words and phrases, such as *really*, *right*, *good*, *quite*, *fair enough* or *that's true*. However, it should be acknowledged at the outset that the division established between one type of token and another may serve to play down the similarity between them in terms of their roles and functions in conversation. For example, as has been discussed in the previous section, *oh* is often regarded as functioning as a change-of-state marker, that there has been for the speaker some kind of "change in his or her locally current state of knowledge or information" (Heritage 1984; 299), a function that is not dissimilar to that of *right*. Gardner (2007: 329) observes that *"[r]ight*s are … response tokens that occur following units of talk that at least appear to progress the epistemic store", but points out that other tokens (including *uhu*, *mhm*, *okay* or *all right*) can also fulfill the same functions. In this regard, two (*right* and *all right*) of the three non-minimal response tokens focused on here have been chosen because they can function as what Gardner

(2007 p. 335) refers to as "epistemic dependency tokens". He describes these tokens in the following terms:

> epistemic dependency tokens … progress the shared epistemic store, extending the common ground between speakers. They are claims on the part of the recipient that he or she recognizes the prior unit of talk as being dependent on some other talk, and that these are part of a complex activity such as an extended informing or advice-giving sequence. Such activities are rich grounds for presenting information (p. 335).

They were thus considered to be of relevance to the academic interactions under consideration here. *Perfect*, on the other hand, was singled out for attention because of its relative frequency in the corpus as a response token used by some of the Spanish Erasmus students.

Figure 3 shows the frequency of use in each of the transcripts.

As can be appreciated, what is particularly interesting about the use of *right* is that 24 of the 27 students (88.8 %) who participated in the study never used this token at all. This is particularly significant in the light of Gardner's remarks on the use of *right* in British and Australian English: the L2 speakers of English recorded at the different universities in Europe showed very little awareness or command of this particular token in signalling understanding of the information they had been given in a prior unit of talk. Nor can the use made of this token be related to greater proficiency in English on the part of the three students who did produce *right*: in the cases of the students participating in the conversations labeled UE2 and UE5, there was no language requirement in place at their host universities at the time the recordings were made, and in the case of the student taking part in the conversation labeled US5, the language requirement was a B2. Considering, then, that some of the other student participants attested a C1 in English, the absence of *right* in the conversations involving the latter cannot be attributed to any prior assessment of

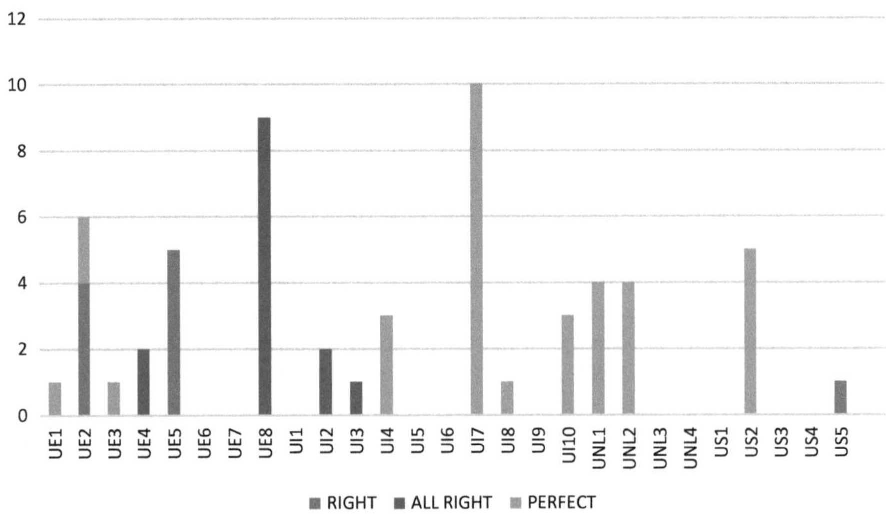

Fig. 3 Number of uses of different non-minimal response tokens by the students individually

their interactional skills in English, but rather seemed to be linked to particular response styles, peculiar to the individual participants as well as to the particular conversations in which they participated.

Likewise, the use of *all right* and *perfect* were very unevenly distributed across the student cohort. In the case of *all right*, only four of the 27 students (14.8 %) produced this token, while ten (37 %) used *perfect* to acknowledge and align themselves with the advice they had been offered. As a consequence of the meaning of *perfect* ("not having any faults" or "as good as possible; the best of its kind", according to the Longman Dictionary), this token functioned not just to signal acknowledgement of the information or advice received but also contained a strong appreciation of it. But again, this token (a very useful one in terms of the interpersonal relations being built in the course of these exchanges) was used by less than half the students and is thus another indication that response styles may vary quite considerably across an otherwise homogeneous group. It also indicates that the individual conversations had specific features that cannot be captured adequately by corpus linguistics methods of analysis: even though all the students spoke with their lecturers about similar topics, the way that each conversation unfolded was different, and the use of *perfect* – or indeed the display of any type of response behaviour – cannot be adequately explained without reference to the whole of the interaction in which it took place. In the case of *perfect*, those who used this token did so either when the information received had cleared up something that appeared to have been particularly worrying them or at the close of conversations as a signal of appreciation of the time and effort expended by the lecturers in giving them the advice and information they sought. However, its absence in other conversation is of equal interest, because it cannot be claimed that those who used *perfect* were more or less worried or more or less appreciative, only that they did not express themselves in this particular way.

4.3 Substantive Recipiency: Reformulating and Jargonizing

Waring (2002a: 454) describes "substantive recipiency" as:

> the verbal resources deployed by discussion participants to indicate "I'm following you" or "I'm trying to follow you" without actually saying so. It involves demonstrating comprehension through the construction of candidate understandings. It reflects the communicative goal of being attentive (by means of continuing an old topic) as opposed to its competing goal of introducing a new topic.

She excluded silence, backchannels or continuers as showing this substantive recipiency, as well as assessments of the prior talk, focusing instead on three ways that speakers (in this case, also university students) may make a minor contribution to the topic without performing actions that change the direction of talk. The three realizations of substantive recipiency focused on in Waring's study were reformulating, extending and jargonizing. Here, I will limit myself to two of these (reformulating and jargonizing) in order to make some remarks on the importance of this kind of verbal behaviour in intercultural academic interaction.

The discourse particle *so* has been approached in different ways by different researchers. Among these, Schiffrin (1987) highlighted the use of *so* in conversation with the relationship between ideas in discourse, when speakers signal that they have inferred something from prior talk ("inferential *so*"). It can thus preface the kind of reformulation discussed by Waring: students may express their understanding of what their lecturers have told them by a reformulation prefaced by *so*. The following extract comes from a conversation between a student of Biomedical Engineering (AG) and a lecturer (PD) teaching in an undergraduate degree in Health and Safety (UI6), a conversation that involved lengthy explanation of the topic of a lecture the student had missed about layer of protection analysis. Throughout the interaction, the student had mostly limited her responses to the explanations offered by tokens such as *yeah* or *okay*. However, about 7 min after the conversation began, this response behaviour changed substantially:

109	AG	okay
110	PD	and then (.) additional to that then (.) is the next layer where
111	AG	yeah
112	PD	you you have a fire-brigade
113	AG	yeah
114	PD	and you have ambulance and you have trained (.) emergency (.) response (.) teams (.) yeah?
115	AG	yeah
116	PD	that's that's what it means
117	AG	so e it's a: every em company have to: do this for each e:m
118	PD	kind of yeah (.) well in in principal yeah

At 117, the student reformulates what the lecturer has said, in order to check that she has understood correctly. As can be seen from the lecturer's response, her inference is not sufficiently well expressed to allow him to concur that this is exactly what he meant. More interesting is that, once the student had found a way to participate more actively in this mentoring session, by expressing her understanding of what the lecturer had told her, she went on to use the same strategy again on another three occasions, one of which closely followed the one already illustrated:

126	PD	and (.) the law in ireland probably the same in spain (.) er requires (.) the the company to show (.) how are you going to protect (.)
127	AG	yeah
128	PD	if the vessel explodes or
129	AG	mhm
130	PD	how will you stop it from exploding first (.) and if it does explode (.) how will you stop it from (.) spreading (.) out of the site and so on
131	AG	so we have different methods to pr- to protect or to
132	PD	yeah

In this second instance, the lecturer ratifies the student's reformulation (expressed as an inference), and this allowed the lecturer to move on to explanation of another aspect of layer of protection analysis.

As was found with the response tokens, the use of *so* by the student cohort was uneven, with five students (18.5 %) never using it in turn-initial position, while one student (UE2) used it a total of 13 times to introduce a reformulation, most often beginning "okay so…". It should also be pointed out that *so* was often used by some students as a stand-alone item or at the end of an utterance, prompting a reformulation by the lecturer, rather than in order to express what they had inferred from his/her talk. This "prompt" or "non-prefatory" use of *so* has been examined by different scholars, who have reached somewhat different conclusions about its functions. Lam (2009), for example, regards it simply as a turn-yielding device, while Schiffrin (1987) similarly saw it as marking a potential turn transition, but also pointed out that the turn could in fact be completed by the current speaker. In relation to L2 speakers of English, two studies (Müller 2005 and Buysse 2014) have examined non-prefatory uses of *so* with somewhat different results, quantitatively speaking. Müller (2005), for example, found German speakers of English used *so* to mark implied result in similar ways to L1 speakers. In contrast, Buysse (2014) found that Dutch learners of English used "prompt" *so* significantly more frequently than in the native speakers' speech. He attributed this to the fact that "the learners' inventory of cues to prompt their interlocutors to draw inferences may be limited" (Buysse 2014, p. 29). The findings of the present study do not confirm this relatively high frequency of non-prefatory *so* in L2 discourse. Rather, as has been seen in the case of the minimal and non-minimal response tokens discussed in Sects. 4.1 and 4.2, the use of *so* varies a great deal in the EuroCoAT student, as shown in Fig. 4.

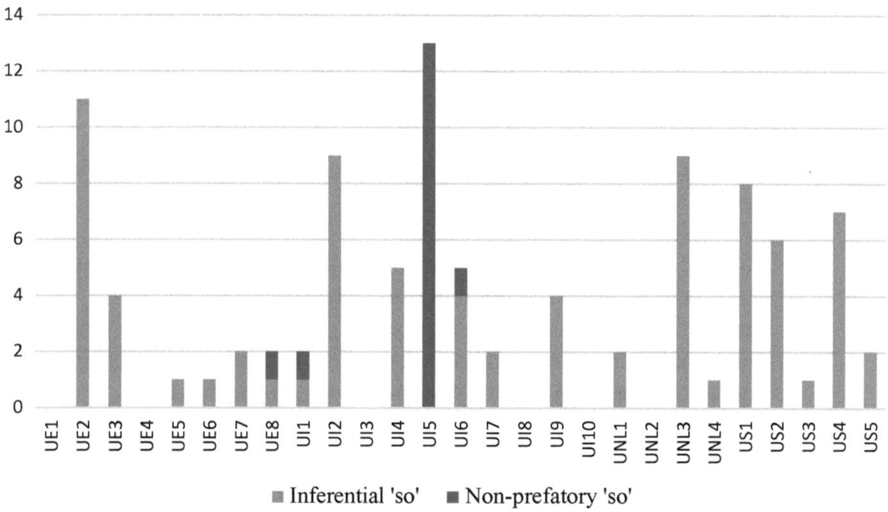

Fig. 4 Number of uses of inferential and non-prefatory ("prompt") *so*

Figure 4 shows a relatively high frequency of use of "prompt" or non-prefatory *so* by the student in UI5. This is quite interesting, given that, as was seen in Sect. 4.1., this particular student used the tokens *yeah* and *okay* quite infrequently, and the difference between the use of these tokens and non-prefatory *so* may indicate a preference for the latter as a turn-yielding device. However, the fundamental difference between non-minimal response tokens like the ones considered earlier and this use of *so* is that this item typically marks main units of the discourse (Schiffrin 1987), which may be "controlled" by either participant in a conversation. Therefore to generalize about its functions as a "lexical teddy bear" (Hasselgren 1994, cited in Buysse 2014, p. 29) may be quite wide of the mark in the case of the office hours' consultations examined here. Rather, as will be seen below, the student participating in the conversation labelled UI5 was among those who displayed greatest substantive recipiency in terms of jargonizing, and the use of non-prefatory *so* in this particular interaction may therefore reveal something quite different from the somewhat passive turn yielding described in previous studies. However, as is the case of the other items described in this article, these different functions of *so* can only be briefly mentioned here, while acknowledging that they deserve closer attention.

Jargonizing, or the specific ability to use the metaphorical language typical of spoken academic discourse, was again found to be extremely uneven across the student cohort, with exceptional ability shown by some students (for example, in transcripts UI2, UI5 or US3) in contrast with a complete absence of any ability to match the lecturers' metaphors in their responses to the advice or information they were being given (for example, in transcript UE2). These findings are reported fully in MacArthur et al. (2015), MacArthur (2016) and MacArthur and Alejo-González (in preparation), and here it will suffice to mention that analysis of metaphorical language uses in the corpus showed that there was a great deal of systematicity in the way that the English-speaking lecturers talked about certain topics. Among the metaphor themes that were identified as particularly significant in these interactions were UNDERSTANDING IS SEEING or WRITING IS SPEAKING. Substantive recipiency could be displayed by the students' repetition or elaboration of the metaphorically-used words and phrases present in the lecturer's talk, such as when a student receiving feedback on an essay responded to a lecturer's talk about how her essay could have been improved:

27 FL so this (.) this ONE thing is something that you need to **pick out**
from your essay (.) **lift out** and **make clearer** (.) this is your
main idea (.) you're not talking about (.) oscar wilde or (.) or or
the (.) article (.) you are talking about how he contraDICTS
himself in the article this is your **point** (.) and you need
to **lift it out** (1)
28 RH yeah (.) I have to be more **clear** (.) I know

The student's summary of the lecturer's metaphorical formulation of the problems he found in her essay shows the kind of substantive recipiency discussed by Waring (2002a) and her involved a near repetition of the lecturers words (*clearer*-

clear). On another occasion during the same conversation, her response to the lecturer's iterative use of saying verbs (*say*, *tell*, *contradict*, *argue*, *talk*) to refer to written communication was equally coherent with the metaphors the lecturer used (for fuller discussion of this conversation, see MacArthur 2015):

40	RH	but what when i **speak** em (.) like being me?
41	FL	mhm
42	RH	e i can't put i or
43	FL	no (.) avoid that

5 Discussion and Conclusions

As has been seen from the overview of the response behaviour examined in the course of this article, the way that Spanish undergraduate students used the verbal resources of English to display understanding varied quite substantially. While there might have been a preference for minimal response tokens such as *yeah* and *okay* to express "I'm following you" among the student cohort, this was by no means uniform, and the presence of other, equally important tokens in the context of conversations aimed at increasing the student's epistemic store, such as *oh* or *right*, was even more uneven.

No attempt has been made in the course of this article to relate this to the attested language proficiency of the students on entry to the host university. This is due, on the one hand, to the fact that two of the universities which the Erasmus students were enrolled in did not, at the time of making these recordings, have a minimum language requirement in place, so in many cases the students had not been formally assessed using the Common European Framework of Reference for Languages (CEFR) scales of competence. On the other hand, there are indications from the corpus that the kind of interactional skills displayed in the transcripts were not related to the students' overall competence in English, as has been seen in discussion of one student's use of *right* in Sect. 4.2. Nevertheless, given the lecturers' subjective impressions of the ease or difficulty of coordinating meanings and understandings in these conversations, it seems clear that students generally need to be able to signal clearly how well they are understanding a lecturer's talk. The students appeared to think they had done so, but the lecturers did not always agree.

I have traced this mismatch to students' response behaviour, looking at two major ways that understanding may be signaled: through the use of response tokens (minimal and non-minimal) and through substantive recipiency. For reasons of space, the descriptions offered have focused only on some salient features of listenership behaviour in a corpus of 27 conversations. Nevertheless, the overview provided draws attention to the need for further research into these and other similar discourse events. For international students generally, the office hours' consultation – or the opportunity to talk to a lecturer or tutor face-to-face about problematic aspects of the academic work being undertaken – is likely to comprise an important learning opportunity, given the differences between the academic cultures of the home and host universities. It will be on those occasions that students may raise (and seek to have resolved) problems relating to their incomplete understanding of course contents, how to do written and other assignments or what assessment systems are in place, among many other topics that have to do with differences between their own and the host university. Such issues will not tend to be dealt with in other types of teaching/learning activities they experience at the host university, since the academic enculturation of undergraduate students tends to take place in the first year of a degree, while Erasmus students do not go abroad until their second or third year. Yet the incoming students need to fully understand these aspects of academic life and be able to consult their lecturers about them.

However, it may turn out that in some cases the efforts having to be made by English-speaking lecturers in these intercultural conversations prove so great that they become unwilling to expend such efforts in the face of the passive recipiency or apparent lack of understanding displayed by L2 students such as those that took part in the present study. The (probably unintentional) lack of engagement displayed by the student who participated in the conversation referred to as US5 (Sect. 4.1.2), for example, might well have had knock-on effects, provoking a negative assessment of the student's understanding or even leading to the lecturer's unwillingness to engage in another consultation session of this kind with this particular student. This is pure speculation, of course, but it can still be stated that it will be necessary for Spanish undergraduate students to master the interactional skills that will enable them to participate actively in this kind of conversation.

As I have tried to show, this active or "engaged" listenership is not displayed only through appropriate use of response tokens: more substantial contributions to an academic conversation also point to how well a student is understanding the advice or information he or she is receiving. Investigating this kind of substantial recipiency is only partially amenable to corpus linguistics techniques (although it is possible to automatically retrieve particular instances of jargonizing if a corpus has been tagged for such uses, as was the case for the metaphorical language present in the corpus). But this limitation is also evident in the analysis of the type of response tokens in small or large corpora that can be identified, retrieved and quantified using appropriate software: even when information becomes available about the variation in the uses of response tokens in different conversations, it will also be necessary to examine each transcript in detail in order to account fully for their presence or absence in any one specific interaction. Apart from anything else, a conversation is the product of the joint production of the participants (in this case lecturer-student dyads) and attention to the input of only one of the pair (in this case, the student) may well prove misleading when seeking to fully account for the relative success of an interaction. The present article has not attempted to provide such an account, given the quantity of data (relatively speaking) that it would be necessary to examine in order to answer the question why – in any given conversation – some tokens have been preferred by certain speakers over others or why some have been frequently used by some students and not at all by others.

However, it seems to me that these difficulties should not deter efforts to further investigate this important aspect of academic talk, even if involves a very lengthy research programme. The investment in mobility programmes – not only financial, but also in terms of the human resources involved – makes it vital to foster successful intercultural dialogue between at least two of the parties involved (students and lecturers) if the experience of study abroad in programmes such as Erasmus are to be as fruitful as could be desired. Learning more about how pairs of lecturers and international students coordinate meanings and understandings more or less successfully in face-to-face conversation would certainly contribute to this.

Acknowledgement The research reported here was made possible by funding of the project (reference: FFI2011-22809) by the Spanish *Ministerio de Ciencia e Innovación.*

References

Beach, W. (1993). Transitional regularities for 'casual' "Okay" usages. *Journal of Pragmatics, 19*, 325–352.

Bernier, A., Larose, S., & Soucy, N. (2005). Academic mentoring in college: The interactive role of student's and mentor's interpersonal dispositions. *Research in Higher Education, 46*(1), 29–51.

Buysse, L. (2014). "So what's a year in a lifetime so". Non-prefatory use of so in native and learner English. *Text & Talk, 34*(1), 23–47.

Chiang, S.-Y. (2011). Pursuing a response in office hour interactions between US college students and international teaching assistants. *Journal of Pragmatics, 43*, 3316–3330.

Coleman, J. A. (2006). English-medium teaching in European higher education. *Language Teaching, 39*(1), 1–14.

Farr, F. (2003). Engaged listenership in spoken academic discourse: The case of student-tutor meetings. *Journal of English for Academic Purposes, 2*, 67–85.

Gardner, R. (1998). Between speaking and listening: The vocalisation of understandings. *Applied Linguistics, 19*(2), 204–224.

Gardner, R. (2005). Acknowledging strong ties between Utterances in talk: Connections through *Right* as a response token. In *Proceedings of the 2004 conference of the Australian linguistic society. http://prijipati.library.usyd.edu.au/bitstream/2123/115/1/ALS-20050630-RG.pdf*

Gardner, R. (2007). The *Right* connections: Acknowledging epistemic progression in talk. *Language in Society, 36*(3), 319–341.

Heritage, J. (1984). A change-of-state token and aspects of its sequential placement. In J. Maxwell Atkinson & J. Heritage (Eds.), *Structures of social action* (pp. 299–347). Cambridge: Cambridge University Press.

House, J. (2013). Developing pragmatic competence in English as a lingua franca: Using discourse markers to express (inter)subjectivity and connectivity. *Journal of Pragmatics, 59*, 57–67.

Jefferson, G. (1984). Notes on a systematic deployment of the acknowledgement tokens "Yeah" and "Mm hm". *Papers in Linguistics, 17*(2), 197–216.

Jefferson, G. (1993). Caveat speaker: Preliminary notes on recipient topic-shift implicature. *Research on Language and Social Interaction, 26*, 1–30.

Lam, P. W.Y. (2009). The effect of text type on the use of so as a discourse particle. *Discourse Studies, 11*(3), 353–372.

Limberg, H. (2007). Discourse structure of academic talk in university office hour interactions. *Discourse Studies, 9*(2), 176–193.

Limberg, H. (2010). *The interactional organization of academic talk.* Amsterdam: John Benjamins.

MacArthur, F. (2015). On using a dictionary to identify the basic senses of words. *Metaphor and the Social World, 5*(1), 124–136.
MacArthur, F. (2016). Overt and covert uses of metaphor in the academic mentoring in English of Spanish undergraduate students at five European universities. *Review of Cognitive Linguistics, 14*(1), 23–50.
MacArthur, F., & Alejo-González, R. (in preparation). The Erasmus challenge: Metaphor in the academic mentoring of undergraduate students.
MacArthur, F., Krennmayr, T., & Littlemore, J. (2015). How basic is "UNDERSTANDING IS SEEING" when reasoning about knowledge? Asymmetric uses of sight metaphors in office hours' consultations in English as academic lingua franca. *Metaphor and Symbol, 30*(3), 184–217.
McCarthy, M. (2002). Good listenership made plain: British and American non-minimal response tokens in everyday conversation. In R. Reppen, S. M. Fitzmaurice, & D. Biber (Eds.), *Using Corpora to explore linguistic variation* (pp. 49–71). Amsterdam: John Benjamins.
McCarthy, M. (2003). Talking back: "Small" interactional response tokens in everyday conversation. *Research on Language and Social Interaction, 36*(1), 33–63.
McCarthy, M. (2009). Rethinking spoken fluency. *ELIA, 9*, 11–29.
Müller, S. (2005). *Discourse markers in native and non-native English discourse*. Amsterdam/Philadelphia: John Benjamins.
Norrick, N. R. (2012). Listening practices in English conversation: The responses responses elicit. *Journal of Pragmatics, 44*, 566–576.
O'Keeffe, A., McCarthy, M., & Carter, R. (2007). *From corpus to classroom: Language use and language teaching*. Cambridge: Cambridge University Press.
Poteat, L. F., Shockley, K. M., & Allen, T. D. (2009). Mentor-protégé commitment fit and relationship satisfaction in academic mentoring. *Journal of Vocational Behavior, 74*, 332–337.
Reinhardt, J. (2010). Directives in office hour consultations: A corpus-informed investigation of learner and expert usage. *English for Specific Purposes, 29*, 94–107.
Romero-Trillo, J. (2002). The pragmatic fossilization of discourse markers in non-native speakers of English. *Journal of Pragmatics, 34*, 769–784.
Romero-Trillo, J. (2015). 'It is a truth universally acknowledged' … you know? The role of adaptive management and prosody to start a turn in conversation. *Pragmatics and Society, 6*(1), 117–145.
Sacks, H. (1992). In G. Jefferson (Ed.), *Lectures on conversation, vols. 1 and 2*. Oxford: Blackwell.
Schegloff, E. (1982). Discourse as an interactional achievement: Some uses of 'uh huh' and other things that come between sentences. In D. Tannen (Ed.), *Analyzing discourse: Text and talk* (pp. 71–93). Washington: Georgetown University Press.
Schiffrin, D. (1987). *Discourse markers*. Cambridge: Cambridge University Press.
Skyrme, G. (2010). Is this a stupid question? International undergraduate students seeking help from teachers during office hours. *Journal of English for Academic Purposes, 9*, 211–221.
Thonus, T. (2007). Listener responses as a pragmatic resource for learners of English. *The CATESOL Journal, 19*(1), 132–145.
Tottie, G. (1991). Conversational style in British and American English: The case of backchannels. In K. Aijmer & B. Altenberg (Eds.), *English corpus linguistics*. London: Longman.
Voice. (2013). *The Vienna-Oxford International Corpus of English* (version 2.0 online). Director: Barbara Seidlhofer; Researchers: Angelika Breiteneder, Theresa Klimpfinger, Stefan Majewski, Ruth Osimk-Teasdale, Marie-Luise Pitzl, Michael Radeka. http://voice.univie.ac.at (24/10/2014).
Waring, H. Z. (2002a). Displaying substantive recipiency in seminar discussion. *Research on Language and Social Interaction, 35*(4), 453–479.
Waring, H. Z. (2002b). Expressing noncomprehension in a US graduate seminar. *Journal of Pragmatics, 34*(12), 1711–1731.
Willemyns, M., Gallois, C., & Callan, V. J. (2006). Conversations between postgraduate students and their supervisors: Intergroup communication and accommodation. In *The first world congress on the power of language: Theory, practice and development*.
Young, R. F. (2013). Learning to talk the talk and walk the walk: Interactional competence in academic spoken English. *Ibérica, 25*, 15–38.

Focusing on Content or Language?: Comparing Paired Conversations in CLIL and EFL Classrooms, Using a Corpus

Keiko Tsuchiya

Abstract This preliminary comparative study examines two dyad interactions of Japanese learners of English in a Content and Language Integrated Learning classroom (CLIL) and a General English class (GE) at a Japanese university, focusing on *discourse framework* and the use of *repair*. Three research questions are addressed here: between these two settings, (1) are there any similarities and differences in numbers of words, turns and speaking time in the learner-learner dialogues?, (2) how do the learners frame *discourses*, and (3) what *repairables* are marked and what *repair strategies* are used in the respective contexts? The findings indicate longer but fewer turns were characterised in the interaction in the GE interaction, while shorter and frequent turn exchanges occurred in the CLIL one, which relates to discourse frameworks in the interactions in the two settings. *Endorsement framework* (topic initiation → suggestion for decision making → (dis-)alignment) was observed in the CLIL conversation with the frequent use of *joint production*, whereas the learners in GE adapted *narrative framework* (topic initiation → narrating → acknowledgement). The students in both contexts paid attention to linguistic/factual repairables. However, procedural repairables were marked only by the participants in the CLIL interaction. To repair the trouble sources, both self-repair and other-repair were used in the CLIL students although the GE participants only used the former. The distinct features in the two learner interactions might derive from differences in types of *communicative action* (c.f. Habermas J, Some further clarification of the concept of communicative rationality. In: Cooke M (ed) On the pragmatics of communication. The MIT Press, Cambridge, MA, pp 307–382, 1996).

Keywords Learner-learner interaction • Framing • Repair • Communicative action

K. Tsuchiya (✉)
International Education Centre, Tokai University,
4-1-1 Kitakaname, Hiratsuka, Kanagawa 2591292, Japan
e-mail: ktsuchiya@tokai-u.jp

J. Romero-Trillo (ed.), *Yearbook of Corpus Linguistics and Pragmatics 2016*,
Yearbook of Corpus Linguistics and Pragmatics 4,
DOI 10.1007/978-3-319-41733-2_9

1 Introduction

The question – what makes learner-learner interactions different in classrooms? – has been one of the themes I am interested in (Taylor and Tsuchiya 2007; Tsuchiya 2013a, 2014, 2015). This paper reports a preliminary comparative study of learner-learner interactions in a Content and Language Integrated Learning classroom (CLIL, hereafter) and a General English class (GE, hereafter) at a Japanese university, focusing on *discourse framework* and the use of *repair.* Three research questions are addressed here: between these two settings, (1) are there any similarities and differences in numbers of words, turns and speaking time in learner-learner dialogues?, (2) how do the learners frame *discourse*, and (3) what *repairables* are marked and what *repair strategies* are used in the respective contexts?

CLIL integrates acquisition of subject knowledge with language learning, either a second or foreign language, simultaneously (Mehisto et al. 2008). Its dual focus on both content and language distinguishes CLIL from immersion and content-based instruction (ibid: 13). CLIL has been implemented in primary, secondary and tertiary education in Europe since the late 1990s to promote the multilingual policy to enhance the mobility of the populations within the EU (Breidback and Viebrock 2013). Recently CLIL has been introduced in other parts of the world, i.e. Asian and Latin American countries, and higher education in Japan is no exception (Ikeda et al. 2013). Although CLIL is a relatively new approach, a large body of research is now available: theories and rationales of CLIL (Coyle et al. 2010; Mehisto et al. 2008); language policies underlying CLIL implementations (Fortanet-Gomez 2013; Smit and Dafouz 2012); CLIL courses in Japanese higher education (Izumi et al. 2012; Sasajima 2011; Watanabe et al. 2011); and research on interactions in CLIL classrooms from perspectives of systemic functional grammar (Dalton-Puffer 2007; Hynninen 2011), discourse/conversation analysis (Llinares et al. 2012; Nikula 2007) and lexical approach (Watanabe 2013).

Communication is one of the core factors in the 4 Cs framework of CLIL, the other three being *Content*, *Cognition* and *Culture* (Coyle et al. 2010, pp.36–38). Nikula (2005) examines classroom discussions in CLIL and EFL learners in lower/upper secondary school in Finland, concluding that the feature of detachment in learner-learner discourse was observed in the EFL classrooms while learners showed more involvement in discussions in the CLIL classrooms. Moore (2011) also compares interactions in paired conversations between learners in CLIL and mainstream (henceforth MS) classrooms in secondary school in Spain, reporting that there were more occurrences of collaborative turns among the CLIL learners than the MS learners (also cited in Nikula et al. 2013). Nikula et al. (2013: 74) categorise discourse research in CLIL classrooms into three categories: (1) CLIL classroom discourse and language use, (2) CLIL classroom discourse and knowledge construction in the L2, and (3) CLIL classroom discourse and language learning. This preliminary study relates to the first category of the classification in Nikula et al. (2013), but an emphasis is placed on the framing of discourse.

The features in learner-learner discussions in higher education are discussed here, considering some other perspectives from social practices, such as learners' agency and their rationality in the wider social communities they belong to. Learners perform social actions through classroom interactions. On the basis of the speech act theory (Austin 1962; Searle 1969), Habermas (1986, 1996) conceptualised *communicative rationality*, categorising social actions into three types: *intentional action*, *communicative action* and *strategic action*.

Exemplary types	Types of action/Modes of language use
Propositional and intentional sentences used "mentally"("pure" representation and "monological" action planning)	Intentional action/Noncommunicative
Normatively nonembedded expressions of will	Weak communication action/Oriented toward reaching understanding
Completely illocutionary acts (expressive, normative, constative)	Strong communicative action/Oriented toward agreement
Perlocutions	Strategic action/Oriented toward consequences (indirect mutual understanding)

Adapted from: Habermas (1996: 333–334)

Intentional action refers to representations of affairs or 'monological' plans of action, which thus is noncommunicative. Strategic action is used to achieve *indirect* mutual understanding without reciprocal processes between the speaker and the addressee, which can be realised through 'moral reproach' or 'legal threats' (Habermas 1996: 331). Communicative action has two sub-categories, *weak* and *strong* communicative actions, which are distinguished from each other according to their orientations: the former aims towards *mutual understanding*, while the latter requires *agreement* among the interlocutors. The notion of the *weak/strong communicative action* are taken into considerations in the discussion.

Another underlying agenda here is to test the feasibility of the research methodology, which integrates a quantitative corpus-based analysis with qualitative discourse and conversation analytic approaches. The integration of corpus study with other qualitative approaches has been attempted by corpus linguists in several studies (Adolphs 2008; Partington et al. 2013; Taylor 2008; Tsuchiya 2013b; Walsh et al. 2011), yet still waits for further development of the methodologies. I adopted both quantitative and qualitative methodologies to reveal the complex phenomena of learner-learner interactions in classrooms as Yang (2014) applied the integrated approach to his study of teachers' use of discourse markers 'to probe into different levels of discourse (ibid: 297)'. Llinares and Romero-Trillo (2008) also conducted a corpus-based analysis to compare the pragmatic use of discourse markers in native/non-native teachers in CLIL classrooms in English and L1 subject teachers, finding that non-native CLIL teachers used instrumental discourse markers more frequently than native CLIL teachers and L1 teachers. As shown in these previous studies, both qualitative and quantitative approaches are applied to this study. The following two sections will review existing studies in *discourse framework* and strategies of *repair*.

2 Framing Discourse

Discourse frameworks, in other words 'the structure of interaction' (c.f. Goffman 1981: 53), in various contexts have been studied in the areas of conversation analysis and discourse analysis. Some conversation analysts have examined discourse framework in the contexts of medical and healthcare communication, such as *online commentary* in Heritage and Stivers (1999) and *the Dallas call*, which is an emergency call analysed in Whalen et al. (1988). Other researchers have investigated discourse frameworks in institutional talk, as Baker et al. (2001), who analysed the organisation of helpline calls from a customer and found a typical sequence of conversational turns in the specific context. On the basis of Tannen and Wallat's (1993) analysis on a medical examination, Poncini (2004: 258) identified three categories of frames in multicultural business meetings: *at-meeting*, *outside-meeting*, and *other* frames. He described 'special' shifts among these three frameworks: one of them was a shift from a 'joking' framework to seriousness, which was indicated by a change in the participants' choices of languages at that moment from English to Italian in the particular context. Saft (2007) identified two discourse frameworks in a faculty meeting at a Japanese university: *reporting framework* and *discussion framework.* One of the faculty members cut in the chair's reporting, which was followed by the chair's response token *un*, which is an equivalent of *uh-huh* or *mhm* in English. This response token seemed to allow the faculty member to continue his speaking, leading the shift from *reporting framework* to *discussion framework* in the meeting.

In pedagogic settings, the seminal study in discourse analysis by Sinclair and Coulthard (1975) provided the IRF framework (teacher's initiation → pupil's response → teacher's follow-up) in language classrooms. At tertiary level, tutor-student dyad conversations in supervisions at British universities were examined in Tsuchiya (2013b), who identified two discourse frames in the academic context: *commentary frameworks*, where the tutors give comments and suggestions to the students, and *explanatory frameworks*, where the students elaborate and explain their ideas. In her data, the tutors frequently cut-in students' explanation to initiate a commentary.

Discourse analysts have also recognised frames in particular genres in discourse, i.e. *narratives* and *endorsement. Narratives* are defined as 'oral versions of personal experiences' (Labov and Waletzky 1967: 13), comprising the distinct pattern of framing organization: orientation → complication → resolution → Coda (ibid: 41). Stubbs (1983) describes three frames of *endorsements*: acknowledge → accept → endorse (ibid: 189–190). Endorsements function 'not merely to convey propositional content, but to take up an alignment, to make a commitment to a position, to claim fellowship or form alliances' (ibid: 188), which affect the orientation of the interaction. Stubbs (1983) also points out the frequent use of *joint production* in endorsement discourse framework, which involves interlocutors' competence 'to make such prediction and interpretations, and to analyse the implications of utterances, in a fraction of a second' (ibid: 22), i.e. co-completion of turns. These framework analyses were applied to this study, with particular attention to the last two discourse frameworks, *narrative* and *endorsement.*

3 Repair in Interaction

Repair is one of the central themes among conversation analysts. Schegloff (2007) defines repair in conversation as 'efforts to deal with trouble-sources or repairables – marked off as distinct within the ongoing talk' (ibid: 101). There are four types of repair sequences, which can be divided into two categories depending on who initiates repair (self-initiated repair and other-initiated repair), and who repairs the repairable (by the self or the other):

	Self-initiated	Other-initiated
Self-repair	Self-initiated self-repair (SISR)	Other-initiated self-repair (OISR)
Other-repair	Self-initiated other repair (SIOR)	Other-initiated other repair (OIOR)

Adopted from Schegloff (2007: 101)

Schegloff et al. (1977) identified a three-turn exchange structure for other-initiated repair sequences, known by the acronym NTRI (next turn repair initiator):

Turn 1: Utterance
Turn 2: NTRI
Turn 3: Response to the NTRI

According to Schegloff et al. (1977), self-repair is unmarked and preferred in interactions while other-repair can be dispreferred and potentially face-threatening. In a study of English as a Lingua Franca (ELF) in academic settings, Kaur (2011) found that self-repair functions not only as corrections of linguistic errors but also as a strategy to 'allow the speaker to make talk more specific, explicit and clear' (ibid: 2712). In workplace discourse in ELF settings, Firth (1996, 2009) examined conversations in international trading companies and found that discourse that is recognised as 'abnormal' and 'extraordinary' by 'native-speaker assessments', is treated as 'normal' and 'ordinary' in the ELF talk (Firth 1996:239–240). The interlocutors did not use or postpone initiation of other-initiated repair and 'let it pass'. In some contexts, however, the use of other-initiated other-repair can be accepted and taken as 'normal', i.e. the frequent use of other-initiated other-repair in an international bridge construction meeting (Tsuchiya and Handford 2014).

In a context of CLIL classrooms, Dalton-Puffer (2007) collected conversation data in secondary schools in Austria, identifying three types of repairables in teacher-learner interactions: *factual* (subject content), *linguistic* (pronunciation, morph-syntax and lexicon) and *procedural repairables* (aspects of activities and their sequencing). The first two are categorised as *instructional register*, the last being *regulative register* on the basis of the functional linguistic classification of classroom interaction in Christie (2000: 29, also cited Dalton-Puffer 2007). Sample 1 is an example of *factual repairable* by a teacher (T) to a student (sf).

Sample 1 Biology, Grade 6[1]

1 T from/what's it made from/cider/it's made from/… it's made from what fruit. what fruit.
2 Sf Zitrone
3 T **no no it's not lemon**…apples it's made of apples right!
(Dalton-Puffer 2007: 247, original emphases)[1]

In her data, factual repair is 'generally unmodified' (ibid) and used even with negative evaluation as shown in line 3 in Sample 1, where the teacher directly corrected the previous utterance by the student without mitigation, saying 'no no it's not lemon'. The second type of repair is *linguistic repair*, which is found in Sample 2.

Sample 2 History, Grade 11[1]

1 Sf1 conf-consisted of the city and s-surrounding countryside? the larged the largest?
2 T Mhm
3 Sf1 polis was Athens, which hm had about..
4 T two thousand five hundred
5 Sf1 two thousand five hundred square kilometres and (?) one thousand square square miles of (xxx) however, most statsh
6 T st-
7 Sf1 were much smaller with many less than two..
8 T **two hundred and fifty square**
9 Sf1 ah two hundred fifty square kilometres…and hundred square miles […]
(Dalton-Puffer 2007: 249, original emphases) [1]

In Sample 2, Sf1 (student) has difficulty in conveying numerical terms in English. At the end of line 7, Sf1 starts to say a number, but this is not completed. The teacher then repairs the utterance at line 8, saying 'two hundred and fifty square', which is followed by a repetition by the student to confirm the repair. The last one is *procedural repair*. Sample 3 is one such example.

Sample 3 Modulated teacher repair on procedural matter in Geography grade 6

you don't have to do anything yet, er the first sheet it er the first sheet is should this really be numer [sic] forty nine and **i [sic] think** the second sheet is numer [sic] fifty
(Dalton-Puffer 2007: 250, original emphases)

[1] 1. T indicates teacher. Sf unidentified female student and Sf1 female student 1. Slash marks '//' indicate the English translation of an utterance made in German. Short pause and long pause are marked with '..' and '…'. The question mark '?' is used for rising intonation. Unintelligible words are indicated with (xxx) (Dalton-Puffer 2007, pp. xi–xii).

Compared to content repair, procedural repair is often 'modulated' to increase indirectness for face-saving (Brown and Levinson 1987), which was also observed in the instance of procedural repair with 'i think' as mitigation in Sample 3.

Dalton-Puffer (2007) also classified the seven repair trajectories for her analysis in reference to Schegloff et al. (1977):

T0	non-repair
T1	same-turn self-repair
T2	transition space self-repair
T3	third-turn self-repair
T4a	other initiation & self-repair in turn 1
T4b	other-initiation in turn 2/self-repair in turn 3
T5a	other-repair in turn 1
T5b	other-repair in turn 2 after trouble
T6	self-initiation other-repair
T7	meta-talk about mistakes

(Dalton-Puffer 2007: 210)

Both categorisations of repair strategies in Schegloff (2007) and Dalton-Puffer (2007) were adapted to the analysis of learner-learner interactions in this study, defining the former (SISR, SIOR, OISR, and OROR) as *forms of repair*, and the latter (factual, linguistic, and procedural repair) as *functions of repair*.

4 Research Data and Methods

As a preliminary study, two conversations were analysed, which were audio-recorded in the two settings, a CLIL and a GE classrooms respectively, at a university in Japan. The two 5-min paired conversations were examined both quantitatively and qualitatively in detail, using a miniature time-aligned corpus (approximately 850 words in total). All of the four participants were Japanese undergraduate students, and their level of English was B1 in the Common European Framework of Reference (CEFR). The CLIL class was an undergraduate module of English Language Teaching (ELT), where the participants, Taka (male) and Mika (female), were preparing for their group presentation assignment. The medium of instruction was English in the class and the students were required to fulfil the assignments in English. They were second grade students enrolled in the School of Arts and Science. In the assignment, they had to present their English lesson plan and teaching materials in a group of three although one of the members was absent on the day of the recording.

CLIL (ELT)	Taka (male) Mika (female)	Arts and Science	Presentation preparation: developing teaching materials
GE (English)	Sota (male) Kazu (male)	Aeronautics engineering	Practice for an oral exam: plan for summer

In the GE class, two male participants, Sota (male) and Kazu (male), were talking about their plans for the coming summer vacation in order to practise for the paired oral test, which was a part of the assessment in the course. They were also second grade students but majored in aeronautics engineering.

The audio-recorded conversations were transcribed and time-stamped using the annotation tool Transana (Fassnacht and Woods 2002). The annotation systems employed in the CANCODE (The Cambridge and Nottingham Corpus of Discourse in English) (Adolphs 2006) was applied to the transcripts since they are sufficient for the analysis in this study (see Appendix for the annotation conventions). Although the time stamps were originally tracked in milliseconds (ms) in Transana, the time scale was reduced and rounded into seconds to simplify the analysis at this stage. The numbers of words and time lengths of speaker turns were examined using the time-aligned corpus. Keyword lists were also extracted from the transcripts using the software application, WordSmith (Scott 2013). Discourse frameworks (i.e. *narrative* in Labov and Waletzky (1967) and *endorsement* in Stubbs (1983)) and strategies of repair (Schegloff 2007) were qualitatively described, applying discourse and conversation analytic approaches.

The following section first looks at the results from the quantitative corpus-based analysis to highlight the areas for the qualitative conversation/discourse analysis.

5 Numbers of Words and Speaking Time

The numbers of words, speaker turns, and average speaking time length of each participant are summarised in Tables 1 and 2.

The students in GE had fewer but longer turns than those in CLIL. The number of speaker turns in Sota is 32 and Kazu 29, and the average time length of a speaking turn in Sota is 8.23 s and Kazu 4.12 s, while Taka and Mika in CLIL took more than

Table 1 Numbers of turns and speaking time in GE

	Turn	Word count	Time	Word/turn (word)	Time/turn (sec)
Sota (male)	32	308	0:02:53	9.63	8.23
Kazu (male)	29	207	0:01:59	7.14	4.12
Pause	–	–	0:00:08	–	–
Total	61	515	0:05:00	–	–

Table 2 Numbers of turns and speaking time in CLIL

	Turn	Word count	Time	Word/turn (word)	Time/turn (sec)
Taka (male)	45	110	0:01:26	2.44	1.90
Mika (female)	47	241	0:02:34	5.13	3.28
Pause	–	–	0:01:00	–	–
Total	92	351	0:05:00	–	–

Table 3 A keyword list of CLIL

Rank	Freq	Keyness	Keyword
1	17	19.997	ah
2	8	14.45	bingo
3	8	14.45	we
4	6	10.837	they
5	6	10.837	think
6	5	9.031	card
7	5	9.031	music
8	5	9.031	students
9	4	7.225	hobby
10	4	7.225	nandaro
11	3	5.419	um
12	3	5.419	filter
13	3	5.419	food
14	3	5.419	idea
15	3	5.419	if

45 speaker turns each although their average time lengths of speaking turns are shorter than those of GE: Taka spoke for 1.9 s in a speaking turn on average and Mika 3.28 s. The total number of words in GE is 515 words, which is about 1.5 times more than that of CLIL (351 words). The miniature corpus was used for the analysis here to see the feasibility of the research methodology although further analysis with a larger corpus is necessary in future research.

Using WordSmith, I first extracted two frequent word lists from the two transcripts. I then created two keyword lists, one for the CLIL transcript and one for the GE transcript, by cross referencing them to each other. The discourse marker *ah* is ranked first in the list of CLIL, which is a Japanese equivalent of *oh* in English and functions as a *change-of-status token* (Heritage 1984), and the Japanese response token *um* is 13th, which seems to function as an acknowledge token i.e. *yeah* in English (O'Keeffe and Adolphs 2008) and also as a turn-holding device (Gardner 2002) in speaker turns. In the list of GE, on the other hand, the continuer response token *mhm* is ranked 5th (Tables 3 and 4).

Table 4 A keyword list of GE

Rank	Freq	Keyness	Keyword
1	34	28.065	so
2	35	9.512	i
3	9	9.355	a
4	8	8.315	want
5	6	6.237	mhm
6	14	6.108	to
7	5	5.197	listening
8	5	5.197	section
9	5	5.197	study
10	15	4.79	and
11	4	4.158	abroad
12	4	4.158	aeronautics
13	4	4.158	studying
14	4	4.158	summer
15	4	4.158	vacation

Two plural pronouns, *we* (2nd) and *they* (3rd), are in the list of CLIL, while the first person singular pronoun *I* is ranked 2nd in the GE list. The terms, *bingo*, *card*, and *music*, are in the CLIL list since the students in CLIL were talking about teaching materials in the conversation, and the term *filter* was used in the collocation *Krashen's [affective] filter theory*. This is a 'content obligatory word' in the subject content, English Language Teaching, and a 'nominalisation', which is a technical term to express a 'prepackaged' meaning that the interlocutors share since it has previously been presented in the class (Llinares et al. 2012: 44). The term *nandaro* at the tenth rank in the CLIL list is a Japanese word, which is a metalinguistic remark and an equivalent of the utterance 'how can I say' in English. The use of these keywords is described qualitatively in the following sections, simultaneously examining specific aspects: discourse framework and repair strategies.

6 Narrative or Endorsement Framework

To look at the data qualitatively, I quote a slightly longer extract from the CLIL interaction here, where Taka and Mika are discussing what teaching materials they will include in their lesson plan.

Extract 1 Endorsement framework in the CLIL learner interaction (at 00:00:32)

1		Mika	What materials will you use?	
2		Taka	Er okay er I think (1.0) it needs to cards or bingo.	
3	→	Mika	Ah yes me too. <$E> laugh </$E>	*acknowledge/accept* (lines 3–5)
4		Taka	Me too. <$E> laugh </$E>	
5	→	Mika	Yes.	
6		Taka	<$E> laugh </$E>	
7	→	Mika	I think, yes, bingo card+	*endorse* (lines 7–9)
8		Taka	<$E> laugh </$E> bingo card.	
9	→	Mika	+ is nice.	*joint production* (lines 9–11)
10		Taka	+ is nice yeah. <$E> laugh </$E>	
11		Mika	Yeah. <$E> laugh </$E>	
12		Taka	Er er I think the bingo card er should be made by students.	
			[several lines are omitted.]	
13		Mika	And er what= and er what is the bingo's theme?	
14		Taka	Ah ah.	
15		Mika	Hobby= er in this book hobby or jobs, but I think it's not ah NANDARO <$E> in Japanese (how can I say) </$E> = is not good+	
16	→	Taka	Um.	*acknowledge*
17		Mika	+Job. Um I think hobby or weekend= what do you do on your weekend?	
18	→	Taka	Ah NARUHODO NARUHODO YABE <$E> in Japanese (I see, I see, I shouldn't [speak in Japanese]) </$E> I see.	*acknowledge* (lines 18–20)
19		Mika	<$E> laugh </$E>	
20	→	Taka	I see. Sorry. Er=	
21		Mika	Because=	
22		Taka	Let's see=	
23		Mika	Er because they= we er NANDARO <$E> in Japanese (how can I say) </$E> we assume that students intro= introduce themselves weekend or hobby?	
24		Pause	(2.0) <$E> looking at the text book </$E>	
25		Taka	Er I think er=	

26		Pause	(2.0)	
27		Taka	Er	
28		Pause	(1.0)	
29		Taka	kind of food?	
30	→	Mika	Ah favourite food.	*acknowledge*
31		Taka	Yeah favourite food+	
32	→	Mika	Ah	
33		Taka	+um bingo.	
34	→	Mika	Ah it's very easy.	*accept/endorse*
35		Taka	Yeah yeah yeah.	
36		Pause	(1.0)	
37	→	Mika	Ah that's nice idea.	

In line 1, Mika initiates the topic of discussion (teaching materials), and Taka suggests a 'bingo game', saying 'Er okay er I think (1.0) it needs to cards or bingo [*sic*]' in line 2. Mika expresses acknowledgement/acceptance with 'Ah yes me too' in line 3 and 'Yes' in line 5, and then utters endorsements in lines 7 and 9, saying 'I think, yes, bingo card is nice'. The last part of the utterance '+ is nice' is uttered by both Mika and Taka at the same time, which is an occurrence of *joint production*, indicating collaboration and endorsement in the discussion. The alignment in the discussion is formed through the endorsement framework.

After the sequence, another endorsement framework follows. Mika initiates a new but related topic (the theme of the bingo game) in line 13, uttering 'And er what = and er what is the bingo's theme?' and expresses her opinion that 'jobs or hobbies', which were on their textbook as examples, do not seem appropriate for their target learners since they are planning a lesson for lower secondary school students in line 15. Then, Mika suggests 'weekend' as a theme of the bingo game in line 17, uttering 'Um I think hobby or weekend = what do you do on your weekend?'. Taka gives several acknowledgements from lines 16 to 20, but does not move to the expected successive frames, *acceptance* and *endorsement*. So, Mika suggests the same opinion again in line 23, saying 'we assume that students intro = introduce themselves weekend or hobby?', which is followed by a two-second pause. During the pause, they are looking at the text book in silence. After several pauses and a mitigation by Taka, 'Er I think er=' in line 25, which are taken as delay strategies before a dispreferred response (Schegloff 2007), Taka suggests a different theme for the bingo game in line 29, saying 'kind of food'.

Mika immediately responds to him with acknowledgement, 'Ah favourite food' in line 30 and 'Ah' in line 32. She then expresses her acceptance and endorsement in line 34, 'Ah it's very easy' and in line 37, 'Ah that's nice idea'. The first part of this sequence frames *dis-alignment* due to the noticeable absence of Taka's acceptance and endorsement to Mika, however, the discussion is repaired with Taka's suggestion and oriented towards *alignment* with endorsement framework at the end.

Thus, from the qualitative analysis, *endorsement framework* was observed in the CLIL interaction, which includes (1) topic initiation, (2) suggestion for decision making, and (3) (dis-)alignment, with the use of *joint production.*

Extract 2 Narrative framework in the GE learner interaction (at 00:00:01)

1		Sota	Wha= so what are you going to do= er= summer vacation?	
2		Kazu	Er in this summer vacation?	
3		Sota	Yeah.	
4	→	Kazu	Er my plan is studying hard= er= this is because I want to study abroad in <$G?> CHAU <$E> in Japanese (it's not [what I meant]) </$E> next September+	*orientation*
5		Sota	Mhm.	
6	→	Kazu	+ er but er= I could= can't study abroad in next seme= next semester. Er because I fail the+	*complication*
7		Sota	Yeah.	
8	→	Kazu	+interview test. Er so= er= I have many choices now= er= such as= er entering another university or studying abroad in (.) a new term.	*resolution*
9		Sota	New term?	
10		Kazu	Or=	
11		Pause	(1.0)	
12	→	Kazu	Er:: or be= (.) doing ARUBAITO <$E> in Japanese (part-time job) </$E> part-time job	*resolution*
13		Sota	Mhm.	
14	→	Kazu	+and= and entering some companies. Um (1.0) er to study abroad and to enter another university. I have to study more and more.	
15		Pause	(1.0)	
16		Sota	Um. Yeah.	
17	→	Kazu	so, in this summer vacation, my plan is studying hard.	*Coda*
18		Sota	I see, I see.	
19	→	Kazu	And you?	

The discourse framework observed in the GE learner interaction differs from the CLIL one. Extract 2 is the first part of the GE interaction, where Sota and Kazu are talking about their plan for the coming summer vacation. Sota initiates the conversation, asking what Kazu is going to do during summer in line 1. Then in line 4, Kazu starts talking about his plan for summer, saying 'Er my plan is studying hard = er = this is because I want to study abroad', which is recognised as the *orientation* of his narrative. Sota utters a continuer response token *Mhm* in line 5, then Kazu continues and adds the reason he had to study hard, saying '+ er but er = I could = can't study abroad in next seme = next semester. Er because I fail the interview test', in line 6 and the first utterance of line 8, which is the second frame of the narrative, *complication*. Sota inserts an acknowledgement token *yeah* without holding the floor of the conversation.

Then, from line 8 to line 14, Kazu states how he is going to deal with the problem he mentioned in the complication part, which is the *resolution*. Sota is listening to Kazu, signalling a continuer response token *mhm* or an acknowledgement token *yeah*. Sota also inserts a clarification 'New term?' in line 9. However, Kazu does not acknowledge or respond to the clarification and continues his talk after a one-second pause. By so doing, Kazu avoids a framework shift and maintains the narrative framework. The last part of Kazu's utterance in line 14, 'I have to study more and more', can be a *coda* but Sota does not take the next floor and, in line 16, utters acknowledgements, 'Um. Yeah', after a pause. So Kazu closes his narrative, saying 'so, in this summer vacation, my plan is studying hard' in line 17, indicating closing of his narrative with the discourse marker *so* (Carter and McCarthy 2006). This functions as the *coda* of his narrative. Sota then provided acknowledgements, uttering 'I see, I see' in line 18, which is followed by Kazu's explicit turn giving to Sota, 'And you?', in line 19. Responding to Kazu's turn-giving, Sota starts to talk about his summer plan, which forms another narrative framework.

Thus, unlike the discourse framework in the CLIL interaction, the learners in GE adapted *narrative framework*, which includes (1) orientation, (2) complication, (3) resolution and (4) coda. These differences in framing in the two learner-learner interactions seem to derive from the distinct learning contexts. This might also imply that the expected learning outcomes from these respective interactions in the CLIL and GE classrooms could vary.

To see features in the interactions more closely in relation to their attention to language and content learning, the next section will explore the repair sequences observed in the two conversations.

7 Repairing Fact, Language or Procedure

Referring to the classifications of repair sequences in Schegloff (2007) and Dalton-Puffer (2007), I manually annotated the four forms (SISR, SIOR, OISR, and OIOR) and three functions of repair (content, linguistic, and procedural repair) to the two transcripts, integrating the conversation analytic approach with the corpus analysis. The numbers of repair in each form and function are illustrated in Figs. 1 and 2.

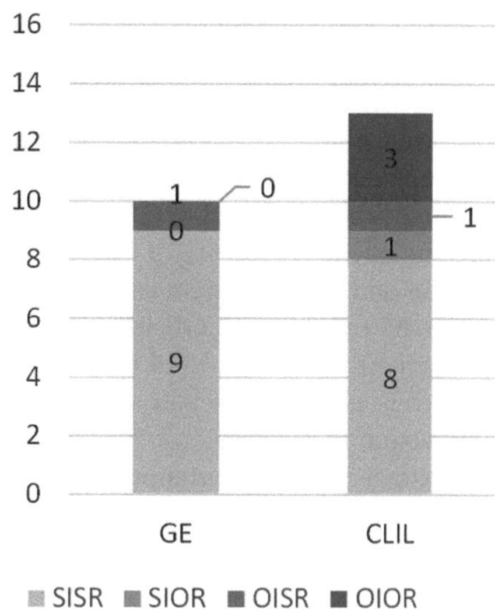

Fig. 1 Forms of repairs

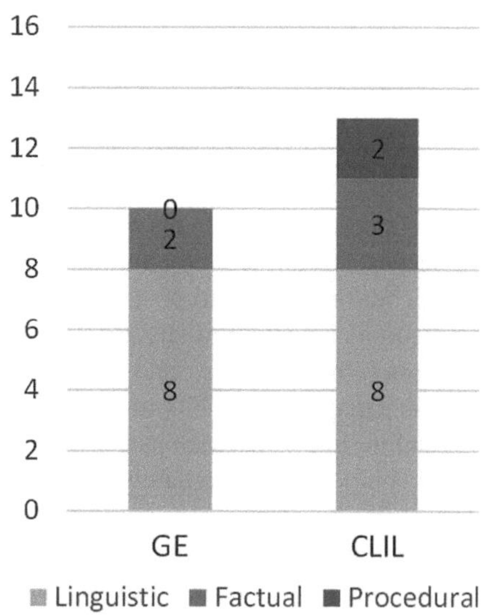

Fig. 2 Functions of repairs

The CLIL learners used more repair sequences than the GE ones. Most of the forms of repair observed in the GE interaction was SISR (9) with only one exception of OISR (1). Similarly, the CLIL interaction included eight SISR and only one occurrence of OISR. However there are differences in the use of other-repair: there was one instance of SIOR and three of OIOR in the CLIL conversation while none of those were observed in GE (see Fig. 1). In terms of the functions of repair, there are similarities in the use of linguistic and content repairs in both interactions: both the GE and CLIL learners used linguistic repair eight times, and content repair was observed twice in the GE interaction and three times in the CLIL one. However, procedural repair was used only in the CLIL interaction twice (see Fig. 2). Thus, occurrences of other-repair and procedural repair were only observed in the CLIL interaction in my data.

Extract 3 is the beginning of the GE interaction, which includes examples of SISR, which function as linguistic repair.

Extract 3 SISR-Linguistic repair in the GE interaction

1		Sota	Wha= so what are you going to do= er= summer vacation?	
2		Kazu	Er in this summer vacation?	
3		Sota	Yeah.	
4	→	Kazu	Er my plan is studying hard= er= this is because I want to study abroad in <$G?> CHAU <$E> in Japanese (it's not [what I meant]) </$E> next September+	*SISR/linguistic*
5		Sota	Mhm.	
6	→	Kazu	+ er but er= I could= can't study abroad in next seme= next semester. Er because [...]	*SISR/linguistic*

In line 4, Kazu starts his narrative, saying, 'Er my plan is studying hard = er = this is because I want to study abroad in<$G?>'. The last word in the sentence is inaudible, but that seems to be a part of the word he wrongly chose. So, Kazu immediately utters a metalinguistic comment 'CHAU' in Japanese to himself, which means 'it's not [what I meant]', and repairs by himself and re-states 'next September'. This is also categorised as T7 (*meta-talk about mistakes*) in Dalton-Puffer's (2007) classification. In line 6, Kazu uses SISR as linguistic repair again. He first says '+ er but er = I could', but immediately repairs the grammatical error in the tense of the axillary verb *can*, saying 'can't study abroad'. This is T1 (*same-turn self-repair*) (ibid). In this analysis, I did not take a simple repetition of a word or a part of a word as repair, i.e. 'in next seme = next semester' in the last part of the utterance in line 6.

In the CLIL interaction, there were several instances of other-repair and procedural repair. In the preceding sequence of Extract 4, Mika and Taka were talking about the bingo game as a teaching material, which was shown in Extract 1. In Extract 4, they decide the details of the teaching materials, and Mika says 'Ah okay. Erm when the = Kota come [*sic*] we will tell him this idea' in lines 1 to 7. Kota was the other group member and absent on that day. She then whispers ‘Finish’ with a soft voice in line 10 after a pause.

Extract 4 OIOR – procedural repair in the CLIL interaction

1	Mika	Ah okay. Erm when the= Kota come+	
2	Taka	Um.	
3	Mika	+ we will tell+	
4	Taka	tell+	
5	Mika	him+	
6	Taka	the+	
7	Mika	+this idea	
8	Taka	+this idea. Okay.	
9	Pause	(1.0)	
10	Mika	Finish.	
11 →	Taka	Next should we do?	*OIOR/procedural* (lines 11–13)
12	Pause	(3.0)	
13 →	Taka	That's all?	
14 →	Mika	That's all? Ah how about music?	*OIOR/procedural*
15	Taka	Music? Ah okay okay.	

Taka marks Mika’s utterance ‘finish’ in line 10 as a *procedural repairable*, which is related to the process of the discussion. Taka mitigates the repair initiation and asks Mika what they should do next with a question form in line 11, ‘Next should we do [*sic*]’. However, there is no response from Mika and a three-second pause follows, so Taka repairs the interaction in line 13, saying, ‘That’s all?’, with a rising tone, which implies that there are more things to do. Thus, Taka’s utterance here is an NTRI. Mika marks Taka’s utterance and takes this as a *procedural repairable* and repeats it ‘That’s all?’ and suggests ‘Ah how about music?’ in line 14. This is another example of OIOR-procedural repair. The first OIOR could be a variation of T4b (*other-initiation in turn 2/other-repair in turn 3*), the second being T5a (*other-repair in turn 2 after trouble*) in Dalton-Puffer (2007).

The CLIL interaction also contained some instances of *factual repair*. In Extract 5, Mika quotes Kota’s opinion from lines 1 to 3. Mika attempts to explain why music as a teaching material is important by referring to *Krashen’s affective filter hypothesis*, which they learned in the previous lectures, but she has difficulty in uttering the content obligatory word.

Extract 5 SISR/SIOR – factual repair in the CLIL interaction

1		Mika	But Kota <$E> another member in their group </$E> said er music is+	
2		Taka	Important.	
3		Mika	+ important.	
4		Taka	Yeah.	
5		Pause	(1.0)	
6	→	Mika	And er if= er if= what? Krashen's filter theory+	*SISR/factual*
7		Taka	Um um.	
8	→	Mika	When= if we use music as material, we can NANDARO <$E> in Japanese (how can I say) </$E> apply the Krashen's filter filter= NANDAKKE <$E> in Japanese (what was it) </$E> hy= hypothesis?	*SIOR/factual* (lines 8–9)
9	→	Taka	Theory?	

In line 6, Mika uses SISR for the *factual repairable* in the utterance 'And er if=er if=what? Krashen's filter theory'. This repair-initiation 'what?' can be categorised as T7 (meta-talk about mistakes) in Dalton-Puffer's (2007) repair trajectories. Mika employs a similar repair-initiation strategy to the previous one (T7) in line 8, uttering NANDAKKE (what was it) in Japanese this time. This is followed by other-repair by Taka in line 9, 'Theory?', which is mitigated with a rising tone to save Mika's face. This can also be classified as T5b (*other-repair in turn 2 after trouble*) (ibid).

The qualitative analysis of the repair strategies in the learners in the two distinct learning contexts shows the tendency that SISR was frequently observed to repair *linguistic repairables* in the GE interaction while both self-repair and other-repair were used not only for *linguistic repairables* but also for *factual* and *procedural repairables* in the CLIL interaction although this is a preliminary small-scale study. Other-repair in the CLIL learners seemed modified and mitigated with a rising tone for face-saving. To grasp what is happening in the interactions in classrooms, the next section will discuss the differences in discourse frameworks and repair strategies in the two learner-learner interactions from a perspective of social and discursive practices, *communicative action* in Habermas (1996).

8 Classroom Interaction as Social Action

Llinares et al. (2012) quoted the theoretical framework of *vertical* and *horizontal discourses* (Bernstein 1999) to describe features of interactions, teacher-student interaction in particular, in CLIL classroom. The former relates to 'uncommonsense knowledge which is learned through formal education', while the latter to 'commonsense knowledge that is acquired through participation in local practices, such as the family and friendship groups' (Llinares et al. 2012: 39). Their conversation data in the CLIL classrooms in secondary schools shows the shifts between the two discourses in the context. The discourse of the GE interaction in my data can be more horizontal and the CLIL one can be more vertical. In addition to the distinctions in types of knowledge the participants exercise in the discourses, the differences in the learner interactions in this study can be explained with these types of *communicative action*, which was reviewed in the introduction.

The GE interaction in my data can be categorised as *weak communicative action* since both the participants narrated their plans for the coming summer vacation *independently* for the purpose of language practices where they acknowledged and understood each other's narratives, though they did not necessarily have to agree with each other's plans. The students were aware of the context of the interaction, which was a practice for the oral English test where they were expected to show their proficiency of the language in front of a rater (the teacher of the class). Therefore, each participant took longer speaking time to let the rater assess their performance, repairing linguistic mistakes by themselves to increase accuracy.

In the CLIL classroom, on the other hand, the interaction seemed more *interdependent* since the participants had to reach the agreements on the procedures of the discussion and the plans for the presentation. Thus, it can be categorised into *strong communicative action*. The agreements were made through the discussion between the participants, who shared the aim of what they, as a group, had to achieve through the discussion. They also shared experiences in the past (i.e. learning subject knowledge in the previous lectures together) and consequences of their actions as a group in the future, (i.e. the result of the group presentation). These underlying discourses might also affect the framing of interactions in the classroom although more analysis is necessary for further discussion.

9 Concluding Remarks

Discursive practices in learner-learner interactions in the two distinct contexts, the CLIL and GE classrooms in higher education, were investigated in this study. Although the data of this study is too small to generalise the features of the two interactions, longer but fewer turns were characterised in the GE interaction, while shorter and frequent turn exchanges occurred in the CLIL one, which relates to discourse frameworks in the interactions in the two settings. *Endorsement framework* (topic initiation → suggestion for decision making → (dis-)alignment) was observed in the CLIL conversation with the frequent use of *joint production*, while the learners in GE adapted *narrative framework* (topic initiation → narrating → acknowledgement). The students in both contexts paid attention to linguistic/factual repairables. However, procedural repairables were marked only by the participants in the CLIL interaction. To repair the trouble sources, both self-repair and other-repair were used in the CLIL students although the GE participants only used the former. These results were discussed from a perspective of social practices, with reference to the theory of communicative action in Habermas (1996), to consider the differences in framing in the two distinct learner interactions.

Although this is a preliminary study and further analysis with a larger set of data is necessary, it reveals that these learning contexts seemed to impact interactions between the learners, framing of discourse and their attention to content and language learning in the particular contexts. These differences imply that different learning outcomes can be expected from CLIL and language classrooms. What differences in learning outcomes can be expected from the two contexts could be explored further in future research, which will eventually help educators to implement optimal teaching approaches to different learning aims. This study also indicates the feasibility and potential of the corpus research integrated with more qualitative research methods i.e. discourse and conversation analysis, and sheds light on areas for further research on discursive practices in classroom interaction.

Acknowledgements This study was supported by JSPS Grant-in-Aid for Young Scientists (B) No. 26870599.

Appendix: Annotation Conventions

Conventions	Symbol	Explanation
Extralinguistic information	<$E>…</$E>	This includes laughter, coughs and transcribers' comments
Unintelligible Speech	<$G?>	Unintelligible speech is marked with these brackets
Guess	<$H>…</$H>	Where the accuracy of the transcription is uncertain, the sequence of words in question is placed between these two angle brackets
Interrupted sentence	+	When an utterance is interrupted by another speaker, this is indicated by using a + sign at the end of interrupted utterance and at the point where the speaker resumes his or her utterance
Unfinished sentence	=	Unfinished sentences of any type are indicated with = sign at the end of unfinished utterances

Adolphs (2008: 137–138)

References

Adolphs, S. (2006). *Introducing electronic text analysis: A practical guide for language and literary studies*. London: Routledge.

Adolphs, S. (2008). *Corpus and context: Investigating pragmatic functions in spoken discourse*. Amsterdam: John Benjamins Publishing Company.

Austin, J. L. (1962). *How to do things with words*. London: The Clarendon Press.
Baker, C., Michael, E., & Alan, F. (2001). Discovering order in opening sequences: Calls to software helpline. In M. H. Alec & R. Mark (Eds.), *How to analyse talk in institutional settings: A casebook of methods*. London: Continuum.
Bernstein, B. (1999). Vertical and horizontal discourses: An essay. *British Journal of Sociology of Education, 20*(2), 157–173.
Breidback, S., & Viebrock, B. (2013). CLIL: Complementing or compromising foreign language teaching?: Effects and perspectives of education policy plans. In B. Stephan & V. Britta (Eds.), *Content and Language Integrated Learning (CLIL) in Europe* (pp. 11–24). Frankfurt am Main: Peter Lang.
Brown, P., & Stephen Levinson, C. (1987). *Politeness: Some universals in language usage*. Cambridge: Cambridge University Press.
Carter, R., & McCarthy, M. (2006). *Cambridge grammar of English: A comprehensive guide spoken and written English grammar and usage*. Cambridge: Cambridge University Press.
Christie, F. (2000). The language of classroom interaction and learning. In L. Unsworth (Ed.), *Researching language in schools and communities: Functional linguistics perspectives* (pp. 184–205). London: Cassell.
Coyle, D., Hood, P., & Marsh, D. (2010). *Content and language integrated learning*. Cambridge: Cambridge University Press.
Dalton-Puffer, C. (2007). *Discourse in Content and Language Integrated Learning (CLIL) classrooms*. Amsterdam: John Benjamins Publishing Company.
Fassnacht, C., & Woods, D. (2002). *Transana. Version 2.12 – Win*. Wisconsin: University of Wisconsin-Medison.
Firth, A. (1996). The discursive accomplishment of normality: On 'lingua franca' English and conversation analysis. *Journal of Pragmatics, 26*, 237–259.
Firth, A. (2009). Doing not being a foreign language learner: English as a lingua franca in the workplace and some implications for SLA. *International Review of Applied Linguistics in Language Teaching, 47*, 127–156.
Fortanet-Gomez, I. (2013). *CLIL in higher education: Toward a multilingual language policy*. Bristol: Multilingual Matters.
Gardner, R. (2002). *When listeners talk: Response tokens and listener stance*. Amsterdam: John Benjamins.
Goffman, E. (1981). *Forms of talk*. Philadelphia: University of Pennsylvania.
Habermas, J. (1986). Communicative rationality and the theories of meaning and action. In M. Cooke (Ed.), *On the pragmatics of communication* (pp. 183–214). Cambridge, MA: The MIT Press.
Habermas, J. (1996). Some further clarification of the concept of communicative rationality. In M. Cooke (Ed.), *On the pragmatics of communication* (pp. 307–382). Cambridge, MA: The MIT Press.
Heritage, J. (1984). A change-of-state token and aspects of its sequential placement. In M. J. Atkinson & J. Heritage (Eds.), *Structures of social actions: Studies in conversation analysis* (pp. 299–345). Cambridge: Cambridge University Press.
Heritage, J., & Stivers, T. (1999). Online commentary in acute medical visits: A method of shaping patient expectations. *Social Science & Medicine, 49*, 1501–1517.
Hynninen, N. (2011). The practice of 'mediation' in English as a lingua franca interaction. *Journal of Pragmatics, 43*(4), 965–977.
Ikeda, M., Pinner, R., Mehisto, P., & Marsh, D. (2013). Editorial. *International CLIL Research Journal 2*(1). Available online from http://www.icrj.eu/21/editorial.html.
Izumi, S., Ikeda, M., & Watanabe, Y. (2012). *CLIL (Content and Language Integrated Learning): New challenges in foreign language education at Sophia University. Volume 2: Practice and applications* (in Japanese). Tokyo: Sophia University Press.
Kaur, J. (2011). Raising explicitness through self-repair in English as a lingua franca. *Journal of Pragmatics, 43*, 2704–2715.

Labov, W., & Waletzky, J. (1967). Narrative analysis. In J. Helm (Ed.), *Essays on the verbal and visual arts* (pp. 13–44). Seatle: University of Washington Press.

Llinares, A., & Romero-Trillo, J. (2008). Discourse markers and the pragmatics of native and non-native teachers in a CLIL corpus. In J. Romero-Trillo (Ed.), *Pragmatics and corpus linguistics: A mutualistic entente* (pp. 191–204). Berlin: Mouton de Gruyter.

Llinares, A., Morton, T., & Whittaker, R. (2012). *The role of language in CLIL*. Cambridge: Cambridge University Press.

Mehisto, P., Marsh, D., & Maria Frigols, J. (2008). *Uncovering CLIL: Content and language integrated learning in Bilingual and multilingual education*. Oxford: Macmillan Education.

Moore, P. (2011). Collaborative interaction in turn-taking: A comparative study of European bilingual (CLIL) and mainstream (MS) foreign language learners in early secondary education. *International Journal of Bilingual Education and Bilingualism, 14*(5), 531–549.

Nikula, T. (2005). English as an object and tool of study in classrooms: Interactional effects and pragmatic implications. *Linguistics and Education, 16*(1), 27–58.

Nikula, T. (2007). The IRF pattern and space for interaction: Comparing CLIL and EFL classrooms. In C. Dalton-Puffer & U. Smit (Eds.), *Empirical perspectives on CLIL classroom discourse* (pp. 179–204). Frankfurt: Peter Lang.

Nikula, T., Dalton-Puffer, C., & Llinares, A. (2013). CLIL classroom discourse: Research from Europe. *Journal of Immersion and Content-Based Language Education, 1*(1), 70–100.

O'Keeffe, A., & Adolphs, S. (2008). Response tokens in British and Irish discourse. In K. P. Schneider & A. Barron (Eds.), *Variational pragmatics* (pp. 69–98). Amsterdam: John Benjamins Publishing Company.

Partington, A., Duguid, A., & Taylor, C. (2013). *Patterns and meanings in discourse: Theory and practice in Corpus Assisted-Discourse Studies (CADS)*. Amsterdam: John Benjamins Publishing Company.

Poncini, G. (2004). *Discursive strategies in multicultural business meetings*. Bern: Peter Lang.

Saft, S. (2007). Conversation analysis and the study of Aizuchi: The organization of argument in Japanese faculty meetings. In Yumiko Ohara (Ed.), *Nihongo disukousu no tayouna apurouchi (Various approaches in Japanese discouse)* (pp. 38–70). Tokyo: Heibonsha.

Sasajima, S. (2011). *CLIL: Content and Language Integrated Learning* (in Japanese). Tokyo: Sanshusha.

Schegloff, E. A. (2007). *Sequence organization in interaction: A primer in conversation analysis, volume 1*. Cambridge: Cambridge University Press.

Schegloff, E. A., Jefferson, G., & Sacks, H. (1977). The preference for self-correction in the organization of repair in conversation. *Language, 53*, 361–382.

Scott, M. (2013). *WordSmith tools. Version 6.0.*. Liverpool: Lexical Analysis Software Ltd.

Searle, J. R. (1969). *Speech acts: An essay in the philosophy of language*. Cambridge: Oxford University Press.

Sinclair, J. M., & Coulthard, M. (1975). *Towards an Analysis of Discourse: The English Used by Teachers and Pupils*. Oxford: Oxford University Press.

Smit, U., & Dafouz, E. (2012). Integrating content and language in higher education: An introduction to English-medium policies, conceptual issues and research practices across Europe. *Association Internationale de Linguistique Appliquée Review, 25*, 1–12.

Stubbs, M. (1983). *Discourse analysis: The sociolinguistic analysis of natural language*. Oxford: Blackwell.

Tannen, D., & Wallat, S. (1993). Interactive frames and knowledge schemas in interaction: Examples from a medical examination/interview. In D. Tannen (Ed.), *Framing in discourse* (pp. 57–76). Oxford: Oxford University Press.

Taylor, C. (2008). What is corpus linguistics? What the data says. *The International Computer Archive of Modern and Medieval English Journal, 32*, 179–200.

Taylor, L., & Tsuchiya, K. (2007). What makes English group discussion relevant in Monolingual classes? In B. Beaven (Ed.), *IATEFL 2007 Aberdeen conference selections*. Aberdeen: IATEFL.

Tsuchiya, K. (2013a). Behaviours in ELF: Analysing interruption sequences in discussions in an EAP course. *Waseda Working Papers in ELF (English as a Lingua Franca), 2*, 59–83.

Tsuchiya, K. (2013b). *Listenership behaviours in intercultural encounters: A time-aligned multimodal corpus analysis*. Amsterdam: John Benjamins Publishing Company.

Tsuchiya, K. (2014). Why bother switching to ELF?: Analysing code-switching in a group discussion in a CLIL class at university in Japan. *Waseda Working Papers in ELF, 3*, 140–157.

Tsuchiya, K. (2015). Analyzing Interruption Sequences in ELF Discussions. In K. Murata (Ed.), *Exploring ELF in Japanese Academic and Business Contexts: Conceptualisation, Research and Pedagogic Implications* (pp. 90–110). London: Routledge.

Tsuchiya, K., & Handford, M. (2014). A corpus-driven analysis of repair in a professional ELF meeting: Not 'letting it pass'. *Journal of Pragmatics, 64*, 117–131.

Walsh, S., Morton, T., & O'Keeffe, A. (2011). Analysing university spoken interaction: A CL/CA approach. *International Journal of Corpus Linguistics, 16*, 325–344.

Watanabe, Y. (2013). Profiling lexical features of teacher talk in CLIL courses: The case of a higher education EAP programme in Japan. *International CLIL Research Journal, 2*(1), 4–18.

Watanabe, Y., Ikeda, M., & Izumi, S. (2011). *CLIL (Content and Language Integrated Learning): New challenges in foreign language education at Sophia University. Volume 1: Principles and methodologies* (in Japanese). Tokyo: Sophia University Press.

Whalen, J., Zimmerman, D. H., & Marilyn, W. (1988). When words fail: A single case analysis. *Social Problems, 35*(4), 335–362.

Yang, S. (2014). Interaction and codability: A multi-layered analytical approach to discourse markers in teacher's spoken discourse. In J. Romero-Trillo (Ed.), *Yearbook of corpus linguistics and pragmatics 2014: New empirical and theoretical paradigms* (pp. 291–313). Dordrecht: Springer.

Writers' Uncertainty in a Corpus of Scientific Biomedical Articles with a Diachronic Perspective

Andrzej Zuczkowski, Ramona Bongelli, Ilaria Riccioni, Massimiliano Valotto, and Roberto Burro

Abstract The communication of the uncertainty of a scientific finding largely determines whether that information will be translated to practice. Unfortunately, our ability to study these phenomena is restricted since existing uncertainty corpora with a diachronic perspective are limited. We analysed a historical corpus through a random sample of 167 years (1840–2007) of articles published in the British Medical Journal. Randomization was stratified according to four distinct time periods. The Uncertainty Markers (UMs) and their linguistic scope were tagged in each full-text article in order to answer the following main questions: (1) which and how many lexical and morphosyntactic UMs are used by writers in order to communicate their own uncertainty? (2) How much uncertainty (UMs + their scope) is present in each article, in each period and in the whole corpus? (3) Is there any significant variation in the use of UMs and their scope along the 167-year span? Although the

The present study has been developed within a PRIN project (Scientific Research Programme of Relevant National Interest), funded by the Italian Ministry of University and Research. The project is coordinated by Andrzej Zuczkowski (University of Macerata) and involves 4 Universities: Macerata, Bari, Rome 3 and Genoa. The study presented here shows some results reached by the University of Macerata (Andrzej Zuczkowski, Ramona Bongelli, Ilaria Riccioni), with the external collaboration of Massimiliano Valotto (University of Udine) for the informatic aspects and of Roberto Burro (University of Verona) for the statistical analyses.

A. Zuczkowski (✉) • I. Riccioni
Department of Education, Cultural Heritage and Tourism, University of Macerata, Macerata, Italy
e-mail: zuko@unimc.it

R. Bongelli
Department of Political Sciences, Communication and International Relations, University of Macerata, Macerata, Italy

M. Valotto
Department of Mathematics, Computer Science and Physics, University of Udine, Udine, Italy

R. Burro
Department of Philosophy, Education, Psychology, University of Verona, Verona, Italy

J. Romero-Trillo (ed.), *Yearbook of Corpus Linguistics and Pragmatics 2016*, Yearbook of Corpus Linguistics and Pragmatics 4,
DOI 10.1007/978-3-319-41733-2_10

analysis revealed significant differences in two of the six categories of UMs (non-verbs and modal verbs in the conditional mood), the amount of certainty and uncertainty along the four periods revealed no significant variation. The manual identification was followed by an automatic detection, whose results showed that UMs and their scope were recognised with good accuracy.

Keywords Biomedical articles • Uncertainty markers • Epistemic stance • Tagging • Scope • Automatic detection

1 Introduction

Uncertainty language in scientific writing represents the degree to which researchers trust their results. This is an essential feature because communicating the same information in a certain or uncertain manner could lead toward the information being implemented or not. For example, national healthcare policies are built on the basis of how certain or uncertain the results from biomedical research might be communicated. Clinical practice guidelines also follow the same rationale, with the adoption of a new therapy, prevention or diagnostic new conduct being implemented on the basis of how certainly or uncertainly previous results might have been communicated.

Given the importance of uncertainty language in determining practical decision-making, the field has received a host of contributions from scholars starting in the 1990s (e.g. Hyland 1994, 1998a, b, 2004; Salager-Meyer 1994, 1997; Crompton 1997, 1998; Hyland and Milton 1997).

More recently, this interest has been shared by researchers in the Natural Language Processing community (e.g. Vincze et al. 2008; Kim et al. 2009; Özgür and Radev 2009; Farkas et al. 2010; Agarwal and Yu 2010; Szarvas et al. 2012; Zou et al. 2013; Zhou et al. 2011, 2015). Specifically, this community is interested in the detection of certainty/uncertainty markers and their linguistic scope.

To date there are a few annotated corpora focusing on certainty and uncertainty, using both manual and automatic protocols. These corpora, however, are limited in a number of aspects. Firstly, corpora focusing on scientific biomedical articles have a small number of full-text articles. For example, Bioscope (Vincze et al. 2008), one of the first annotated corpora for uncertainty, is composed only of nine full-text articles. Secondly, they lack a historical perspective to evaluate how uncertainty has evolved over time.

Furthermore, as regards the methodological approaches, authors like Holmes (1988), Hyland (1995) and Hyland and Milton (1997) adopted mainly not a bottom-up, but top-down approach, i.e., the uncertainty markers were initially extracted from grammar books and dictionaries and subsequently applied in their analysis.

Unlike the aforementioned studies, in a previous research (Bongelli et al. 2012, 2014) we analysed a wide corpus of 80 full articles from the British Medical Journal (henceforth BMJ) and 167 years, from 1840 to 2007. Our approach was mainly bottom-up: the uncertainty markers were manually identified in each article on the basis of prior discussion of individual analyses (see Sect. 3.2) and were grouped into five categories: *verbs, non-verbs, if, modal verbs both in the simple present and in the conditional mood.*[1] This manual detection was followed by an automatic identification (Bongelli et al. 2012),[2] whose results showed that most of the uncertainty markers were recognised with good accuracy (overall precision = 68.67 %; recall = 90.42 % and F1 score = 78.06 %).[3] Only the results of the *if* category were substantially lower than those of the other categories (precision = 26.42 %; recall = 93.99 % and F1 score = 41.24 %). Maybe this unsatisfactory result was due to the complexity of the *if* category (see Sect. 4.2).

More recently three of the authors reviewed, refined and implemented the previous manual analysis of the uncertainty markers in the whole corpus, adding a sixth category (*uncertain questions*) and identifying the linguistic scope of all six categories.

New experiments of automatic annotation[4] were carried out to assess the results of this second manual analysis, specifically (1) to improve the results of the *if* category, (2) to test the new category of the *uncertain questions* and (3) to test the linguistic scope of the uncertainty markers of all six categories.

In the first part of this article we present the theoretical and methodological background applied both to the previous and current research and, in the second part, we show the results of the second manual and automatic annotation.

---

[1] In our corpus there were only three occurrences of the epistemic or conjectural use of will (Celle 2005). However we were unable to agree upon their epistemic interpretation. For these reason, this possible category (epistemic future) was excluded.

[2] The experiments were carried out using YamCha to train a classifier for recognizing the Uncertainty markers and the documents were processed using TreeTagger.

YamCha is an open source text chunker. http://chasen.org/~taku/software/yamcha/.

Treetagger is a language-independent PoS tagger http://www.cis.uni-muenchen.de/~schmid/tools/TreeTagger/

[3] The precision, recall and F1 are measures defined as follows:

precision = TP/(TP + FP)

recall = TP/(TP + FN)

F1 = 2 * [(precision * recall)/(precision + recall)]

True positive (TP) are uncertainty markers correctly tagged by the software, False Negative (FN) are uncertainty markers not tagged by the software and False Positive (FP) are tags incorrectly identified by the software as uncertainty markers. The *precision* is the accuracy of the software in identifying uncertainty markers: an accuracy of 75 % means that 3 out of 4 automatic tags are uncertainty markers. The *recall* measures how many uncertainty markers the software is able to automatically identify in the corpus: a recall of 75 % indicates that the software is able to automatically identify 3 uncertainty markers out of every 4 in the corpus. The *F1 score* is a measure that gives a weighted average of the precision and recall (Goutte and Gaussier 2005).

[4] In the present study we adopted a different approach, based on grammatical and syntactical rules. Partially similar approaches were previously adopted in Kilicoglu and Bergler 2010, Velldal et al. 2010. The proposed architecture and processing workflow are more cognitively plausible than the classification-based sub-symbolic approach exploited in our previous experiments (Bongelli et al. 2012). For a detailed description of the software architecture see Omero et al. (in preparation).

2 Linguistic Background

2.1 *Atomic Text*

Our linguistic theoretical background is based on J.S. Petöfi's *Theory of Text Structure and World Structure* (1973, 2004),[5] in particular his model of deep structure, the so-called *Atomic Text*. Petöfi's model has been chosen among possible others not only because it is textual but mainly because it takes into account and fully represents the perceptual and cognitive processes through which speakers/writers *in the here and now of communication* gain access to the information they are communicating. Perception refers to the five senses and proprioception (meaning "the ability to sense stimuli arising within the body regarding position, motion, and equilibrium", *Webster's New World Medical Dictionary* 2008, 305); cognition refers to thought, memory, imagination etc. For this reason, cognitive markers are not only verbal expressions such as *I remember, I know…*, but also *I think, I believe, I imagine, I suppose…*, because opinions, beliefs, imagined scenarios, suppositions etc. are also considered to be "modes of knowing" (Willett 1988) and, therefore, sources of information.

An Atomic Text is formed by three propositions hierarchically ordered in the following way:

- A *performative proposition* (pp), i.e., a well-formed representation of the particular *illocutionary act* (Austin 1962) that a speaker/writer (from now on S/W) performs in speaking/writing (S/W states, asks, orders…);
- A *world-constitutive proposition* (wcp), i.e., a well-formed representation (i) of how S/W gains perceptual or cognitive access to the piece of information represented in the descriptive proposition (S/W sees, remembers, believes…) and/or (ii) of her/his commitment towards its truth (for S/W it is certain/probable/possible that …);[6]
- A *descriptive proposition* (dp), i.e., a well-formed representation of the piece of information that constitutes the core of the communication.

These propositions form the theoretical representation of the three main parts constituting the basic structure of any communication.

Consider the following two examples:

(1) *I see* that Pam is on the beach
(2) *I think* that Pam is on the beach

[5] We limit ourselves to only quote two of Petöfi's works.

[6] These two aspects refer to what in linguistic literature is respectively called 'evidentiality' and 'epistemicity', which we are going to discuss in Sect. 2.3.

Their Atomic Texts would be represented as follows:[7]

(1a)
pp: Here and Now I (S/W) communicate[8] to you (the listener/reader) that
wcp: Here and Now I see that
dp: (Here and Now) Pam is on the beach

(2a)
pp: Here and Now I communicate to you that
wcp: Here and Now I think that
dp: (Here and Now) Pam is on the beach

The Atomic Texts (1a) and (2a) show that Here and Now (i.e., in the place where and at the time when communication occurs) S/W communicates respectively that it is through visual perception (*I see*) and through thought (*I think*) that Here and Now s/he gains access to the piece of information *Pam is on the beach*.

The expression Here and Now, the first person singular, the present tense and the indicative mood characterize the performative and the world-constitutive propositions, i.e., they indicate the simultaneity of communicating and experiencing [= perceiving in (1a) and thinking in (2a)] in relation to the time when and the place where communication occurs. On the contrary, the tense of the descriptive propositions can vary, i.e., it can be simultaneous with (as in (1a) and (2a)), previous to (as we will see in (3a) down here) or following the moment in which S/W communicates. That is why in the above representations (1a) and (2a) of the descriptive propositions the expression Here and Now is within brackets.

2.2 *World-Constitutive vs. Descriptive Use of Perceptual and Cognitive Verbs*

In the examples (1) and (2) the perceptual verb *to see* and the cognitive verb *to think* are used by S/W in a world-constitutive way as they are in the present indicative and their grammatical subject is the first person singular; as a matter of fact, in the Atomic Texts (1a) and (2a) they appear in their respective world-constitutive propositions.

---

[7] The Atomic Text can be represented by using natural language or the canonical language of Petöfi's Text Theory. In this paper, for the sake of simplicity, we use natural language representations.

[8] In particular, the syntactic structures of (1) and (2) communicate that, from the performative viewpoint, S/W *states*; for the aims of this paper, we prefer to use the more generic verb *to communicate*.

Now, let us imagine that S/W says/writes:

(3) I remember I have seen that Pam was on the beach

In (3) the cognitive verb *to remember* is used in a world-constitutive way as *to see* in (1) and *to think* in (2), as it is expressed in the present indicative and its subject is the first person singular; but the verb *to see* is not used in a world-constitutive way as instead it was used in (1): *I have seen* is a *descriptive use* of the verb *to see*, because, though its subject is the first person singular, its tense is not the present. In fact, the Atomic Text of (3) is the following:

(3a)
pp: Here and Now I communicate to you that
wcp: Here and Now *I remember* that
dp: (There and Then)[9] *I have seen* that
dp: (There and Then) Pam was on the beach

In this representation, the cognitive verb *to remember* is in the world-constitutive proposition whereas the perceptual verb *to see* is in the descriptive one. In the act of communicating (Here and Now), S/W *remembers* something of which s/he has had a previous (There and Then) visual perception. Therefore, *remembering* refers to the cognitive process simultaneous to the act of uttering and the world of visual perception (*seeing*) is embedded in the world of memory (*remembering*).

In principle, in written or spoken utterances verbs expressing how speakers/writers gain access to an informational content are used in a world-constitutive way if they are in the simple present and their subject is the first person singular (*I think that…*) or is linked somehow to the first person singular (*It seems to me that…*). On the contrary, they are used in a descriptive way if their subject is not the first person singular (e.g.: Ann *sees/thinks* that Pam is on the beach) or, even though their subject is the first person singular, their tense is not the present, but the future or the past (e.g.: I *saw/thought* that Pam was on the beach).

The asymmetry of the perceptual and cognitive verbs between their world-constitutive use (for example: *I see*) and the descriptive one (*I have seen/I will see/Ann sees*, etc.) is analogous to the asymmetry typical of the performative verbs between their performative use (for example: *I promise*) and their descriptive ('constative' in Austin's terminology) use (*I promised/I will promise/Ann promises*, etc.).

From a methodological point of view, we did not apply Petöfi's Atomic Text as a generative grammar model (as it was originally conceived), but as a theoretical frame of reference. Namely, during the analysis, each sentence of a BMJ article was compared to Petöfi's model of deep structure in order to single out its performative, world-constitutive and descriptive aspects by making explicit, complete, unambiguous what may be left implicit, incomplete, ambiguous in the sentence.

---

[9] In this descriptive proposition and in the next one, *There and Then* are used instead of *Here and Now* since the former show that the place (*There*) where *I have seen* is assumed to be different from the one (*Here*) where *I remember* and the time (*Then*) when *I have seen* is assumed to be previous to the one (*Now*) when communication occurs.

2.3 Communicating Certainty or Uncertainty

The world-constitutive proposition is the most interesting for us in the context of this study since, as we have seen above, it represents the speaker/ writer's attitude, either evidential[10] or epistemic,[11] towards the descriptive proposition (i.e., the piece of information). These two aspects are related to the communication of certainty and uncertainty, as we are going to show.

According to our definition (Zuczkowski et al. 2011; Bongelli et al. 2012, 2013; Philip et al. 2013; Riccioni et al. 2013; Dorigato et al. 2015), a piece of information is communicated as *certain* when the speaker/writer's commitment to its truth is at the maximum or high level, such as in the above mentioned examples (1) and (3) and in the following ones:

(4) Pam is *surely* on the beach
(5) *I know* that she is on the beach
or simply:
(6) She is on the beach

answering the question 'Where is Pam?' in a plausible context.

In the examples (1), (3) and (5) the evidential verbs *I see*, *I remember* and *I know* indicate how speakers/writers gain access to the piece of information, i.e., they specify their sources of information or modes of knowing (Willett 1988). Although there are no lexical epistemic markers in these utterances, these evidential verbs are enough to communicate certainty. On the contrary, in the example (4) there is no evidential verb and certainty is communicated by the epistemic adverb *surely*.[12]

In example (6) there are neither epistemic nor evidential lexical markers, but its declarative structure in the simple present functions as a morphosyntactic marker of certainty.[13]

---

[10] Authors focusing on evidentiality provide definitions, which can be largely classified into two main types: the first considers evidentiality in terms of linguistic devices that refer to *sources of information* (see for example, De Haan 1999; Fitneva 2001); the second one considers evidentiality in a broader sense including *modes of knowing* (see for example, Chafe and Nichols 1986; Willett 1988; Cornillie 2007).

[11] Epistemicity has different definitions in the literature, some authors referring to the speaker's *attitude regarding the reliability of the information* (Dendale and Tasmowski 2001; González 2005), others to the *judgment of the likelihood of the proposition* (Nuyts 2001a, b; Plungian 2001; Cornillie 2007), and yet others to the *commitment to the truth of the message* (Sanders and Spooren 1996; De Haan 1999; González 2005).

[12] In the world-constitutive proposition the epistemic adverbs, adjectives etc. are represented by the corresponding verbal expressions: the example (4) would be represented in the following way: 'Here and Now *for me it is sure* that...' or 'Here and Now *I'm sure* that...'.

[13] The example (6) would be represented in the world-constitutive proposition in the following way: 'Here and Now *I know* that...'.

Vice-versa, according to our definition, a piece of information is communicated as *uncertain* when the speaker/writer's commitment to its truth is at the minimum or low level, such as in the above mentioned example (2) and in the following ones:

(7) *Probably* Pam is on the beach
(8) She *may* be on the beach
(9) Pam *must* have flown from home to Berlin yesterday
(10) In this moment Pam *will* be walking along the beach

The cognitive verb *I think* (example (2)) communicates uncertainty, since in this context it is used to perform a conjecture, supposition, etc.

In examples (7), (8), (9) and (10) uncertainty is communicated respectively by:

- an epistemic adverb (*probably*);
- two modal verbs (*may* and *must*, the latter being used epistemically);
- an epistemic future, i.e., a specific morphosyntactic structure.[14]

All these examples show that the communication of certainty or uncertainty is carried out not only through epistemic (such as in (4), (7), (8), (9)) but also evidential markers (1), (3), (5), both lexical and morphosyntactic ((6) and (10)).

Our operational assumption is that speakers/writers, normally, can only communicate either certainty or uncertainty, but not both at the same time.

Summing up, according to our view, lexical certainty markers include, first, evidential verbs in the first person singular or plural of the simple present such as the verbs *I/we know*, *I/we remember*, *I/we see* or in the third person singular or plural such as *one sees* (inclusive of the I/we), *it reminds me* or *they recall me*.

Second, they include epistemic adverbs, such as *undoubtedly*, *surely*, *certainly*, or adjectives such as *sure*, as well as verbal expressions such as *I am sure*, *I have no doubt*, and *I am convinced*. What is certain is normally communicated morphosyntactically also through declarative sentences in the present, past and future indicative with no lexical evidential or epistemic markers (Lyons 1977; Aijmer 1980; Kamio 1994, 1995, 1997; Labinaz and Sbisà 2014).

What is uncertain is usually communicated by:

- cognitive verbs in the first person singular and plural, such as *I/we suppose*, *I/we think*, *I/we believe*, *I/we imagine*, *I/we doubt* or in the third person singular or plural when they semantically refer to the first person such as *it seems to me*, *they appear to me*;
- verbal epistemic expressions such as *it is probable*, *it is possible*, *I am not certain*, *I am uncertain*, *I am not sure*;
- adverbs such as *probably*, *perhaps*, *likely*, *possibly*;
- adjectives such as *likely*, *possible*;
- modal verbs in their epistemic use,

[14] The examples (7), (8), (9) and (10) would be represented in the world-constitutive proposition respectively in the following way: 'Here and Now *for me it is probable* that…'; 'Here and Now *for me it is possible* that…'; 'Here and Now *I think* that/pd: Pam has flown from home to Berlin yesterday'; 'Here and Now *I think* that/pd: in this moment Pam is walking along the beach'.

but also through morphosyntactic markers such as modal verbs in the conditional mood, if clauses, and epistemic future.

2.4 Certainty/Uncertainty and Truth/Falsehood

Certainty/uncertainty is different from truth/falsehood. In everyday communication truth/falsehood is usually associated with the result of a comparison between what speakers/writers affirm and the corresponding state of affairs. For example, when speakers/writers state that 'Pam is at home' (= *p*), both speakers/writers and hearers/readers will evaluate *p* as true if Pam is indeed at home. In other words, if the utterance corresponds to the communicated state of affairs, it will be considered true. If this is not the case, then the utterance is evaluated as false. Irrespective of *p* being true or false, *p* is communicated as if it were true, therefore as a certain statement. This certainty is conveyed by the declarative structure in the indicative mood, which as we said above is the main morphosyntactic marker of certainty.

In sum, certainty and uncertainty are independent concepts from truth and falsehood. Usually, in order for hearers/readers to know whether the information provided by a speaker/writer is either true or false, they will need iterative cycles of proof, especially when the information is new to them. However, when attempting to evaluate whether the information is communicated in a certain or uncertain manner, hearers/readers need no iterative proof cycles. In contrast with truth/falsehood, certainty and uncertainty are *encoded* within the communication, depending on evidential or epistemic markers, be they lexical or morphosyntactic. Certainty and uncertainty are therefore inherent to the means of communication, while truth and falsehood are extrinsic, external to communication, in the sense that they cannot be simply verified by communication alone.

2.5 Whose Uncertainty?

In a text, uncertainty markers can refer either to the author's uncertainty or to somebody else's uncertainty. Both types of uncertainty can refer to the present or past or future.

An essential point in our study is that we specifically aimed at identifying the uncertainty markers of the writer in the Here and Now of her/his communication, which in our study was identified as the author of the article at the time the article was written.

In other words, we are exclusively interested in studying what in a previous section we called the 'world-constitutive' use of the uncertainty markers, not the 'descriptive' one, i.e., we are interested in what in the current literature, specifically in Conversation Analysis, is called *epistemic position* or *epistemic stance* (cf. for example Heritage 2012a, b, 2013). For this reason, we excluded from our analysis

(1) the uncertainty markers of the writer in the past or in the future, and (2) the uncertainty markers of somebody else different from the author of the article.

Consider the following examples:

(11) "*I am not quite sure* whether it was Dieffenbach or Jobert who first exposed the error of former operators" (Wells, BMJ, 1861).

or

(12) "*Perhaps* this is the most popular notion entertained upon the subject" (Hingeston, BMJ, 1875).

or

(13) "In fine, *my opinion* is that an absolutely satisfactory means of recording at the bedside the various blood pressure data has yet to be discovered" (Dally, BMJ, 1913).

In each of these examples the author communicates that he is currently uncertain about the information that follows the uncertainty markers.

Let us just consider example (11). If the sentence had been '*I was not quite sure* whether…' or '*I will not be quite sure* whether…' instead of '*I am not quite sure* whether…', the uncertainty markers would again refer to the author's uncertainty but, unlike the example, in the past and in the future and not in the present. If the sentence had been 'Doctor Collins *is not/was not/will not be quite sure* whether…' the uncertainty markers in the present, past or future would refer to Doctor Collins and not to the author. Again the difference is in the world-constitutive or descriptive use of the verbal expression 'to be not quite sure'.

As a result, our analysis would only detect uncertainty under the first case (the author's uncertainty in the present), and not the other two (the author's uncertainty in the past or future and somebody else's uncertainty in the present, past or future).

3 Method

3.1 Corpus and sampling structure

We analyzed 80 articles (total tokens 187,882) randomly selected from the British Medical Journal (BMJ) and available at PubMed Central (http://www.ncbi.nlm.nih.gov/pmc/journals/3/, last access February 2012).[15] Randomization was stratified in four distinct time periods, namely 1840–1880, 1881–1920, 1921–1960, and 1961–2007.[16] Each time period contains 20 articles. The average number of tokens is

[15] A total of 58 articles were written by a single author, 16 by two or more authors, and 6 are articles where the authors were not disclosed.

[16] 1840–1880: a fascinating period for medicine in that physiology and experimentation were beginning to come up in Europe and this might be reflected in the certainty/uncertainty and hedging language; 1880–1920: the turn of the century, with all the excitement about the apparent lack of boundaries regarding what science could do and the belief that it could predict everything; 1920–1960: times of war, with the good and the bad they brought to science; 1960–2007: what we do now.

2348.52 per article. We identified 6 types of articles: reviews, clinical cases, original researches, reports, lectures, letters.

Table 1 shows, for each period and for the whole corpus, the amount of tokens, the types of articles and the absence or presence of the IMRAD (Introduction, Method, Results and Discussion) structure (Gross et al. 2002).

The texts were edited manually and converted into plain text files (.txt). The corpus included: titles and main texts. Reference lists, figures, tables, authors' names and affiliations, etc., were excluded to facilitate the data set processing through the use of software (WordSmith and Knowtator).

3.2 Uncertainty Tagging Process

In Bongelli et al. (2012, 2014) ten language specialists analyzed and tagged 4 full text articles separately using Petöfi's Atomic Text as the main theoretical frame of reference. They then met and discussed each individual result, line by line. On the basis of this comparison a provisional reading-grid, containing the markers so far found, was elaborated. Then, the remaining 76 full text articles were analyzed in pairs by the same 10 specialists using the reading-grid. Pair tagging was chosen so that consensus could be achieved when questions arose (inter-observer agreement=0.89). A final re-analysis was conducted by 5 of the 10 previous analysts to ensure that all markers had been appropriately identified. In this phase, specialists used the WordSmith Tools software in order to improve the quantitative analysis, checking that all occurrences of uncertainty markers had been detected.

All results were placed on a cloud environment so that it could be accessible by the researchers in real time. During the analysis, all language specialists gathered to discuss (1) the detected uncertainty markers in detail to ensure that they all agreed on each of them and (2) their possible classification into five different categories, three lexical (verbs, modal verbs in the simple present, non-verbs, i.e., adjectives, adverbs, nouns, expressions) and two morphosyntactic (modal verbs in the conditional mood, if).

More recently three of the authors reviewed, refined and implemented the previous manual analysis of the uncertainty markers in the whole corpus, adding a sixth category (*uncertain questions*) and identifying the linguistic scope of all six categories.

3.3 Research Questions

In this paper we aim at the answering the following research questions:

(1) Which and how many lexical and morphosyntactic uncertainty markers are used by writers in order to communicate their own uncertainty?
(2) How much uncertainty (uncertainty markers+their scope) is present in each article, in each period and in the whole corpus?

Table 1 Corpus and subcorpora size, types of articles, IMRAD

			Types of articles						IMRAD	
Period	Articles	Tokens	Reviews	Clinical cases	Original researches	Reports	Lectures	Letters	Absence	Presence
1st	20	47,093	4	12	1	–	1	2	20	–
2nd	20	51,915	4	8	2	2	4	–	20	–
3rd	20	54,518	6	2	9	3	–	–	9	11
4th	20	34,356	9	–	10	–	–	1	9	11
Total	**80**	**187,882**	**23**	**22**	**22**	**5**	**5**	**3**	**58**	**22**

(3) Is there any significant variation in the use of the uncertainty markers and/or in their uncertainty scope along the 167-year span?
(4) Are the scores of the second automatic detection of the *if* category better than the previous ones (see Introduction)? Furthermore, which are the scores of the new category of the *uncertain questions* and of the linguistic scope of all six categories?

4 Qualitative Results

Among the 80 articles analyzed in BMJ, uncertainty markers (henceforth UMs) were grouped according to the following seven categories (the first three are lexical categories, the last four are morphosyntactic categories), as shown in Fig. 1.

4.1 Lexical UMs

Verbs These are evidential and epistemic verbs conjugated on the first person singular or plural of the simple present such as *I believe*

(14) "*I believe* that the hernia was, at the beginning at all events, incarcerated, not strangulated" (Bartleet, BMJ, 1875).

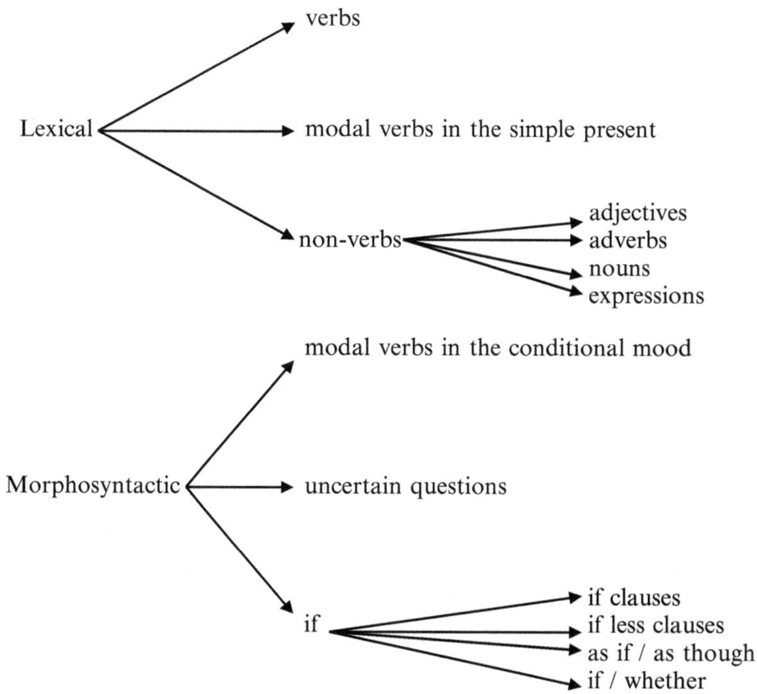

Fig. 1 Categories of lexical and morphosyntactic UMs

I suppose, *we think*, as well as on the singular or plural third person, when they include the author: these can be presented in both a non-personal use such as *one hopes*

(15) "*One hopes* this will be true, but there are reasons for not being too sanguine" (Witts, BMJ, 1948).

as well as under a passive one such as *it is believed*

(16) "*It is believed* by many surgeons that the predisposition to the first occurrence of hernia is due to the fact that there is a slight pouch or dimple of the peritoneum" (Davies, BMJ, 1913).

The verb *to seem* (and its synonyms) has been consistently classified as a verb in any person (I, you, s/he, it, we, they) as it indicates uncertainty with any pronoun

(17) "The observations *do not seem* to us to support Berkson's thesis" (Doll and Hill, BMJ, 1956).

Modal Verbs in the Simple Present These include modal verbs in the present tense used to communicate uncertainty or possibility (Halliday 2014). We labeled them as markers of uncertainty including *can*, *may*, *may not*, *must*, and *must not*. We did not label the negative form of *can* because it communicates impossibility, and therefore certainty. For example

(18) "We *cannot* from this result deduce that the deaths of doctors have been incompletely recorded in our inquiry" (Doll and Hill, BMJ, 1956).

All other negative forms of modal verbs have been labeled as uncertainty/possibility markers. The modal verb *must* deserves a separate discussion since it can have an epistemic or a deontic meaning. For example, in

(19) "The effect of this transfer *must have been* to increase the disparity between the two groups" (Wilson, BMJ, 1947).

the word *must* has an epistemic meaning since it can be paraphrased as "I believe that the effect of this transfer has been to increase…"

In contrast, in

(20) "The infants of tuberculous mothers *must* be separated at birth, or, if taken away at a later age, they must be separated for at least 6 weeks to exclude the possibility of their having already acquired tuberculous infection by the natural route before they can be vaccinated" (Wilson, BMJ, 1947).

the two *must* have a deontic meaning.

Non-verbs (Adjectives, Adverbs, Nouns, Expressions) They are grouped in one and the same category:

- **adjectives**: Include examples such as *possible* and *unlikely*. These were included only when they indicated the author's uncertainty in the present as stated in a previous section. For example, *possible* was tagged in

(21) "It is, however, *possible* that future refinements of bacteriological technique may necessitate some modification of this view" (Colebrook, BMJ, 1933).

In this example *possible* refers to the uncertainty stated by the author at the time when the statement was written. A counter-example is that the word *possible* was not tagged in

(22) "The adhesions over the front of the bladder were also broken down, so that it was *possible* to pass a rubber tube across and flush out the left iliac fossa" (Roper, BMJ, 1908).

because it refers to the uncertainty stated by the author when the action was performed, i.e., in the past;

- **adverbs**: Include examples such as *perhaps* and *likely*:

(23) "The possibility arises that the examination was *perhaps* biased towards the more serious diseases under study" (Harvey et al. BMJ, 1989).

In this case, although the verb is in the past ('was'), the adverb *perhaps* refers to the author's uncertainty at the time when the article was written, specifically in relation to the information the author is reporting about the examination. The adverb *perhaps* also boosts the previous uncertainty marker "the possibility arises that…";

- **nouns**: Include examples such as *impression* and *doubt* when they refer to the author's uncertainty at the time the article was written. For these reasons, we tagged *little doubt* in

(24) "There is *little doubt* that in earlier days transfer of infection from another septic case by way of the hands or clothing of doctor or nurse was a common event, but I think there is not much evidence that it is so today" (Colebrook, BMJ, 1933).

because it refers to the author's uncertainty at the moment when the article was written. In contrast, we did not tag the term *impression* in

(25) "The eyeballs were pulped, the eyelids torn, and the whole appearance *gave the impression* that the eyes had been gouged out" (Davis, BMJ, 1940).

because it refers to the author's uncertainty, but not at the time when the author wrote the statement;

- **expressions:** Include examples composed not by one word, as for the previous categories, but by several ones such as *speaking for myself*; *according to my view*, *there is reason for belief* or *in my opinion*:

(26) "Syphilis may be a factor, but *in my opinion* this as a cause of intrauterine death is greatly overrated" (Oliver, BMJ, 1907).

(27) "The antibodies responsible for physiological jaundice, *according to my hypothesis*, are the cold auto-antibodies normally present in every individual's blood" (Wiener, BMJ, 1951).

4.2 Morphosyntactic UMs

Modal Verbs in the Conditional Mood[17] Include *could*, *might*, *ought*, *should*, and *would*. These can be used in positive as well as negative forms, both of them indicating uncertainty. The verb *could* deserves a separate discussion since it can be used to communicate a possibility in the conditional mood such as in

(28) "At first near the neck, they *could* be seen moving actively in all directions" (Morgan, BMJ, 1916).

or to refer to past such as

(29) "the respiratory movements were imperceptible, and the pulsations of the heart, which *could* scarcely be felt, were from 60 to 70 in the minute" (Duvard, BMJ, 1842).

Contextual elements, such as the presence of another verb in the past tense or temporal deixis, can help in disambiguating the interpretation. Only the former case has been taken into account and tagged as uncertain.

Uncertain Questions Yes/no questions, alternative questions and the like (i.e., all questions that can in principle be answered by *yes* or *no*) are considered uncertain in that they come from a "not-knowing-whether" epistemic position of the questioner, since they present, explicitly or implicitly, two or more possible alternatives that the questioner is uncertain about; on the contrary, wh-questions come from a "not-know-

[17] While *would* and *should* are auxiliary verbs of the conditional mood, *could* and *might* mean also possibility, i.e., they add the meaning of possibility to the conditional mood. In this sense, as uncertainty markers, *could* and *might* have both lexical and morphosyntactic features. We treat them as morphosyntactic markers, since we decided to focus on moods rather than on lexical aspects.

ing" (= "unknowing") epistemic position, since they expect an open-ended answer that gives (more) information (than a simple yes or no) concerning something the questioner knows nothing about. For this reason, they are considered unknown instead of uncertain (Zuczkowski et al. 2014a; Dorigato et al. 2015). Examples:

(30) "The four main questions to which we have sought answers are: (1) What are the relative risks of lung cancer associated with the smoking of different amounts of tobacco by different methods? (2) Is there a reduction in the risk if smoking is given up? (3) What is the most likely explanation of the observed association? (4) Is there a relationship between smoking and any other cause of death?" (Doll and Hill, BMJ, 1956).

Questions (1) and (3) come from a "not-knowing" position, while questions (2) and (4) come from a "not-knowing-whether" position. If they were to be transformed into their corresponding indirect forms, we could place before (1) and (3) the expression "I do not know" and before (2) and (4) the expression "I do not know whether", giving rise to four linguistically acceptable sentences: (1) "I do not know what the relative risks [...] are", (2) "I do not know whether there is a reduction in the risk if smoking is given up", (3) "I do not know what the most likely explanation of the observed association is", (4) "I do not know whether there is a relationship between smoking and any other cause of death". Obviously, the same would not hold if we placed before (1) and (3) the expression "I do not know whether" and before (2) and (4) the expression "I do not know".

As shown in the above examples, this "linguistic test" helps to distinguish between uncertain and unknown questions, both direct and indirect. The morphosyntactic category of UMs "uncertain questions" includes the uncertain *direct* questions found in the corpus. The uncertain *indirect* questions are included in the underlying morphosyntactic category *if*, in particular in the sub-category *if and whether*.

If In this category we have included:

If Clauses In the English language, there are different forms of *if clauses*. The zero conditional occurs when *if* is accompanied by simple present in the protasis as well as simple present in the apodosis. This is the only situation in which we did not classify the 'if clause' as uncertain since *if* can be paraphrased by a temporal conjunction, for example 'when' and 'every time,' all of which communicate certainty. An example is

(31) "*If* non-smokers *are compared* with smokers *it is found* that for all causes of death the observed difference is not quite statistically significant (P=0.06)" (Doll and Hill, BMJ, 1956).

All other forms were considered as markers of uncertainty, namely:

– Simple present + simple future, such as in

(32) "*If* all causes of death *are taken* first, it *will be seen* that the mortality is highest among men who smoked 25 g. or more of tobacco a day (18.84 per 1000), and that the rates for light smokers (14.92 per 1000) and moderate smokers (14.49 per 1000) are 10 to 13 % above the rate for non-smokers (13.25 per 1000)" (Dally, BMJ, 1913).

In other cases, the present tense is not in the indicative mood, as it was in the previous example, but in the subjunctive mood, as in

(33) "*If* a vaccinated sheep *be inoculated* with anthrax within a few days of the operation, it *will die* of splenic fever" (Lister, BMJ, 1880).

– Simple present + present conditional, such as in

(34) "*If we are content* to record systolic pressures alone, unquestionably we *should say* that the man with a systolic pressure of 140 ran the graver risk" (Dally, BMJ, 1913).

– Simple past + present conditional, such as in

(35) "*If* the association suggested by the upper part of the table were due merely to a bias in our method investigation, we *would expect* to see that bias operating to some extent in all, or nearly all, causes of death" (Doll and Hill, BMJ, 1956).

– Past perfect + perfect conditional, having as an example

(36) "These age rates for a smoking category were then applied to the corresponding U.K. population in 1951 to obtain the death rate at all ages that *would have prevailed* in the U.K. population *if it had experienced* the rates at specific ages of the particular smoking group" (Doll and Hill, BMJ, 1956).

If-Less Clauses We also tagged the implicit *if clauses*, i.e., the constructions without the explicit *if*, such as

(37) "*Had I regarded* the systolic pressures alone, *I should have said that* the aortic case had the higher blood pressure, and that his arteries were in a condition of greater stress than those of the man with granular kidney" (Dally, BMJ, 1913).

In this example the initial expression 'Had I regarded' is equivalent to 'if I had regarded'.

Comparative constructions introduced by as if and as though (Swan 2005; Zuczkowski et al. 2014b) including the following examples:

(38) "She died *as if* struck by lightning" (Snow, BMJ, 1852).

(39) "If the stones look *as though* they may be difficult to remove endoscopically the surgeon should convert to open exploration of the bile duct" (Scott-Coombes and Thompson, BMJ, 1991).

If and whether introducing propositions indicating possibility or alternative conditions, i.e., introducing indirect uncertain questions (see above). In this function *if* and *whether* are preceded generally, in our corpus, by a perceptual or cognitive verb, as in the following examples:

(40) "We have scheduled a 2 year follow up to see *if* this occurs, but our analysis on change in stage between the arms (data not presented) showed no benefit of the intervention for this outcome either" (Aveyard et al., BMJ, 1999).

(41) "To that end it should be insisted upon that every nurse or doctor who develops a sore throat, a definite tonsillitis, laryngitis, or an antral infection, should be temporarily excluded from all contact with parturient women, and a swab taken to ascertain *whether or not* that infection is due to haemolytic streptococci" (Colebrook, BMJ, 1933).

To sum up, as the above mentioned lexical and morphosyntactic uncertainty markers demonstrate, our operational definition of uncertainty includes, in addition to the *narrow sense* of uncertainty (I do not know whether; I'm not certain that; I'm uncertain about), also *possibility* (as expressed, for example, by the epistemic use of the modal verbs *can* and *may*, both in the present indicative and in the conditional mood, and expressions such as *it is possible/probable*, etc.)[18] and *subjectivity* (i.e., the communication of the speakers'/writers' point of views, such as the expressions *in my opinion, according to my view, I think*, etc.).[19] Since these concepts partially overlap, we prefer to use the more generic term 'uncertainty', which encompasses them all.

4.3 Uncertainty Scope

After the manual identification of all UMs, through the use of Knowtator text annotation tool,[20] we tagged also their linguistic scope (Quirk et al. 1985), using the same software. For instance, in the above quoted excerpt

[18] For the epistemic use of modal verbs in English see for example, Palmer (1986) and Papafragou (2000).

[19] 'Because the mental state predicates are inherently subjective, they are frequently used as mitigating or hedging devices' (Nuyts 2001a, 391. Cf. also Nuyts 2014).

[20] @inproceedings{1225791, author={Ogren, Philip V.}, title={Knowtator: a prot\'{e}g\'{e} plug-in for annotated corpus construction}, booktitle={Proceedings of the 2006 Conference of the North American Chapter of the Association for Computational Linguistics on Human Language

(14) "*I believe* that the hernia was, at the beginning at all events, incarcerated, not strangulated" (Bartleet, BMJ, 1875).

15 tokens were tagged, because the linguistic scope of the UM "*I believe*" extends over the whole sentence.

5 Quantitative Results

5.1 Lexical and Morphosyntactic UMs

Out of the 2808 manually annotated UMs, 1739 were lexical and 1069 were morphosyntactic (see Table 1). Their difference is statistically significant ($\chi^2=159.86$, df=1, p-value<0.0001; Cramer's V=0.238, effect size moderate, Cohen 1988),[21] as shown also by the percentages: Ws use more frequently lexical than morphosyntactic UMs.

The ratios between lexical and morphosyntactic UMs in each of the four periods (see Table 3) are consistent with the total ones (Table 2): in all four periods, lexical markers are more used than morphosyntactic ones.

Table 2 Frequency and percentage of lexical and morphosyntactic UMs 1840–2007

UMs 1840–2007	Frequency	%
Lexical	1739	61.93
Morphosyntactic	1069	38.07
Total	**2808**	**100**

Table 3 Frequency and percentage of lexical and morphosyntactic UMs in the four periods

	Lexical		Morphosyntactic		Total	
Period	Frequency	%	Frequency	%	Frequency	%
1st	344	58.80	241	41.20	585	100
2nd	515	62.80	305	37.20	820	100
3rd	582	60.81	375	39.19	957	100
4th	298	66.81	148	33.19	446	100
Total	**1739**	**61.39**	**1069**	**38.07**	**2808**	**100**

Technology}, year={2006}, pages={273–275}, location={New York, New York}, doi={http://dx.doi.org/10.3115/1225785.1225791}, publisher={Association for Computational Linguistics}, address={Morristown, NJ, USA},}

[21] Because statistically significant differences are more likely to occur with large sample sizes, effect sizes are necessary to understand if the differences are meaningful. In order to assess the effect sizes for our χ^2 analyses, we used Cramer's V test. The guidelines to determine the magnitude of the effect sizes (Cohen 1988) are in Appendix.

[22] We included under the label "seem/s" the occurrences of: *seems* (50); *seem* (29); *does not seem* (6); *do not seem* (2).

Table 4 Frequency and percentage of lexical UMs 1840–2007

Lexical UMs 1840–2007	Frequency	%
Modal verbs	885	50.89
Non-verbs	492	28.29
Verbs	362	20.81
Total	**1739**	**100**

Table 5 Frequency and percentage of lexical UMs in the four periods

	Modal verbs		Non-verbs		Verbs		Total	
Period	Frequency	%	Frequency	%	Frequency	%	Frequency	%
1st	160	46.51	88	25.58	96	27.90	344	100
2nd	300	58.25	119	23.10	96	18.64	515	100
3rd	282	48.45	184	31.61	116	19.93	582	100
4th	143	47.98	101	33.89	54	18.12	298	100
Total	**885**	**50.89**	**492**	**28.29**	**362**	**20.81**	**1739**	**100**

Table 6 Frequency and percentage of modal verbs 1840–2007

Modal verbs 1840–2007	Frequency	%
May	628	70.96
Can	210	23.73
Must	30	3.38
May not	17	1.92
Total	**885**	**100**

5.1.1 Lexical UMs

Specifically, out of the 1739 lexical UMs, 885 were modal verbs in the simple present, 492 were non-verbs, and 362 were verbs (see Table 4).

The difference among them is statistically significant ($\chi^2 = 255.82$, df = 2, p-value < 0.0001; Cramer's V = 0.271, effect size moderately strong): among lexical UMs the writers seem to prefer modal verbs.

The ratios among modal verbs, non-verbs and verbs in each of the four periods (see Table 5) are consistent with the total ones (Table 4), except for the first period where verbs are lightly more used (27.90 %) than non-verbs (25.58 %).

Table 6 shows that, out of the 885 modal verbs used in an epistemic manner, we found 628 occurrences of *may* and 210 of *can*. These are followed by *must* (30) used in epistemic manner and by the negative forms of *may* (*may not* with n = 17). The verb *may* prevails over all markers of the same type.

The ratios among the different modal verbs in each of the four periods (see Table 7) are consistent with the total ones (Table 6): *may* is the most used in all four periods.

Table 7 Frequency and percentage of modal verbs in the four periods

	May		Can		Must		May not		Total	
Period	Freq.	%	Freq.	%	Freq.	%	Freq.	%	Freq.	%
1st	122	76.25	25	15.62	6	3.75	7	4.37	160	100
2nd	210	70	73	24.33	13	4.33	4	1.33	300	100
3rd	186	65.95	84	29.78	8	2.83	4	1.41	282	100
4th	110	76.92	28	19.58	3	2.09	2	1.39	143	100
Total	**628**	**70.96**	**210**	**23.73**	**30**	**3.38**	**17**	**1.92**	**885**	**100**

Table 8 Frequency and percentage of the main verbs 1840–2007

Verbs 1840–2007	Frequency	%
Seem/s	87	24.03
I/we think	61	16.85
Appear/s	46	12.70
Suggest/s	40	11.05
I/we believe	31	8.56
Other verbs	97	26.80
Total	**362**	**100**

As for the uncertainty verbs, we detected 362 occurrences. As shown in Table 8 the most used are *seem/s* (87 occurrences),[22] *I/we think* (61 occurrences),[23] *appear/s* (46 occurrences),[24] *suggest/s* (40 occurrences)[25] and *I/we believe* (31 occurrences).[26]

As shown in Table 9, *seem/s* increases in the last two periods as well as *suggest/s*; *appear/s* instead decreases as well as *I/we think* and *I/we believe.*

If we add, on the one hand, *think* and *believe* and, on the other hand, *seem/s, appear/s, suggest/s*, the difference between the *I/we* verbs and *non-I/we* verbs is more evident (see Table 10): the former are almost twice the latter.

Table 11 shows that in the four periods *I/we* verbs (*think* and *believe*) progressively decrease, whereas *non-I/we* verbs (*seem/s, appear/s, suggest/s*) increase.

Table 12 shows that, out of the 492 occurrences of uncertainty non-verbs, the most commonly used are the adverbs *probably* (59) and *perhaps* (49), the adjective *possible* (58) and *likely* (57) used both as adverb and adjective.

Table 13 shows that *perhaps* and *apparently* progressively decrease, whereas *probably* and *likely* tend to increase, and *possible* fluctuates along the 4 periods.

---

[23] We included under the label "I/we think" the occurrences of: *I think* (44); *we think* (4); *I'm/we are inclined to think/one is tempted to think/we are bid to think* (7); *I cannot help thinking* (2); *It is difficult to think* (2); *I do not think* (1); *I venture to think* (1).

[24] We included under the label "appear/s" the occurrences of: *appears* (20); *appear* (17); *appear to me* (3); *appears to me* (2); *do not appear* (2); *does not appear* (2).

[25] We included under the label "suggest/s" the occurrences of: *suggest/s* (30); *suggesting/to suggest* (8); *it is suggested* (1); *does not suggest* (1).

[26] We included under the label "I/we believe" the occurrences of: *I believe* (19); *believing* (4); *we believe* (2); *it is generally believed* (1); *we are justified in believing* (1); *we do not believe that* (1); *we have every reasons to believe* (1); *induce us to believe* (1); *there is reasons to believe* (1).

Table 9 Frequency and percentage of the main verbs in the four periods

Period	Seem/s		I/we think		Appear/s		Suggest/s		I/we believe		Other verbs		Total	
	Freq.	%	Freq.	%	Freq.	%	Freq.	%	Freq.	%	Freq.	%	Freq.	%
1st	21	21.87	26	27.08	15	15.62	2	2.08	16	16.66	16	16.66	96	100
2nd	19	19.79	21	21.87	14	14.58	3	3.12	5	5.20	34	35.41	96	100
3rd	32	27.58	12	10.34	13	11.20	16	13.79	9	7.75	34	29.31	116	100
4th	15	27.7	2	3.70	4	7.40	19	35.18	1	1.85	13	24.07	54	100
Total	**87**	**24.03**	**61**	**16.85**	**46**	**12.70**	**40**	**11.05**	**31**	**8.56**	**97**	**26.80**	**362**	**100**

Table 10 Frequency and percentage of *non-I/we* verbs vs. *I/we* verbs 1840–2007

Non-I/we verbs vs. *I/we verbs* 1840–2007	Frequency	%
Non-I/we verbs	173	47.79
I/we verbs	92	25.41
Other verbs	97	26.80
Total	**362**	**100**

Table 11 Frequency and percentage of *non-I/we* vs. *I/we* verbs in the four periods

	Non-I/we verbs		I/we verbs		Other verbs		Total	
Period	Freq.	%	Freq.	%	Freq.	%	Freq.	%
1st	38	39.58	42	43.74	16	16.66	96	100
2nd	36	37.50	26	27.07	34	35.41	96	100
3rd	61	52.58	21	18.09	34	29.31	116	100
4th	38	70.37	3	5.55	13	24.07	54	100
Total	**173**	**47.79**	**92**	**25.41**	**97**	**26.80**	**362**	**100**

Table 12 Frequency and percentage of the main non-verbs 1840–2007

Non-verbs 1840–2007	Frequency	%
Probably	59	11.99
Possible	58	11.79
Likely	57	11.59
Perhaps	49	9.95
Apparently	28	5.69
Other non-verbs	241	48.99
Total	**492**	**100**

5.1.2 Morphosyntactic UMs

Out of the 1069 occurrences of the morphosyntactic markers, 714 are modal verbs in the conditional mood, 313 are occurrences of *if* category and 42 are occurrences of uncertain questions (see Table 14). The difference between modal verbs in the conditional mood, if and uncertain questions is significant ($\chi^2=641.56$, df=2, p-value<0.0001; Cramer's V=0.547, effect size very strong): writers seem to prefer modal verbs in the conditional mood rather than if and uncertain questions.

Table 15 shows that in the four periods modal verbs in the conditional mood increase, while if category and uncertain questions decrease.

Table 16 shows that, out of the modal verbs in the conditional mood (total occurrences=714), the most used are *would* (246+ 24=270) and *should* (239+8=247), followed by *might* (110+ 5=115) and *could* (52+7=59).

Table 17 shows fluctuating values of all modal verbs in the conditional mood, except for *ought/ought not* that decrease up to disappear.

Table 13 Frequency and percentage of the main non-verbs in the four periods

Period	Probably		Possible		Likely		Perhaps		Apparently		Others		Total	
	Freq.	%	Freq.	%	Freq.	%	Freq.	%	Freq.	%	Freq.	%	Freq.	%
1st	10	11.36	6	6.81	8	1	11	12.5	7	7.95	46	52.27	88	100
2nd	13	10.92	16	13.44	10	8.40	16	13.44	7	5.88	57	47.89	119	100
3rd	18	9.78	26	14.13	28	15.21	16	8.69	9	4.89	87	47.28	184	100
4th	18	17.82	10	9.90	11	10.89	6	5.94	5	4.95	51	50.49	101	100
Total	**59**	**11.99**	**58**	**11.79**	**57**	**11.59**	**49**	**9.95**	**28**	**5.69**	**241**	**48.99**	**492**	**100**

Table 14 Frequency and percentage of morphosyntactic UMs 1840–2007

Morphosyntactic UMs 1840–2007	Frequency	%
Modal verbs in the conditional mood	714	66.79
If	313	29.27
Uncertain questions	42	3.93
Total	**1069**	**100**

Table 15 Frequency and percentage of morphosyntactic UMs in the four periods

	Modal verbs in the conditional mood		If		Uncertain questions		Total	
Period	Freq.	%	Freq.	%	Freq.	%	Freq.	%
1st	159	65.97	69	28.63	13	5.39	241	100
2nd	192	62.95	104	34.09	9	2.95	305	100
3rd	257	68.53	105	28	13	3.46	375	100
4th	106	71.62	35	23.64	7	4.72	148	100
Total	**714**	**66.79**	**312**	**29.27**	**42**	**3.93**	**1069**	**100**

Table 16 Frequency and percentage of modal verbs in the conditional mood 1840–2007

Modal verbs in the conditional mood 1840–2007	Frequency	%
Would + Would not	246 + 24 = 270	37.81
Should + Should not	239 + 8 = 247	34.59
Might + Might not	110 + 5 = 115	16.10
Could + Could Not	52 + 7 = 59	8.26
Ought + Ought not	22 + 1 = 23	3.22
Total	**714**	**100**

Table 18 shows that, out of the 313 instances of the class labeled *if*, there were 195 instances of *if clauses* stricto sensu (plus 24 instances of *if-less clauses* = 219), followed by *whether* and *if* (87) and by *as if* and *as though* (6 + 1 = 7).

Table 19 shows that *if clauses* and *if-less clauses* decrease along time, while *if/whether* increases and *as if/as though* remains stable in its small quantity.

Table 20 is a synoptic frame of the six categories of UMs 1840–2007. The most used categories are modal verbs in the simple present and in the conditional mood. If we add them together, we obtain 1599 occurrences (56.95 %), i.e., more than half of all UMs.

Table 21 shows that in the four periods modal verbs both in the simple present and in the conditional mood are fluctuating; non-verbs tend to increase, verbs tend to decrease, if category decreases and the uncertain questions remain stable in their very limited quantity.

Table 17 Frequency and percentage of modal verbs in the four periods

	Would + Would Not		Should + Should Not		Might + Might Not		Could + Could Not		Ought + Ought Not		Total	
Period	Freq.	%	Freq.	%	Freq.	%	Freq.	%	Freq.	%	Freq.	%
1st	58+2=60	37.73	39	24.52	28+2=30	18.86	15+2=17	10.69	12+1=13	8.17	**159**	100
2nd	72+8=80	41.66	72+3=75	39.06	22	11.45	6+3=9	4.68	6	3.12	**192**	100
3rd	84+12=96	37.35	91+4=95	36.96	41+3=44	17.12	17+1=18	7	4	1.55	**257**	100
4th	32+2=34	32.07	37+1=38	35.84	19	17.92	14+1=15	14.15	0	0	**106**	100
Total	**270**	**37.81**	**247**	**34.59**	**115**	**16.10**	**59**	**8.26**	**23**	**3.22**	**714**	**100**

Table 18 Frequency and percentage of *if* category 1840–2007

If 1840–2007	Frequency	%
If clauses	195	62.30
If/whether	87	27.79
If-less clauses	24	7.67
As if/as though	7	2.23
Total	**313**	**100**

Table 19 Frequency and percentage of *if* category in the four periods

	if clauses		if/whether		if-less clauses		as if/as though		Total	
Period	Freq.	%	Freq.	%	Freq.	%	Freq.	%	Freq.	%
1st	41	59.42	16	23.18	10	14.49	2	2.89	69	100
2nd	78	75	14	13.46	10	9.61	2	1.92	104	100
3rd	66	62.85	35	33.33	2	1.90	2	1.90	105	100
4th	10	28.57	22	62.85	2	5.71	1	2.85	35	100
Total	**195**	**62.30**	**87**	**27.79**	**24**	**7.67**	**7**	**2.23**	**313**	**100**

Table 20 Synoptic frame of lexical and morphosyntactic UMs 1840–2007

UMs categories 1840–2007	Frequency	%
Modal verbs in the simple present	885	31.52
Modal verbs in the conditional mood	714	25.43
Non-verbs	492	17.52
Verbs	362	12.89
If	313	11.14
Uncertain questions	42	1.49
Total	**2808**	**100**

5.2 *Uncertainty Scope*

Out of 187,882 tokens (i.e., the total amount of tokens), 36,680 are the uncertainty tokens (i.e., UMs + their linguistic scope). This means that the uncertainty communicated in our biomedical corpus is about the 20 % of the total (see Fig. 2).

In order to test if there were significant differences in the amount of certainty and uncertainty tokens along the four periods ranges, we applied the Generalized Linear Mixed-Effects Models (GLMMs).

GLMMs are an extension of the class of generalized linear models in which random effects (effects that are associated with individual experimental units drawn at random from a population and account for variations between groups that might affect the response) are added to the linear predictor (the so-called fixed effects). This allows the modeling of correlated, possibly non-normally distributed data with flexible accommodation of covariates. Such data include clustered observations,

Table 21 Synoptic frame of lexical and morphosyntactic UMs in the four periods

Period	Modal verbs in the simple present		Modal verbs in the conditional mood		Non-verbs		Verbs		If		Uncertain questions		Total	
	Freq.	%	Freq.	%	Freq.	%	Freq.	%	Freq.	%	Freq.	%	Freq.	%
1st	160	27.35	159	27.17	88	15.04	96	16.41	69	11.79	13	2.22	585	100
2nd	300	36.58	192	23.41	119	14.51	96	9.60	104	12.68	9	1.09	820	100
3rd	282	29.46	257	26.85	184	19.22	116	12.12	105	10.97	13	1.35	957	100
4th	143	32.06	106	23.76	101	22.64	54	12.10	35	7.84	7	1.56	446	100
Total	**885**	**31.52**	**714**	**25.43**	**492**	**17.52**	**362**	**12.89**	**313**	**11.14**	**42**	**1.49**	**2808**	**100**

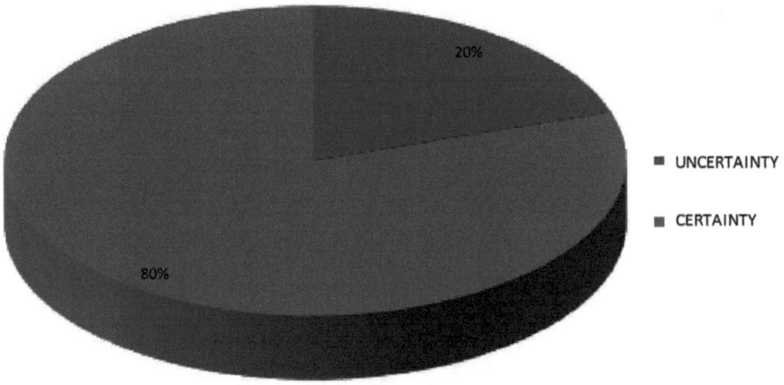

Fig. 2 Percentage of certainty and uncertainty 1840–2007

Table 22 Amount and percentage of uncertainty and certainty tokens in the four periods

Period	Uncertainty tokens	%	Certainty tokens	%	Total tokens	%
1st	7446	15.81	39,647	84.18	47,093	100
2nd	11,018	21.22	40,897	78.77	51,915	100
3rd	12,545	23.01	41,973	76.98	54,518	100
4th	5671	16.50	28,685	83.49	34,356	100
Total	**36,680**	**19.52**	**151,202**	**80.47**	**187,882**	**100**

repeated measurements, longitudinal measurements, multivariate observations, etc. For this purpose, we used the glmer function in the lme4 package of the R-software environment for statistical computing and graphics (Bates et al. 2015).

To be specific, two models were fitted using as dependent variable the proportion of certainty and uncertainty tokens in the four periods ranges (their frequencies weighted in relation to the total number of words in each article), therefore considering the four periods variable as fixed-effect, the articles variable as random-effect and the binomial error family with logit link function. Link function specifies the link between random and fixed components. It says how the expected value of the response relates to the linear predictor of explanatory variables. As Dobson and Barnett (2008) pointed out, linear regression assumes that the response variable is normally distributed. GLMMs can have response variables with distributions other than the Normal distribution – they may even be categorical rather than continuous. Thus they may not range from $-\infty-\infty$ to $+\infty+\infty$; the relationship between the response and explanatory variables need not be of the simple linear form. This is why we need the link function as a component of the GLMMs. It links the mean of the dependent variable to the linear term in such a way that the range of the non-linearly transformed mean ranges from $-\infty-\infty$ to $+\infty+\infty$. Thus we can actually form a linear equation and use an iteratively reweighted least squares method for maximum likelihood estimation of the model parameters.

To assess any significant effects, we used Wald χ^2 tests on GLMMs (Fox and Weisberg 2011).

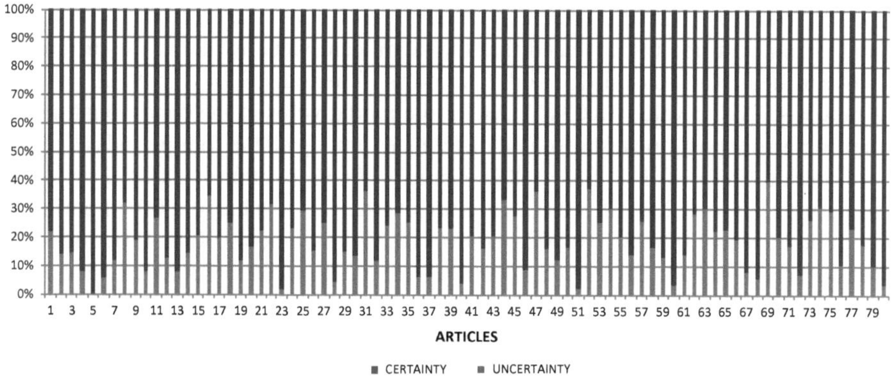

Fig. 3 Proportion of uncertainty and certainty in each article

As shown in Table 22, the percentage of uncertainty in the four periods ranges, in a non-significant way (Wald χ^2=5.9907, df=3, p-value=0.112), from 16 to 23 %.

The analysis did not reveal any significant variation not even with regards to the amount of certainty (Wald χ^2=5.874, df=3, p-value=0.117).

Figure 3 shows the ratio of certainty (in red) and uncertainty (in blue) for each article of our corpus. In 17 articles the percentage of uncertainty ranges from 0 to 10 % (=17 articles have as a maximum 10 % degree of uncertainty), in 26 from 10 to 20 % (=26 articles have as a maximum 20 % degree of uncertainty), in another 26 from 20 to 30 % (=26 articles have as a maximum 30 % degree of uncertainty), in 11 from 30 to 40 % (=11 articles have as a maximum 40 % degree of uncertainty). This means that in all the 80 papers the percentage of uncertainty is always less than the percentage of certainty and ranges from a minimum of 0 % (see article number 5) to a maximum of 40 % (see article 69).

To sum up, the percentage related to uncertainty in the whole corpus is about 20 %, in the four periods it ranges from 16 to 23 % and in each paper from 0 to 40 %.

5.3 *Variation in the Use of UMs*

In order to test if there were significant differences in the use of the six categories of lexical and morphosyntactic UMs (verbs, non-verbs, modal verbs in the simple present, modal verbs in the conditional mood, if, uncertain questions) between the four time periods taken into account, we applied the GLMMs.

The models were fitted using as the dependent variable the proportion of markers of the six categories (their frequencies weighted in relation to the total number of words in each article), and considering the time-periods variable as fixed-effect, the articles variable as random-effect and the binomial error family with logit link function.

The analysis revealed significant differences in two of the six categories: non-verbs (Wald χ^2=9.388, df=3, p-value=0.024) and modal verbs in the conditional mood (Wald $\chi^2=1256.2$, df=3, p-value<0.0001). As for the non-verbs, the Bonferroni post-hoc test revealed that the significant value is due to the difference between the first and the third period (I period vs III period: EST=−0.549, SE=0.202, z-ratio=−2.708, p-value=0.0341). As for the modal verbs in the conditional mood, the Bonferroni post-hoc test revealed differences among all the four periods (I period vs II period EST=−0.110, SE=0.002, z-ratio=47.636, p-value=0.0001; I period vs III period EST=−0.233, SE=0.002, z-ratio=−100.877, p-value=0.0001; I period vs IV period EST=0.024, SE=0.002, z-ratio=10.561, p-value=0.0001; II period vs III period EST=−0.344, SE=0.003, z-ratio=−105.037, p-value=0.0001; II period vs IV period EST=−0.085, SE=0.003, z-ratio=−26.217, p-value=0.0001; III period vs IV period EST=0.258, SE=0.003, z-ratio=78.806, p-value=0.0001).

Although these differences in two categories of Ums, the statistical analyses of the amount (scope) of certainty and uncertainty along the four periods did not reveal any significant variation (see Sect. 5.2). It is very difficult, if not impossible, to explain the differences in the above mentioned two categories of UMs, since the possible involved variables are so numerous (type of article, author's style, IMRAD presence or absence and so on).

5.4 *The Automatic Annotation*

The new experiments of automatic annotation clearly improved the results of the *if* category (precision=82.26 %; recall=81.47 %; F1=81.86 %) and were able to identify with good accuracy both the *uncertain questions* (precision=81.58 %; recall=73.81 %; F1=77.5 %) and the linguistic *scope* of the uncertainty markers of all six categories (precision=75.56 %; recall=74.87 %; F1=75.21 %).

6 Discussion

As for the lexical UMs, the preference for modal verbs, adverbs and adjectives of possibility and non-I/we verbs is functional to minimize the writer's presence according to the "predominant view of science as an impersonal, inductive enterprise" as Hyland claims (1998b, 364).

These results suggest that writers prefer to communicate their uncertainty with markers of possibility rather than with markers of subjectivity (see the end of Sect. 4.2). Specifically, they prefer using a third person subject followed by modal verbs such as *may* or *seem* rather than using a first person subject followed by verbs such as *think* or *believe.* In the latter case, writers show their own 'face' (Brown and Levinson 1987; Myers 1989; Hyland 1998b, 2004), i.e., they demonstrate their personal, explicit commitment toward the informational content. In the former case, there is a sort of *eclipse of their ego*, i.e., their commitment is communicated in an impersonal, implicit way.

In this context (biomedical scientific writing), a cautious way (using possibility markers) of communicating a piece of information seems indeed more appropriate than an explicit personal way (using subjectivity markers).

As far as we know, in terms of the morphosyntactic UMs, our study is the first that explicitly takes into consideration *if clauses, if less clauses, as if/as though, if/whether and uncertain questions*, in addition to modal verbs in the conditional mood. The results from comparing the modal verbs in the conditional mood with the *if* category and *uncertain questions* suggest that scientific writers prefer to mitigate their statements, formulating assumptions and creating hypotheses through the conditional mood rather than resorting to the *if clauses* and even less to the uncertain questions.

According to the results from the Generalized Linear Mixed-Effects Models the number of UMs and their rate over the total number of words in each article have remained essentially unmodified over a period of 167 years, i.e., the proportion of certainty (80 %) and uncertainty (20 %) is the same over the 167-year span. These results are very intriguing. They could be related to the specific genre, scientific and specifically biomedical, that requires an imbalance between certainty and uncertainty in favor of the former. In other words, to be published the submitted scientific biomedical articles need in principle, among other things, to be neither too certain nor too uncertain.

Our initial hypothesis was that the level of uncertainty communication would have increased secondary to the increase in the knowledge-based of biomedical science, leading to an increase in the number of possible explanations. In addition, one would have expected that given the increase in size of the scientific community, authors would have been more cautious and therefore decreased their degree of certainty in their communication.

However, none of these explanations agree with our findings.

One possibility is that, although these factors might have indeed contributed to an increase rate of uncertainty, they were counterbalanced by, first, the pressure from journals on authors to make their results seem nearly flawless, since too much uncertainty would lead to a perception of weakness.

Second, from a cognitive perspective, communicating a fact as uncertain opens up a large number of possibilities regarding what could be certain, while communicating a fact as certain opens up a single possibility. Therefore, uncertain communication quickly leads toward cognitive burden given the large number of possibilities, and is therefore less preferred by editors, readers, and even by authors themselves (cf. Gross and Chesley 2012).

The results from the new automatic detection seem to be very encouraging. The most important result of the experiments is related to the automatic identification of the scope: the F1 score of 75.21 % (cf. Sect. 5.4) improves the best F1 score of 71.92 % obtained in Zhou et al. (2011).

7 Conclusion

In 80 articles of BMJ over a 167-year span, we analyzed the lexical and morphosyntactic markers (and their scope) used by writers to communicate their own uncertainty in the Here and Now of their communication, i.e., at the time the articles were been written (cf. Sect. 2.5).

We found that lexical markers are more frequent than morphosyntactic markers and this rate remains stable in all four periods.

Among the lexical markers, the most frequent are modal verbs followed by non-verbs and verbs, also in each period.

Among modal verbs, the most frequent (also in each period) is the verb *may*, which is in agreement with Hyland (1998b).[27]

Among non-verbs, adverbs and adjectives such as *probably*, *possible, likely* are more frequent than expressions such as *in my (own) opinion*, *personally*, *according to my view*.

Among verbs, the most frequently used is *seem/s*, followed by *appear/s* and *suggest/s*. While *seem/s* and *suggest/s* increase in the four periods, *appear/s* instead decreases. The non-I/we verbs (*seem/s, appear/s* and *suggest/s*) result to be more frequently used (not only in the total year-span, but also in each period) than the expressions of mental states, such as *I/we think*, *I/we believe*, which considerably decrease.

Among the morphosyntactic markers the most frequent are modal verbs in the conditional mood also in each of period: the most used are *would* and *should*. Occurrences of the *if* category are less frequent, while uncertainty questions are even less so. Specifically, in the four periods, *if clauses* and *if-less clauses* decrease while *if/whether* introducing indirect uncertain questions considerably increase, inversely to the decrease of *direct uncertain questions*.

The number of UMs and their rate over the total number of words in each article have remained essentially unmodified over a period of 167 years.

The Generalized Linear Mixed-Effects Models revealed significant differences in two of the six categories of UMs: non-verbs and modal verbs in the conditional mood. This means that, roughly speaking, non-verbs' occurrences in the first and third periods deviate from the expected mean value; as for modal verbs in conditional mood, their occurrences deviate from the expected mean value in all four periods. It is very difficult, if not impossible, to explain these data since the possible involved variables are very numerous (type of article, author's style, IMRAD presence or absence and so on).

Although these differences in two categories of UMs, the statistical analyses of the amount (scope) of certainty and uncertainty along the four periods did not reveal

[27] Hyland (1995) compared the use of hedges and boosters in eight different academic disciplines that were divided in hard (in this class, for example, he included biology) and soft sciences (in this one he included, for example, philosophy). The main result was the preference for impersonal strategies (see for example, Rundblad 2007) of hedging in hard sciences.

any significant variation. This means that the proportion of certainty (80 %) and uncertainty (20 %) is the same over the 167-year span; scientific writers have been using uncertainty in an unaltered way and always in a smaller percentage respect to certainty.

The results from the new automatic identification of both the six categories of UMs and their scope are better than our previous ones and very encouraging.

Acknowledgment Sections 1, 2, 2.1, 2.2, 2.3, 2.4 and 2.5 are mainly based on Bongelli et al. (2014) *BioUncertainty. A Historical corpus evaluating uncertainty language over a 167-year span of biomedical scientific articles*, in *Communicating Certainty and Uncertainty in Medical, Supportive and Scientific Contexts*, edited by Andrzej Zuczkowski, Ramona Bongelli, Ilaria Riccioni and Carla Canestrari, pp. 309–339, with kind permission by John Benjamins Publishing Company, Amsterdam/Philadelphia www.benjamins.com

Appendix

Guidelines to determine the magnitude of effect sizes (Cohen 1988)

Effect size value (Cramer's V test)	Description	Comments
0.00	No Relationship	Knowing the independent variable does not help in predicting the dependent variable
.00–.15	Very Weak	Not generally acceptable
.15–.20	Weak	Minimally acceptable
.20–.25	Moderate	Acceptable
.25–.30	Moderately Strong	Desirable
.30–.35	Strong	Very Desirable
.35–.60	Very Strong	Extremely Desirable
.60–.70	Worrisomely Strong	Either an extremely good relationship or the two variables are measuring the same concept
.70–.99	Redundant	The two variables are probably measuring the same concept
1.00	Perfect Relationship	If we the know the independent variable, we can perfectly predict the dependent variable

References

Agarwal, S., & Yu, H. (2010). Detecting hedge cues and their scope in biomedical literature with conditional random fields. *Journal of Biomedical Informatics, 43*(6), 953–961.

Aijmer, K. (1980). *Evidence and the declarative sentences*. Stockholm: Almqvist & Wiksell International.

Austin, J. (1962). *How to do things with words*. Oxford: Oxford University Press.

Bates, D., Mächler, M., Bolker, B., & Walker, S. (2015). Fitting linear mixed-effects models using lme4. *Journal of Statistical Software, 67*(1), 1–48.

Bongelli, R., Canestrari, C., Riccioni, I., Zuczkowski, A., Buldorini, C., Pietrobon, R., Lavelli, A., & Magnini, B. (2012). A corpus of scientific biomedical texts spanning over 168 years annotated for Uncertainty. In N. Calzolari, K. Choukri, T. Declerck, M. Ugur Dogan, M. Bente, J. Mariani, A. Moreno, J. Odijk, & S. Piperidis (Eds.), *Proceedings of the eighth international conference on Language Resources and Evaluation (LREC'12)* (pp. 2009–2014).

Bongelli, R., Riccioni, I., & Zuczkowski, A. (2013). Certain-uncertain, true-false, good-evil in Italian political speeches. In I. Poggi, F. D'Errico, L. Vincze, & A. Vinciarelli (Eds.), *Multimodal communication in political speech* (pp. 164–180). Berlin: Springer.

Bongelli, R., Riccioni, I., Canestrari, C., Pietrobon, R., & Zuczkowski, A. (2014). BioUncertainty. A historical corpus evaluating uncertainty language over a 167-year span of biomedical scientific articles. In A. Zuczkowski, R. Bongelli, I. Riccioni, & C. Canestrari (Eds.), *Communicating certainty and uncertainty in medical, supportive and scientific contexts* (pp. 309–339). Amsterdam/Philadelphia: Benjamins.

Brown, P., & Levinson, S. (1987). *Politeness. Some universals of language usage*. Cambridge: Cambridge University Press.

Celle, A. (2005). The French future tense and English will as markers of epistemic modality. *Languages in Contrast, 5*(2), 181–218.

Chafe, W., & Nichols, J. (1986). Evidentiality in English conversation and academic writing. In W. Chafe & N. Johanna (Eds.), *Evidentiality. The linguistic coding of epistemology* (pp. 261–272). Norwood: Ablex.

Cohen, J. (1988). *Statistical power and analysis for the behavioral sciences* (2nd ed.). Hillsdale: Lawrence Erlbaum Associates, Inc.

Cornillie, B. (2007). *Evidentiality and epistemic modality in Spanish (Semi-) auxiliaries: A cognitive–functional approach*. Berlin: Mouton de Gruyter.

Crompton, P. (1997). Hedging in academic writing: Some theoretical problem. *English for Specific Purposes, 16*(4), 271–287.

Crompton, P. (1998). Identifying hedging: Definition or divination? *English for Specific Purposes, 17*(3), 303–311.

De Haan, F. (1999). Evidentiality and epistemic modality: Setting boundaries. *Southwest Journal of Linguistics, 18*(1), 83–101.

Dendale, P., & Tasmowski, L. (2001). Introduction. Evidentiality and related notions. *Journal of Pragmatics, 33*(3), 349–357.

Dobson, A. J., & Barnett, A. (2008). *An introduction to generalized linear models* (3rd ed.). Abingdon: Chapman & Hall/CRC.

Dorigato, L., Philip, G., Bongelli, R., & Zuczkowski, A. (2015). Knowing, unknowing, believing stances and characters' dialogic identities in the Harry Potter books. *Language and Dialogue, 5*(1), 62–89.

Farkas, R., Vincze, V., Móra, G., Csirik, J., & Szarvaset, G. (2010). The CoNLL-2010 shared task: Learning to detect hedges and their scope in natural language text. In *Proceedings of the fourteenth conference on computational natural language learning – Shared task*, pp. 1–12.

Fitneva, S. A. (2001). Epistemic marking and reliability judgments. Evidence from Bulgarian. *Journal of Pragmatics, 33*(3), 401–420.

Fox, J., & Weisberg, S. (2011). *An R Companion to Applied Regression* (2nd ed.). Sanford Weisberg – University of Minnesota, USA: Sage.

González, M. (2005). An approach to Catalan evidentiality. *Intercultural Pragmatics, 2*(4), 515–540.

Goutte, C., & Gaussier, E. (2005). A probabilistic interpretation of precision, recall and F-score, with implication for evaluation. In D. E. Losada & J. M. Fernández-Luna (Eds.), *Proceedings of the 27th European conference on Advances in Information Retrieval Research (ECIR'05)* (pp. 345–359). Berlin/Heidelberg: Springer-Verlag.

Gross, A., & Chesley, P. (2012). Hedging, stance and voice in medical research articles. In K. Hyland & C. Sancho Guinda (Eds.), *Stance and voice in written academic genres* (pp. 85–100). London/New York: Palgrave MacMillan.

Gross, A., Harmon, J., & Reidy, M. (2002). *Communicating science. The scientific paper from the 17th century to the present*. New York: Oxford University Press.
Halliday, M. A. K. (2014). *Halliday's introduction to functional grammar* (4th ed.). London/New York: Routledge.
Heritage, J. (2012a). Epistemics in action: Action formation and territories of knowledge. *Research on Language and Social Interaction, 45*(1), 1–29.
Heritage, J. (2012b). The epistemic engine: Sequence organization and territories of knowledge. *Research on Language and Social Interaction, 45*(1), 30–52.
Heritage, J. (2013). Epistemics in conversation. In J. Sidnell & T. Stivers (Eds.), *Handbook of conversation analysis* (pp. 370–394). Boston: Wiley-Blackwell.
Holmes, J. (1988). Doubt and certainty in ESL textbooks. *Applied Linguistics, 9*(1), 20–44.
Hyland, K. (1994). Hedging in academic writing and EAP textbook. *English for Specific Purposes, 13*(3), 239–256.
Hyland, K. (1995). The author in the text: Hedging scientific writing. *Hong Kong Papers in Linguistic and Language Teaching, 18*, 33–42.
Hyland, K. (1998a). *Hedging in scientific research articles*. Amsterdam/Philadelphia: Benjamins.
Hyland, K. (1998b). Boosting, hedging and negotiation of academic knowledge. *Text, 18*, 349–382.
Hyland, K. (2004). *Social interactions in academic writing*. Ann Arbor: The University of Michigan Press.
Hyland, K., & Milton, J. (1997). Qualification and certainty in L1 and L2 students' writing. *Journal of Second Language Writing, 6*(2), 183–205.
Kamio, A. (1994). The theory of territory of information. The case of Japanese. *Journal of Pragmatics, 21*, 67–100.
Kamio, A. (1995). Territory of information in English and Japanese and psychological utterances. *Journal of Pragmatics, 24*, 235–264.
Kamio, A. (1997). *Territory of information*. Amsterdam/Philadelphia: Benjamins.
Kilicoglu, H., & Bergler, S. (2010). A high-precision approach to detecting hedges and their scopes. In *Proceedings of the fourteenth conference on computational natural language learning – Shared task* (pp. 70–77). Uppsala: Association for Computational Linguistics.
Kim, J. D., Ohta, T., Pyysalo, S., Kano, Y., & Tsujii, J. (2009). Overview of BioNLP'09 shared task on event extraction. In *Proceedings of the workshop on BioNLP: Shared task* (pp. 1–9). Boulder: Association for Computational Linguistics.
Labinaz, P., & Sbisà, M. (2014). Certainty and uncertainty in assertive speech acts. In A. Zuczkowski, R. Bongelli, I. Riccioni, & C. Canestrari (Eds.), *Communicating certainty and uncertainty in medical, supportive and scientific contexts* (pp. 31–58). Amsterdam/Philadelphia: Benjamins.
Lyons, J. (1977). *Semantics*. Cambridge: Cambridge University Press.
Myers, G. (1989). The pragmatics of politeness in scientific articles. *Applied Linguistics, 10*(1), 1–35.
Nuyts, J. (2001a). *Epistemic modality, language and conceptualization*. Amsterdam/Philadelphia: Benjamins.
Nuyts, J. (2001b). Subjectivity as an evidential dimension in epistemic modal expressions. *Journal of Pragmatics, 33*(3), 383–400.
Nuyts, J. (2014). Subjectivity in modality, and beyond. In A. Zuczkowski, R. Bongelli, I. Riccioni, & C. Canestrari (Eds.), *Communicating certainty and uncertainty in medical, supportive and scientific contexts* (pp. 13–30). Amsterdam/Philadelphia: Benjamins.
Omero, P., Valotto, M., Bellana, R., Bongelli, R., Riccioni, I., Zuczkowski, A., & Tasso, C. (in preparation). *Uncertainty identification in scientific biomedical texts: A tool for automatic if-clause tagging*.
Özgür, A., & Radev, D. (2009). Detecting speculations and their scopes in scientific text. In *Proceedings of the 2009 conference on empirical methods in natural language processing* (pp. 1398–1407).

Palmer, F. (1986). *Mood and modality*. Cambridge: Cambridge University Press.
Papafragou, A. (2000). *Modality: Issues in the semantics-pragmatics interface*. Oxford: Elsevier.
Petöfi, J. S. (1973). Towards an empirically motivated grammar theory of verbal texts. In J. S. Petöfi & H. Rieser (Eds.), *Studies in text grammar* (pp. 205–275). Dordrecht: Reidel.
Petöfi, S. J. (2004). *Scrittura e Interpretazione. Introduzione alla Testologia Semiotica dei Testi*. Roma: Carocci.
Philip, G., Bongelli, R., Canestrari, C., Riccioni, I., & Zuczkowski, A. (2013). Negotiating narrative. Dialogic dynamic of known, unknown and believed in Harry Potter and the Deathly Hallows. *Language and Dialogue, 3*(1), 7–33.
Plungian, V. (2001). The place of evidentiality within the universal grammatical space. *Journal of Pragmatics, 33*(3), 349–357.
Quirk, R., Greenbaum, S., Leech, G., & Svartvik, J. (1985). *A comprehensive grammar of the English language*. London: Longman.
Riccioni, I., Bongelli, R., & Zuczkowski, A. (2013). The communication of certainty and uncertainty in Italian political media discourses. In A. Fetzer (Ed.), *The pragmatics of political discourse* (pp. 135–165). Amsterdam/Philadelphia: Benjamins.
Rundblad, G. (2007). Impersonal, general, and social. The use of Metonymy versus passive voice in medical discourse. *Written Communication, 24*(3), 250–277.
Salager-Meyer, F. (1994). Hedges and textual communicative function in medical english written discourse. *English for Specific Purposes, 13*(2), 149–170.
Salager-Meyer, F. (1997). I think that perhaps you should: A study of Hedges in written scientific discourse. In T. Miller (Ed.), *Functional approaches to written text: Classroom applications* (pp. 105–118). Washington, DC: United States Information Agency.
Sanders, J., & Spooren, W. (1996). Subjectivity and certainty in epistemic modality: A study of Dutch epistemic modifiers. *Cognitive Linguistics, 7*(3), 241–264.
Swan, M. (2005). *Grammar*. Oxford: Oxford University Press.
Szarvas, G., Vincze, V., Farkas, R., Móra, G., & Gurevych, I. (2012). Cross-genre and cross-domain detection of semantic uncertainty. *Computational Linguistics, 38*, 335–367.
Velldal, E., Øvrelid, L., & Oepen, S. (2010). Resolving speculation: MaxEnt Cue classification and dependency-based scope rules. In *Proceedings of the fourteenth conference on computational natural Lan-guage learning – Shared task* (pp. 48–55). Uppsala, Sweden.
Vincze, V., Szarvas, G., Farkas, R., Móra, G., & Csirik, J. (2008). The bio-scope corpus: Biomedical texts annotated for uncertainty, negation and their scopes. *BMC Bioinformatics, 9*(11), S9. http://doi.org/10.1186/1471-2105-9-S11-S9.
Willett, T. (1988). A cross-linguistic survey of the grammaticalization of evidentiality. *Studies in Language, 12*(1), 51–97.
Zhou, H., Huang, D., Li, X., & Yuansheng, Y. (2011). Combining structured and flat features by a composite Kernel to detect hedges scope in biological texts. *Chinese Journal of Electronics, 20*, 476–482.
Zhou, H., Huijie, D., Huang, D., & Minling, Z. (2015). Hedge scope detection in biomedical texts: An effective dependency- based method. *PLoS One, 10*(7), 1–16.
Zou, B., Zhou, G., & Zhu, Q. (2013). Tree Kernel-based negation and speculation scope detection with structured syntactic parse features. In *Proceedings of the 2013 conference on empirical methods in natural language processing* (pp. 968–976).
Zuczkowski, A., Bongelli, R., & Riccioni, I. (2011). Proposizione costitutiva di mondo e indicatori linguistici percettivi e cognitivi. In K. Hölkerm & C. Marello (Eds.), *Dimensionen der Analyse von Texten und Diskursen. Festschrift für János Sándor zum achtzigsten Geburstag. Dimensioni dell'analisi di testi e discorsi. Festschrift für János Sándor Petöfi in János Sándor Petöfi in occasione del suo ottantesimo compleanno* (pp. 41–61). Berlin: Li.
Zuczkowski, A., Bongelli, R., Vincze, L., & Riccioni, I. (2014a). Epistemic stance. Knowing, unknowing, believing (KUB) positions. In A. Zuczkowski, R. Bongelli, I. Riccioni, & C. Canestrari (Eds.), *Communicating certainty and uncertainty in medical, supportive and scientific contexts* (pp. 115–136). Amsterdam/Philadelphia: Benjamins.

Zuczkowski, A., Gianluca, C., Riccioni, I., Bongelli, R., & Canestrari, C. (2014b). Italian come se 'as if': Evidential and epistemic aspects. In S. Cantarini, W. Abraham, & L. Elizabeth (Eds.), *Certainty-uncertainty – and the attitudinal space in between* (pp. 297–323). Amsterdam/ Philadelphia: Benjamins.

BMJ References

Aveyard, P., Cheng, K. K., Almond, J., Sherratt, E., Lancashire, R., Lawrence, T., Griffin, C., & O. Evans. (1999). Cluster randomised controlled trial of expert system based on the transtheoretical ('stages of change') model for smoking prevention and Cessation in schools. *British Medical Journal.*

Bartleet, T. H. (1875). Clinical remarks on a case of strangulated Femoral Hernia. *British Medical Journal.*

Colebrook, L. (1933). Puerperal fever: Its aetiology and prevention. *British Medical Journal.*

Dally, J. F. H. (1913). A clinical lecture on maximal and minimal blood pressures and their significance. *British Medical Journal.*

Davies, W. T. F. (1913). A method for operating for radical cure of Inguinal Hernia. *British Medical Journal.*

Davis, E. D. D. (1940). Treatment and primary suture of face wounds. *British Medical Journal.*

Doll, R., & Hill, A. B. (1956). Lung cancer and other causes of death in relation to smoking. *British Medical Journal.*

Duvard, C. (1842). Case of Catalepsy with transposition of the senses. *British Medical Journal.*

Harvey, I., Shalom, D., Marks, R. M., & Frankel, S. J. (1989). Non-melanoma skin cancer. Distribution and natural course are still open questions. *British Medical Journal.*

Hingeston, J. A. (1875). On revaccination. *British Medical Journal.*

Lister, J. (1880). Remarks on micro-organisms: Their relation to disease. *British Medical Journal.*

Morgan, W. P. (1916). The treatment of wound infections. *British Medical Journal.*

Oliver, J. (1907). The determinants of abortion and how to combat them. *British Medical Journal.*

Roper, A. C. (1908). Perforated gastric ulcer: Operation 44 hours after perforation: Recovery. *British Medical Journal.*

Scott-Coombes, D., & Thompson, J. N. (1991). Bile duct stones and laparoscopic cholecystectomy. Selective intraoperative Cholangiography is the best strategy. *British Medical Journal.*

Snow, J. (1852). On the cause and prevention of death from Chloroform. *British Medical Journal.*

Wells, T. S. (1861). Lecture on Vescico-vaginal and Recto-vaginal fistula. *British Medical Journal.*

Wiener, A. S. (1951). Aetiology of physiological jaundice of the newborn. *British Medical Journal.*

Wilson, G. S. (1947). The value of B. C. G. vaccination in control of Tuberculosis. *British Medical Journal.*

Witts, L. J. (1948). The problems of clinical research. *British Medical Journal.*

Chinese University Students' Development of Pragmatic Skills in L2 Italian: A Corpus-Based Study

Andrea Scibetta

Abstract This work focuses on Chinese University students' acquisition of L2 Italian from the point of view of pragmatics. Data gathered from a study consisting of empirical observations as well as quantitative and qualitative analyses of relevant *corpora* of Chinese students of L2 Italian at the University for Foreigners of Siena (Italy) will be introduced.

According to an interdisciplinary theoretical background, mainly about Chinese learners' acquisition of L2 Italian (Valentini 1992; Banfi 2003; Galli 2007; Diadori and Di Toro 2009; Rastelli 2013 *inter alia*), Pragmalinguistics and Intercultural Pragmatics (Kasper and Blum-Kulka 1993; Wierzbicka 2003; Bührig and Ten Thije 2006; Kecskes 2014 *inter alia*), the results of a series of experimental written and oral activities about specific pragmatic skills performed by 85 Chinese learners of L2 Italian will be introduced and analysed.

The main purpose of the above-mentioned study is first of all to deepen the knowledge about the difficulties as well as the specificities of this category of students in developing particular pragmatic skills in Italian. Secondly, to suggest some effective teaching techniques, in order to help these students develop their pragmatic competence faster, which could be also adapted to other categories of learners.

Keywords Pragmatic competence • L2 Italian • Chinese learners • Development of pragmatic skills

A. Scibetta (✉)
Linguistica e Didattica Della Lingua Italiana a Stranieri, Università per Stranieri di Siena (University for Foreigners of Siena), Siena, Italy
e-mail: scibetta.andrea@gmail.com

J. Romero-Trillo (ed.), *Yearbook of Corpus Linguistics and Pragmatics 2016*,
Yearbook of Corpus Linguistics and Pragmatics 4,
DOI 10.1007/978-3-319-41733-2_11

1 Introduction

The total number of Chinese people in Italy has sharply risen since the end of the 1980s (cf. Istituto Nazionale di Statistica – Istat- 2015). The Chinese population in Italy was about 70,000 people in 2003, 188,000 people in 2010 and 265,000 people in 2015 (*ibid.*).

This data confirms, on the one hand, that Italy is one of the most chosen European destinations by Chinese migrants, on the other hand that Chinese people have constantly represented one of the most present nationalities in Italy in the past few years (cf. Ceccagno 2009).

In the last 10 years, in particular, the number of Chinese learners of L2 Italian within universities and academies has sharply risen. Such a considerable increase is the result of some relevant projects implemented by Italian and Chinese institutions, among which the "Marco Polo Program", started in 2007 and integrated in 2009 with the "Turandot Project", is worthy of mention.

An increasing attention towards Chinese migrants' acquisition processes of L2 Italian has contributed to produce some preliminary research studies since the beginning of the 1990s. Two of the most relevant studies were conducted by Valentini (1992) and Banfi (2003), who mainly focused on the analysis of the most frequent morphosyntactic and phonological irregularities of Chinese learners in spontaneous contexts.

Some more recent contributions were carried out from the point of view of different fields of study, and analysing *corpora* of data related to more homogeneous categories of learners (cf. Galli 2007; Diadori and Di Toro 2009 for L2 Italian Acquisition in classroom contexts; Rastelli 2010 for applied linguistics; Rastelli 2013 for the input processing).

Nevertheless, although the international scientific literature has already attributed a crucial importance to the development (and to the teaching) of pragmatic skills, this aspect seems to be underestimated with regard to Chinese learners' acquisition of L2 Italian.

As regards the literature on this specific aspect of the acquisition of other Second Languages, in particular German and English, on the contrary, monographs and detailed works on the development of communicative and pragmatic skills by this specific category of learners have already been published (cf. Hong 2002 and Wang 2007 for German; Wang 2011; Leung and Ruan 2012 for English, *inter alia*).

This work introduces the main results of a corpus-based research study about Chinese university students' development of pragmatic competence in L2 Italian carried out from January 2014 to August 2015 within classroom–learning contexts, namely "Marco Polo – Turandot courses", at the University for Foreigners in Siena, Italy.

During the period January–August 2014 I selected a target group of 80 Chinese learners with a language-communicative competence at B1 level (CEFR), divided into four different classes. I spent an initial period of 4 months conducting empirical, non-participant observations of the selected group during spoken activities in classroom and I transcribed and analyzed a corpus of speech acts performed by the learners.

Further observations were conducted during the period January–April 2015 with a group of 85 Chinese learners in the same learning contexts, with the same language-communicative level.[1]

After that, on the basis of the gathered information, I planned, realized and conducted in class a series of experimental activities addressed to 56 of the observed students (while the other group of 29 students worked as a control group). These activities, both written and oral, were about specific pragmatic skills and their main purpose was to verify the students' level of pragmatic competence, as well as the development of their meta-pragmatic awareness in a short time span.

1.1 The "Marco Polo – Turandot Program"

The "Marco Polo Program" (*Make Boluo jihua* 马可波罗计划) was started in 2007 as a result of an international agreement signed in 2006 by the Italian and the Chinese governments, and modified integrating the "Turandot Program" (*Tulanduo jihua* 图兰朵计划) in 2009.

The main purpose of such a project is to give Chinese students the opportunity to attend L2 Italian intensive courses in Italy for a period of at least eight months. After having attended the language courses and after having obtained a language proficiency certificate at B1 or B2 level (CEFR), "Marco Polo – Turandot" students can start a degree course in their disciplines within Italian universities and academies. The difference between the "Marco Polo" and "Turandot" programs lies on the fact that the former is mainly for students specializing in scientific subjects, while the latter is mainly for students specializing in arts and music.

2 Theoretical Considerations About Some Key-Concepts

Some important key-concepts that deal with the theoretical background of the current study will be briefly analysed in this section.

First, since one of the purposes of this study is to measure the pragmatic competence of the observed learners, a brief account on some of the most influent definitions of "pragmatic competence" will be introduced.

[1] Observations could not be carried out in the period August 2014–January 2015 because the period of stay of "Marco Polo – Turandot students" in Italian universities usually starts in January and finishes in August. This is also the reason why I conducted observations on two different groups of students.

Afterwards, taking into consideration that the cultural and the intercultural dimensions have a considerable influence on the development of pragmatic competence in an L2, as regards students involved in this research in particular, some of the most influent connotations of "culture" (with particular references to "Italian culture" and "Chinese culture") and "interculture(s)" will be analysed.

2.1 *Pragmatic Competence in a Second Language*

Various and heterogeneous definitions of the concept of "pragmatic competence" have been given by different scholars (cf. Koike 1989; Bachman 1990; Kasper and Blum Kulka 1993; Thomas 1995; Kecskes 2014 *inter alia*).

Each scholar has proposed a model of definition of this concept focusing on one or more crucial aspects: Bialystok, e.g., asserts that "pragmatic competence entails a variety of abilities concerned with the use and interpretation of language in context" (Bialystok in Kasper and Blum-Kulka 1993: 43), stressing the importance on the subject as utterer and hearer at the same time, and emphasizing also the key-role played by the context of interaction. According to Bachman (1990), the most relevant characterizations of pragmatic competence are represented by sociolinguistic and illocutionary competence, the latter including the ability to express a series of communicative functions.

Numerous theoretical contributions concerned also the development of pragmatic competence as well as the interplay between pragmatic competence in the L1 and pragmatic competence in an L2.

In particular, I consider the theoretical model adopted by Kecskes' Socio-Cognitive Approach in order to define such notions to be one of the most objective and reliable ones.

Pragmatic competence in the L1, defined by Kecskes (2014: 63–65) as the result of the "language socialization" and, at the same time, the result of the "conceptual socialization",[2] develops through the interplay of both language knowledge and knowledge of the socio-cultural norms of a specific language community.

The substantial difference between the development of pragmatic competence in the L1 and that in an L2 is that in the former the above-mentioned socializations take place since the very beginning of an individual's life, while in the latter they take place later and generally in a more limited time span. Moreover, pragmatic competence in an L2 seems to be built on the basis of one's language and socio-cultural experience in the L1.

For this reason it is important to investigate to what extent "the preferred ways of saying things and the preferred ways of organizing thoughts" (Kecskes 2007, 2014)

[2] This expression, adopted also in Ochs 1988, Willett 1995 e Mitchell and Myles 1998, has had a broad use in linguistic anthropology.

in one's L1 have an influence on and interact with pragmatic competence in an acquired L2.

It is also important to pay attention to the fact that such a procedure can be quite complex: since pragmatic competence in the L1 is characterized by diatopic, diachronic and diaphasic variations, the development of pragmatic competence in an L2 can be influenced by such kind of changes, as well.

It is scientifically recognized by many scholars that "pragmatic competence of nonnative interactants plays a significant role in second and foreign language use and intercultural communication" (Kecskes 2014: 61).

However, the question about which kind of relationship there is between linguistic competence and pragmatic competence in a Second Language, in particular whether the former constitutes only a support for the latter or vice versa, seems still unsolved. The complex question "first pragmatics and then grammar or first grammar and then pragmatics?" has been investigated by various scholars (i.e. Kasper and Blum-Kulka 1993; Bardovi-Harlig 1999; Bettoni 2006), who gave different answers.

Whilst analyzing Second Language Learners' performances it is often visible that even students with high morphosyntactic and lexical competencies produce systematic pragmatic irregularities (Scibetta 2013).

In the process of teaching an L2, the precocious or late development of learners' pragmatic competence can be highly influenced by the teaching approach and method used by the teacher: grammar- and translation-centered methods, for instance, contribute to a quicker development of morphosyntactic skills, while communicative methods could be more useful to let students develop faster their pragmatic skills, creating a good balance between grammar and pragmatics (cf. Vedovelli 2010).

In any case, the knowledge of the socio-cultural norms of the language community (or communities) who speak the acquired L2 (specifically, the norms of the "mainstream culture" of a certain language community, with all its possible variations) is fundamental for the development of pragmatic competence in that language.

As far as the research about the development of pragmatic competence is concerned, and in particular in this work, I argue that there are fuzzy boundaries between pragmatic competence and intercultural pragmatic competence, because the role played by the culture(s) related to the acquired Second Language, as well as the role played by interculturality, is crucial.

2.2 The Concept of "Culture" Beyond Its Definitions

"Culture" is a concept whose use appears in numerous fields of research and that, at the same time, is broadly used in everyday communication within a multifaceted range of contexts.

However, it seems that every attempt to give an objective definition of such a concept does not succeed. A first, insurmountable difficulty emerges when carrying out a comparative analysis of the connotations that this concept assumes in different languages: it is easily observable that its connotations vary according to different language communities. In Italian, for instance, the word "culture" is generally translated as "cultura". According to the *Treccani* Italian language dictionary, this word corresponds to a range of connotations that goes beyond those of the English word "culture".[3]

Analyzing the *Xiandai Hanyu Cidian* ("Contemporary Chinese dictionary"),[4] on the other hand, we observe that the range of connotations attributed to the word *wenhua* 文化 – nearest translation to the English word "culture" – is much more restricted compared with Italian (there are totally six entries in the Italian dictionary, while there are only three entries in the Chinese dictionary).

After carrying out an analysis like the one described above, some crucial questions that come out can be:

(a) to what extent do the connotations attributed to 'culture' change from one language to another?
(b) supposing that there is a "common ground" among the various connotations that "culture" can assume in different language communities, what kind of connotations is this common ground composed by?
(c) supposing that the concept "culture" can be conceived differently according to different language communities, which kind of conceptual and practical misunderstandings can rise when talking about "culture" in another language?[5]

As far as research in different disciplines is concerned, many scholars who belong to different fields of study have tried to give their own definition of "culture", yet none of them can be considered as the definitive one.

Taking into account the heterogeneity of connotations that this concept can be given, as well as the numerous interpretations that it can imply, I shall argue that it could be more fruitful trying to historicize the most influent definitors of the word "culture", contextualizing them in their time and space and trying to understand which pre-comprehension processes are at the basis of their definitions, rather than searching for an objective definition (or "the most objective one").

This is not to argue that trying to define the concept of "culture" does not make sense, rather that no definition tends to be satisfactory enough in order to be consid-

[3] Cfr. Vocabolario della lingua italiana Treccani, www.treccani.it "cultura".

[4] Cfr. Cao, X. (ed.). 2008. Xiandai Hanyu Cidian (di 5 ban) 现代汉语词典(第5版). Beijing: Shangwu Yinshuguan 商务印书管.

[5] A more detailed analysis of the definitions of "culture" contained in dictionaries of different languages in a specific space of time, investigating continuity and change phenomena, could be of great interest.

ered objective. For this reason, I think that it could be quite interesting to adopt an interdisciplinary approach, being able to benefit from the various connotations that the word "culture" has assumed within different disciplines.

Therefore, what we can do when analyzing such a complex and multifaceted concept, is to put in evidence some important aspects of connotations that have been given by different influential scholars.

Investigating "culture" through the above-mentioned methodological pattern, I would like to emphasize some of its connotations that can be useful in interlanguage and intercultural pragmatics research.

First, the role played by the dynamic aspect of culture must be emphasized. Cultures, as well as languages, must be observed in their diachronic dimension: in fact,

> the core of cultural models that people in the same speech community share changes diachronically through systematic and repeated shifts that can come from socio-political changes, technological changes, environmental changes and the like (Kecskes 2014: 92).

Because of the crucial role played by dynamicity, I shall argue that "culture" should be considered as a process rather than as a concept.

Therefore, when observing and studying cultural models, a researcher must contextualize them in time and space. On the other hand, the criteria through which a researcher may pre-comprehend and analyse cultural models can be affected by the socio-historical situation (s)he is contextualized in: (s)he must be aware that (s)he cannot escape from her/his *Zeitgeist*[6] (or "spirit of the time"), the interplay of the restrictions and the imperatives imposed to individuals by the predominant representations during the time in which they live, as well as from her/his *Lebenswelt*[7] (or "lifeworld"), the set of preliminary, already-existing conditions of the individuals' experience. The limitations imposed by our *Zeitgeist* and our *Lebenswelt* also represent limitations for research.

Secondly, according to Durkheim's dichotomy "individual representations" - "collective representations", initially used in order to investigate the concepts of "spirituality" and "religion" and successively applied also to the concept of "culture" (Durkheim 1898), I argue that shared cultural norms and values are not the result of the sum of individual cultural norms and values. On the one hand the former are something more than the sum of the latter, while on the other hand individuals internalize cultural norms and values in their specific ways, creating their specific cultural models (Berger and Luckmann 1966).

Thirdly, it is important to emphasize that cultural boundaries, as well as language boundaries, do not usually coincide with national boundaries (cf. Nocentini 2004).

---

[6] The term *Zeitgeist* dates back to the end of eighteenth century – beginning of the nineteenth century, when it was used by influent European thinkers and philosophers like Hegel, Goethe, Herder, Fichte, Hölderlin.

[7] Among the scholars who used and analysed the term *Lebenswelt*, Hohl and Habermas are worthy of mention.

Several different cultures can coexist within the same nation. In fact, there is a series of socio-historical facts that highly influence the developing of cultural models and that may contribute to differentiate even regions that are very close one to another. For instance, an Italian from Sicily has cultural norms and models characterized by considerable differences from those possessed by an Italian from Venice (before the unification of Italy in 1861, Sicily and Venice had been characterized by completely different socio-historical events); the same happens when comparing cultural models of a Chinese from Beijing and a Chinese from Canton, as well as a Chinese from Inner-Mongol and a Chinese from Yunnan. For this reason, it should be useful and more precise to speak about "Italian cultures" or "Chinese cultures" in the plural rather than in the singular.

What is usually meant by "Italian culture" or "Chinese culture", especially in studies of cross-cultural and intercultural pragmatics, is "Italian or Chinese mainstream culture", a set of shared cultural norms, usually promoted and encouraged by institutions with the purpose of building a national identity. However, at the same time a series of co-existing "not-dominating cultures" that may have a considerable influence on the mainstream culture both on the diatopic and on the diachronic dimensions, must also be taken into consideration.

According to what explained above, I argue that several scholars who conducted relevant and precious works of cross-cultural pragmatics and of intercultural pragmatics have sometimes underestimated the internal complexity of the investigated "cultures", tending to analyse them as generic, pre-constructed entities (i.e. Wierzbicka 2003).

2.3 *From Culture(s) to Interculture(s)*

The concepts "interculturality" and "intercultures" have been investigated by different scholars, particularly in the fields of cross-cultural pragmatics and interlanguage pragmatics. The most part of them, even with different approaches, rejected the idea that such concepts represent phenomena of simple, static encounters between two or more "cultures", or between two or more interactants who belong to different "cultures" (e.g. Nishizaka 1995; Mori 2003; Markee and Kasper 2004; Blum-Kulka et al. 2008; Kecskes 2007). In particular, Kecskes' (2007, 2010 and 2014) and Kecskes and Zhang's (2009) Socio-Cognitive Approach appears justified, according to which there is a basic difference between such two concepts. In fact, the Socio-Cognitive Approach takes "interculturality" into consideration

> as a phenomenon that is not only interactionally and socially constructed in the course of communication but also relies on relatively definable cultural models and norms that represent the speech communities to which the interlocutors belong (Kecskes 2014: 98).

According to Kecskes' Socio-Cognitive Approach, "Intercultures" differ from the key-concept of "Interculturality". While the latter can be also considered as a general phenomenon, the former notion must, instead, be considered only as an emerging situation produced within an interaction between members belonging to two or more different socio-cultural backgrounds. "Intercultures", in fact, are

> ad hoc creations. They are produced in a communicative process in which cultural norms and models brought into the interaction from prior experience of interlocutors blend with features created ad hoc in a synergetic way. The result is intercultural discourse in which there is mutual transformation of knowledge and communicative behaviour rather than transmission. The emphasis is on transformation rather than on transmission (ivi: 99).

For the same reason Rehbein (1985) as well as Koole and Ten Thije emphasize the importance of "culture constructed in cultural contact" (Koole and ten Thije 1994: 69) when describing "intercultures". These two scholar also attribute a crucial importance to the aspect of immanent, emerging co-construction within intercultural communication.

Rehbein, in particular, states:

> Interkulturelle Verständigung ist an das Verstehen des sprachlichen Handelns des anderen gebunden. Dieses setzt an am sprachlichen und nonverbalen Ausdruck als der Inskription des zugrundeliegenden sprachlichen Musters und dessen Handlungsdimensionen. Daraus entsteht das Problem interkultureller Verständigung, denn die Inskription lässt sich nur verstehen, wenn ein gemeinsames Wissen zugrundeliegt; andernfalls wird das (normalerweise automatisch ablaufende) Verstehen zu einem kommunikativen Entziffern bzw. zu einem Projizieren eigenen Wissens in den anderen, zu einem tastenden Etablieren ein gemeinsames Wissens im Diskurs (Rehbein 1985: 10).[8]

Intercultural communication has often been investigated through the analysis of a series of misunderstandings due to cultural differences; thus, intercultural communication has often been considered essentially different from intracultural communication. However, a few scholars carried out studies of intercultural communication beyond misunderstanding (e.g. Clyne 1994; Koole and ten Thije 2001; Bührig and ten Thije 2006), focusing on the similarities between intracultural and intercultural communication rather than on the differences (in particular Kecskes 2014, according to whom the two concepts build a continuum, and not a dichotomy).

In such analyses, some important concepts emerged in order to deepen understanding about methodological mechanisms, beyond misunderstanding, which

---

[8] EN: "Intercultural understanding (*Verständigung*) is linked to the mutual understanding of the other's speech actions. This estimates the verbal and nonverbal expression to be the inscription of the underlying speech action patterns and its dimensions for action. This results in the problem of intercultural understanding, since the inscription can only be understood when there is a basis of common knowledge; otherwise the process (which normally develops automatically) becomes a communicative deciphering process (*Entziffern*) or leads to the projection (*Projektion*) of one's own knowledge onto the other, leading to a feeling for the establishment (*Etablieren*) of common knowledge in discourse" (Translation of ten Thije in Bührig and ten Thije 2006: 114–115).

investigate intercultures. Of particular relevance is Rehbein's concept of "cultural apparatus"; in his words,

> the cultural apparatus deconstructs those standardized forms of acting and speaking which bring about the actors' getting entangled in aporetic ways of communication and it constructs means of an understanding by making recourse to a higher level of mediation, "generating" productive and receptive new forms on the part of speaker and hearer and giving rise to innovative forms of communication (Rehbein in Bührig and ten Thije 2006: 44).

Other key-concepts that could be of great relevance in order to investigate intercultural communication beyond misunderstanding are those related to the notion of "perspective" in intercultural pragmatics, and particularly to the "ability to shift perspective" through the mechanism of the "communicative apparatus of perspectivising" (Bührig and ten Thije 2006: 4), or, in other words, "perspectivising as a communicative apparatus" (Bührig and ten Thije 2006: 112).

3 Methodology, Data Analysis and Results

3.1 Adopted Methodologies

This work is mainly divided into two parts. The first part consists of empirical, non-participant observations of a selected group composed by 80 B1 Level "Marco Polo –Turandot students", for a total amount of 100 hours, during the period January–August 2014 at the University for Foreigners of Siena. Further observations of the same kind were conducted with another group of 85 "Marco Polo – Turandot students" in the same place and with the same language-communicative competence from January to April 2015. During the observations I transcribed a large corpus of different kinds of speech acts performed by the learners during classroom oral activities, like simple dialogues in groups or with the teacher, or role plays.

The second part was carried out from the point of view of L2 Italian teaching from April to August 2015. In this period I planned, realized and carried out a series of ten mutually related and logically connected pragmatic activities in class with 56 of the 85 students observed in the previous 4 months, while the other 29 learners constituted a control group. My main purpose was to analyse the development of their pragmatic competence.

The first two activities were characterized by written tasks and the total estimated time allowed to learners for completing each activity was 25–30 min. The first activity was about communicative formal and informal contexts and some categories of speech acts used in such kinds of situations within Italian mainstream culture and it was conducted both with the target group and with the control group; the second one was specifically about the use of pragmatic markers both in formal and in informal contexts.

The main aim of these two preliminary activities was to verify the target group's level of competence in these specific pragmatic skills, as well as to identify their most common difficulties.

In addition, no activity contained explanations for the underlying norms of usage for specific speech acts or expressions in particular contexts, with the purpose of stimulating learners' meta-pragmatic reasoning. In fact, every ability was divided into two macro-parts: a preliminary one for the "focus on form" and a consequent one in which students were required to classify some speech acts according to pre-existing definitions or to explain with their own words the meaning they attributed to certain speech acts or pragmatic markers, in order to let them move from form to function inductively.

Although methodologies usually adopted in pragmatic and intercultural pragmatic research focus on spoken data, in this part of the study I preferred opting for written data analysis. In order to better "measure" the observed students' metapragmatic awareness, and, in particular, the interplay between pragmatic competence and metapragmatic awareness, I considered written activities more reliable.

Afterwards, I planned and realized a series of seven pragmatic oral activities essentially based on the notions contained within the first two written activities (formal and informal contexts in Italian mainstream culture and pragmatic markers used in both kinds of contexts). In addition, a new aspect was also introduced in the last three activities, namely metaphoric expressions and their contextualization in formal and in informal contexts: the main purpose of this last aspect was to let students familiarize with the use of some kinds of metaphoric expressions in specific formal and informal contexts and with appropriate pragmatic particles.

The seven oral activities experimented with the target group consisted of role-plays or simulations of talk shows and the total estimated time allowed to students for the planning-phase and the performing phase of each activity was about 15–20 min. In each case students were divided into groups and every group was given a piece of paper, on which some indications and some essential information about the setting of the role-play or of the talk show simulation were written; furthermore, each group received also a list of speech acts that had to be performed and contextualized in their activity.

Each oral performance of each group was audio-recorded, transcribed and analysed: the adopted method for the transcription is the "Jeffersonian transcription system" (cfr. Jefferson 1985, 1996). While audio-recording the performances I also accurately took notes about single students' adopted para-verbal and non-verbal languages; the transcription of the performances was integrated also with this further information.

The last oral activity was not experimented only with the target group of 56 students, but also with the control group of 29 students, who did not carry out the previous seven activities. After that, a final written activity about metaphoric expressions[9] contextualized in formal and informal contexts and with appropriate pragmatic particles was conducted in class both with the target group and with the control group.

The main reason why the first activity and the last two activities were experimented also with the control group was to compare the performances (and, as

[9] For more detailed information about the role and the use of metaphors across languages, both from a linguistic and a cognitive point of view, cf. Gola and Ervas (2016).

regards the oral activities in particular, the transcriptions of the performances) as well as to compare pragmatic skills of different groups.

3.2 *Data Analysis and Results*

In this paragraph I will analyse some speech acts transcribed during the empirical non-participant observations of the target group, as well as some results from the pragmatic written activities carried out in class.

The obtained results put in evidence students' generalized difficulties in the comprehension of the norms of appropriateness of different speech acts, most of all in relation with different typologies of possible interlocutors, as well as in the usage of appropriate speech acts and pragmatic markers in different situations.

In terms of methodology, introducing the use Mey's concept of "pragmeme" could be of great importance (Mey 2001). According to Mey's Pragmatic Acts Theory, "there are no speech acts, but only situated speech acts, or instantiated pragmatic acts" (Mey 2001:218). For this reason, more attention should be focused not on individual speech acts, but on "characterizing a general situational prototype (what Mey calls a "pragmeme") that can be executed in the situation" (Kecskes 2014: 38). "Pragmemes" are defined as "prototypes" that "can be substantiated and realized through individual pragmatic acts" (*ivi*: 93) or "practs".

Moreover, according to Wierzbicka (2003), particularly in line with her theory of "universal semantic metalanguage",[10] in order to avoid to use concepts that could be understood as "culture specific", I will not give specific connotations of speech acts like "direct/indirect", "polite/impolite". On the other hand, I will emphasize that some specific speech acts could be perceived as "direct/indirect" or "polite/impolite" in a certain language community (in this case I am focusing only on Italian and Chinese language communities and "mainstream cultures").

As regards the data collected and transcribed through empirical observations, I will here briefly analyse two "pragmatic acts" as examples of particularly diffused pragmatic irregularities.

The first case is about kind requests made in formal contexts. The following pragmatic act is representative of a generalised kind of pragmatic irregularities in the observed Chinese students' performances in Italian. The analysis of the following act, performed in April 2014 by a female student who had to pretend to be in a formal situa-

[10] According to Wierzbicka, the "natural semantic metalanguage" is "is a technical, artificial language, not a natural language (…) because it is derived entirely from natural language and because it can be understood via natural language without any additional arbitrary signs and conventions. Arbitrary signs and conventions are not allowed in this metalanguage, because their meaning would have to be explained – and these explanations, in their turn, would not be intelligible unless they were couched in immediately understandable natural language. (On the other hand, it is allowed to use 'iconic' conventions, such as spatial arrangement of components, the use of separate lines for different chunks of meanings, and the like)." (Wierzbicka 2003: 7)

tion during a role-play, shows that the used utterance could be perceived as "too direct", so as "inappropriate" in such a context within Italian mainstream culture.

(1)[11] PRAGMEME: [making a kind request]
PRACT: *Va bene io ora uso dizionario, o no?*
It's ok I now use dictionary or not
'Is it ok if I use the dictionary now, or not?'

However, taking into consideration the following corresponding Chinese expression (realised through a construction that is analogous to the above-shown one), such an act can be considered as perfectly appropriate in a formal situation within Chinese mainstream culture.

(2) PRAGMEME: [making a kind request]
PRACT: 我现在用词典,好不好? *wo xianzai yong cidian, hao bu hao?*[12]
I now use dictionary good no good
'I'm using the dictionary now, ok?'

The second case is related to the use of pragmatic particles. During my empirical observations I registered numerous difficulties concerning the use of such particles. Those difficulties, as previous personal studies put in evidence, tend to persist also in students with higher communicative competence in L2 Italian. Since the main irregularities are related with the position of the particles within the utterances, I hypothesized that such generalized standard-deviations can be due to the completely different position of the most part of pragmatic particles within Italian and Chinese utterances: in the former ones they are usually dislocated in the initial part of the utterance, while in the latter ones they are mainly dislocated in the final part, as the following comparison emphasizes (pragmatic particles are in **bold**):

PRAGMEME: [complimenting a child]
PRACT:
IT. **Ma** com'è carino questo bambino!
CHIN. 这个孩子这么可爱啊! *Zhe ge haizi zheme ke'ai* ***a*** *!*

The following utterance, performed in March 2014 by a male student during a role play, constitutes one of the numerous examples that may represent the above-described irregularity (the pragmatic particle is in **bold**):

[11] For the analysis of every single pragmatic act I opted for the transcription of the utterance, a literal translation in English of every single word and a possible translation of the utterance in English.

[12] Every time that a Chinese expression is reported in this work, the expression in Chinese characters and its translation through the *pinyin* are both reported.

(3) PRAGMEME: [complimenting a third person]
PRACT: *Questa donna come bella* ***eh!***
This woman how beautiful eh
'What a beautiful woman!'

Taking here into account the corresponding Chinese expression reported below, it can be noted that the pragmatic particle has been maintained in the same position, while in Italian it could be expected to be at the beginning of the utterance (***Ma*** *com'è bella questa donna!*).

(4) PRAGMEME: [complimenting a third person]
PRACT: 这位女人这么漂亮啊!*Zhe wei nüren zheme piaoliang* ***a*** *!*
This GENERIC CLASSIFIER FOR A PERSON woman so beautiful ah
'What a beautiful woman!'

According to what registered during the periods of empirical, non-participant observations carried out from January to August 2014 and from January to April 2015, I planned to realize a series of specific pragmatic activities, the main purpose of which was to reinforce and to develop students' performance of speech acts in formal and in informal contexts as well as their use of appropriate pragmatic particles in such situations. I chose to focus on these two aspects because the results of the observations confirm that learners produced a big amount of generalized irregularities related to these specific skills.

I also postulated that at the basis of such kinds of irregularities there can be "pragmatic transfer" phenomena from the L1 to the L2.[13] Such phenomena consist in the use of expressions that probably correspond to common speech acts in Chinese language and "mainstream culture", but may not result as appropriate for Italian language use.

As regards the analysis of the pragmatic written activities carried out in class about common speech acts in formal and in informal contexts and about pragmatic markers, in fact, diffused irregularities were registered, a part of which could have been identified as "pragmatic transfers".

For instance, a task within the activity about speech acts in formal and informal contexts asked to complete some sentences in a dialogue choosing the correct expressions among some options in brackets. Below is reported a part of this task, with the correct solutions in **bold**.

(5a)[14] PRAGMEME: [drawing someone's attention]
PRACT: *(* ***Mi scusi*** */ scusa / Prego), può dirmi dov'è l'aula 12?*
(FORM. **Excuse me** / INFORM. Excuse me / Please)
FORM. Can you tell me where is the classroom 12
'Excuse me, could you tell me where the classroom 12 is?'

[13] For a detailed definition of the concept of "pragmatic transfer", cf. Kasper and Blum-Kulka (1993).

[14] The translation in English has been added in this work, but it was not included in the original version of the task. Moreover, the methodological terminology ("PRAGMEME" and "PRACT") was not present in the original format.

(6a) PRAGMEME: [Asking someone to repeat]
PRACT: *(**Prego** , / grazie, / Cosa?) può ripetere per cortesia?*
(**Sorry**, / Thank you, / What?) FORM. can you repeat please
'Sorry, could you please repeat?'

(7a) PRAGMEME: [Explaining something already asked]
PRACT: *(Certo / Sì / **Chiedevo**) se sa dove si trova l'aula 12.*
Of course / Yes / **I was asking**) whether FORM. you know where is located the classroom 12
'I was wondering whether you know where the classroom 12 is'

(8a) PRAGMEME: [answering affirmatively]
PRACT: *(**Certamente** / Sì / Diciamo di sì), la terza porta sulla destra.*
(**Of course** / Yes / Let's say yes), the third door on the right
'Of course I do, the third door on the right'

Here below, instead, is reported the pattern that was most frequently chosen by the observed students (learners' correct choices are marked in **bold**, while learners' pragmatic irregularities are <u>underlined</u>):

(5b) PRAGMEME: [drawing someone's attention]
PRACT: *(**Mi scusi** / scusa / Prego), può dirmi dov'è l'aula 12?*
(FORM. **Excuse me** / INFORM. Excuse.me / Please)
FORM. can you tell me where is the classroom 12
'Excuse me, could you tell me where the classroom 12 is?'

(6b) PRAGMEME: [Asking someone to repeat]
PRACT: *(Prego, / grazie, / <u>Cosa?</u>) può ripetere per cortesia?*
(Sorry, / Thank you, / <u>What?</u>) FORM. can you repeat please
'Sorry, could you please repeat?'

(7b) PRAGMEME: [Explaining something already asked]
PRACT: *(<u>Certo</u> / Sì / Chiedevo) se sa dove si trova l'aula 12.*
(<u>Of course</u> / Yes / I was asking) whether FORM. you know where is located the classroom 12
'I was wondering whether you know where the classroom 12 is'

(8b) PRAGMEME: [answering affirmatively]
PRACT: *(**Certamente** / Sì / Diciamo di sì), la terza porta sulla destra.*
(**Of course** / Yes / Let's say yes) the third door on the right
'Of course I do, the third door on the right'

First of all, the second speech act used in the pattern above is not appropriate to the represented communicative situation. Since the context of this part of the task is formal, the communicative gambit[15] cosa? (EN. "what?") in order to ask to repeat could be perceived as impolite by some native speakers, while it can be appropriate in informal situations.

Moreover, the use of *certo* (EN. "of course") in the third statement, besides being inappropriate in such a communicative context, makes the Italian sentence non-grammatical.

It could be argued that at the basis of these kinds of irregularities there can be pragmatic transfer phenomena realised through the use of structures that correspond to typical Chinese speech acts that would be appropriate in such communicative situations in Chinese language and mainstream culture. Below a comparison between the two above-shown pragmatic irregularities in Italian and the corresponding Chinese expressions are exemplified:

(5c) PRAGMEME: [Asking someone to repeat]
PRACT: Italian: *Cosa? può ripetere per cortesia?*
What FORM. can you repeat please
Chinese: 什么?能不能再说一遍?
Shenme? Neng bu neng zai shuo yi bian?
What PRO DROP can not can again say once

(6c) PRAGMEME: [Explaining something already asked]
PRACT: Italian: *Certo se sa dove si trova l'aula 12*
Of course whether FORM. you know where is located the classroom 12
Chinese: 当然, 您知道12号教室在哪儿吗?
Dangran , nin zhidao 12 hao jiaoshi zai naer ma?
Of course FORM. you know 12 number classroom to be located where INTERR. PARTICLE

However, although I argue that the above-described irregular speech acts could represent transfer phenomena, it may be difficult to understand whether in such cases students only produce pragmatic transfers or the used expressions are the result of further co-occurring factors beyond the transfer.

Some researchers in the fields of interlanguage and intercultural pragmatics, in fact, even argue that although the phenomenon of "pragmatic transfer" has been and is still being broadly analysed, such phenomenon can hardly be validated (Kecskes 2014). According to Kecskes' Socio-Cognitive Approach,

> "Transfer" may not exactly be the right term to describe what takes place in the bi- and multilingual mind. What really happens is that the non-native speakers use their L1 (or Lx) cultural models, norms, and way of thinking about the world to formulate or interpret an utterance in another language, which may result in grammatical, lexical, and pronunciation errors at a lower level of proficiency, and grammatically correct but odd utterances or inappropriate use of expressions and formulaic units at a higher level of proficiency. So "transfer" does not seem to be the best way to describe this phenomenon (Kecskes 2014: 78).

[15] As regards the definition and a possible taxonomy of "communicative gambits", cf. Wang (2007).

The analysis conducted comparing the performances of the target group and of the control group put in evidence generalised difficulties and irregularities in both groups. The charts below represent the statistical results of the performances of the students of both groups related to the different parts of the first written activity (a sample of the whole activity can be found in the Appendix 1). Performances of every single student were evaluated in each part of the written activity; the marks attributed to the performances range from UNSATISFACTORY to EXCELLLENT.

Observing the comparison of the results obtained by both groups in each single part of the activity, it can be clearly seen that there are not substantial differences in terms of percentages related to success/failure; students of the control group sometimes obtained even better results than those of the target group (cf., for instance, Figs. 1, 2 and 3).

The analysis of the results obtained from the evaluation of the last activity (a sample of the last activity can be found in the Appendix 1), on the contrary, puts in evidence that the students of the target group, who had already carried out several experimental pragmatic activities in class, produced visibly better performances in comparison with those of the students of the control group. From the charts below it can be clearly observed that the percentage of students of the target group who

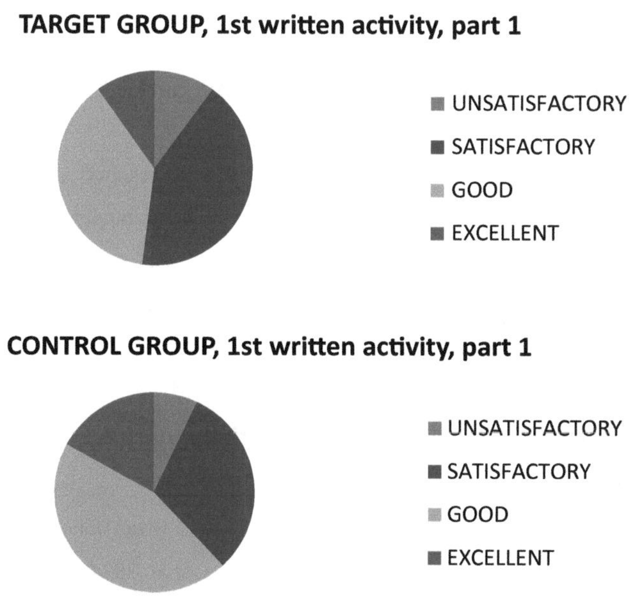

Fig. 1 Comparison between evaluations of target group's and control group's performances: 1st written activity, part 1

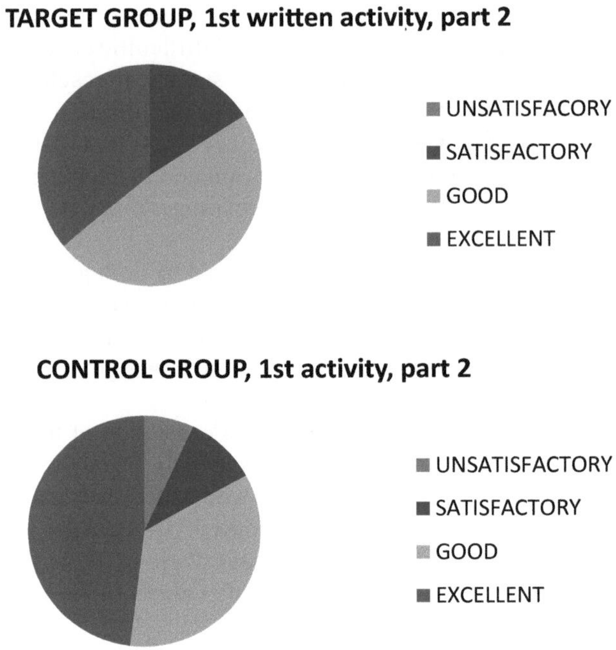

Fig. 2 Comparison between evaluations of target group's and control group's performances: 1st written activity, part 2

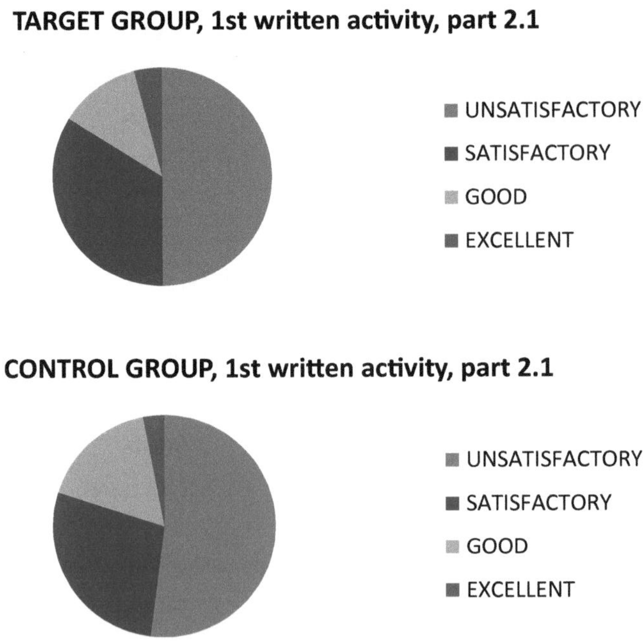

Fig. 3 Comparison between evaluations of target group's and control group's performances: 1st written activity, part 2.1

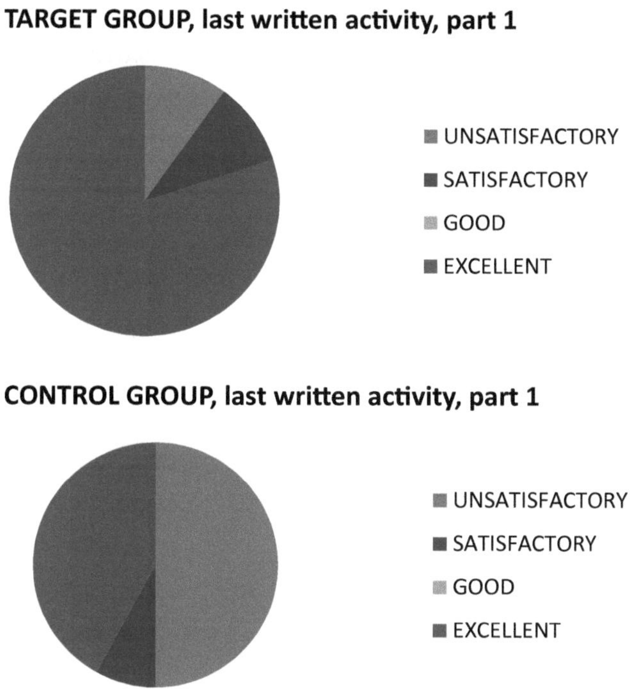

Fig. 4 Comparison between evaluations of target group's and control group's performances: last written activity, part 1

obtained GOOD or EXCELLENT results in each single part of the activity is remarkably higher than the corresponding percentage of students of the control group (Figs. 4, 5, 6 and 7).

As regards the comparative analysis of the oral performances of the students, similar results can be noted. Below is reported an excerpt of a conversation between some students of the target group while performing the first experimental oral activity. Such an activity was a role play in which learners had to pretend to be in a famous luxury restaurant; moreover, they had to use and to contextualize in their conversation a list of speech acts suggested by me (the pattern of the activity can be consulted in the Appendix 2). The excerpt has been transcribed through the Jeffersonian transcription system.

Stud. 1: Eh (0.2) salve benvenu:ti
Stud. 2: °benvenudi° grazie siamo in quattro quale siamo:: ↑ (0.5) tavolo
Stud. 1: mm prego sedetevi a tavo:lo tre
Stud. 2: ok andiamo ↓
Stud. 3: eh (0.3) ah (0.2) came (0.3) camelie (0.2) cam (0.1) cameliele ah (0.2) cameliele dammi il menù ↓

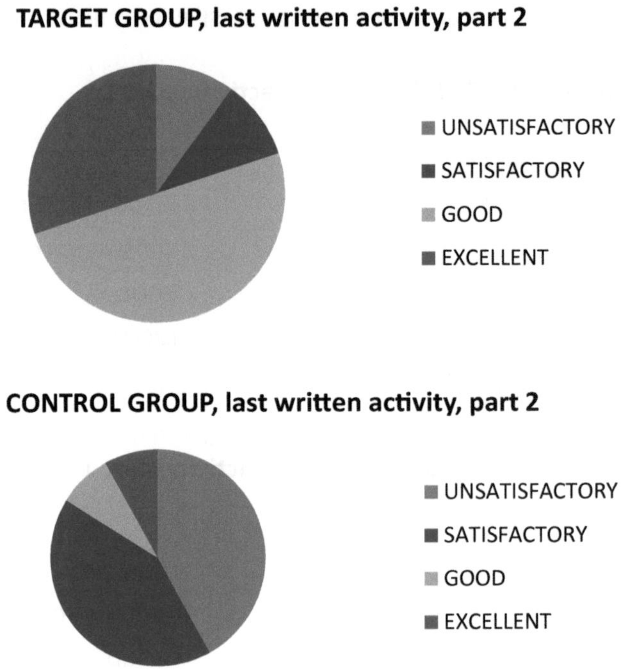

Fig. 5 Comparison between evaluations of target group's and control group's performances: last written activity, part 2

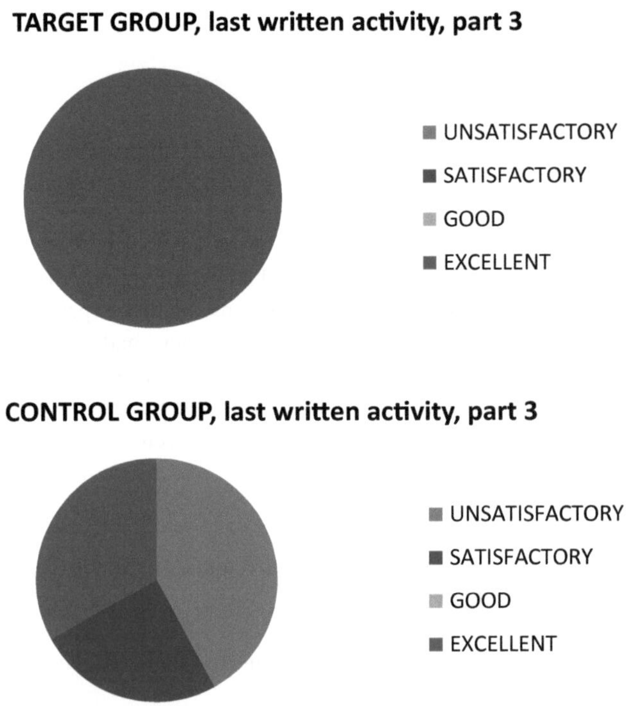

Fig. 6 Comparison between evaluations of target group's and control group's performances: last written activity, part 3

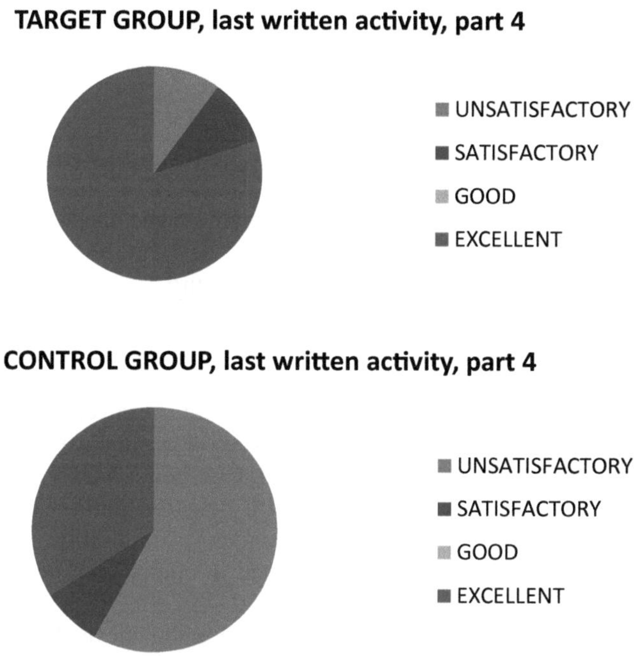

Fig. 7 Comparison between evaluations of target group's and control group's performances: last written activity, part 4

Stud. 1: eh (0.2) aspettate (0.2) eh (0.1) ecco↓
Stud. 2: °grazie°
Stud. 3: c'è un lasania? (.) °c'è°
Stud. 1: (.) eh (0.3) sì (0.4) sì sì sì *(laughs and looks down)*
Stud. 2.: una lasania pel favore↓ *(laughs)*
(.) e anche bodilia di l'acqua↓

As it can be observed from the students' performances, most of the speech acts produced are not appropriate for that communicative context (e.g. "cameliele dammi il menù↓", that can be translated "waiter, give me the menu"; or "c'è un lasania? (.)", that can be translated "is there a lasagna?").

The analysis of an excerpt from a conversation of the same group of students while performing the last experimental oral activity, on the contrary, shows considerable general improvements in the performances related to different pragmatic skills. This activity was also a role play, in which learners had to pretend to bargain the price of an object; also in this case they had to use a list of speech acts, including pragmatic particles and metaphoric expressions, suggested by me (a sample of the activity can be consulted in the Appendix 2).

Stud. 1:	Che bello que:sto museo:: ↓ quindi () forse posiamo::: ah comprare qualcosa per questo ↓
Stud. 2/Stud. 3:	Sì Sì andiamo andiamo ↓
Stud. 4:	Buongiorno [benvenute: ragazze ↓
Stud. 1/ Stud. 2:	[Buongiorno
Stud. 3:	**[Ciao**
Stud. 1:	Che bello: ombrello (0,2) quanto viene questo?
Stud. 4:	°Sì sì° speciale ↓ (0,5) questo↑ (0,4) que ah questa ombre ah ombrella (0,4) costa↑duecento euro ↓ (*laughs*)
Stud. 1/2/3:	Oh mamma mia ()
Stud. 2:	Ma quanto costa! (0,2) sembra fatto d'oro (*opens the hands*)

In this case learners' performance seems to reflect improvements in their pragmatic competence: a relevant part of their speech acts, for instance, is perfectly appropriate for that communicative context ("Che bello: ombrello (0,2) quanto viene questo?" that can be translated "What a beautiful umbrella, how much is this?"; or "Oh mamma mia" to show astonishment); in addition, prosodical elements and intonations are generally better used in comparison with the previous performance.

Particularly remarkable is the difference between the above-shown exceprt and the exceprt below, performed by students of the control group. In this case learners had to perform the same kind of dialogue, including the same list of speech acts, but it was their first and only time they took part in an experimental oral activity.

Stud. 1:	Quanto costa questo ↓ °so° (0,4) sovie (0,2) eh [sov
Stud. 2:	[souvenir
Stud. 1:	Souvenir
Stud. 2:	eh (0,3) cento euro ↓ (*laughs*)
Stud. 3:	Da da dai troppo caro ↓ (0,5) ah abbassa °un° po' il pazzo ↓
Stud. 1:	Eh () si sie sie siete () es (.) tres tristi (.) siete triste in vacanza eh (0,3) eh vo voliamo comprate pro: propi::o
Stud. 4	Eh () ascolta (.) io almeno () io almeno devo:: guada:gnarci un po' (.) eh (0,4) venticinque euro ↓ (*laughs*)

The analysis of the excerpt above puts in evidence generalised difficulties related to the appropriateness of the performed speech acts (e.g."eh vo voliamo comprate pro: propi::o", that could be translated "we really want that you buy", even though the expression performed sounds rather ambiguous) as well as to prosodic elements and intonation. There seems to be evidence that the quality of the target group students' performance is better than that of the control students' performance.

4 Conclusions

Some important information has emerged from the corpus-based study described in this work.

The results gathered from the experimental pragmatic activities carried out with a corpus of 85 B1 level students show that at the beginning the observed learners had generalized difficulties in the comprehension and use of the norms of appropriateness of different kinds of speech acts and pragmatic markers.

Some of the common irregularities observed could be analysed as the result of pragmatic transfer phenomena, even though it is not clear whether there are further co-occurring factors beyond the transfers.

Furthermore, the comparison of the experimental pragmatic activities performed by the target group and by the control group shows that, although students of both groups seemed to have similar pragmatic competences at the beginning, the performances of the target group in the last two activities gave results that were visibly better than those of the control group. This means that learners who took part in a series of experimental pragmatic activities developed some pragmatic skills better and faster.

However, some limitations of this kind of research should also be mentioned. First, it is not clear to what extent the L2 environment outside the class influenced the observed learners' development of pragmatic skills in L2 Italian; yet, it is sure that interactions with Italian language speakers and Italian learning in spontaneous contexts play a crucial role for the development of their language-communicative competence. Secondly, the experimental activities conducted in class were only simulations of real communicative situations: therefore also "intercultures", conceived as "*ad hoc* creations" (cf. Sect. 2.3), had to be re-created and simulated.

Having brought to bear the crucial importance of the pragmatic dimension in the L2 Italian acquisition process of "Marco Polo – Turandot" students, I emphasize the necessity of developing a specific pragmatic syllabus for this category of learners. At the same time, there is the need to deepen the knowledge about all the factors outside the class that can influence the students' development of pragmatic skills: longitudinal studies on single learners could be helpful.

Appendices

Appendix 1

1st Experimental Written Activity

1. Secondo te queste figure rappresentano situazioni formali o informali? Metti accanto ad ogni figura una F per "FORMALE" o una I per "INFORMALE", poi collega l'immagine con la frase che meglio la caratterizza.

1) 

2) 

3) 

4) 

5) 

Prego, ci parli della Seconda Guerra Mondiale.

Dai che ce la facciamo!!!

Marco, passami un altro pezzo.

Professore, qual è la Sua opinione sulla riforma dell'istruzione?

È stato un piacere conoscerla. Mi farò risentire al più presto.

2. Osserva le seguenti espressioni e prova a inserirle nelle colonne giuste. Guarda l'esempio.
   2.1 Lavora con un compagno. Per ogni espressione formale dell'esercizio 2 provate a scriverne una informale corrispondente, e viceversa.

Salve Professore   Grazie mille   Ci vediamo

Piacere di conoscerla   Può ripetere, per favore?   Salutami Marco

Cosa mi racconti di nuovo?   Le chiedo cortesemente di rispondermi al più presto

Sei stato un grande!   Manteniamo i contatti, mi raccomando

ESPRESSIONI FORMALI	ESPRESSIONI INFORMALI
Salve Professore	

Saluti/ congedi	Richieste/ richieste di informazioni	Espressioni di apprezzamento	Ringraziamenti
Salve Professore			

Last experimental written activity

1. Osserva le metafore (比喻) qui sotto e prova a collegarle ai loro significati, come nell'esempio.

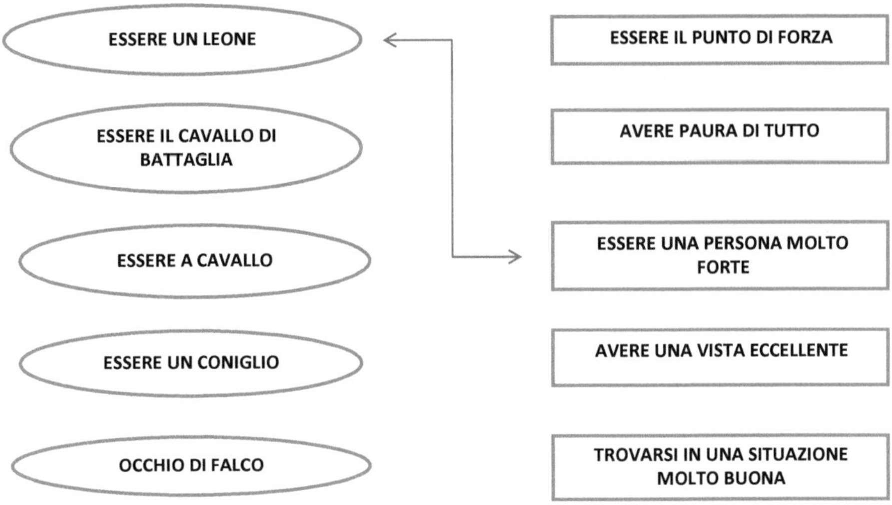

2. Leggi il testo qui sotto e prova a sottolineare le metafore. In tutto ce ne sono 7.

Quella sera pioveva pesantemente e senza sosta. Un tempo da lupi, per niente adatto ad un'iniziativa all'aperto. Eravamo quattro gatti, qualche amante della musica e qualche persona semplicemente curiosa di vedere un nuovo concerto.

Io ero insieme ad un paio di miei conoscenti: una certa Maria, che poi si è rivelata una vera iena, un certo Pino, proprio un cervello di gallina, ed un tale Claudio, che sembrava continuamente con la testa fra le nuvole e non apriva mai bocca. Insomma, non una gran compagnia. La serata era già iniziata male.

Il concerto partì con un'ora di ritardo per colpa del maltempo, ma la cosa che mi fece andare in bestia fu che la banda smise di suonare dopo soli 10 minuti, perché la pioggia non cessava. Appena capii che il concerto era stato annullato, rimasi di stucco per qualche minuto, ma poi realizzai subito che avevo buttato via la serata irrimediabilmente.

3. Leggi il breve dialogo qui sotto e prova a inserire le metafore giuste, scegliendo fra quelle proposte in fondo.

A: Ciao Marco! Come stai? Ti vedo molto dimagrito, ____________________________! Cos'è successo?
B: Ciao Antonio! Guarda, lascia perdere. Mi sono ripreso ora da una ____________________________________. Sono stato male una settimana.
A: Davvero? E cosa hai avuto?
B: Mah, non lo so esattamente. Forse una banale influenza. Ho dovuto prendere_______________________________________ di antibiotici per farmi passare tutto. E ancora non sono guarito al cento per cento. Fra l'altro domenica devo anche giocare una partita importante di calcio.
A: Dai, che piano piano passa tutto. Ti auguro una buona guarigione e___________________________________ per la partita!

una dose da cavallo	in bocca al lupo
sei un'acciuga	febbre da cavallo

4. Osserva ancora il dialogo dell'esercizio 3 e prova a spiegare a parole tue il significato delle seguenti metafore.

ESSERE UN'ACCIUGA:____
____

AVERE UNA FEBBRE DA CAVALLO:_______________________________
____

Appendix 2

1st Experimental Oral Activity

Siete un gruppo di amici ad un ristorante di lusso. Avete prenotato un tavolo e in questo momento il cameriere vi accoglie.

Usate tutte le espressioni qui sotto:

- Prego, accomodatevi qui
- Vorrei stare vicino alla finestra, è possibile?
- Vi chiedo di aspettare qualche minuto
- Vorremmo ordinare anche del vino

Last Experimental Oral Activity

Siete un gruppo di turisti in vacanza. Volete comprare dei *souvenir*, ma i venditori vi propongono prezzi troppo alti. Quindi iniziate a contrattare i prezzi.

Usate tutte le espressioni qui sotto:

- Ma dai! Troppo caro! Abbassa un po' il prezzo.
- Ok, ultima proposta. Facciamo 10 euro, che ne dite?
- Mamma mia! Da quanto costa sembra fatto d'oro!
- Ascoltate, io almeno devo guadagnarci un po'...
- Sei proprio uno stupido. Sei impazzito!

Works Cited

Bachman, L. F. (1990). *Fundamental considerations in language testing*. Oxford: Oxford University Press.

Banfi, E. (2003). *Italiano L2 di cinesi- Percorsi acquisizionali*. Milano: Franco Angeli.

Bardovi-Harlig, K. (1999). Exploring the interlanguage of interlanguage pragmatics: A research agenda for acquisitional pragmatics. *Language Leaning, 49*(4), 677–713.

Berger, P. L., & Luckmann, T. (1966). *The social construction of reality: A treatise in the sociology of knowledge*. Garden City: Anchor Books.

Bettoni, C. (2006). *Usare un'altra lingua. Guida alla pragmatica interculturale*. Bari: Laterza.

Blum-Kulka, S., Blondheim, M., House, J., Kasper, G., & Wagner, J. (2008). Intercultural pragmatics, language and society. In P. van Sterkenburg (Ed.), *Unity and diversity of languages* (pp. 155–173). Amsterdam: John Benjamins.

Bührig, K., & ten Thije, J. (Eds.). (2006). *Beyond misunderstanding. Linguistic analysis of intercultural communication*. Amsterdam/Philadelphia: John Benjamins.

Cao, X. (Ed.). (2008). 现代汉语词典 (第5版) *Xiandai Hanyu Cidian (di 5 ban)*. Beijing: 商务印书管 *Shangwu Yinshuguan*

Ceccagno, A. (2009). La diaspora cinese. In G. Samarani & M. Scarpari (Eds.), *La Cina – Verso la modernità* (pp. 297–311). Torino: Einaudi.

Clyne, M. (1994). *Inter-cultural communication at work: Cultural values in discourse*. Cambridge: Cambridge University Press.

Diadori, P., & Di Toro, A. (2009). Come insegnare italiano agli studenti di madrelingua cinese? Un'introduzione. In P. Diadori (Ed.), *La DITALS risponde 6* (pp. 67–77). Perugia: Guerra Edizioni.

Durkheim D. E. (1898). *Représentations individuelles et représentations collectives*. Revue de Métaphisique et de la Morale.

Galli, S. (2007), *Dal cinese all'italiano. L'italiano per studenti sinofoni, con elementi di lingua cinese*, Cremona: Quaderni del Centro Studi, 2007 1.

Gola, E., & Ervas, F. (2016). *Metaphor and communication*. Amsterdam: John Benjamins.

Hong, W. (2002). *Request patterns in Chinese and German: A cross-cultural study*. Munich: Lincom GmbH.

Jefferson, G. (1985). An exercise in the transcription and analysis of laughter. In T. A. Van Dijk (Ed.), *Handbook of discourse analysis* (Vol. 3, pp. 25–34). London: London Academic Press.

Jefferson, G. (1996). A case of transcriptional stereotyping. *Journal of Pragmatics, 26*, 159–170.

Kasper, G., & Blum Kulka, S. (1993). *Interlanguage pragmatics*. New York: Oxford University Press.

Kecskes, I. (Ed.). (2007). *Explorations in pragmatics. Linguistic, cognitive and intercultural aspects*. Berlin/New York: De Gruyter.

Kecskes, I., & Zhang, F. (2009). Activating, seeking and creating common ground: A socio-cognitive approach. *Pragmatics and Cognition, 17*(2), 331–355.
Kecskes, I. (2010). The paradox of communication: a socio-cognitive approach. *Pragmatics and Society, 1*(1), 50–73.
Kecskes, I. (2014). *Intercultural pragmatics*. New York: Oxford University Press.
Koike, D. A. (1989). Pragmatic competence and adult L2 acquisition: Speech acts in interlanguage. *Modern Language Journal, 73*, 79–89.
Koole, T., & ten Thije, J. D. (1994). *The construction of intercultural discourse: Team discussions of educational advisers*. Amsterdam/Atlanta: RODOPI.
Koole, T., & ten Thije, J. (2001). The reconstruction of intercultural discourse: Methodological considerations. *Journal of Pragmatics, 33*, 571–589.
Leung, C., & Ruan, J. (Eds.). (2012). *Perspectives on teaching and learning English literacy in China* (Vol. 3). Dordrecht, Heidelberg, New York, London: Springer, Multilingual Education.
Markee, N. P., & Kasper, G. (2004). Classroom talks: An introduction. *Modern Language Journal, 88*(4), 491–500.
Mey, J. L. (2001). *Pragmatics: An introduction* (2nd ed.). Oxford: Blackwell.
Mitchell, R., & Myles, F. (1998). *Second language learning theories*. London: Arnold.
Mori, J. (2003). The construction of interculturality: A study of initial encounters between American and Japanese students. *Research on Language and Social Interaction, 36*(2), 143–184.
Nishizaka, A. (1995). The interactive constitution of interculturality: How to be a Japanese with words. *Human Studies, 18*, 301–326.
Nocentini, A. (2004). *L'Europa linguistica. Profilo storico e tipologico*. Firenze: Le Monnier Università.
Ochs, E. (1988). *Cultural and language development: Language acquisition and language socialization in a Samoan village*. Great Britain: Cambridge University Press.
Rastelli, S. (Ed.). (2010). *Italiano di cinesi, italiano per cinesi*. Perugia: Guerra Edizioni.
Rastelli, S. (Ed.). (2013). *Il processing nella Seconda Lingua. Teorie, dati sperimentali, didattica*. Roma: Carocci.
Rehbein, J. (Ed.). (1985). *Interkulturelle Kommunikation*. Tuebingen: Narr.
Scibetta, A. (2013). 意大利中国移民语言学习现状的调查与分析 *(Analysis of the current situation of Chinese migrants' acquisition of Italian)*. In 八桂侨刊, Guangxi, 2013 1.
Thomas, J. (1995). *Meaning in interaction. An introduction to pragmatics*. New York: Routledge.
Valentini, A. (1992). *L'italiano dei cinesi. Questioni di sintassi*. Milano: Guerrini Studio.
Vedovelli, M. (2010). *Guida all'italiano per stranieri. Dal Quadro comune europeo per le lingue alla sfida salutare*. Roma: Carocci.
Wang, Y. (2007). *Mündliche kommunikative Fähigkeiten chinesischer Deutschlerner*. Hamburg: Iudicium Verlag GmbH.
Wang, V. X. (2011). *Making requests by Chinese EFL learners*. Amsterdam/Philadelphia: John Benjamins.
Wierzbicka, A. (2003). *Cross-cultural pragmatics. The semantics of human interaction*. Berlin: De Gruyter.
Willet, J. (1995). Becoming first graders in an L2: An ethnographic study of L2 socialization. *TESOL Quarterly, 29*(3), 473–503.

Websites Cited

www.istat.it. ISTAT (Istituto Nazionale di Statistica), Dossier immigrazione in Italia 2015.
www.treccani.it. Vocabolario della lingua italiana Treccani, "cultura".

Part III
Book Reviews

Review of Bamford, J., Cavalieri, S. and Diani, G. (Eds). (2013) *Variation and Change in Spoken and Written Discourse: Perspectives from Corpus Linguistics*. Amsterdam: John Benjamins

Claire Childs

Abstract Bamford et al. (2013) edited volume comprises 16 studies of language variation and change in speech and writing, spanning both corpus-driven and corpus-based approaches. Although some of the studies have unfortunate methodological issues or lack sufficient discussion of the implications of the findings, the volume comprises an interesting set of investigations which together showcase the diversity of corpus linguistic research. The volume would be particularly useful to researchers working on variation within the discourse of academia, business, arts/culture and the media (all of which are well-represented in the book), as well as corpus compilers

Keywords Corpus linguistics • Variation and change • Discourse • Genre • Methodology

Given recent technological advancements in linguistic analysis, it is no surprise that corpus linguistic methods have become increasingly embraced in the study of language variation and change. Although corpus size must be balanced with careful design to ensure representativeness and comparability (e.g. Biber 1990; Sinclair 2005; Reppen 2010), the efficiency of computers in analysing large datasets 'has made possible unrestricted access to the observation of language in use' (Tognini-Bonelli 2001: 5). Corpora are therefore an invaluable resource for the investigation of language variation and change, particularly within or across different modes/genres, which is central to Bamford, Cavalieri and Diani's (2013) edited volume.

C. Childs (✉)
School of English Literature, Language and Linguistics,
Newcastle University, Newcastle Upon Tyne, UK
e-mail: claire.childs@ncl.ac.uk

J. Romero-Trillo (ed.), *Yearbook of Corpus Linguistics and Pragmatics 2016*,
Yearbook of Corpus Linguistics and Pragmatics 4,
DOI 10.1007/978-3-319-41733-2_12

The book is part of John Benjamins' *Dialogue Studies* series which focuses on inter-disciplinary approaches to dialogicity in language use. The 16 chapters were selected for inclusion from papers given at the CLAVIER (Corpus and Language Variation in English Research group) Conference on 'Corpus Linguistics and Language Variation', which took place in Modena, Italy in November 2009. As Diani notes in her introduction, the chapters differ in terms of scope and approaches, but all focus on language variation and/or change, using corpus linguistic methods to explore the 'dialogic interactivity between the spoken and the written' (ix).

The book is split into two main parts, 'Part I: Corpus analysis of spoken dialogue' and 'Part II: Using corpora to analyse written discourse: A diachronic perspective', with further sub-sections. The first sub-section of Part I comprises two chapters on variation within speech in an academic setting. Chapter 1 ('Speaking professionally in an L2: Issues of corpus methodology') by Mauranen provides detailed description of the development of the *English as a Lingua Franca in Academic Settings* (ELFA) corpus and its advantages as the first corpus of ELF speech in academia. Mauranen subsequently discusses three potential methods for beginning corpus linguistic analysis (brainstorming, concordance software and reading transcripts) which she evaluates in terms of their reliance on data versus intuition, stressing the importance of researchers not bringing preconceptions to ELF analyses. In Chapter 2 ('Common features and variations in the use of personal pronouns in two types of monologic academic speech'), Okamura examines the use of personal pronouns in undergraduate versus public lectures in the *Michigan Corpus of Academic Spoken English*. Okamura finds that the frequency and discourse context of personal pronouns varies according to the lecture type, especially the relationship between speaker and audience. However, the results must be considered with caution as Okamura presents raw numbers of occurrence, rather than normalised frequency measures that would account for the difference in length (c. 10,000 words) between the two datasets.

The second sub-section consists of two chapters comparing variation between spoken and written business texts. In Chapter 3 ('Variation across spoken and written registers in internal corporate communication: Multimodality and blending in evolving genres'), Bowker compares how businesses convey messages in audio-conference presentations (both orally and in accompanying slides) and staff e-newsletters. Bowker finds that nominalisation, text organisation features (e.g. *so*) and imagery are used to convey the company's discourse message and suggests that the written texts adopt a conversational style. In Chapter 4 ('Using grammatical tagging to explore spoken/written variation in small specialized corpora'), Crawford Camiciottoli similarly studies language in business texts, comparing financial earnings presentations with written earnings releases. The research highlights the advantage of POS-tagging in corpora, as it allows Crawford Camiciottoli to study the lexical density and use of evaluative adjectives in the two text types, which would be painstaking with an unmarked corpus. The two corpora have similarly high lexical density scores indicative of the 'strong transactional dimension of message/goal-oriented financial disclosure' (73), but the higher frequency and wider range of evaluative adjectives in the presentations highlights their interactivity and 'more purposeful and sophisticated rhetorical style' (73).

The third sub-section comprises chapters on 'Dialogic variation and language varieties'. Savino's study in Chapter 5 ('Exploring regional variation in Italian question intonation: A corpus-based study') addresses a clear research question: is there geographical differentiation in Italian dialects with respect to *yes/no* question intonation? Some prior studies suggest that falling-rising intonation is characteristic of Standard Italian as well as most Northern and Central dialects, while rising-falling is typical in the South (e.g. D'Imperio 2002), but others have found little geographical distinction (e.g. Canepari 1980). Arguing that the lack of consensus amongst previous studies is mainly due to their consideration of different speech styles (e.g. read versus spontaneous), Savino presents a detailed technical analysis of intonation in a corpus of spontaneous speech recorded during participants' completion of a Map Task (*Corpora e Lessici di Italiano Parlato e Scritto*, "Corpora and Lexicons of Spoken and Written Italian"). She demonstrates that a rise on the nuclear syllable is the most common intonation pattern in all 15 Italian dialects studied and that a final rise is infrequent overall. Thus, the results show that there is no geographical pattern in this regard and emphasise the impact of speech style on intonation.

Chapter 6 ('Estonian emotional speech corpus: Content and options') by Altrov and Pajupuu discusses the construction of the *Estonian Emotional Speech Corpus*. The corpus contains passages from Estonian press which, when read aloud, had been judged to express a particular emotion either independently or dependently of subject matter. Although primarily designed to 'provide units to be selected for speech synthesis' (119), the corpus can also be used in studies of emotional speech. Chapter 7 ('Using movie corpora to explore spoken American English: Evidence from multi-dimensional analysis') similarly highlights practical applications of corpora, but in language teaching. Forchini compares the frequency of spoken language features in the *Longman Spoken American Corpus* and the *American Movie Corpus* to test previous claims that film dialogue is dissimilar to real-life speech. Forchini finds that the two corpora score similarly on Dimension 1 of Biber's (1988) Multi-Dimensional Analysis in having an interactive style, suggesting similarity between film and real-life dialogue. The author subsequently tests whether film dialogue can aid Italian student learners of English in acquiring conversational features. The students were asked to write a dialogue based on a story from a film that they were told. In later sessions, the students watched film scenes and were asked to recreate their initial dialogues. Comparing the two sets of dialogues revealed increased use of colloquial features (e.g. pauses, interjections, discourse markers) in the second which, as Forchini suggests, indicates that film is a useful resource in L2 language tuition. However, as the frequencies of the colloquial features are presented in aggregate, potential differences in students' individual performance are obscured, which are important to consider given the small sample (nine students).

In the final chapter of this sub-section (Chapter 8: "But that's dialect, isn't it?" Exploring geographical variation in the SCOTS corpus'), Anderson discusses the 4-million word *Scottish Corpus of Texts and Speech*. The range of text types/genres, timespan (1945-present) and detailed meta-data make this corpus an excellent dialectological resource, as Andersen demonstrates through her small-scale study on the use of *bide* and her qualitative investigation of attitudes towards language use in Scotland.

Part II comprises research taking a diachronic perspective within written corpora. The first sub-section of four chapters focuses on historical data. In Chapter 9 ('Variation in the language of London newspapers: January 1701'), Fries focuses on a set of newspapers from 1701 to 1702, an extension to the *Zurich English Newspaper Corpus*. He observes that different newspapers have varying preferences for *hath* versus *has* and *wrote/writ/written*, though the latter analysis is limited by the variable's low frequency (N=35). He supplements the analysis with a qualitative examination of the length, structure and topics of pieces in different newspapers.

Moving from the eighteenth into the nineteenth century, in Chapter 10 ('From letters to guidebooks: Ruskin's *Mornings in Florence*') Del Lungo Camiciotti presents discourse analysis of Ruskin's titular (1875) travellers' guidebook for art historians and visitors to Florence. Del Lungo Camiciotti's primarily qualitative analysis explores the way that Ruskin creates a relationship between writer and reader and adopts the readers' view of artefacts through the use of instructional language and orientation phrases. Similarly focusing on cultural texts, in Chapter 11 ('Justificatory arguments in writing on art: Toulmin's model tested on a small corpus of eighteenth- and nineteenth-century exhibition reviews') Tucker examines whether Toulmin's ([1958] 2003) model of justificatory arguments applies to a sub-corpus of art criticism from 1771 to 1893. He finds that the model does apply, but that there is synchronic and diachronic variation in the use of warrants in the argumentation, i.e. statements that create a link between data and subsequent claim (Toulmin [1958] 2003: 91). Chapter 12 ('Analysing discourse in research genre: The case of biostatistics') meanwhile concerns texts within the field of biostatistics. Prosperi Porta compares three specialist texts (a scientific report (1662), theoretical textbook (1930) and manual (2003)) to establish how discourse in the field has changed diachronically. The author's one-by-one consideration of the three texts somewhat hinders the reader's comprehension of connections between them, but the study shows how language varies 'according to the respective discourse communities and diverse communicative purposes across time' (217).

The second sub-section of Part II focuses on diachronic studies of language change, beginning with Chapter 13 ('The difference a word can show: A diachronic corpus-based study of the demonstrative 'this' in tourism research article abstracts') by Godnič Vičič, a corpus-driven study of the use of *this* in abstracts from tourism studies papers. The results reveal that determiner *this* increases in frequency between the 1980s and 2000s. Furthermore, there is a rise in the use of *this study/research* but relative stability in the frequency of *this paper/article*, which may indicate a diachronic change from 'abstracts as summaries to abstracts as advertisements' (235).

Chapter 14 ('Changing trends in Italian newspaper language: A diachronic, corpus-based study') marks a return to newspaper language, where Spina examines media influence on language change using a corpus of Italian newspapers from 1985 to 2000. Spina's initial hypothesis ('the main hypothesis is that these 16 years highlighted significant changes emerging in newspaper language' (242)) leaves the reader uncertain as to what constitutes a "significant change" (see Gries 2013: 10–14 on the importance of clarity in hypothesis formulation), but it is subsequently explained that Biber's (1988) characteristics of informal registers were used as a starting point for the analysis. From 1985 to 2000, Spina finds that dislocations and sentence-initial connectives increase in frequency, while sentences become shorter, lexical density decreases and subordinators are used less. As it has been previously noted that newspapers are 'adopting more oral features in an effort to appeal to a wider reading audience' (Biber 2003: 170), Spina's results may indeed be indicative of language change, as she suggests. However, her conclusion that they represent newspapers' 'attempt to reproduce forms of communication which are typical of television' (251) is not convincing, as there is insufficient evidence that television output in particular forms a model for newspaper prose.

In one of the few chapters on a language other than English (Chapter 15: 'A corpus-based analysis of some time-related aspects of contemporary Japanese'), Tanomura presents four case studies of variation within a corpus of transcribed minutes from the National Diet of Japan (1947-present) and two major Japanese newspapers (1987–1997 and 1991–2005). Highlighting the shortcomings of existing corpus software in handling Japanese characters, Tanomura uses his own tool to study the morphology of the verb *suru* ("do"), the adjectivalizing suffixes *–na* and *–no*, the permissive construction *V sasete itadaku* and some seasonal changes in lexical frequency. It is difficult for the reader to understand the figures in minute detail due to the use of greyscale to distinguish lines representing the diachronic frequency of different construction types, but as Tanomura groups together semantically-similar items with helpful labels, the overall diachronic trends can be seen nonetheless. The final chapter (Chapter 16: 'It's always the same old news! A diachronic analysis of shifting newspaper language style, 1993–2005') also considers newspaper language, but in a British context. Clark investigates the extent of "tabloidisation" of newspapers in recent decades using the *SiBol 93* and *SiBol 05* corpora of *The Times*, *Daily Telegraph* and *The Guardian* from 1993 to 2005. Between the two corpora, Clark identifies a decrease in the frequency of honorifics and an increase in the use of taboo words, contractions, pronouns and direct speech, which she argues are indicative of increasing tabloidisation in newspapers over time.

Considering the array of topics and approaches in these chapters, the volume is relatively well-structured. However, it is perhaps misleading that while Part I and Part II's titles suggest they concern speech and writing respectively, Chapters 3 and 4 compare both speech and writing. Chapters may have therefore been better categorised by genre/focus, e.g. academia (chapters 1, 2, 12, 13), business (3, 4), press (9, 14, 16), arts and culture (7, 10, 11) and language varieties (5, 6, 8, 15). There are also some typographical or grammatical errors in the text, e.g. 'is the only responsible for' (80), 'stands in fronts of' (174), '[t]rends in frequency data have showed' (232), '88 % of instances of *that this* is preceded' (233), 'a lower weight of content words in newspapers texts' (248).

As evident from the above discussion, some studies in this volume are corpus-driven (where the corpus is the starting point for the analysis, rather than existing theory) while others are corpus-based, with a more explicit theoretical basis (see Tognini-Bonelli 2001). In this volume some of the corpus-driven studies in particular may strike the reader as overly-descriptive as at times there is little explanation of the observed patterns or discussion of wider implications, which will disappoint some readers hoping for more substantial analysis. In addition, some authors' use of non-normalised frequency counts undermines the conclusions that can be drawn from their analysis (see Pichler 2010). These criticisms aside, however, this volume will undoubtedly be interesting and informative to linguists working on variation within particular settings (e.g. academia, business) or genres (e.g. newspapers). Furthermore, as the majority of chapters include at least some discussion of issues such as corpus representativeness and comparability that are so central to corpus linguistics, the book also offers important methodological insights that will be particularly useful to corpus compilers.

References

Biber, D. (1988). *Variation across speech and writing*. Cambridge: Cambridge University Press.

Biber, D. (1990). Methodological issues regarding corpus-based analyses of linguistic variation. *Literary and Linguistic Computing, 5*, 257–269.

Biber, D. (2003). Compressed noun-phrase structures in newspaper discourse: The competing demands of popularization vs. economy. In J. Aitchison & D. M. Lewis (Eds.), *New media language* (pp. 169–181). London: Routledge.

Canepari, L. (1980). *Italiano Standard e Pronunce Regionali*. Padova: CLEUP.

D'Imperio, M. (2002). Italian intonation: An overview and some questions. *Probus, 14*, 37–49.

Gries, S. T. (2013). *Statistics for Linguistics with R: A practical introduction* (2nd ed.). Berlin: Mouton de Gruyter.

Pichler, H. (2010). Methods in discourse variation analysis: Reflections on the way forward. *Journal of Sociolinguistics, 14*, 581–608.

Reppen, R. (2010). Building a corpus: What are the key considerations? In A. O'Keeffe & M. McCarthy (Eds.), *The Routledge handbook of corpus linguistics* (pp. 31–37). London: Routledge.

Ruskin, J. (1875). *Mornings in florence*. Chicago: Homewood.

Sinclair, J. (2005). Corpus and text: Basic principles. In M. Wynne (Ed.), *Developing linguistic corpora: A guide to good practice* (pp. 1–16). Oxford: Oxbow Books. http://www.ahds.ac.uk/creating/guides/linguistic-corpora/chapter1.htm

Tognini-Bonelli, E. (2001). *Corpus linguistics at work*. Amsterdam: John Benjamins.

Toulmin, S. E. ([1958] (2003)). *The uses of argument*. Updated edition. Cambridge: Cambridge University Press.

Review of Kruger, A., Wallmach, K. and Munday J. (2011) *Corpus-Based Translation Studies: Research and Applications*. London and New York: Bloomsbury

Sofia Malamatidou

Abstract A significant addition to the theoretical and descriptive accounts of corpora in translation studies is Corpus-Based Translation Studies: Research and Applications, an edited volume by Alet Kruger, Kim Wallmach, and Jeremy Munday. This review aims at examining this edited volume in detail, focusing on each chapter, and highlighting specific strengths and limitations. Overall, the book delivers its aim to describe how corpus-based studies have assisted translation scholars, and reports on a wide range of research using corpora. As such, it should be of interest to any academic interested in the use of corpora in translation and interpreting research, but also to postgraduate modules or programmes on corpus-based translation and interpreting studies

Keywords Translation • Interpreting • Comparable corpus • Parallel corpus • Corpus tools

Ever since corpora were first introduced in translation by Baker (1993), corpus-based translation studies has developed into a major paradigm in Translation Studies and is now a fast growing discipline holding a prominent place in the academy. A variety of monographs are available on corpus-based translation studies, including studies with corpora and translation in specific languages (e.g. Chesterman 2005; Bosseaux 2007; Hansen-Schirra et al. 2012), guides on the applications of corpora in translation training (e.g. Bowker and Pearson 2002; Zanettin et al. 2003; Tengku et al. 2010) and accounts of the theoretical and descriptive aspects of corpora (e.g. Olohan 2004; Zanettin 2012).

S. Malamatidou (✉)
Department of Modern Languages, University of Birmingham, Birmingham, UK
e-mail: s.malamatidou@bham.ac.uk

J. Romero-Trillo (ed.), *Yearbook of Corpus Linguistics and Pragmatics 2016*,
Yearbook of Corpus Linguistics and Pragmatics 4,
DOI 10.1007/978-3-319-41733-2_13

A significant addition to the theoretical and descriptive accounts of corpora is *Corpus-Based Translation Studies: Research and Applications*, edited by Alet Kruger, Kim Wallmach, and Jeremy Munday, leading researchers in the area of corpus-based translation and interpreting studies, and practising translators and/or interpreters. The composition of the editing team is worth commenting on: two of the editors come from South African universities (Kruger and Wallmach), while one from the UK (Munday). This perhaps demonstrates how far-reaching corpus-based studies are, having developed firstly in the UK and now reaching the international academy.

Kruger, Wallamach and Munday begin with an introduction to the field of corpus-based translation and interpreting studies, where they offer a brief historic overview and examine the different strands of corpus research, situating their volume in the strand of research-oriented corpus-based studies, as opposed to those focusing on training and learning. The volume is then divided into three parts, each consisting of a number of contributions from an impressive array of leading international figures in corpus-based translation and interpreting studies. Part I (chapters 1–5) is the largest of the three, and examines core concepts and tools in corpus research. Part II (chapters 6–8) is the shortest, and focuses on corpus methods for the qualitative analysis of contrastive patterns in large corpora. Finally, Part III (chapters 9–12) consists of studies in specific sub-fields.

The volume begins with two chapters, one from Laviosa, a pioneer of corpus-based translation research, and one from Robin Seton, a professional conference interpreter, which very skilfully set the background for the rest of the book, providing comprehensive overviews of corpus-based translation and interpreting studies respectively. Although Laviosa's chapter is an excellent introduction to the field and is one of the most detailed, yet concise, in the literature, Seton's contribution, which is the longest in this volume, might give the impression of being slightly overambitious, as it tries to cover different aspects of corpus-based interpreting studies, including its history, tools, approaches and applications, some more successfully than others.

Moving away from historical overviews, Chapter 3 is a contribution by Kenny, one of the prime movers of corpus-based translation studies. She employs empirical data to assess the potential of corpus-based translation studies, addressing the controversial, yet important, concept of translation units. Through a focused examination of a relatively small (approximately 2 million words) by today's standards parallel corpus of German-English texts, she concludes that there is not always a correspondence between translation units and units of meaning and advocates for the use of much larger corpora in translation studies.

Chapters 4 and 5 specifically address tools in corpus-based studies and work very nicely together. Chapter 4 is a contribution by Zanettin, one the most prominent names in the field, and addresses the most important topic of corpus annotation, which is often ignored in corpus-based translation studies, not least because of the technical difficulties associated with it. He manages to present the many advantages of employing corpus annotation, which are nicely summarised at the end of the chapter. In doing so, he tries to answer some basic questions, which are crucial for anyone that wants to get an understanding of corpus annotation: why annotate, what to annotate and how to annotate. The last chapter of Part I is by Luz, a computer scientist, who has extensive expertise in computational linguistics and corpus-based projects. Although at points perhaps too technical, this chapter discusses recent advances in tools, technologies and standards that are valuable for web-based corpus research and offers some examples from the Translational English Corpus (TEC). It is a very useful chapter for anyone interested in gaining a better understanding of how web-based corpus software might be designed or using the TEC software more efficiently. It is also a valuable addition to the present volume, as it allows it to address the topic of corpus-based translation studies from complementary perspectives, including that of computer science.

Part II opens with Chapter 6, a brilliantly written chapter by Hoey, a renowned linguist, who puts forward the intriguing hypothesis that changes in lexical priming might be related to language change and provides some, admittedly little, evidence from the analyses of actual translations of an English sentence into Brazilian Portuguese, but validates his observations with reference to larger corpora (100 million for English and 6 million for Brazilian Portuguese). This is an informative chapter that addresses a topic that has generally been neglected in translation studies and Hoey is right to observe that the implications of translation for diachronic linguistics have not been fully exploited.

Chapter 7 is written by Munday, a leading translation scholar, who discusses semantic prosody, describing how it can be analysed cross-linguistically using comparable corpora from English and Spanish, and offering a discussion of its potential for translation studies. The corpora analysed are large, all over 100 million words, and the linguistic items chosen for analysis, *loom large* and *cernerse*, are well justified. Most important is the final section of this chapter, where the potential of this analysis for translation studies is (unfortunately only briefly) discussed. Indeed, corpora are likely to become important tools for the investigation of similar phenomena and semantic prosody is an area where collaboration, in terms of methods and theories, is likely to flourish. These final observations, paving the way to the future, are certainly the most valuable contribution of this chapter, and one of the most significant of the book.

The final chapter of Part II, Chapter 8, is by House, a distinguished translation scholar, who has extensively used corpora in her research. The aim of this chapter is to provide an answer to the intriguing question of whether English, as a dominant language, can initiate change through contact in translation, namely in German, and offers an example of novel corpus research. The corpus analysed for the purposes of the project presents an impressive design, consisting of a number of sub-corpora that allow validation of the results. The chapter makes two major contributions. Firstly, it offers a number of hypotheses for explaining the role of translation in language contact situations and, secondly it offers an informed discussion of the possible benefits and drawbacks of qualitative and quantitative multilingual translation-related corpus work, stressing the importance of using corpora in translation not as a goal, but rather as a methodological tool to gain a better understanding of translation.

Chapter 9 by Bowker opens successfully Part III and examines the impact that corpora have had on terminological research and in particular on the working practices of terminologists and translators. This chapter is a welcome addition to the number of theoretically-oriented contributions in this volume, as it addresses the topic of electronic corpora from a very practical perspective and explains how these might be employed in professional translation, i.e. in the day-to-day job, and how training reflects recent developments in corpus research. Compared to the previous chapters in the volume that see corpora as a methodological tool for understanding the process of translation, this chapter nicely compliments them by focusing on corpora and their application to translation practice.

Chapter 10 is by Saldanha, who uses a corpus to reveal patterns in the use of foreign words in literary translations from Spanish and Portuguese into English. After a relatively short and concise literature review, a longer section is dedicated to methodology, which makes good use of Baker's (2000) suggestion for a similar methodology for investigating translator's style. From all the chapters in this book, this is perhaps the one that clearly focuses on corpus methods, and dedicates most of its space to corpus results. As such, it is a valuable contribution, which fits both the theme of the book and of Part III in which it appears. However, there is little discussion of how such corpus methods might have facilitated the analysis and how they have helped to uncover rather important implications about translators' style.

The next chapter is by Moropa and examines the use of corpus methods with less widely spoken languages, namely Xhosa in South Africa. The aim of this chapter is to examine whether the rather unique concordial system of Xhosa might create a link between the translators' tendency to simplification and explicitation. Although this chapter is significant in terms of the angle of less widely spoken languages and how corpus methods might be used with these, it, unfortunately, does not provide any quantitative data, including statistics, to allow the reader to infer how strong the relationship between simplification and explicitation is. While corpus methods are explained at the beginning, with some rather detailed technical information on corpus analysis, we seem to forget about them as we move towards the end of the chapter. As with the previous chapter, some brief reference to how corpus methods might have assisted in revealing the links between simplification and explicitation would have been welcome.

The final chapter is a study involving interpreting data and ties nicely with Chapter 2. Bendazzoli, Sandreli, and Russo examine a corpus of interpreting (European Parallel Interpreting Corpus) in order to compare instances of mispronunciations and truncated words between the source and the target texts, and across different language combinations. The aim of their study, which is to examine whether speakers and interpreters repair their output, is well justified, and the hypothesis put forward, i.e. that simultaneously interpreted speeches are likely to contain more instances of the above features and fewer repairs, is a valid one. A short section on methodology is included and a detailed presentation of the results is offered. What is, unfortunately, missing from this chapter (as well as from others in Part III) is a more detailed presentation of the methods employed to analyse the corpus. The writers state that data have been extracted *by means of specific procedures* (p.290), but these procedures are not explained. This does not impede the reader from gaining some useful insights of the nature of interpreting activities, but it is something that one would expect to find in such a volume.

Through a careful selection of contributions, the editors successfully provide an outlet that has a number of strengths, making it a worthy read for academics and postgraduate students, both MA and PhD, interested in gaining a better understanding of the wide range of research questions, approaches and tools used in corpus research. Most importantly, this volume does not only address issues in corpus-based translation studies, but also examines the much neglected field of corpus-based interpreting studies. Although translation occupies most part of the volume, explicit reference to interpreting is a much needed addition in the field that tends to be monopolised by corpus-based translation studies.

Another important strength of the volume is that it is one of the few that manage to address the topic from a range of different angles, namely theoretical, technical and practical, offering a comprehensive account of the field. By not focusing on only one of these angles, which is the tendency in existing books, especially those is the research-oriented strand of corpus-based studies, this volume presents a comprehensive overview of the field and reflects its diversity. A final advantage can be found in the different parts of the volume that specifically address the potential of corpora for translation and interpreting studies and how they could be explored in the future. While this feature of the volume could have been further elaborated (i.e. be an integral part of each contribution), specific references to the advantages of corpora as a methodological tool is a considerable advantage.

In terms of the weaknesses, the selection of specific sub-fields in Part III would benefit from a clearer rationale, as it is not obvious why these specific sub-fields have been chosen among the many others available. What is more, while this part is certainly more focused on the results of corpus-based studies, most chapters it consists of make only brief references to how corpora have assisted them in reaching these results. More specific references to the methodological potential of corpora would have allowed the different parts of the volume to be linked together tighter.

While including contributions from the field of corpus-based interpreting studies is without a doubt a particular strength of the volume, these could have been more in number. One cannot fail to notice that there is no contribution from the perspective of interpreting in Part II of the volume. As it stands, the reader might get the impression that two chapters on interpreting have simply been added to what is primarily a translation studies volume, something that is also prominently reflected in the title of the book. Although it is true that corpus-based studies in interpreting are not as developed as those in translation, a volume that attempts to account for both in relatively equal measure would have been welcome. This would have made an already strong volume, much stronger and clearer in terms of rationale.

A final weakness is that of the time of its publication (2011), as some contributions seem to refer to research that has taken place some years prior to 2011, and/or more updated versions of the papers can already be found. The chapters involved are Kenny's, which seems to be related to her 2001 book, Zanettin's (see Zanettin 2012), House's (see Kranich et al. 2011 and 2012), and Saldanha's, which is related to her 2005 thesis. To an extent this is something that cannot be prevented in edited collections such as the present one, and this is perhaps a point to be addressed to the publishers, rather than the editors, but it is rather unfortunate that an important contribution such as the present volume would become outdated so quickly after being published.

Overall, the book delivers in terms of its aim to describe how corpus-based studies have helped *translation studies researchers in the investigation of key questions of translation and interpreting* (p.1) and it provides a comprehensive account of the diverse nature of corpus research. As such, it is bound to be relevant to any academic in corpus-based translation and interpreting studies, but also in the related disciplines of linguistics, computational linguistics, stylistics and lexicography among others. It is also a valuable resource for any Higher Education postgraduate module or programme on corpus-based translation and interpreting studies, although perhaps more as an advanced resource, rather than a key reading.

References

Baker, M. (1993). Corpus linguistics and translation studies: Implication and applications. In M. Baker, G. Francis, & E. Tognini-Bonelli (Eds.), *Text and technology: In honour of John Sinclair*. Amsterdam/Philadelphia: John Benjamins.

Baker, M. (2000). Towards a methodology for investigating the style of the literary translator. *Target, 12*(2), 241–266.

Bosseaux, C. (2007). *How does it feel? Point of view in translation: The case of Virginia Woolf into French*. Amsterdam/New York: Rodopi.

Bowker, L., & Pearson, J. (2002). *Working with specialized language: A practical guide to using corpora*. London/New York: Routledge.

Chesterman, A. (2005). *On definiteness: A study with special reference to English and Finnish*. Cambridge: Cambridge University Press.

Hansen-Schirra, S., Neumann, S., & Steiner, E. (2012). *Cross-linguistic corpora for the study of translations: Insights from the language Pair English-German*. Berlin/New York: Mouton de Gruyter.

Kenny, D. (2001). *Lexis and creativity in tranlsation*. London/New York: Routledge.

Kranich, S., Becher, V., & Höder, S. (2011). A tentative typology of translation-induced language change. In S. Kranich, V. Becher, S. Höder, & J. House (Eds.), *Multilingual discourse production*. Amsterdam & Philadelphia: John Benjamins.

Kranich, S., Becher, V., & House, J. (2012). Changing conventions in English-German translation of popular scientific texts. In K. Braunmüller, C. Gabriel, & B. Hänel-Faulhaber (Eds.), *Multilingual individuals and multilingual societies*. Amsterdam/Philadelphia: John Benjamins.

Olohan, M. (2004). *Introducing corpora in translation studies*. London/New York: Routledge.

Saldanha, G. (2005). *Style of translation: An exploration of stylistic patterns in the translations of Margaret Jull Costa and Peter Bush*. PhD thesis. Dublin: Dublin City University.

Tengku, M., Tengku, S., Vaezian, H., & Akbari, M. (2010). *Corpora in translation: A practical guide*. New York/Bern: Peter Lang.

Zanettin, F. (2012). *Translation-driven corpora: Corpus resources for descriptive and applied translation studies*. Manchester: St. Jerome Publishing.

Zanettin, F., Bernardini, S., & Dominic, S. (Eds.). (2003). *Corpora in translator education*. Manchester: St. Jerome Publishing.

Review of Hyland, K., Huat, C. M. and Handford, M. (2012). *Corpus Applications in Applied Linguistics*. London: Bloomsbury

Karen Kinloch

As the title suggests, this volume brings together chapters on a range of areas of interest in Applied Linguistics (AL), from the analysis of conventional data such as language learning/pedagogy and institutional discourse to the more unusual, such as photographic images and short message service (SMS) texts, and examines the potential contribution of Corpus Linguistics (CL) to these areas.

As a corpus linguist I found this book an excellent exemplar of the diversity of topics within applied linguistics which can benefit from the use of corpus methodology. Each of these chapters very much treats corpus linguistics as a methodological tool, a way of "doing linguistics", rather than a theoretical standpoint (McEnery and Hardie 2012. p 6) and a practical approach dominates. To get the most from this book one would need, I felt, at least a basic knowledge of corpus terminology and methodology as the explanations of terms varied greatly from chapter to chapter, as did the level of technical background required. However, it would be of use certainly from MA level upwards and as a postgraduate researcher I found it to be both accessible and informative.

The structure of these chapters also suggests that it is intended to dip in and out of as a particular need or interest arises, and the volume spans a variety of linguistic areas from sociolinguistics, pragmatics to genre. There are mostly clear links between the chapters in each section with the first and last section being the most internally cohesive. This book does not challenge the many corpus and applied linguistics handbooks (e.g. McEnery and Hardie 2012) which are available, rather it acts as a complement to them by providing expertise and case studies in specified areas.

The volume consists of five parts, including a comprehensive introduction to the uses of corpus methods for applied linguistics by the editors. These five sections are

K. Kinloch (✉)
Linguistics and English Language Department, Lancaster University, Lancaster, UK
e-mail: k.kinloch@lancs.ac.uk

J. Romero-Trillo (ed.), *Yearbook of Corpus Linguistics and Pragmatics 2016*,
Yearbook of Corpus Linguistics and Pragmatics 4,
DOI 10.1007/978-3-319-41733-2_14

"bookended" by the two of the most common areas for applied linguistics, "Institutional Uses of Language" and "Language Learning and Pedagogy", with the mid sections covering a wider range of potential spheres of study.

Although Chapter 2 is titled "Professional Communication and Corpus Linguistics" this chapter also examines the use of professional discourse corpora to inform language pedagogy. In doing so Handford highlights the need for contextual data when using corpora for applied linguistics and give examples of how such context may be provided. Although examples are given of possible methodology and data at least half of the chapter looks at how a corpus of authentic professional discourse can improve language learning materials.

In Hyland's chapter on "Corpora and Academic discourse" the importance of contextual data is also foregrounded, through the combination of corpus with other more qualitative methods. This recurring focus on context is a common theme throughout the book and provides a thread which holds the sometimes disparate chapters together. Rather than presenting academic discourse as a monolith this chapter presents a range of academic discourses, varying across text and context. Hyland also gives a case study which presents an interesting challenge to the essentialist view of gender and demonstrates the potential of corpus applications for identifying differences in rhetorical style.

In contrast to Handford who focuses on the pedagogical applications of corpus studies into professional discourse, Koester's chapter on workplace discourse is concerned with identifying pragmatic features. While both these chapters look at spoken discourse and utilise data from CANBEC corpus, Koester presents examples of lexical and pragmatic items which are distinctive features of workplace discourse. There does seem to be a conflation here of workplace and business as the data in the examples presented is drawn from a commercial environment rather than public sector, however this is addressed in descriptions of potential uses of this methodology.

Part three of this book addresses the use of corpora to study traditional applied linguistic domains of translation, forensic linguistics, gender and media, demonstrating the breadth of possible corpus applications.

Whilst other chapters have more in common with research papers, Laviosa's description of the use of corpora for translation studies provides more of a textbook approach giving detailed background information on the history of translation studies as a discipline. There is perhaps an expectation that readers will be less familiar with this area than other domains, I include myself in that category, and I found both this description and the overview of contemporary issues in translation studies and how corpora may be used to address them a useful feature. This chapter does not confine itself to the issue of translation but rather addresses the practical issue of using corpora to train translators in specialist business language. This study therefore provides a pleasing congruence with the chapters on both pedagogy and business.

Olsson's chapter on Forensic Linguistics provides a fascinating example of the use of corpora to authenticate authorship in a legal context. Whilst many of the other chapters provide at least an overview of corpus linguistics at the start Olsson deviates from this structure and begins with the presentation of a case study prior to any description of the field and I felt that the reader who does not have at least a basic knowledge of corpus linguistics may find this off putting. As a regular corpus user I found this a really helpful insight into an "applied" technique and noted with interest the use of "Web as Corpus" as this is the only chapter to address this.

In addressing the question of corpus linguistics and gender studies Baker provides considerable background on gender/corpus and, while advocating the potential of corpus methods, gives a robust critique of their limitations. Whilst initially looking at gendered usage of language, Baker moves on from this to using corpora to uncover gendered representations by combining corpus methods with critical discourse studies. Looking at discursive representations in a corpus of news texts, this chapter provides a good example of Baker's method of triangulating the quantitative corpus method with more qualitative techniques.

The chapter on media studies and corpus by O'Keeffe links nicely with Baker's work as it also deals with media texts albeit in the case of O'Keeffe the data is spoken rather than written. This section provides a good overview on the issues of gathering and analysing spoken data using corpus methods, although the author acknowledges that it is light on discussion of the wider application of CL in the study of media discourse. The bulk of the chapter covers an example study looking at differencing types of media interactions. There are lots of textual examples and tables of the different types of corpus analysis including keywords and concordances, this does make the chapter quite dense in terms of data presentation and I would have been interested in more explanation of the analysis.

While the previous chapters generally clustering around a particular domain or type of discourse the section on "New spheres of study" is necessarily less internally similar, with a variety of text types which have not received as much attention from corpus linguistics previously, including new language varieties and non-linguistic corpora.

In this section I found the chapter by Seidlhofer particularly interesting as it clearly sets out the author's intent to look at what ELF can contribute to corpus studies reversing the aim of most of the other chapters. This work focuses on a speech community not usually addressed in "mainstream" corpus building and challenges assumptions about language and language learning, specifically the privileging of "standard English". While Seidlhofer addresses conventional sociolinguistic and pragmatic concerns faced by those who study ELF, she also gives a good coverage of the issue of corpus design common to anyone who is building a specialist corpus of new text types. This chapter includes many references to studies of ELF but fewer actual linguistic examples so unless this is an area of particular interest further reading may be required to see how the pragmatic functions of ELF are realised.

Tagg's chapter on compiling a corpus of SMS texts also raises issues of corpus building, some of which have been addressed by others in particular issues of data collection which are closely related to those faced by compilers of spoken language corpora. Several of the issues presented however are unique to this text type, such as, the negative public perception of the form and dealing with non-standard orthography when using automated analysis techniques. The examples given combine sociolinguistics and corpus methods and give a fascinating insight into the creativity of this text type which reaches beyond the constraints of form and technology. I also felt that this chapter demonstrated well how conventional approaches can be used to shed light on new genres.

While most of the chapters in this volume tend to look at findings of studies which combine CL and AL, Yueguo's account of building a photographic corpus is very much a methods chapter and would be a useful read for anyone engaged in corpus building of this nature. The issues of automated processing of multimedia texts are perhaps too wide in scope for a single chapter and the chapter is rather heavy on technical detail but it is written in a way which is easy enough to follow for a novice in this area. Most of the chapter deals with issues of annotation which are general to any corpus building, in this case they are applied to the problem of how to extract images from a corpus rather than how to analyse such images in the way a more conventional corpus would be used. As such it may seem like an unusual fit for this book, however the author does include a description of how such techniques may benefit AL in terms of language pedagogy.

In a return to more conventional AL study the final section of this book addresses "Corpora, language learning and pedagogy" beginning with a chapter by Haut on learner corpora. In this case the focus is on EFL learners and examines the role of the L1 on linguistic practices of advanced level L2 speakers and how corpus methods can be used to elucidate this. The background provided in this chapter is very good with a range of clear examples and an overview of the methodological and philosophical challenges of studying L2 language learners. The chapter includes a range of potential directions for corpus based learner corpora which are well illustrated by a case study and could be followed without a great deal of prior knowledge.

Similarly the chapter by Flowerdew on "Corpora in the Classroom" also provides an excellent summary of this area and in grounded in a (relatively) long tradition of the use of corpora in language teaching. Rather than focusing on examples of the methodology one may use, this chapter is more of a literature review of the area and examines in some detail various frameworks and language learning theories. As anyone familiar with Flowerdew's work would expect, this chapter is clearly and fluently written and could be utilised in PG or UG teaching within this area. While maintaining a critical stance the author is cautiously optimistic about the usefulness of CL approaches to language pedagogy.

The final contribution in this section maintains close links with the previous chapter in terms of providing an overview of debates in this area rather than a focus on a particular case study, although practical examples are provided to illustrate the authors points. McCarthy gives a balanced account of the use of corpora in language teaching over the last decade, presenting arguments both for and against, addressing for example Widdowson's (2004) criticism of the decontextualisation of corpus data. He also discussed the practical challenges of creating learning materials using corpus methods and offers suggestions of how to do this using several corpus tools; frequency lists, keywords and collocates. The author is keen to explore the offerings of CL but with the caveat that the corpus is a beginning not a complete solution – a statement which most CL academics would support.

In addition to summarising the contributions to the volume, Susan Hunston's afterword nicely brings together some of the synergies between CL and AL, while maintaining that their strength lies in their identities as two separate but complementary disciplines.

I did not feel that this book presumed to be the last word on CL and AL and all chapters necessarily provided a brief overview of a large area. However, this proved to be one of the strengths of this volume by giving necessary depth in a particular area but the range of chapters leading to breadth overall. By providing a range of critiques into the possibilities of combining two distinct branches of linguistics this is not so much a "how to" book but a "how one might do" book.

References

McEnery, T., & Hardie, A. (2012). *Corpus linguistics: Method, theory and practice.* Cambridge: Cambridge University Press.

Widdowson, H. G. (2004). *Text, context, pretext: Critical issues in discourse analysis.* Oxford: Blackwell.

Author Index

J. Romero-Trillo (ed.), *Yearbook of Corpus Linguistics and Pragmatics 2016*,
Yearbook of Corpus Linguistics and Pragmatics 4,
DOI 10.1007/978-3-319-41733-2

Z

Subject Index

J. Romero-Trillo (ed.), *Yearbook of Corpus Linguistics and Pragmatics 2016*,
Yearbook of Corpus Linguistics and Pragmatics 4,
DOI 10.1007/978-3-319-41733-2

MIX
Papier aus verantwortungsvollen Quellen
Paper from responsible sources
FSC® C105338

If you have any concerns about our products,
you can contact us on
ProductSafety@springernature.com

In case Publisher is established outside the EU,
the EU authorized representative is:
Springer Nature Customer Service Center GmbH
Europaplatz 3, 69115 Heidelberg, Germany

Printed by Libri Plureos GmbH
in Hamburg, Germany